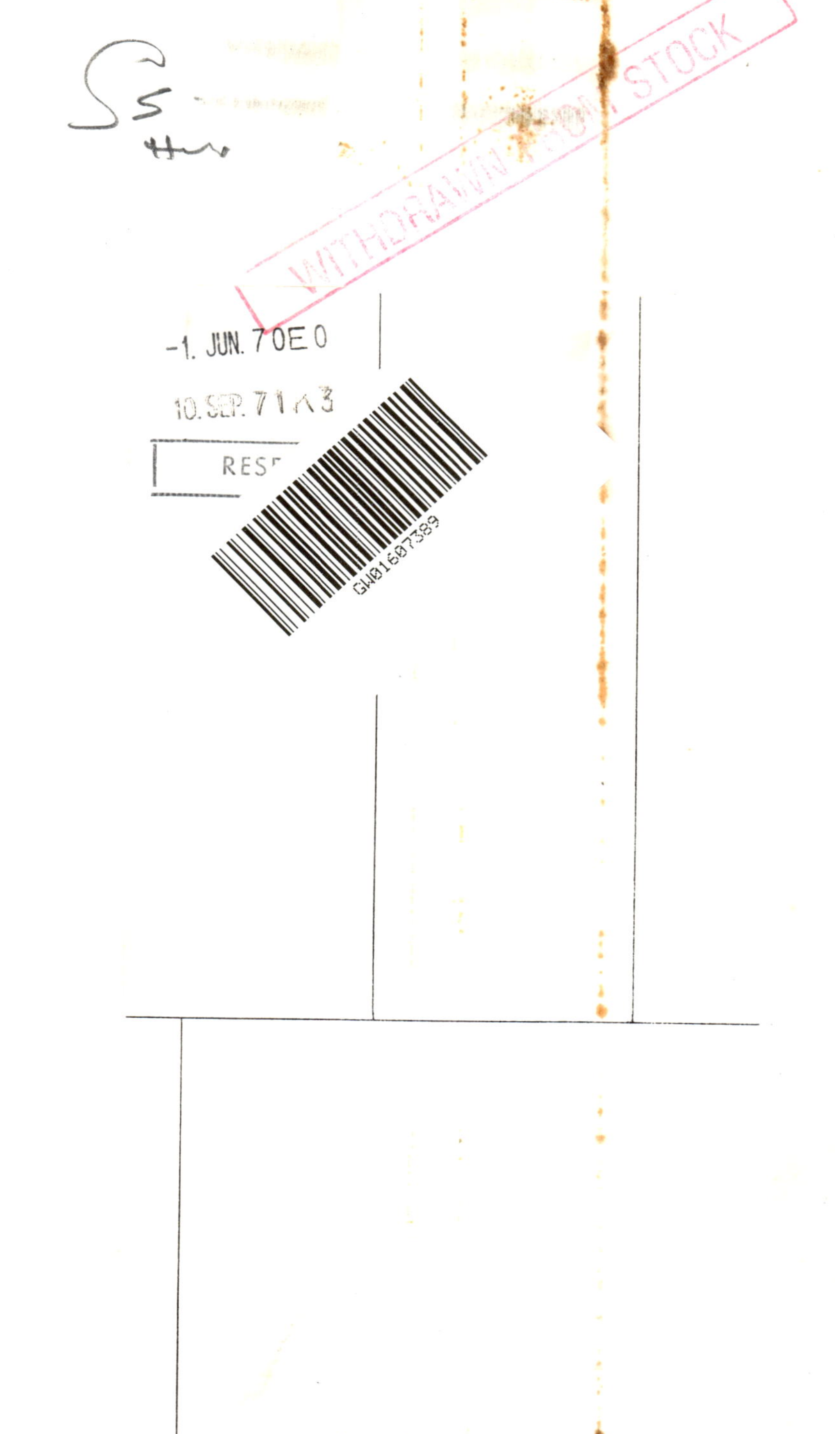
WITHDRAWN FROM STOCK
-1. JUN. 70E0
10. SEP. 71 ^3
RESE
GW01607389

Industrial Archaeology 1969

Industrial Archaeology 1969

Volume 6 of *Industrial Archaeology: The Journal of the History of Industry and Technology*

Editor: John Butt
Assistant Editor: Ian Donnachie

DAVID & CHARLES: NEWTON ABBOT

7153 4758 6

Printed in Great Britain by
Latimer Trend & Company Limited Plymouth
for David & Charles (Publishers) Limited
Newton Abbot Devon

Contents

Volume 6 Number 2

Contents

Volume 6 Number 3

Contents

Volume 6 Number 4

Contents

ANTHONY TRIGGS

The Windmills of Hampshire

HAMPSHIRE has never been a windmill county, since its long chalky rivers have always provided enough power, putting watermills well to the fore. Even today the existing watermills in Hampshire outnumber the existing windmills by over ten to one. Many of the windmills that have stood in the county in the past were probably too small to be of any consequence—often standing for such short periods that they have left no record of their passing. With the development of the tower mill at the beginning of the sixteenth century the mills were speedily changed, leaving no post mills. Hampshire millers kept abreast of progress by installing fantail stagings in the mid-eighteenth century, and abandoning the common sail for patent sails in 1807. Unfortunately the mills were never considered really important, probably owing to the lack of worthwhile sites and the watermill competition, and therefore records are scarce. This article is intended to present an account of all the Hampshire windmills that have stood or still stand in the county, and I have, for simplification, divided it into four distinct parts: Hampshire in general; Portsmouth, which has the most consistent windmill history in Hampshire; the Isle of Wight; and Hayling Island.

Hampshire

A number of mills stood on the coastline near Lymington, and a larger example stood at Buckler's Hard, all dating from the late eighteenth century. I have seen a reference to this latter mill, stating that it was used as a saw mill for the timbers of the mighty wooden walls that were built at the Hard. Also Gilbert White, in his *Natural History of Selborne* (1789), mentions a windmill in his area that had disappeared even then. He also includes a view of the village from Windmill Hill.

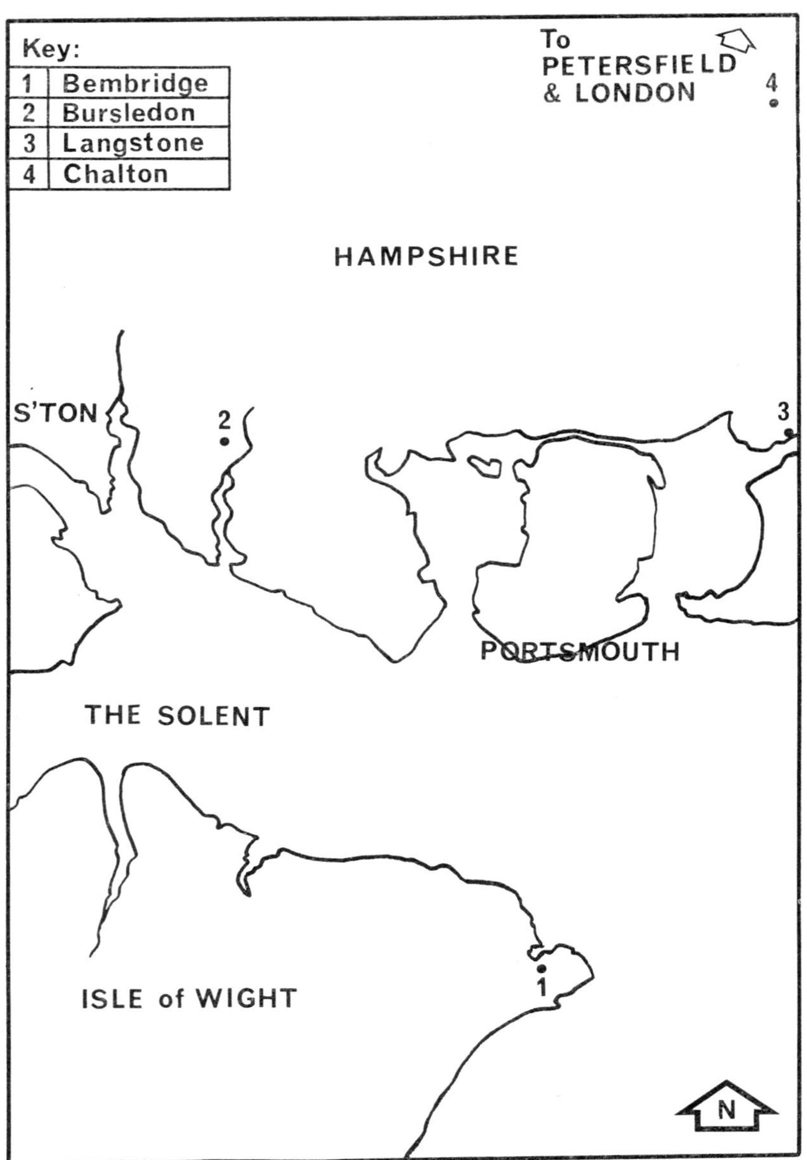

Map showing windmills of any consequence still standing in Hampshire

There is a 'Windmill Hill' at Stockbridge (168: SU408348), and 'The Windmill' is seen on modern maps at Hythe, near Southampton (180: SU418065), tantalising references to be left to the imagination, for I could find no other mention of either. The demolition of the tower mill that stood somewhere near the position of the present day Gosport to Fareham road took place in 1790. The Prideaux Brune family owned a mill at Rowner, which they used to grind corn for the monks at Quarr Abbey, on the Isle of Wight, with whom they had connections. A small tower mill also stood at Haslar, on the outskirts of Gosport. Arthur A. Walford, the famous Gosport bookseller and historian, states in *Historic Sketches of Gosport, Alverstoke and Rowner* that the mill together with the mill farm was demolished in 1746 when the Haslar hospital was built.[1] The hospital was completed in 1762.

A small tower mill, known as the Wicor mill stood at Portchester, the stump remaining until fairly recently. A public house of the same name, with a row of model windmills along the roof, stands near the old site. At Portchester the author recently found remains of a tower mill not shown on any map except the Ordnance Survey of 1870. A smock mill once stood at Otterbourne, and a small tower mill at Chawton. The map of Hampshire, executed by Isaac Taylor in 1759,[2] clearly shows a post mill at Fareham and another shown as Burrant windmill on high ground between Fareham and Portchester. A third post mill is also shown north of the county, at Stoke Charity.

Even the great city of Southampton has a short windmill history. In 1550 the Court Leet commanded one Thomas Wykes to 'scoure his Ditch in Kayneshut by the Wyndmille by Michaelmas upon pain of 3/4d'. This mill was later taken over by a Mr Caplin, and by 1612 a lease had been granted to Denis Rowse for 90 years for 'the wyndmille and a voyde plot of ground'. By 1771 the mill had disappeared. The site was where the present day Regent Street (formerly Caneshut Lane) stands. Another windmill is mentioned in 1600, but no further details are available; and there is very little written about the Castle windmill which supplied flour to Simnel Street, when that area was the Baker's Quarter. The fourth and last mill of Southampton stood on the causeway road across the saltmarsh, and in 1600 it is recorded that the public collected funds to mend the highway from the mill to the Itchen ferry.[3]

The old mill at Chalton (181: SU716162), overlooking the Portsmouth to Petersfield road, is still a landmark although in the very advanced stages of decay. The mill itself was built about the beginning of the nineteenth century, but it is said that a series of mills have stood in the same position since 1289, thus making the site the oldest in the county. The mill building is of brick and despite its dilapidation part of the fantail staging remains, as does the main shaft, 50 ft high with a circumference of over 8 ft. The beautiful metal cupola-shaped cap is now missing, but the metal curb which was used to rotate the cap is still in place. According to that indefatigable enthusiast for windmills of the 1930s, J. B. Paddon, the mill is supposed to be haunted, but his is the only reference to that fact I have found.[4] From Chalton mill once could be seen the revolving sweeps of four other mills—one at Weston, near Petersfield, one at Denmead, and two at Hambledon.

The small tower mill at Weston must be mentioned only shortly, for, as with many Hampshire mills, there is no documentary evidence of its life. The stump could be seen until recently built into a farmhouse and completely forgotten. The Denmead mill would have been the next in line, and was built in 1819. It was often called the Barn Green mill after the old name for the village, and was pulled down by a Mr Silvester in 1922. The bricks were used to build the road bridge over the railway at Cosham in Portsmouth.[5]

Hambledon boasted two mills, on either side of the village. The first stood on Windmill Down and the second on Speltham Hill. They were both said to have been built by the same millwright, this worthy also constructing the Chalton mill. The first mill was demolished years ago, but the Speltham Hill mill stood, overgrown and decayed, until about five years ago.

Remaining in the southern half of the county we next examine the tower mill, the remains of which still stand in private ground just off the Southampton road, at Bursledon (180: SU483109). A short walk up Windmill Lane is all that is required to see the mill, which has been in the hands of a Mr Pollard since 1965. A century ago the mill was purchased, together with the windmill house, by a local Methodist preacher, Mr George Gosling. Today the fantail, cap and sweeps are gone, the top being covered by a flat roof. As in the case of the Chalton mill the runner is still in place. When in its prime the mill boasted three pairs of stones, for wheat, oats, and barley, all of which were removed c 1930. Recently, the owner put forward a proposal to the planning committee to convert the mill into a dwelling house.[6]

The Old mill at Langstone Harbour, just off the road to Hayling Island from the mainland (181: SU720050), has already been converted and has been inhabited for many years. A combined water- and windmill, it was last at work sometime during the last half of the nineteenth century. An old photograph showing Langstone Harbour completely iced up in 1890 shows the mill to be in a similar state to the Chalton mill, with its cap and sweeps missing.[7] Later, in 1927, J. B. Paddon reached Langstone and sketched the mill, showing it slightly renovated as far as the tower, but with the fantail staging removed completely.[8] It has always had a rather infamous reputation owing to early associations with smugglers; and there is still said to be a secret passage running between the mill and the Royal Oak Inn some yards away.

To the north of the county lies the village of Grately, and here stands the stub of a tower mill, used until recently as a storehouse (167: SU269418). The mill was completed in 1849 and lived a short life as a windmill proper, as the sweeps were removed on Easter Monday 1889. A steam engine was then installed, but the boiler burst soon after, and an oil engine replaced it.

Just south of Winchester stands Owslebury, which had two windmills for a time. The first of these, remembered by the 'Old Mill Stores' was demolished by bombing during the first world war. The second, known as Bridle's mill, was a water-pumping mill and had a shaft some hundreds of feet deep sunk below it. The sails on the 40-ft-high tower were removed in 1914 and a traction engine was installed. The remains could be seen until recently.

Portsmouth

The earliest record of windmills in Portsmouth is an old map showing a line of them along the slopes of Portsdown Hill. These were almost certainly tiny post mills, so small in fact that the body of the mill only consisted of one room, and there was no roundhouse to cover the base of the post. These certainly cannot be listed as mills of any permanence, as they were probably blown down and rebuilt many times during the course of the years. The first mill of any importance was built on the northern shore of Portsmouth Harbour in the year 1212, or earlier, and apparently had some connection with a similar one at Gosport.

The next to be built was situated at Southsea, near the cattle pond which lay on the site of the present Canoe Lake. Known as Lumps mill, it stood on land belonging to Lumps Farm. According to an ancient deed, one Philip, son of Peter de Esteneye, held one acre of land at Esteneye (Eastney) under Ralph Lumpe and his wife Cecily. This mill was almost certainly a post mill in early times but was replaced by a tower mill at a later date. This second mill was known as the White mill, probably because of its colour, and was still standing c 1800. Part of Lumps Fort can still be seen at Southsea, and it is interesting to note that the mill was still standing when the fort was constructed.[9]

The present Queens Hotel covers the site of a mill—Ballards mill, which stood near a farmhouse and an inn. It has been said that the miller owned another mill in Sussex, and there is a record of a post mill at Patcham, at about the same time and of the same name. Some plans show another windmill nearby, which was probably Denison's mill. A small mill also stood on the site of the present Portsmouth Guildhall, but its history seems to have been extremely short-lived, since references to it are scanty.

The area known as Stamshaw once boasted a mill called Emery's mill, and Kingston had its own known as Byerly mill.[10] Byerly Road still runs from Kingston to Fratton, and memories of the old windmill could have had some bearing on its name.

An old water-colour painting of 'The Lime Mill, Portsmouth' recently came to light at the Southsea Castle Museum, which was passed to me by Mr A. Corney of that establishment. After some searching a map dated 1830 revealed a mill on the shore of the harbour known as Rudmore mill.[11] Rudmore Wharf is still used for the loading of gravel, cement and other materials, and the Stamshaw brick kilns once stood just north of the area. It seems conclusive that the lime mill and Rudmore mill are one and the same.

At the close of the eighteenth century, bread had become so expensive that to help the poor the Portsmouth Dockyard shipwrights built their own windmill. Then known as the Shipwrights mill, this is shown on a plan of the city to be standing just north of the dockyard of the time. It proved to be a blessing to the poor for many years until 1816, when the land was required by the Admiralty to enlarge the dockyard and naval establishments. It was this action that started the story of the most famous windmill ever to be built in Portsmouth.[12] With the resounding success of their first mill behind them, the shipwrights put their heads together, started a collection, and formed the Dockyard Co-operative Mill Society. They then constructed their own new windmill at Southsea, and even started a commercial bakery. The big black windmill, known fondly as the Dock mill, stood 100 ft high and 40 ft across the base, and was the largest of its type in England. The Army Board of Ordnance supplied one million bricks for it, all of which were used. A publication of the time states that the mill had a statue as a finial on the cap, and the following legend engraved upon the door:

This mill is the equal property of subscribers 1817.

Both rich and poor,
A friend will find,
Who standeth here,
Their corn to grind.

In spite of all its superlatives the Dockyard Mill Society went to the wall in 1834, as a direct result of increased wages. After standing derelict for thirty-five years, the Dock mill was purchased in 1869 by Mr Maurice Welch, a miller of renown; he had previously been in charge of the King's mill, the Admiralty tide mill that stood at the Quay Gate, and was destroyed by fire in 1868. Mr Welch had to fight his way through thick undergrowth that had accumulated through the years, and to get his wagons to the mill he even had to construct his own road! In later years the road came to Mr Welch, and it could be said that the Dock mill stood on the corner of Napier Road and Wisborough Road, Southsea. As soon as he arrived, Mr Welch installed steam power for grinding, with original wind power as a standby. In 1900 the mill stones were replaced by the most modern Hungarian steel rollers, and in 1905 the sails revolved for the last time when wind power was completely dispensed with. At this time the seven-storey mill was turning out 60–70 tons of flour per week, and its quality was known far and wide. In 1905 a medal was awarded at the International Bakeries Exhibition for the quality of the bread made from Dock mill flour, and two years later another was awarded for the cakes made with the 'Purity' brand flour ground by Mr Welch.[13] The Dock mill was put up for auction in 1922, but was not sold, and was eventually demolished in 1923, the last of the windmills of Portsmouth.

Only a few things remain in Portsmouth to remind us of these hard-working giants of the past. The Dock mill cottages still stand in Napier Road, but the fast rate of demolition for new developments in the city hints that they will not stand for much longer.[14] Perhaps a more lasting memento of the mill can be seen at the school situated only a few yards from the mill site, where the design of the school badge has been based around the Dock mill.

Across the city at Elm Road, Mile End, stands a public house called 'The Windmill', and its position is such that it could have been named from the mill that would have towered over it—the old Shipwrights mill. Almost the same explanation could apply to the 'Windmill and Sawyer' which stands near the Unicorn Gate of the Dockyard. According to students of inn signs there were many of that name standing in England, and they date back to 1770 when Dutch millwrights built a windmill in London in order to work a saw mill. Apparently the sawyers, who made their living sawing the giant beams for the Navy, thought they would be put out of work and so destroyed the new mill with their axes. Later a law was passed suffering the mills to work unmolested—and at this time public houses were named after events of the period. This may be so, but I like to think that the sawyers were the Portsmouth Dockyard men, and the windmill was their own Shipwrights mill, grinding corn as a defence against hunger for the poor people scraping a living around it.

The Isle of Wight

An early seventeenth-century map of the Isle of Wight shows four windmills very clearly, all illustrated by little post mills, which they undoubtedly were. A large one was shown at 'Shaucome', now Shalcombe; and another of considerable size was situated at Cheverton Down. A third was shown at 'Kington', now Knighton, just north of Newchurch; and the last was a small mill at Shanklin.

By 1682 Captain Grenville Collins was appointed by King Charles II to make a survey of England. When Collins came to surveying the Solent he wrote: 'When the windmill on the Isle of Wight beareth S.W. by W., then you are abreast of the Buoy of Horse.'[15] This windmill could have been the one that stood at Upton, Ryde, until about fifty years ago. Other mills stood at Mill Hill, Cowes, at Freshwater and at East Cowes. Today only one remains on the island, but this, the 40-ft tower mill at Bembridge, has the honour of being the only mill in Hampshire to be preserved in its original condition.

If Captain Collins had waited a mere eighteen years before coming to the Solent he would have been able to see the Bembridge mill, as it was built in 1700. It was situated then, not at Bembridge, but on Binbridge Isle, now a name of the past owing to the reclamation of Brading Harbour some eighty years ago. The cap of the mill had been leaking even then for the original roof of straw was replaced with one of wood in about 1720. Inside the tower, on a beam, can be seen the carved name of one of the mill boys—E. Beker—and the date '1746 AC'. Apparently the Pope was so unpopular in England at that time that the English AC (After Christ) replaced the usual Latin AD.

The mill was constructed of local stone, was built upon the orders of the Lord of the Yaverland Manor, and worked until about 1914, the last miller being Mr A. Morris. Gradually it became more decayed, the inside machinery rotting and becoming infested with woodworm and death-watch beetle. It was used for a time as a cowshed and a store until the second world war when the Home Guard took it over as an observation post, during which time lightning destroyed one of the sweeps.

When Mr Morris died, he left the mill to his niece, Mrs E. Smith of the nearby Mill Farm. She offered it to the National Trust who accepted it. In 1958, the Island National Trust Properties Management Committee launched an appeal for restoration funds, which was magnificently subscribed to by many of the island's town councils and private individuals. Restoration was started in 1959, and the mill was actually taken over by the National Trust in 1961. Drawings for the new sweeps were prepared by Mr R. C. Durden and the actual carpentry was undertaken by Mr F. Cheverton. The original mill stones had been removed, but luckily the stones from the now demolished tide mill at Wootton Bridge fitted exactly.[16] The sails are the canvas-covered type as used by the original miller in 1700. Since its opening the windmill has been visited by an estimated 15,000 people per year, between the months of April and September.[17]

Hayling Island

According to records there were once three windmills on Hayling Island, the last one being destroyed as late as 1886. The old Hayling Tide Water mill, which stood directly opposite the present Maypole Inn, was mentioned as being part of the Hayling Priory as far back as 1294 and was valued at £3. By 1325 the inventory of the priory mentions another mill, obviously a windmill. In this year a petition was made to the Crown asking for a remission of taxation and a lower valuation of the mills. The petition was heard by Ralph de Bereford and Richard de Westcote who were described as 'wardens of the alien religious house in the County of Southampton'. The value of the mills dropped to £1 per annum. The site of the windmill had always been known as Windmill Hill Field, and in the early 1930s during an excavation of a tumulus in this area, Mr E. S. McEuan came across the remains of what appeared to be two windmills on the top of the Neolithic burial place.[18] The first one could have been the remains of the windmill mentioned above and was obviously a post mill as the charred remains of the main post cross-braces were discovered. Close by, the distinctive cross shape of a later post mill, this time not destroyed by fire, was found.

So far two of the three Hayling mills have been accounted for, leaving the famous North Hayling windmill, which was a well-known feature of the landscape for many years. Owned by Mr George Sparks, it stood as the only mill on the island until it was destroyed by fire in 1886, as was the old water-mill nine years before.[19] I have an old blurred print of the North Hayling windmill, which shows it to be a tower mill of about three storeys with a neat beehive-shaped cap. The sails were the common canvas-covered type and the fantail staging is short with the fan itself missing. The photograph shows the mill with a small 'lean-to' constructed at the side, and a small driveway to a neat five-barred gate in the foreground. Unfortunately the print is too poor for reproduction.

Acknowledgments

I would like to take this opportunity to thank the following for their invaluable assistance towards making this article possible: Mr A. Corney, of the Portsmouth City Museums; Mrs Guy, the staff of the Portsmouth City Library, and Mr Alan Howard.

Notes

1 Published by Walford & Sons, The Library, High Street, Gosport, 1887. See also W. Tait, MB, *A History of Haslar Hospital*, Portsmouth, 1912.

2 This was reprinted at a reduced scale for the Hampshire Field Club, 1933.

3 R. A. Pelham, *The Old Mills of Southampton*, Southampton Corporation.
4 J. B. Paddon, 'Windmills in Hampshire', *Hampshire Observer*, 13 August 1937. 'Clanfield Mill Fades Away', *Portsmouth Evening News*, 15 November 1962.
5 A. Keeble Shaw, 'Windmills and Watermills in Hampshire', *Proceedings of the Hampshire Field Club*, vol 21, 107–9.
6 'The Future of Bursledon Windmill', *Hampshire Chronicle*, 7 January 1967, Winchester.
7 *Hayling and Havant Town Guide*, Havant, 1895, 5.
8 J. B. Paddon, 'Windmills in Hampshire', *Hampshire Observer*, 13 August 1937.
9 W. G. Gates, *Records of the Corporation*, 1835–1927, Portsmouth.
10 W. G. Gates, *An Illustrated History of Portsmouth*, Portsmouth, 1900, 279. W. G. Gates, *The Portsmouth that has Passed*, Portsmouth, 1949, 209.
11 Betty R. Masters, *Portsmouth: A Brief Outline of its Development*, Portsmouth Corporation, 1964, 5.
12 James Bayes, 'The Dock Mill', *Portsmouth Evening News*, 24 August 1962.
13 Messrs Welch and Son, *The Gentleman's Journal*, 2 November 1907, 12.
14 Ian Dillow, 'Historic Cottages wait for Bulldozer', *Portsmouth Evening News*, 6 September 1968, 31.
15 D. Phillips Birt, *The Waters of Wight*, 1967.
16 The original stones were later found in the ornamental garden of a house at St Helens. The owner had purchased them in 1920.
17 'A Showpiece for Visitors', *Portsmouth Evening News*, 7 January 1965, 14 & 15.
18 F. G. S. Thomas, *The King Holds Hayling*, Havant, 1961, 42.
19 'The Mills of Hayling Island', *Hampshire Telegraph and Post*, 22 January 1932, Portsmouth, 3.

Plates, pages 33–5

Notice

John Hammerton in *Industrial Archaeology*, vol 5, no 3 (August 1968), 303, unfortunately stated that the price of the offprint of J. D. Marshall and M. Davies-Shiel's 'Industrial Archaeology in the Lake Counties and Furness', reprinted from *Northern History*, vol 2, 1967, was 25s. This is, in fact, the price of *Northern History* as a volume. The correct price of the offprint is 4s. Copies may be obtained from the School of History, University of Leeds. Subscriptions to *Northern History* should be sent to the Secretary, *Northern History*, University of Leeds, Leeds 2.

ALAN SMITH

The Herculaneum China and Earthenware Manufactory, 1796–1840

IT is rare to find, amongst documents of industrial history, first-hand accounts of factory organisation and management as accurate and well-observed as one which has survived concerning the Herculaneum Pottery Company in Toxteth, near Liverpool. The document describes a visit made to the works by a reporter on the staff of the *Liverpool Albion* and it appeared in print on 9 July 1827. Its opening paragraph reads:

> THE HERCULANEUM POTTERIES
>
> This extensive manufactory of earthenware and china, which gives employment to from three to four hundred persons, men, women, and children, is carried on in a mass of irregular low brick buildings, close to the river. The buildings are enclosed by a high wall, and are distinguishable by several conical chimneys (as at glass houses), or hovels, as they are technically termed, to convey aloft the smoke from the ovens within them, in which the ware is exposed to the action of the furnaces. There is a commodious basin, or dock, attached, for the convenience of landing the clay and other materials, or embarking the ware. The site and some of the buildings were, some thirty years ago, used as a copper work, which was removed, having become a nuisance to the town, from the spot on which now stands the old tobacco warehouse, and was here carried on for upwards of twenty years. Large blocks of the copper dross are still seen about the present buildings and in the neighbourhood, and are still used in walls or pavement.

This was by far the largest of the twenty-five or so potteries which worked in Liverpool during the eighteenth century. As mentioned above, the site of the pottery had already been developed industrially by the erection of a copper-smelting works which belonged to Charles Roe & Company. This firm had, before 1771, worked in Liverpool but had been requested to move by the city fathers because of the smoke and dirt produced by their process. At this time the Earl of Sefton was granting leases on his estates in Toxteth Park for industrial development, alongside which was to be built a new town:

> The new town is intended to be called Harrington in reference to the family of the present countess dowager of Sefton, the daughter of the earl of Harrington; and the proposed streets take their names from friends and relatives of the family.[1]

By 1792 Charles Roe was contemplating removal from the Toxteth site in view of the difficulties he was having in obtaining the necessary supplies of coal. An advertisement in *Gore's General Advertiser* for 3 July 1794 announced that the works were for sale and by the end of that year Charles Roe & Company had removed their business to Neath in South Wales.

Our knowledge of the first use of the copperworks' buildings as a pottery during the years 1794–6 is very vague indeed. Tradition has it that a pottery here was started by Richard Abbey and Andrew Graham, though the only reference to this which is at present known to exist appears in Joseph Mayer's *History of the Art of Pottery in Liverpool*, first published in 1854. Richard Abbey was a well-known figure in the history of potting in Liverpool. He was primarily an engraver and decorator of pottery, using prints transferred to the surface of the finished pots. Apprenticed in his early years to that famous inventor of transfer-printing on earthenware, John Sadler, he worked in Liverpool, Glasgow and for a time in France, ultimately coming to Toxteth for the last two years of his working life, retiring in 1796 and dying at Aintree in 1801, aged eighty-one. Nothing is known about Graham apart from the fact that he seems to have come from a family of Liverpool potters.[2] Whether or not they actually made pots at Toxteth we shall perhaps never know, but they may have been simply engaged in decorating, by the transfer-printing method, plates, jugs, mugs and so forth acquired from other Liverpool and perhaps even Staffordshire manufacturers.

Firm evidence about the early years of the Herculaneum Pottery becomes available from 1796 when the establishment was purchased by three merchants, Samuel Worthington of Llwynan, near Bangor (who already had an interest in the site from 1772 and appears to have been the leading member of the concern), Michael Humble of Shooters Hill near Bawtry, and Samuel Holland of Liverpool. These gentlemen evidently had great faith in the ultimate success of a pottery on this site, for they not only employed local labour but brought to the works about forty operatives, men, women and children from the Staffordshire Potteries. Joseph Mayer gives a most colourful description of the journey and arrival in Liverpool of these people,[3] and *Gore's General Advertiser* of 13 December 1796 contains the following description:

> On Saturday last the new pottery, formerly the copper works, near this town was opened, and a plentiful entertainment given by Mr Worthington, the proprietor, to upwards of sixty persons employed in the manufactory, who were preceded by a military band from the works, along the docks and through Castle Street. Two colours were displayed on the occasion—one representing a distant view of the manufactory. We have pleasure to say these works are very likely to succeed which, if they do, from their extent and situation will be of infinite advantage to the merchants of Liverpool.

Williamson's Liverpool Advertiser on 6 March 1797 gives us an even more important clue as to the faith the investors had in the ultimate success of the works, the key being the ease of transport of both raw materials and the export of finished goods:

> Samuel Worthington & Co. Herculaneum Pottery
>
> Late the copper works, near Liverpool. Manufactures all kinds of earthenware, and will supply merchants, Captains and Wholesale at the regular trade prices. From the situation of their works they will have it in their power to ship goods without pilferage or breakage; the evils which are of such magnitude when crates are conveyed by inland navigation.

A further advertisement in *Gore's General Advertiser* of 7 June 1798 mentions that a constant supply of Bangor slates, for home consumption and exportation, is always kept on hand and the same journal of 28 December 1797 puts us clearly in the picture as to the goods which were manufactured and the advantages which the proprietors felt were to be derived from the location of their works:

Herculaneum Pottery

Late Copper Works near Liverpool.

Samuel Worthington and Co. having by great pains and attention established their manufactory of earthenware, take upon themselves in the first place, to acknowledge their obligations for the favour of their friends. They have, and mean always to keep by them a large assortment, consisting of useful cream-coloured, enamelled, painted and printed ware, which will enable them to execute large orders in the shortest notice. Exclusive of all other advantages to merchants, captains, and others, they trust those derived from their situation are such as must give peculiar pleasure and satisfaction, for without expense goods may be inspected, approved and packed under the eye of the merchant's clerk. Other advantages will be explained on application.

The earliest pictorial view of the works which survives today is illustrated on page 36. This engraving was specially commissioned as the heading for a set of share certificates which were issued in 1806, of which more details will be given later. The view shows the workshop buildings neatly grouped together on the shore of the Mersey estuary, surrounded by open fields and with the workmen's cottages on the extreme left which are also marked on the plan on page 17 (figure b). Power for grinding the flints and other materials was, at this time, provided by the post windmill on the left of the factory (near to the dock) while to the right of the mill the spars and rigging of a ship in the dock may clearly be seen. Seven pottery kilns or ovens dominate the long low line of buildings which, with their regularly spaced chimney stacks, were part of the copper-smelting establishment (figure a). On the right of the group lies a small building with three lancet windows which formed the private chapel attached to the works and which is referred to in various places amongst the records of the factory. On 25 November 1811 it is recorded in the Herculaneum Minute Book[4] that 'power is granted to the Committee to make such allowance to the Sunday School as they shall, in their discretion, from time to time see fit and think reasonable and proper', and on 5 December of the same year they 'resolved that ten shillings and sixpence per month be paid as a gratuity from the Proprietors to the Sunday School at the Pottery

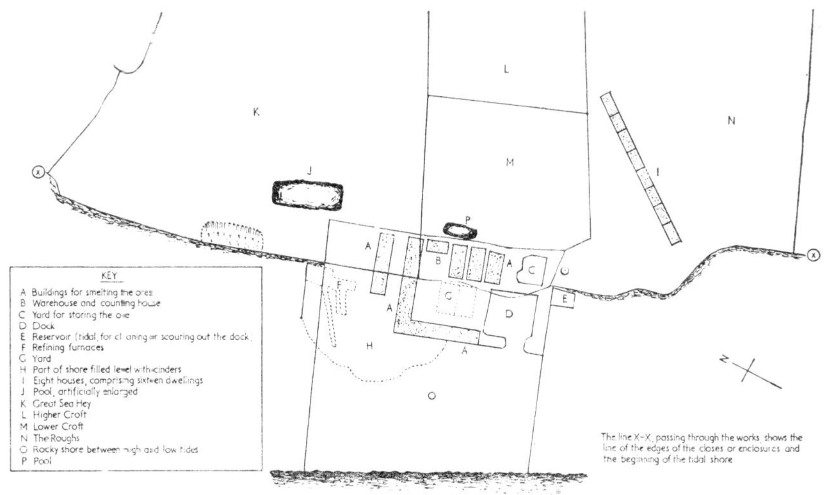

(*a*) *Plan of the copperworks of Charles Roe & Company from the map of part of Toxteth c 1790 (Lancashire Record Office DDM 14/62)*

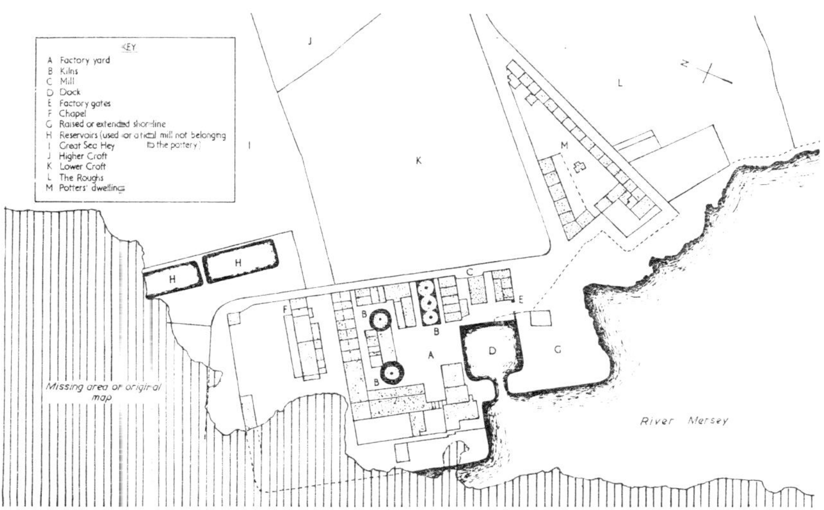

(*b*) *Plan of the Herculaneum Pottery from the map of part of Toxteth c 1800 (Lancashire Record Office DDM 14/61)*

towards the support of that institution'. J. A. Picton gives us an interesting note on the religious life of the community:[5]

> The potters long continued a separate and isolated people, preserving their own manners and customs, and retaining their Mercian dialect. Being principally of Weslyan Methodist persuasion, a small chapel was erected for their use by the proprietors, where Dr Adam Clarke, Jabez Bunting, Robert Newton, and many other eminent men of the denomination, have occasionally officiated.

while the *Liverpool Albion* of 1827 also mentions:

> There is within the walls a neat little chapel, where sermons are preached evry Sunday; and here there is a Sunday School, attended by about 100 scholars. The females, by their attendance at the chapel and their being together, are many of them good singers, both of church music and of songs. We heard their voices several times as they joined in glees over their work.

Of the share certificates themselves, issued to expand the capital of the factory in 1806, a good deal of information survives. Fifty shares valued at £500 each were sold to some twenty-eight shareholders representing the very considerable sum of £25,000 capital. The original shareholders are listed as follows, though in the years following 1806 many certificates changed hands. Three of the original documents, printed on vellum, may be seen in the archives of the Liverpool Museum and Liverpool Record Office.

> Samuel WORTHINGTON: Michael HUMBLE: Samuel HOLLAND: Archibald KEIGHTLEY: Samuel BEREY: John MENZIES: Edward BLACKSTOCK: William FAUCETT: Adam STEUART: William FRENCH: Robert JONES: John HARDING: George ROWE: George ORRED: Richard SUTTON: Richard HOLDEN: Latham HANMER: Henry LAWRENCE: William CARTWRIGHT: William HARDING: Anna HIRD: William HUTCHINSON: Benjamin RAWSON: John HOLLAND: John MOORE: John HOLLINS: Ralph MANSFIELD: James PARR.

Of these shareholders nine are described as 'gentlemen', twelve as 'merchants', two as 'silversmiths', one as a book-keeper, Anna Hird as a spinster, while the professions of two are not given at all. The remaining shareholder was Ralph Mansfield who at the time of the issue was the manager of the pottery and appears to have been the senior member of the group of potters who came from Staffordshire in 1796.

An interesting source of revenue during these early days of the factory's existence was that involving the sale of copper slag of which large deposits remained in the area of the works. The principal customer for this material was John Clare & Company who, between October 1809 and December 1817, purchased some 5,517 tons. As the years went by and the supply diminished the price increased from about 2s 8d a ton in 1809 to about 7s a ton in 1816. The accounts show that by the end of the transaction John Clare was buying his slag (for road and other foundations) in tons, hundredweights and quarters and not in round figures of tons as in former days! They also show that Samuel Worthington made a profit of about £1,000 over the original £600 he had paid for the right to dispose of the slag.

The years between 1806 and about 1820 were undoubtedly the most prosperous for the Herculaneum Pottery Company. Some idea of the range of goods produced may be gained from the following list, selected at random from a surviving account book in the Liverpool Museum.[6]

> TUREENS; SAUCE TUREENS; STANDS & COVERS; VEGETABLE DISHES; COVERED DISHES; COMPOTEERS; SHELLS; TOOTH TRAYS (with and without covers); CHEESE DISHES; CHEESE TOASTERS; OPEN BAKERS; SOAP BOXES; URINALS; CREAM VASES; GOOSE POTS; EWERS; COACH POTS; SUPPER DISHES; EGGSTANDS; CHEESE STANDS; PICKLE SETS; CANDLESTICKS; BUTTER TUBS; CRUIT FRAMES; STEWPOTS; CREAM BOWLS; FOOT BATHS; BARBERS BASINS; TEAPOTS; SUGARS; CHAMBERS; JUGS; PEPPERS; PORRINGERS; COFFEEPOTS; BUTE CUPS; BUTE BOWLS; MUSTARDS; SAUCE LADLES; STONE JUGS; SOUP LADLES. . . .

Although much of the foregoing was simple domestic pottery of the day, many pieces were made of high artistic excellence, particularly between 1806 and about 1815. It has frequently been stated that most of the pottery produced was indistinguishable from that made in Staffordshire at the time, and although in principle we accept that most of the wares made were similar to those from the large establishments of Stoke-on-Trent, following the fashions of the day, at best the Herculaneum products were as good as any produced elsewhere.

The present article is not the place for a detailed appraisal of the pottery made at the Herculaneum factory, an example of which, however, may be seen in the illustration on page 38. It is important to note that probably as much as 75 per cent of the total products of the factory were exported abroad, directly from the factory dock, and an advertisement of 1840[7] (when the factory was closing and the stock was for sale), describes wares produced especially for the United States, Canada, Brazil, Chile, Peru, East India and African markets. The writer has just purchased a piece of Herculaneum ware discovered in western Spain. It is also of particular note that the company acted as an agent for many Staffordshire firms and in the account books are to be found entries for such well-known and important firms as Hicks & Meigh (Shelton), T. & J. Hollins (Shelton), Wood & Cauldwell (Burslem) and Josiah Spode (Stoke), on whose behalf they acted as forwarding agents. Staffordshire pieces were also sold directly to the public from the warehouse in Duke Street, and in the common absence of marks it is frequently difficult to know whether certain specimens of pottery were made at Herculaneum or in Staffordshire.

The various stages in the making of pottery are somewhat complicated and difficult to describe. The reporter of the *Liverpool Albion*, however, was a keen observer of the processes and it seems useful to quote at least that portion of his text which describes the shaping of the wares:

> We next saw the operation of 'throwing' or forming the several articles, jugs, basins, and round vessels. The operation is performed on an horizontal flat wheel, or 'block', turned rapidly by means of a larger wheel and cord, like a common lathe. The workman seizes a piece of clay, the size regulated by constant practice, and, throwing it on the centre of the horizontal wheel, turns it with his hands, hollows it out, thinning it up in a straightish form, and, with his fingers, gives it the required bulge or shape. The operation is performed in a few moments; and it is cut from the block by a piece of wire, and placed carefully upon boards, to be carried to the drying house. Other round articles are formed with equal rapidity, and a piece of thin horn is used to give them the proper polish or shape where the hand is not applicable.

The finer jugs, cups, bowls, and other articles are, when sufficiently dried, though still in a very fragile state, turned on common lathes with iron tools; and it is curious to observe the clay shavings curling off. They are afterwards polished. Coarse jugs and other articles are coloured in stripes and irregular ornaments while on the lathe. The colouring is put into pots with two spouts, one of them having a very small aperture. The workman blows through the other, directing the stream to the article, which is instantly encircled by the colouring liquid. Some of these pots have divisions, and will eject a mixture of colours for coarse ornaments.

The plate and dish makers next attracted our attention. The mould, or block, upon which these are turned is exactly of the shape of the inside of the article, with notched, waved, or plain edges, as required. The clay is beated, till like a pancake, on a tablet of plaster of Paris with a flat block of the same material, having an iron handle in it, and placed on the mould, which is fixed on a spindle; a twirl of the hand sends it round, and it is smoothed over the mould, and finished with a bit of horn. . . . Oval or round cornered dish-making is a more difficult art; it is performed in the same manner, with a delicate jerking of the elbow to meet the shape as it turns, and render the article of equal thickness throughout. When they are taken from the mould, to which they do not stick, from its spongy nature, the inside of the plate or dish is very smooth; yet these are all, after drying a little, repolished by boys.

The next object of curiosity is the operation of the pressers, or moulders of hollow and finer table ware, which cannot be formed by the throwers; such as oval tureens, tubbs, vases, oval sugar-basins, articles having relieve mouldings or ornaments &c. These are all formed in plaster moulds, opening in the centre, and when finished are, many of them, very rich and beautiful. Handles of common articles are cut from long lengths of clay, and turned by hand; finer embossed or ornamental handles are formed in the moulds; and the fixing of these and spouts, &c. to the pieces, is a neat branch of the trade. Here every class of workmen has a peculiar and exclusive department, and has little or no experience in other branches.

When the articles are formed, they are carried on boards to what is termed the green-house, to be dried, and there are stoves to accelerate the operation. They are then packed with more or less care into 'Jaggers', or cylindrical vessels, made of fire clay or marl, with lids, not unlike band-boxes. These are piled one on the other in the ovens, which are of considerable height, and the fires below are put in force, to a white heat, for many hours. Tea-cups and other slender-edged articles are protected from warping, or becoming crooked, by a ring of crockery ware, shaped like a quoit, being placed on the top. The china is much thicker and larger when put into the oven first than when it comes out, and, that it may shrink evenly, it is carefully packed in calcined flint, which has the quality of resisting vitrification.

After describing the manner in which the cheaper pots are decorated the reporter draws to the end of his account, of which the following further extracts are worthy of note:

> Progressing to witness the higher branches of the trade, we were conducted to the china-painting or enamelling room. Here we found a clever young artist painting fine showy ware (fruit plates), for the American market, after some elegant new patterns. He had, with a fine pencil, being [sic] laying on the gold upon a superb tea-service, of china, destined to swell out the splendour of the sumptuous civic feasts given by our worthy Mayor. The workmanship is rich, yet chaste. Each piece has the Liverpool coat of arms on each side, in gold, and, when completed, they will do honour to the purchasers as encouragers of the fine arts, as well as to the furnishers as a creditable specimen of their skill and taste. The gold, when laid on the china, with a pencil, looks like dirty brown paint; it comes from the oven of a dead or frosted-gold colour, and is afterwards burnished with agates to the lustre of the genuine metal.
>
> We concluded our inspection by visiting the pattern room, which is plenished with a number of beautiful specimens of the skill of the potter, chiefly in china. We observed many landscapes and fancy pieces, in glowing colours, on the enamelled chimney ornaments, baskets, plates, &c. but, as these may be seen at the ware-rooms of the establishment, in Duke Street [page 37], we shall not detain our readers with further particulars.
>
> We must not, however, close our sketch, without noticing the great regularity and order that prevail throughout the establishment, and the great cheerfulness and civility of the people. All of them seem too busy for debate or conversation, and silently attend to their several vocations. The females employed apparently exceed in number the males; and, amongst them, are many who are not without considerable personal attractions. . . .
>
> In the last apartment which we visited, there is placed a box, for the reception of donations, to the Benefit Society of the workmen and their families, from those who visit the works, no one being allowed to receive a gratuity. We should be glad, if this hasty and imperfect account of their labours should be the means of increasing the little fund set apart for the sick and infirm of this interesting community.

From the description of the works just quoted, it would reasonably appear that the pottery was a happy and flourishing concern. Other material available, however, shows that all was not as well as it might have been in the 1820s owing to the increasing competition from the ever-expanding potteries of Staffordshire and the difficult economic circumstances of the day. From the Herculaneum Minute Book we find that on 7 August 1821 it was resolved:

> That Mr Barlow [John Barlow of Hanley was engaged as foreman of the works 12 November 1820] be directed to take a journey to the potteries in Staffordshire in order to enquire the price given there to the various artists and workmen, and also as to what artists and workmen may be proper to engage....

also on 5 March 1822 it was resolved:

> That Mr Richard Holden and Mr Archibald Mansfield [Ralph Mansfield's son] do take a journey into Staffordshire to order two sets of copper plates for tea ware, to enquire as to table services of blue ware and to make such observations and to obtain the best information of the general manufactories there....

Even more poignantly the problem may be seen from a roughly scribbled entry in Joseph Tomkinson's notebook:

1. What am't of capital w'd be sufficient to enable us to carry on the Blue business with Credit and profit.
2. What w'd be the probable am't pr year of the sale of blue in the Potteries.
3. What is a fair average of the profits upon the manufactory of blue.
4. What servants do you think you sh'd want in the business.

Joseph Tomkinson's notebooks and other papers are full of tests and trials which were clearly designed to offset the demands of keen competition in the 1820s and he resigned his position as manager in 1826, following a disagreement with the proprietors on the value of continuing his experiments. (The proprietors wished him to continue.) About 1825 Archibald Mansfield, after a career at the works in which he was recognised as being a man of unusual skill, started a pottery of his own in Canning Street, off Bevington Bush, Liverpool, which survived until his death in 1840. From such details as the foregoing it would seem, therefore, that the Herculaneum firm was approaching the end of the road, and this was ultimately confirmed by the following advertisement which appeared in the *Staffordshire Advertiser* of 16 March 1833:

> HERCULANEUM POTTERY LIVERPOOL
>
> To be let or sold
>
> All that valuable Freehold and improving PROPERTY known as the HERCULANEUM POTTERY, Earthenware and China Manufactory; to-

gether with Ovens, Kilns, Steam Engine, Mill, Workshops, Crate Sheds, Manager's House, and 62 Cottages and Houses, now tenanted by the workmen, and occupying 30,900 square yards of land.

Also the Copper-plate Engravings, Blocks, Moulds, &c. and all other utensils complete for carrying on the Earthenware and China Manufacture, all in excellent working condition.

A large and useful Dock, with a powerful Crane and other appurtenances for loading and unloading of Goods, &c. comprising 1089 square yards of Land.

The whole situated on the South Shore of the River Mersey, within half a mile of Brunswick Dock, and adjoining the improvements now making by the Trustees of the Liverpool Dock Estate.

The Premises are in a good state of repair, and well calculated by their local facilities to carry on the manufacture of Earthenware and China to considerable advantage, as well as any other manufactory where space and easy access to the river are required.

By a recent admeasurement, this eligible property contains a total of 54,245 square yards of Land, including 22,222 square yards, being the Strand of the River Mersey down to low water mark, which may be made available for Timber Yards, Ship-building, and other purposes.

For further particulars, apply to Thomas Case, Esq., Exchange Street East, and at the Manufactory, Toxteth Park, Liverpool, where plans of the Property may be seen.

Settlement in this sale did not take long to reach for the old proprietorship was dissolved and an agreement was entered into to sell the property to Ambrose Lace, Gentleman, of Liverpool, for £25,000, to pay £4,000 as a deposit and to come into possession on 1 November 1833. Ambrose Lace immediately let the property to Thomas Case (who already had at least £1,500 invested in the company and was, in fact, chairman of the committee responsible for running the works) and James Mort. Some three years later another change came about when the lease passed to James Mort and John Simpson, for a further seven years.

This last seven-year lease was destined never to run its complete period for in December 1840 the works were advertised for sale once more. The following notice in the *Staffordshire Advertiser* for 5 and 12 December gives an interesting analysis of much of the machinery which had been used by the factory:

IMPORTANT SALE
AT THE HERCULANEUM POTTERY
LIVERPOOL

(now about to be pulled down for the erection of docks)

EXTENSIVE and valuable STOCK OF EARTHENWARE, consisting of printed table, tea and toilette ware; and painted, edged, dipt, and cream colour ware, of all descriptions; potters' FIXTURES, MATERIALS, valuable copper plate ENGRAVINGS, being of choice patterns and shapes, blocks and moulds, superior draught horses, gearing, carts, lorry, and other miscellaneous effects.

Also the mill work, &c. which will be found suitable for manufacturers, engineers, millwrights, grinders of plaster, barytes &c., consists of two flint pans of 13 feet diameter, three ditto of nine feet, two ditto of five feet, and six colour pans, each 1½ feet in diameter, plaster mill, a pair of rollers 20 inches wide, clay mill three feet eight inches by two feet one inch, a large cistern with water pumps, pipes etc. hoisting tackle, a large wash tub, and fan nine feet six inches in diameter, a pump, connecting rods, uprights &c., with all the needful machinery, crown spur, driving and cog wheels, shafts and collars, arms and drivers in connection with a THIRTY HORSE POWER ENGINE, with everything requisite for working the above.

WILL BE SUBMITTED TO SALE BY AUCTION
by Mr Johnson

On the premises, at the Herculaneum Pottery, Liverpool.

On Tuesday, December 15th. 1840 and following days until all is sold.

Descriptive catalogues of sale are now in circulation, and may be had on application of the HERCULANEUM POTTERY COMPANY, Liverpool, or from the Auctioneer, Burslem.

Of the various items mentioned in this advertisement the steam engine is perhaps the most important. This engine was constructed by one Mr Kirk and the work begun in November 1817. Apart from the fact that a steam engine could be used to reduce enormously the hand manipulation formerly required in many grinding processes, the real cause of its introduction was the urgent need for the factory to be independent for its supplies of ground flint—a material of great importance in the composition of both the clay bodies and the glazes used at the pottery. Until this date the potters had had to rely on purchasing their flint in an already-ground condition. Apparently the idea of a steam engine had been discussed as early as 1811, the machine in question to have cost £2,500, but the proprietors seem to have disagreed about putting up the money during those difficult times of the war with France. After 1815 there was an appreciable improvement in the amount of work produced at Herculaneum and the consequent capital in hand to cover such improvements to the plant.

The name Herculaneum for a Merseyside pottery of 1796 was no doubt chosen because of the evident success of Josiah Wedgwood's pottery called by another ancient Italian name, Etruria. Unlike Etruria, however, the fame of Herculaneum was relatively short-lived since the company lasted, as we have seen, rather less than fifty years. The location of the factory was primarily based on the advantages of good transport for raw materials and finished goods. For a time the works prospered and success seemed assured. The rising pottery industry of Staffordshire, however, with most of its raw materials close to hand and its canal system already established between the Mersey and the Trent (first pioneered by Wedgwood in 1766), coupled with the difficulties of the Napoleonic wars, the nation-wide recession of trade in the 1820s and finally the expanding needs of Liverpool's warehousing and shipping interests, brought about the end of this interesting pottery. On the site where the factory originally stood there is now nothing to be seen except docks and railway sidings. A few old houses on Grafton Street which were reputedly used by the potters, the Herculaneum Docks, the Herculaneum Bridge Hotel and the Herculaneum Steel Fabrication Works are the only reminders which exist today of the Herculaneum Pottery.

It was not the last pottery to work on Merseyside. The experiment of siting the workshops near the means of ready transport was tried in the field of ceramic production once more in 1851, when the Staffordshire potter Henry Goodwin established his factory at Seacombe on the Cheshire Wirral. Economically this factory, in spite of its modern planning and up-to-date methods, rested on a knife-edge throughout the short twenty years of its life, and the wares it produced were poor indeed compared with the products of Herculaneum.

One small subsidiary of the Herculaneum factory, begun in 1836 by

Messrs Mort & Simpson, should be noted. This was a small factory at St Helens, known in that town as the Liverpool Pottery. Sited close to the coal mines and alongside the Sankey Canal, it worked until the summer of 1841 when it passed into other hands, though still continuing as a pottery. A few fragments of unglazed shards were recently found in the area of the potworks on ground now occupied by the timber yards of Messrs Pilkington Brothers' glassworks, and the Sankey Canal itself, in that section, is remembered by the name Canal Street which now follows the line of the original cut.

Notes

1 J. Aikin, *A Description of the Country from Thirty to Forty Miles Round Manchester*, 1795, 375 (reprinted 1968).
2 In 1767 'William Graham & Company, Mug Warehouse, N. side Old Dock' is recorded in *Gore's Directory* and an Andrew Graham, potter at 2 East Street in 1810.
3 Joseph Mayer, *History of the Art of Pottery in Liverpool*, 1854.
4 Liverpool Record Office, Herculaneum Minute Book 1806–22.
5 J. A. Picton, *Memorials of Liverpool*, 1875, vol II, 466.
6 Tomkinson Papers, Liverpool Museum.
Joseph Tomkinson (b 1784, d New York 1836) was employed at the Herculaneum Potteries for many years, becoming manager from 1821 to 1826 when he emigrated to the United States.
7 *Staffordshire Advertiser*, 31 October 1840.

Plates, pages 36–8

P. S. RICHARDS

The Holywell Textile Mills, Flintshire

A study of the relationship of these North Wales mills to the Welsh flannel industry and the Lancashire cotton industry

To obtain a complete picture of an industry, the study of both literary and archaeological evidence is essential; the two sources of information complement each other.[1] Thus in preparing this paper the writer visited the Holywell mills in order to obtain first-hand information about them.[2] The study of a single plant can be very interesting, but to obtain a satisfactory picture, it is essential to see how the single plant fits into the larger pattern of what is known about the industry.[3] Hence this study of the Holywell mills will be made in relation to both the Welsh flannel industry and the Lancashire cotton industry.[4]

I

There are nearly four-and-a-half million sheep in Wales; this represents a density of something like one per acre. The most important breed, numerically and economically, is the Welsh mountain sheep which is well suited to the rough terrain of much of upland Wales,[5] and which can survive severe weather better than cattle can. They do not require the daily attention which is given to dairy animals; they graze closer than do cattle, and are capable of living on poor or coarse pasture.[6] Wool from the sheep and the lambs is marketed by the Wool Marketing Board; some is consumed by the Welsh woollen industry and the remainder is sent to England. The characteristic Welsh wool is obtained from the upland sheep and because of its rough texture (it contains kemp), it is blended for manufacturing purposes with other wools such as merino.[7] Even as early as 1341 Welsh wools were stated to be of the poorest quality in the country, and were described as 'coarse and of little value'.[8] Welsh frieze (coarse woollen cloth with a nap) was shipped from Lymm by Hanseatic merchants in 1467.[9] Today the Flintshire mills use wool from many sources, including overseas.

Many parts of Wales formerly had a considerable domestic woollen industry.[10] It is one of the oldest rural industries in the country, having grown in response to local needs, and was based on local raw material. Moorland sheep provided the wool, and many clear swift-running streams supplied pure water for washing and cleaning it, and for the fulling processes and dyeing. These streams were also harnessed to provide power for turning the waterwheels. Thus many of the woollen mills, including those at Holywell, are sited near supplies of water.

The settlement of European refugees in certain parts of Wales was a factor in determining the location of the industry. The Flemings, who settled in South Pembrokeshire, and the French Protestants, who came to Montgomeryshire, Breconshire, and north-east Wales and who later moved to the Teifi valley, were skilled weavers and introduced new methods for the manufacture of wool. Their influence on the Flintshire mills, however, was very limited.

The Industrial Revolution, which slowly changed the character of the woollen industry in many parts of England, hardly influenced the industry in Wales. The development of steam power was of little advantage, since the centres of woollen production were remote from the coal-producing areas, and the facilities for the transport of coal were inadequate. Flintshire, however, seems to be an exception: the Holywell mills are on a coalfield (very near to many disused pits) and therefore they could use steam power to drive the machinery. (Today, however, electricity from the national grid is used.) The isolated nature of Wales partly explains why the Welsh manufacturers were slow to introduce new machinery, but the main reasons were that they lacked the capital necessary for the purchase of new equipment. Although the Flintshire mills were short of capital, they were much more open to English influences than the rest of Wales—a factor which led to the development of the woollen industry there. Thus in many ways the Holywell textile mills are not typical of Welsh woollen mills.

Until about 1850 the Welsh woollen industry, which depended on local markets, was fairly prosperous, but after 1850 there was competition from Lancashire and Yorkshire and the industry began to decline. Although the number of employees in the Flintshire woollen industry fell between 1861 and 1871, this was only a temporary setback. Otherwise the number of workers increased considerably between 1851 and 1891—again Flintshire is untypical of Wales as a whole where the number of persons employed in the woollen industry fell from 9,000 in 1851 to about 2,300 in 1911. This was in spite of the demand by the miners of South Wales and the quarrymen of North Wales in the latter half of the nineteenth century for Welsh flannel; Holywell was able to meet much of this demand, and prosper in so doing. With the changing fashions of the twentieth century even the demand for Welsh flannel rapidly declined. However, these mills are the largest and most modern in Wales today and consume one-third of the wool used in the industry.[11] Why the Holywell mills survived will be the subject of the latter part of this paper.

II

The precursors of the present Holywell woollen mills were the cotton factories which were established at both Holywell and Mold in the eighteenth century. The factory at Holywell was concerned entirely with, and that at Mold mainly with, the spinning of cotton and not its weaving.[12] The industry migrated from Lancashire, attracted by St Winefred's Well: the reputation of this well in Roman Catholic circles was high and well known to the West Lancashire people among whom the Catholic element was strong. St Winefred's Well rises from the Holywell Stream (or Holywell River) and was reliable—the mills (and there were many: paper mills, snuff mills etc) upon the stream were never retarded by floods and the water never froze. It was also close to the River Dee, and there were regular sailings from Bagillt to Liverpool, Chester and Parkgate.[13] The district was not as remote as some which became cotton-spinning centres for a period; this probably accounts for the fact already noted that the Holywell mills are untypical of those of the rest of Wales.

There were many attractions for John Smalley, formerly a partner of Arkwright in his struggling days at Preston, to establish himself independently of Arkwright at Holywell and so in 1777 inaugurate the cotton-spinning industry in Wales.[14] He set up, in partnership with John Chambers of Holywell, the Yellow Mill, a replica of the typical Lancashire warehouse of pre-power days, to which a waterwheel had been added.[15] Spinners were probably brought from England to work the mills—at a later date, at any rate, the bulk of the employees were English.[16]

The years 1783–7 were prosperous ones for the cotton industry: imports of raw cotton doubled within four years of the ending of the American War of Independence. The expiry of Arkwright's patents in 1785 and the introduction of cylinder printing by Livesay, Hargreaves & Company also contributed to this prosperity. However, the great panic of 1787–8, with the failure of this firm and of Allen's Bank in Manchester, shook the young industry to its foundations.[17]

The boom of the previous years, however, had its repercussions in Holywell, despite Smalley's death in 1782 and the bankruptcy of Chambers;[18] Smalley's widow continued with the business and soon found supporters, who invested fresh capital. In 1783 the Upper mill was built and in 1785 a third, the Lower mill, was constructed. Both were much larger than the original mill and the whole concern was known as the Holywell Cotton Twist Company.[19] This company continued to expand. In 1790 a fourth mill, the Crescent mill, was built, rather smaller than the Upper and Lower mills.[20] At this time, according to Pennant, there were over 1,225 employees, including over 500 women and children, as well as 300 parish apprentices housed in the company's own 'Commodious houses'. In Denbigh the company had taken over a building previously used as a woollen mill and built by Mostyn, Pigot & Company in 1749. There the cotton was picked and sorted. Mule spinning was carried on in addition to spinning by the water frame.[21]

The Cotton Twist mills, variously known as Douglas, Smalley & Company, and later Douglas & Company, continued to depend on water power until the thirties. In 1816 the number of employees was 736, of whom 20 were under ten years of age and 297 between ten and eighteen years.[22] This reduction in the number of employees was probably due to the economic dislocation which followed the Napoleonic wars. The whole of the cotton industry marked time after the financial crises of 1825 and 1826; but by the 1830s power-loom weaving had extended. In 1833 the mills depended on 'the improved machinery of Sir Richard Arkwright'; the Upper mill worked 12,218 spindles, the Lower mill 7,492 and the Crescent mill 8,286; 26,096 pounds of thread were produced weekly. Many manufacturers had added weaving sheds to their factories and installed steam engines to supplement or replace their waterwheels. By 1835, as has already been seen, the Flintshire factories employed five steam engines and four waterwheels, all the steam engines being at the Holywell mills.[23]

This period of apparent prosperity was short-lived and the slump of 1837 contributed to the downfall of the Douglas family (the Smalleys withdrew from the firm in 1828). Before this, the Cotton Twist Company had survived both the war and the many trials of the post-war years—including serious damage by floods in 1821 (the River Holywell evidently flooded at least once!) and attempts to burn down the mills in the same year.[24]

There were four reasons for the failure of the enterprise. The banking house which the partners had set up collapsed in 1838.[25] The River Dee had been silting up and this made the import of raw cotton from overseas more expensive.[26] The 1833 Factory Act, which prevented the employment of young persons in textile factories and appointed inspectors to enforce this, had the effect of increasing labour costs. The introduction of steam power had failed to maintain the prosperity of the Holywell firm against the increasing dominance of South Lancashire. This competition was met by commercial impotence. Contravention of the Factory Act in an effort to compete with other products was followed by a prosecution in 1837.[27] By 1841 only fourteen people were employed[28] and apparently at this time the firm soon went into liquidation only to rise again, however, as woollen mills.[29]

The Dock mill, Portsmouth

An old line illustration of the Dock mill

The Rudmore lime mill, Portsmouth (Courtesy: Portsmouth City Museums)

The derelict mill at Owslebury (1930)

The windmill at Chalton in the 1930s. Note the cupola-shaped cap then still in existence

A recent photograph of the Chalton mill, showing how the decay has set in. It is now a pigsty

Bursledon mill

The Old mill at Langstone

The Chalton mill in the late 1950s

The mill at Speltham Hill, Hambledon, in the 1930s. Even at that time it was an overgrown ruin.

For all preceding plates, see 'The Windmills of Hampshire', pp 1–12

View of the Herculaneum Pottery from an engraving of 1806 by George Codling. This engraving formed the heading of share certificates issued that year and printed upon vellum. (Courtesy: Liverpool Museum)

Water-colour drawing of the Herculaneum Pottery by Joseph Mayer, 1825 (Courtesy: Liverpool Record Office)

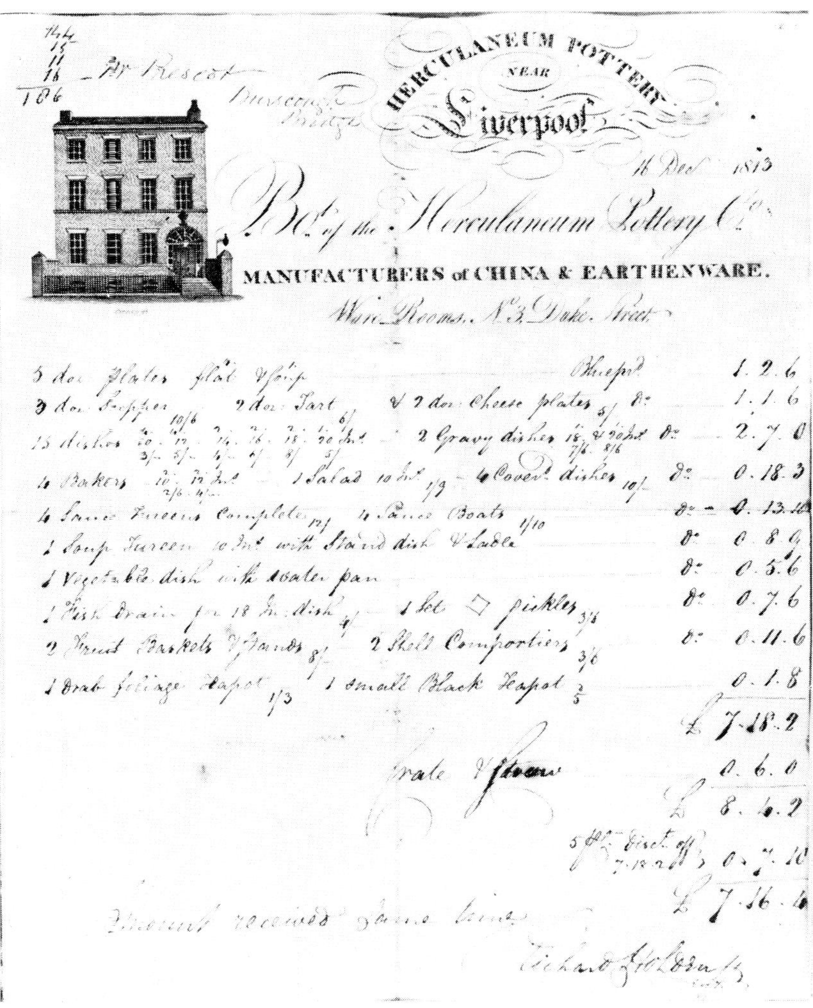

Mr Prescot
Burscough Bridge

HERCULANEUM POTTERY NEAR Liverpool

16 Dec 1813

Bot. of the Herculaneum Pottery Co.

MANUFACTURERS of CHINA & EARTHENWARE.

Ware Rooms, No. 3 Duke Street

5 doz plates flat & soup	Blue print	1. 2. 6
3 doz Supper 2 doz Tart & 2 doz Cheese plates 5/	Do	1. 1. 6
15 dishes … 2 Gravy dishes	Do	2. 7. 0
4 Bakers … 1 Salad 10 Inch 1/9 4 Cover'd dishes 10/	Do	0. 18. 3
4 Sauce Tureens Complete 12/ 4 Sauce Boats 1/10	Do	0. 13. 10
1 Soup Tureen 10 Inch with Stand dish & Ladle	Do	0. 8. 9
1 Vegetable dish with water pan	Do	0. 5. 6
1 Fish drain for 18 In. dish 4/ 1 Set ◇ pickles 3/6	Do	0. 7. 6
2 Fruit Baskets & Stands 8/ 2 Shell Comportiers 3/6	Do	0. 11. 6
1 Drab foliage Teapot 1/3 1 small Black Teapot 5		0. 1. 8
		£ 7. 18. 2
Crate & Straw		0. 6. 0
		£ 8. 4. 2
5 p Ct Disct off 7.18.2		0. 7. 10
		£ 7. 16. 4

Amount received same time

Richard Holden

Bill of 1813 issued by the Herculaneum Pottery Company with an illustration of the Duke Street Warehouse and signed by Richard Holden, cash and book-keeper (Courtesy: Liverpool Museum)

For plates on these two pages, see 'The China and Earthenware Manufactory, 1796–1840', pp 13–27

Coffee pot, stoneware, maroon ground with cream-coloured relief decoration, 1805–10 (Courtesy: Liverpool Museum)

See 'The Herculaneum China and Earthenware Manufactory, 1796–1840', pp 13–27

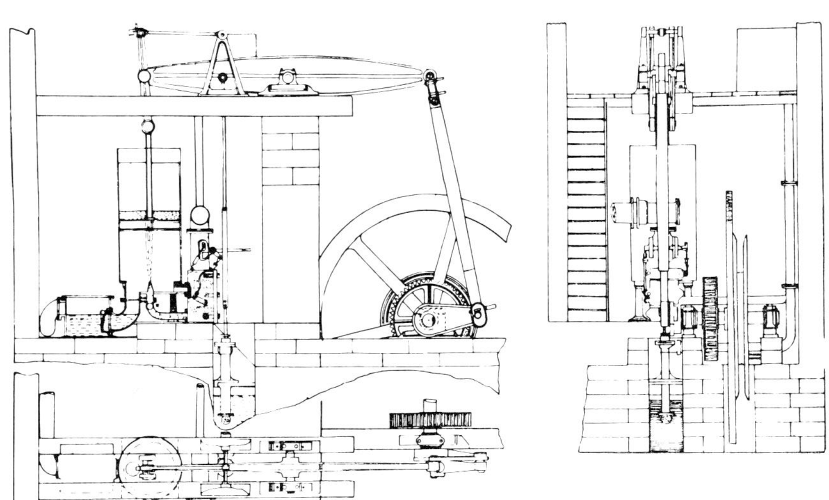

This Newcomen rotative engine, erected in the first decade of the nineteenth century at Farme Colliery, operated for a century. Its date is of course later than those in the list in 'Early Application of Steam Power at Scottish Collieries: A Note and Query', pp 70–3 *(Courtesy: Glasgow Museums)*

Milestone at Cockadilly, on re-alignment (1784) of Old Bath Road near Nympsfield (ST 797003)

Milestone at Stepping Stone Lane, Painswick (SO 864088), probably late 1770s

See 'Aids to Recording (2): Some Problems of Dating Milestones', pp 60–9

Fall Ings Foundry, Wakefield: eighteenth-century engine house

Fall Ings Foundry, Wakefield: nineteenth-century foundry building

See 'Fall Ings, Wakefield: Some Notes on an Eighteenth-Century Foundry', pp 74–9

The other centre of cotton manufacture in Flintshire was the mill at Mold, a product of the boom years of 1790–4 when the Smalleys, amongst others, extended their mills. The flourishing state of the Holywell company drew the attention of other Lancashire manufacturers towards the Welsh valleys and inspired Welsh landowners to offer likely sites for industrial concerns.[30] In 1792 Messrs Samuel & James Knight of Manchester set up near Mold a 'handsome and stupendous cotton factory' which, twenty years later, gave an example to North Wales in the use of gas for lighting. By 1820, 300 hands were employed and the premises were greatly enlarged during the boom of 1825.[31]

Like the Smalleys, the Knights combined banking with cotton spinning, but their resources do not seem to have been equal to the strain of the years of slack trade which followed the boom. There are no references to this bank after 1828 and by 1833 operations at the cotton mill were at a standstill. It was reopened, however, when trade improved. By 1836, 236 hands were employed and in 1838, despite the slump, sixty more. More than half the employees were now women and more than half were under eighteen: they were paid less than men. This increase was partly due to the fact that the new proprietors, Messrs Inman & Son, had extended their operations by installing thirty power looms, which were worked by a staff of fourteen women, under the supervision of two male weavers from Manchester. The Mold factory had long sent its cotton waste to Manchester. It was now able to send bales of the state calicoes known as 'domestics'. It had also ceased to be a mere watermill. One steam engine came in with the power looms, and a second followed soon after, giving the mill, between water and steam, a total capacity of 112 hp.

Having survived the worst troubles of the early years of the nineteenth century, the Mold cotton mill was able to maintain itself for another generation. In 1841 there were 246 cotton workers in Flintshire; of these 14 worked in Holywell and the rest in Mold. During the next decade, the number fell to 48, but it had risen again to 171 by 1861; of these nearly 70 per cent were females. In 1866, however, the works were completely destroyed by fire, and as trade had not yet recovered from the cotton famine of 1861–5 they were not rebuilt. At the time of the fire, there were 250 employees and 25,000 spindles; weaving, however, had apparently been abandoned and the mill had reverted to water power. This factory was not to enjoy resurrection as a woollen mill. The estate and ruins were bought by a steel tinplate firm and later passed to the Pontypool Iron & Tinplate Company.

III

A few years after the cotton mills had ceased production, a Mr John Jones, of Newtown, took over one of the disused cotton mills to use it for flannel weaving. He developed here the first practicable power loom for the Welsh woollen industry which was in use by 1850. Before that time handloom weaving was the usual practice; the use of the power loom doubled the output.[32] The explanation for the rise of this industry here lies in the fact that, according to local tradition, John Jones had not been allowed to set up weaving machinery at home.[33] Both Flintshire and Denbighshire had been very slow to develop a woollen textile industry despite the large number of sheep reared in these counties. A contemporary writer stated that the inhabitants of these two counties were not disposed to exercise the wheel and the loom; they either sold their fleece wool to adjoining manufacturers or took it to Chester and Shrewsbury sales to meet the more crafty clothiers of the north.[34]

Besides the existence of the mills there were, however, numerous advantages in the choice of this site. There was a never-failing cheap water supply—generating 30 hp—which the lessor, Sir Pyers Mostyn, was prepared to let for the modest rent of about £120 per annum. There were plenty of operatives who inherited their skill from the days of cotton manufacture.[35] In those days labour had been cheap because of the low cost of living compared with other areas.[36] There were excellent railway communications—the main line from London to Holyhead and a branch line up the Greenfield Valley to Holywell had recently been built. The River Dee provided access to Liverpool. St

Winefred's stream (Greenfield River) was not thought to be so suitable for textile finishing processes as the Severn tributaries but was superior to the rivers of Lancashire.[37] Despite all these advantages the venture of John Jones failed for lack of capital. Another citizen of Newtown, Richard Baldwin, followed him and failed for the same reason.

The industry did not flourish in the rest of Wales—Flintshire was the only county in the Principality where the number of employees did not decline during the second half of the century. Originally it had the smallest production of woollens in the whole of Wales but by 1901 it was second only to Montgomeryshire. By that time there were normally over 200 employees in Flintshire engaged in woollen manufacture, most of them in the Holywell textile mills. Since then, the coming of the artificial silk industry has made Flintshire the leading textile county in North Wales.[38] The following table shows the number of employees in the woollen industry in Flintshire during the latter part of the nineteenth century and the early part of the twentieth century:[39]

Year	Employees	Year	Employees
1831	40	1881	65
1841	5	1891	205
1851	32	1901	140
1861	88	1911	215
1871	49	1914	300

The decline during the years 1831 and 1851 was the result, as has already been stated, of two successive owners going bankrupt. The large increase in the number of workers in the woollen industry was explained by the opening of one of the largest woollen mills in Wales at Holywell.[40] The temporary decline in the numbers of employees in 1901 was the result of a serious fire at the works.

The early failures of woollen manufacturing in Flintshire were the result of shortages of working capital. It was the individual who had to supply the necessary capital for his business, but after 1862 the joint-stock company form came into being. Thus the way was open for industries to be supported by ample capital. The woollen industry was not firmly established in Holywell until the arrival of a limited liability company, which came in 1874 and was called the Welsh Flannel Manufacturing Company. This was accompanied by an increase in the number of workers in the industry. This company was the joint creation of a Welshman, Urias Bromley, who was without capital, and William Brown (owner of a famous retail store, Brown's of Chester), who was not. Brown wanted to supply work for the inhabitants of Holywell, and at this time there was much unemployment in the town.[41] They started to manufacture Welsh flannel, which had long been the staple product of the Welsh woollen industry at Holywell and for which the demand at this time was substantial. Because of the special properties of Welsh wool, the shrinkage of the cloth was limited and it readily absorbed perspiration. Thus it was ideally suited for underwear and nightgowns, a fact which was acknowledged in the days of Queen Victoria by everyone from the royal household down to the humblest cottager in the land.

The new company, which brought fresh hope to 'the decaying town of Holywell', showed commendable enterprise in developing the industry. A new pipe was laid, a new waterwheel constructed, 28 ft in diameter developing 24 hp, and modern machinery was installed. In 1874 a contemporary account records that there were eighty looms for the manufacture of flannel and elastic cloth—all with the requisite machinery and appliances for milling, dyeing and finishing Welsh flannel.[42] At the same time St Winefred's stream provided seven million gallons every twenty-four hours and this was reinforced by a new source of water playing on wheels coming from the old Holway mines. The Upper factory, on the Greenfield–Holywell Road, constructed entirely of brick and surmounted by a wooden cupola and bell, was six storeys high. On the ground floor there was a machine for 'willowing' and oiling wool. On the second storey there were twelve carding machines and two others in the rear of the mill. The third storey was devoted to roving and spinning: here there were two mules and one roving machine. Altogether there were 3,315 spindles, fourteen carding machines, six mules, two roving engines and two warping mills. The Upper mill was used for wool sorting, carding and spinning and supplied the Crescent mill where the weaving and finishing was done. Fifty to sixty pieces could be turned out in a week—one piece was 170 yd long.

On 19 February 1883 a disastrous fire occurred, causing serious damage and much consternation in the town,[43] largely because it was rumoured that the mill would not be rebuilt. Consequently 170 people were thrown out of work. However, the textile machinery was saved and was moved to the Town Hall, where work was resumed. A new mill was in production by 1884.[44] This was built of local brick from the Victoria brickworks and the small mill 'race' was carried under the building on its way to the Crescent mills. On the basement floor was a carding room (87 ft × 78 ft) and a willow room. The sorted wool went to the willow or teasing machine and then when it was opened out, was ready for carding. On the second and top floors there were spinning and roving machines and warping mills. The machinery was still worked by a high-breast waterwheel with the water from St Winefred's well and the Holywell level stream; there were now 5,200 spindles.[45] Rebuilding was finished by September 1884 and the day of the opening ceremony was declared a public holiday in Holywell—which reflects the very great importance of the woollen industry in the economy of this small market town. Once the mills had recovered from the dislocation caused by the fire of 1883, their output began to rise enormously, and a large number of the workers were in the industry by 1901. Long-term contracts were undertaken for leading wholesale houses in London and the provinces, and for a time the company enjoyed steady profits and expanding trade.

But in the closing years of the century both external and internal problems affected its fortunes. Because of the popularity of Welsh flannel, English manufacturers, mainly in the town of Rochdale, began to produce imitation Welsh flannels which severely competed with the native product.[46] Taste also affected the industry: flannel was no longer fashionable for underwear, for knitted goods made of wool and cotton, and later artificial silk, were more popular. This trend was eventually to result in the closing of scores of little Welsh factories which could not change from a traditional and now outmoded style because of the limitations of their machinery. It was only the ability of the Welsh Flannel Manufacturing Company to overcome these problems, an aspect of geographical inertia, which enabled the industry to survive, with varying fortune, up to the present day.

As if these external problems were not sufficiently threatening, the progress of the Welsh Flannel Manufacturing Company was again impeded by domestic tragedy. In 1898, fire completely destroyed the carding and spinning plant, and for several years afterwards strenuous efforts were needed to gain lost ground. In 1902 the management of the Holywell mills changed. Thomas H. Waterhouse, a Yorkshireman, who had joined the company at its inception and had been successively secretary and general manager, died and was succeeded by his son, Thomas Waterhouse. The new general manager set about modernising and expanding the plant. The number of carding machines was increased from two to eight; sixteen additional spinning mules were installed; the loom capacity rose by 60 per cent and, in 1913, the mills were completely electrified. It was during this period, too, that the name of the firm was altered to Holywell Textile Mills Ltd, a change which reflected the declining demand for Welsh flannel and the development of new products such as tweeds and union shirting cloths.

The 1914–18 war brought intensive activity to the Holywell mills as they were mainly engaged in producing flannel for the British and French armies. The war was followed by a brief boom, culminating in 1920–1 in a disastrous slump which spread over the whole of British industry. The mills went through a difficult period, but whereas in the following two decades 400 woollen firms in Yorkshire were compelled to close, the Holywell factory clung on tenaciously. By 1925 there were

8,000 spindles and more than 200 looms, and the mills were equipped with the most modern electrically-driven machines. Large numbers of workpeople were housed in the company's dwellings. The cloth produced had a world-wide reputation, and the company possessed agencies throughout the British Empire.[47] During the inter-war years, further new products were developed. Union shirtings, composed of cotton and wool, were an important product, but they were supplemented by Welsh tweeds which found markets abroad, notably in South Africa, and by white and coloured blankets, which became increasingly important and competed successfully with the products of Whitney and Yorkshire. This was, however, a period of cut-throat competition and profit margins throughout the British woollen industry were narrowed to vanishing point, with the result that no adequate provision could be made for capital replacement and improvement.

With the outbreak of war in 1939, the situation was again changed overnight In a matter of months the demand for woollen goods far exceeded the industry's productive capacity; consequently, the years that followed saw the renaissance of the Holywell textile mills. In 1951, production reached the highest peak in the firm's history and the extensions to plant and buildings carried out from 1947 to 1950 constituted the most hopeful development in the Welsh woollen industry since 1900. Products were drastically changed: flannel disappeared completely from the looms; even blankets were now a minor item. In their place the greater part of the machinery was turning out women's coating cloths—velours, Bedford cords, whipcords, checks and fancy tweeds—which were supplied to the leading merchants and coat manufacturers in both London and the provinces.[48] Overseas markets were not neglected, the Holywell cloths being exported to the United States, Canada, South Africa, Rhodesia, Norway, Denmark, Cyprus, the Lebanon, Turkey and even the South Sea Islands. A subsidiary but potentially important trade was also developed in woollen upholstery and curtain materials. Some of these luxurious and strikingly designed fabrics graced a number of Cunard and White Star liners, notably the *Queen Mary* and the *Caronia*.[49] Also it was hoped to use them to furnish theatres and to upholster railway carriages and motor cars.

However, in 1952, the mills, in common with much of the textile trade, suffered another severe setback when the post-war boom came to an abrupt stop, and once more the firm had to struggle to keep going. During this period many textile firms in Lancashire and Yorkshire had to close down; others never really recovered and are still struggling. In 1957 a private investment company acquired the bulk of the shares, purely to keep the old-established and largest Welsh firm in existence. A new manager was appointed and the mills, once again, are making a profit. To do this they have changed their products: blankets, travel rugs, tapestry and honeycomb bedspreads are produced. These are largely made from 'shoddy' and are of very high quality. The factory, today, however, is but a shadow of its former size.

IV

A Geographical Analysis of Woollen Manufacture in Flintshire

Wool is almost the only fibre used by the Holywell textile mills. It comes from a variety of sources: the finest wools suitable for ladies' clothing and mantle cloths from Australia; the wool used for the manufacture of tweeds and furnishing fabrics from New Zealand. In addition, a small amount is obtained from sheep reared in the Vale of Clwyd. Much of the wool imported into this country arrives in a greasy state just as it has been shorn from the sheep's back. It has to be 'scoured'—washed in alkali (sodium carbonate) and soap, sorted and graded into standard qualities, and tightly compressed into bales, each about 200 lb in weight. This initial processing is done in the Bradford or Huddersfield areas. Some arrives already processed—thus saving the expense of transporting 'waste and dirt' half-way round the world. This is in partial harmony with Weber's theory that industries whose products weigh less than the raw materials from which they are made (in which, in other words, there is loss of weight in manufacture) are tied in location to their raw materials. Once the raw materials are prepared for use, there will be relatively little further loss of weight, although some might be lost in the teasing process. The wool arrives at Holywell ready for teasing, ie opening out, because in tightly packed bales the wool is unfit for spinning into yarn. Another raw material is the 'oil', a highly saponified fatty acid base, which is used to lubricate the wool fibres for the combing process (80 per cent of the oil content will react with sodium carbonate to form a soap). The grease is then washed out. By law a special oil with a high flash point is used; this is to prevent spontaneous combustion. This process does not upset Weber's theory since it involves an addition and a subtraction which cancel each other out in the course of manufacture. Some of the wool for checked and fancy patterns is already dyed in Yorkshire immediately after the scouring process and sent to Holywell in that state. The remainder is sent back to commission dyers and finishers operating in Lancashire.

Electricity from the national grid runs the machinery. Somewhat fewer than one hundred people are employed, drawn mainly from the Holywell district. Training is given within the factory. Men are employed for the heavy manual work and the maintenance of machinery, but women do most of the actual manufacture. The weekly output of yarn averages about 12,000 lb in weight or approximately 21,000 miles; when converted into cloth, this is up to 4 miles in length and $1\frac{1}{2}$ miles in width.[30]

This industry obviously has a very precarious basis: it relies almost entirely on raw materials imported from overseas which have been semi-prepared elsewhere. Thus transport costs are high. Maximum efficiency in the use of raw materials is a feature of the mill organisation: any wool lost in the course of manufacture is recovered and used again. The industry flourishes today because it produces, by mechanised processes, a very high-grade and expensive product, for which there is a steady demand, especially from high-class hotels and shipping firms. In addition there is a strong human feeling for the industry on the part of the board of directors: they have striven to keep it going and there was, and still is, a will to see it survive.

These mills are obviously an example of geographical or industrial inertia—a contrast to other existing industries of Deeside, since only the paper mills, and to a lesser extent the one surviving coal mine at the Point of Ayr, can boast anything like a long and continuous history.

Notes

1 K. Hudson, *Handbook for Industrial Archaeologists*, 1967, 10.
2 I am indebted to P. P. Dudek, the managing director of the Holywell textile mills, for much of the information on which this paper is based.
3 K. Hudson, op cit, 28.
4 I am indebted to K. Hudson for suggesting this line of approach.
5 M. E. Hughes and A. J. James, *Wales: A Physical, Economic and Social Geography*, 1961, 91.
6 G. Dury, *The British Isles: A Systematic and Regional Geography*, 1961, 204.
7 M. E. Hughes and A. J. James, op cit, 92.
8 D. T. Williams, 'Medieval Foreign Trade: Western Ports' in *The Historical Geography of England before 1800*, H. C. Darby (ed), 1948, 290.
9 Public Record Office, Customs Accounts 97/8; N. S. B. Gras, *Early English Customs System*, 1918, 615, cited by R. A. Pelham, 'Medieval Foreign Trade: Eastern Ports' in H. C. Darby, op cit, 299.
10 L. D. Stamp and S. H. Beaver, *The British Isles: A Geographic and Economic Survey*, 1963, 490.
11 M. E. Hughes and A. J. James, op cit, 179–82.
12 E. J. Foulkes, 'The Cotton-Spinning Factories of Flintshire 1776–1866', *Journal of the Flintshire Historical Society*, XXI, 1964, 91.
13 *The Chester Chronicle*, 30 April 1802; 4 February 1825, cited by Foulkes, op cit, 91.
14 Pennant, *History of the Parishes of Whiteford and Holywell*, 1796, 201–3. Espinasse, *Lancashire Worthies*, I, 384–7, cited by Foulkes, op cit, 91.
15 Pennant, op cit, 214, cited by Foulkes, op cit, 92.
16 M. L. Louis, *Gleanings of a Tour in North Wales*, Liverpool, 1824, 29, and A. H. Dodd, *The Industrial Revolution in North Wales*, 1951, 284.
17 Ellison, *Cotton Trade of Great Britain*, 1886, 49–50. Grindon, *Manchester Banks and Bankers*, 1872, 45–7. *Manchester Mercury*, 29 April 1788; 20 May 1788, cited by Foulkes, op cit, 92.
18 *London Morning Chronicle*, 17 March 1780, cited by Foulkes, op cit, 92.
19 Foulkes, op cit, 92.
20 Pennant, op cit, 213.
21 *Manchester Mercury*, 5 April 1791; 3 May 1791, Pennant, op cit, 216, *Manchester Chronicle*, 9 October 1790.
22 *Select Committee on Children employed in Manufactories*, 1816, 374.
23 A. Ure, *Philosophy of Manufactures*, 1835, 480.
24 A. H. Dodd, op cit, 286.
25 *Manchester Gazette*, 24 February 1838; Foulkes, *Daniel Owen y Nofielydd*, 25, cited Foulkes, op cit, 94.
26 J. P. Bethell, *The Dee Estuary—an Historical Geography of its use as a Port*, unpublished thesis for the degree of MSc, University of Wales, 1952–3.

27 *Reports of Inspectors of Factories* (T. J. Howell), 12 November 1837, cited by Foulkes, op cit, 94.
28 *Census Returns*, 1841.
29 *Bolton Free Press*, 27 November 1841, cited by Foulkes, op cit, 94. *Census Returns*, 1841. Lewis, *Topographical Dictionary*, I, 426, cited by A. H. Dodd, op cit, 287.
30 Foulkes op cit, 95.
31 E. Pugh, *Cambria Depicta*, 1816, Cambro-Briton II (1820), 258. A. H. Dodd, op cit, 287–8.
32 P. T. Williams, *Industrial History of Flintshire*, unpublished thesis for the degree of MA, University of Liverpool, 1933, 253.
33 A. H. Dodd, op cit, 273.
34 W. Davies, *Survey of North Wales 1799* cited by Anna M. Jones, *The Characteristics of Wool production and Woollen manufacture in Wales in relation to the geographical features of the Principality*, unpublished thesis for the degree of MSc, University of Wales, 1925, 4; cf D. T. Williams in H. C. Darby, op cit, 295.
35 P. T. Williams, op cit, 231.
36 Ibid, 216.
37 Ibid, 231.
38 P. S. Richards, 'The Artificial Silk and Rayon Industries of Flintshire' (in the press).
39 C. R. Williams, *A Dissertation on the Industrial Changes and Developments in the County of Flint from 1815–1914*, unpublished thesis for the degree of MA, University of Wales, 1950, 185.
40 Anna M. Jones, op cit, 9, 11, 14.
41 C. R. Williams, op cit, 185.
42 *The Flintshire Observer*, 26 September 1873, cited P. T. Williams, op cit, 253.
43 C. R. Williams, op cit, 185.
44 Ibid.
45 'The Opening of the New Flannel Mill', *The Flintshire Observer*, 25 September 1884, cited by P. T. Williams, op cit, 236.
46 C. R. Williams, op cit, 185.
47 L. B. Cundall and T. Landman, *Wales: An Economic Geography*, 1925, 98.
48 H. W. Crellin, *County of Flint: County Development Plan*, 1954, 27.
49 Hughes and James, op cit, 182.
50 Megan Fox, 'The Welsh mills are "with it" ', *Liverpool Daily Post*, 26 May 1965.

IAN L. DONNACHIE

Aids to Recording (1)

The Classification of Industrial Monuments: A Guideline

GROWING activity in industrial archaeology fieldwork on local, regional and national levels throughout the British Isles, and the establishment of systematic records or archives at each of these levels in recent years, has emphasised the need for increased cooperation and coordination of effort among researchers. Efforts to bring about systematic coordination would undoubtedly be much aided by the existence of a standard classification system for industrial monuments. Such a system, if broadly accepted, could be of enormous potential value to present and future studies in industrial archaeology.

The following classification, essentially derived from the *Standard Industrial Classification*, makes no pretensions to general acceptability, but merely sets out to provide a working model. The SIC is already widely accepted and used by economists and statisticians both in Britain and abroad, being first issued almost twenty years ago to promote uniformity and comparability in official statistics. It provides a good example of a classification system which is simple and workable and at the same time can be expanded to take account of new industries or modes of production.

The order and numbering system of the SIC has been retained as far as possible, though it was often necessary to substitute other headings to take account of the needs of the industrial archaeologist. Subdivisions of many industrial activities were also necessary, particularly under the main headings of Engineering, Textiles and Communications.

The basis of this classification, as in the SIC, is a simple three-digit code number for each type of industrial building, site or physical feature associated with a particular industrial activity. There are a total of sixteen main headings, under which a variety of associated industries or features are classified:

1 Power Sources & Prime Movers
2 Agriculture & Rural Industry
3 Mining & Quarrying
4 Food Processing
5 Chemicals & Associated Industries
6 Metallurgy
7 Engineering
8 Textiles
9 Leather & Leather Working
10 Clothing & Footwear
11 Bricks, Tiles, Pottery, Glass, etc.
12 Timber & Paper
13 Other Manufacturing Industry
14 Public Utilities
15 Communications
16 Other Features (including Housing)

The majority of these headings follow the standard industrial classification almost exactly, but some have been added and others slightly altered to suit the present purpose. Although the main headings have been numbered in the above list, there is no need to use these numbers in classification, since each industrial building or site has its own three-digit code number within the main heading. In some cases a simple decimal-point system has been introduced where a particular industrial feature exhibits the need for further subdivision, in order to classify some important aspect of that feature (eg roads or other mining or quarrying).

The classification is simple to use, as the following examples show:

002 Waterwheel
101 Coal mine
231 Brewery
311 Puddling furnace
413.1 Handloom weaving shop (cotton)
431.2 Skin works
601 Gasworks
702.4 Turnpike or post road

In many cases the three-digit code identifies one particular feature (eg

216, sugar refinery), but in others it classifies in addition other features directly associated with it or with the production processes involved (eg 461, brick kiln; 701, railway tunnel).

Although the simplicity of the system lies in the fact that each industrial site can be classified by a single three-digit or at most four-digit number, this does not exclude the possibility of combining certain code numbers on a decimal system, as the following examples illustrate:

002.211	Water-powered grain mill
001.050	Horse-driven threshing mill
004.415	Steam-powered jute mill
006.462	Electrically-fired pottery kiln

Since prime movers are so fundamental to industrial archaeology, they merit an important place in any classification system for industrial heritage, but it would also be possible to combine code numbers in many other ways, providing a standard methodology was followed.

In the classification the words 'factory', 'works', 'making' and 'manufacture' are often missed out, but in all cases it is the actual premises where the particular activity is carried on which is referred to. Many of the industrial sites or buildings referred to in subheadings will be obvious, but examples have been given where necessary to show the scope of the classification.

The Classification

1 Power Sources & Prime Movers

000	Human power: tread mill
001	Animal power: horse-gin or mill
002	Water power: vertical or horizontal wheel or mill
003	Wind power: windmill
004	Steam power
005	Oil
006	Electricity
007	Gas

2 Agriculture & Rural Industry

050	Farm buildings and machinery
060	Rural industry not otherwise classified

3 Mining & Quarrying

101 Coal mine
102 Stone and slate quarrying and mining (general)
102.1 Stone quarry: sandstone, granite, limestone, marble etc
102.2 Slate quarry or mine
103 Sand, gravel, chalk and clay pit or mine
109 Other mining and quarrying (general)
109.1 Iron-ore mine or quarry: iron ore, bog ore, ironstone
109.2 Other metalliferous mine or quarry: lead, silver, zinc, copper, bauxite, other metalliferous or non-ferrous ores
109.3 Salt mine, salt or brine pit, salt pan or works
109.4 Oil shale mine or oil-well
109.5 Other non-metalliferous mining and quarrying: alum, graphite, barytes

4 Food Processing

211 Grain milling (general)
211.1 Wheat milling
211.2 Other milling: oats, barley, rye etc
212 Bakery or bakehouse
214 Bacon curing, meat and fish products factory
215 Milk product processing plant: creamery
216 Sugar refinery or works
217 Sugar, chocolate and cocoa processing
218 Fruit and vegetable processing: jam and jelly works, canning works
219 Animal and poultry food
229 Other food industries: margarine works
231 Brewing and malting: brewery, malt-barn
239 Other drink industries (general)
239.1 Distilling
239.2 Wine and cider: cider mill
239.3 Soft drinks: lemonade works
240 Tobacco

5 Chemicals & Associated Industries

261 Coke oven
262 Mineral oil refinery
271 Chemicals and dyes (general): tar kiln, kelp kiln
273 Explosives: gunpowder works
274 Paint and printing-ink manufacture
275 Animal and vegetable fats, oils, soap and detergents, tallow, soap works

6 Metallurgy

311 Iron and Steel (general)

311.1 Wrought iron: wrought-iron works, puddling furnaces
311.2 Steel: steel works, blast furnace
313 Iron castings (general)
313.1 Pig-iron furnace
313.2 Refining pig iron
313.3 Engineers' castings: foundry producing iron castings
313.4 Other iron castings: foundry producing cast-iron goods or fittings
321 Light metal working
322 Copper, brass and other base metal working: casting shop

7 Engineering

331 Agricultural and rural machinery: agricultural machine shop, country smithy or forge
332 Machine-tool production
334 Prime mover and industrial engine production: works manufacturing and repairing all types of engines except those classified under 370 and 381–4
335 Textile machinery
336 Earth-moving and contracting equipment
337 Mechanical handling equipment
339 Other machinery manufacture (general)
339.1 Mining machinery
342 Ordnance and small-arms manufacture: lead-shot works
351 Scientific instrument manufacture
352 Watch and clock making
361 Electrical machinery manufacture
370 Shipbuilding and marine engineering: shipyards and associated features
381 Motor vehicle manufacture
382 Motor and pedal-cycle manufacture
383 Aircraft building and repairing
384 Railway workshops: premises manufacturing and repairing locomotives and railway machinery
385 Railway coachworks: manufacturing and repairing coaches, trucks, wagons, tramcars, colliery wagons etc
391 Tool and implement making: shovel forge, tilt hammer etc
392 Cutlery making
393 Nuts, screws, bolts manufacture (nails under 394)
394 Wire and wire manufacture
399 Other metal industries

8 Textiles

411 Preparation of plant and man-made fibres: linen-scutching mill
412 Cotton and flax spinning: cotton, linen mill

413 Cotton, linen and man-made fibre weaving (general)
413.1 Handloom weaving: cottage or workshop
413.2 Weaving factory
414 Wool manufacture (general)
414.1 Wool sorting, combing, cleaning and blending
414.2 Worsted spinning
414.3 Worsted weaving
414.4 Wool recovery
414.5 Wool spinning and weaving: wool mill, tweed mill
414.6 Pressed felt manufacture
415 Jute spinning and weaving: jute mill
416 Rope, twine and net making: rope walk, net weaving shop
417 Hosiery and knitted (general)
417.1 Domestic stocking frame
418 Lace making
419 Carpet manufacture: carpet mill
421 Narrow fabric making
422.2 Canvas making
423 Textile finishing: bleaching, dyeing, printing and finishing: bleach-field or works, dye and print works
429 Other textiles: asbestos, vegetable fibres

9 Leather & Leather Working
431 Tanning and fellmongering (general)
431.1 Leather tanning: tannery
431.2 Fellmongery: skin works
432 Leather-goods manufacture

10 Clothing & Footwear
440 Clothing manufacture (general)
450 Footwear

11 Bricks, Tiles, Pottery, Glass, etc
461 Brick and tile making: brick and tile works, brick kiln etc
462 Pottery: pottery kiln
463 Glass making: glass kiln
464 Cement making
469 Other stone or mineral working

12 Timber & Paper
471 Timber working (general): sawmill
472 Furniture making
475 Wooden container manufacture: coopering, basket, box making
479 Wood and cork manufacture

481 Paper making: paper works or mill

13 Other Manufacturing Industry
491 Rubber
492 Linoleum

14 *Public Utilities*
601 Gas: gasworks, retorts, gas-holders, condensers etc
602 Electricity: all electric power plant
603 Water supply and sewerage

15 Communications
701 Railways (general)—track and all associated features: earthworks, bridges, tunnels, stations, signal boxes, engine sheds, water towers etc
701.1 Wagon-ways
701.2 Narrow-gauge railway
701.3 Standard-gauge railway
701.4 Broad-gauge railway
702 Roads (general)
702.1 Pack way or road and associated features
702.2 Drove road
702.3 Military road
702.4 Turnpike or post road—road and associated features: bridges, toll-houses, tollbars, milestones, change-houses, inns etc
703 Road transport (general)
704 Docks and harbours—and all associated features: warehouses, railway connections, lighthouses etc
705 Canals and inland navigation: canals, locks, aqueducts, overbridges, tunnels, wharves, warehouses, slipways, inclines, drydocks, lock and bridge-keepers' houses

16 Other Features (including Housing)
800 Industrial housing—workers' housing of all kinds: tenements, miners' rows, planned villages

This classification can be considered as little more than tentative. There are many obvious gaps and undoubtedly many omissions, since the system was first evolved in an essentially Scottish context and afterwards revised to include features common elsewhere. However, if we recognise that industrial archaeology will continue to expand as a study in its own right, with increased activity at all levels throughout

Britain, then the need for some standard system of classification is made the more urgent. Indeed there is already a clear case for far more standardisation in all types of industrial recording, using a simple coding system. Although we are concerned with the recording of past industrial techniques, there is no excuse for rejecting a more systematic approach to recording, or even modern computer analysis of that past.

Notes

Central Statistical Office, *Standard Industrial Classification*, HMSO, 1958 (revised ed 1966).

CSO, *Standard Industrial Classification: Alphabetical List of Industries*, HMSO, 1959.

E. E. Hagen, *Handbook for Industry Studies*, Free Press, Glencoe, Illinois, 1958.

J. P. M. Pannell, *Techniques of Industrial Archaeology*, David & Charles, 1966.

C. C. Fagg & G. E. Hutchings, *An Introduction to Regional Surveying*, Cambridge 1930.

John Butt, *Industrial Archaeology of Scotland*, David & Charles, 1967.

CHRISTOPHER COX

Aids to Recording (2)

Some Problems of Dating Milestones

MR W. Branch Johnson, writing on Hertfordshire milestones in vol 2 no 4 of *Industrial Archaeology*, pointed out that some milestones may have been erected before the actual turnpiking of a particular road. S. & B. Webb in *The Story of the King's Highway* wrote that 'it is to the turnpike roads that we owe the general establishment of milestones'. I had not previously known of a series pre-dating turnpiking, other than the stones recorded by W. B. Crump in *Huddersfield Highways Down the Ages*. There were of course single stones denoting mileage or direction. For example, in the Stroud district in Gloucestershire, of the milestones which were surveyed in 1963–4 for the National Survey of Industrial Monuments, there is one just off Old Hill at Avening inscribed AUENEING 1721 (ST 886981). This is thought to be associated with the building of the adjacent house, which may have been an early coaching inn on the Tetbury-Minchinhampton-Birdlip route, which was not turnpiked till 1758 by 31 Geo II c 98. There is also a broken stone set in a wall at Hyde (SO 855017) on a branch of the same route, inscribed 'To TETBURY VI Miles', which also might pre-date turnpiking, and there is a tradition of a Roman milestone at Alkerton, near Eastington.

In general it proved difficult to date turnpike milestones in the Stroud district. The dating of those in Hertfordshire might well be more straightforward, perhaps from that county's proximity to London. The cast-iron milestones mentioned by Mr Johnson may be those of the Metropolitan Roads North of the Thames, roads amalgamated in 1827, one example of which is the Kensington milestone by Milestone Hotel opposite Kensington Gardens. The placement of iron plates on pre-existing stone pillars is found also near Stroud.

My attempts to date Stroud milestones were based on the following: the date of the original turnpike Act, the style of the stone itself, the style of the inscription (whether cut into the stone, inscribed on an iron plate, or cast in relief on a plate), the style of lettering—including the use of the upright form of a medial S (f) and the eighteenth-century spelling of Gloucester, and evidence from documentary or oral sources. In most cases dating had to be very tentative; little evidence to fix a reliable date was found.

Unlike in Hertfordshire, no iron mileposts as such were found. Some parish boundary markers were found in cast iron; for example, the 1880s 6-in Ordnance map marks BS at Stanley Downton near Stonehouse (SO 802044), where there is now a hollow-backed, triangular cast-iron post bearing the parish names on the sides, with the letters WH/D on the top face. There are several such posts in the district, and the foundry name appears below the parish names as 'JM BUTT & Co/IRONFOUNDERS/GLOUCESTER'. WHD presumably indicated Wheatenhurst Highway District and the post therefore may be dated to the 1860s (ref GRO Q/AH 6). A similar post along Stroud Road in Gloucester nearly opposite Tuffley Avenue has GHD, which would indicate Gloucester Highway District. A solid stone parish marker of similar shape near Fostons Ash (SO 914126) has the date 1880 on the top face, instead of a Highway District abbreviation.

It was virtually impossible to determine dates from a stylistic sequence. Most milestones are of the 'gravestone' type, that is an upright slab of varying thickness with an arched head. But each Trust seems to have had its own style, with stones of different dimensions in width and thickness, while the shape of arch varies from flattish to semicircular. One of the oldest series, along the ancient Cirencester-Bisley-Painswick road, was of a nearly rectangular section with a flat head, though not all of these stones were of identical shape. It may indicate a local character when we find that many gateposts in the Bisley area share this shape and dimensions, while elsewhere most stone gateposts have an arched head, and usually taper from base to head.

Other Trusts departed from the 'gravestone' type. Along the road from Ashel Barn towards Tetbury two stones have a square section and a pyramidal head. A similar stone appears in one of Blake's woodcuts of a scene near Felpham in Sussex, where he stayed in the early 1800s. Other stones on the road north from Tetbury had triangular section with flat heads. From cartographical evidence and their general similarity to milestones on adjacent roads which were not turnpiked till the 1820s, it would seem likely that the existing Tetbury–Avening–Minchinhampton road milestones replaced an earlier series. Along the old Stroud–Painswick–Gloucester road, which received separate turnpike status in 1778, is a series of tall, rather slender stones with heads of a low pyramidal shape with the apex cut off. These had plates, but otherwise closely resemble the milestone to be seen in Hogarth's painting *An Election IV: Chairing the Member* of 1754–5.

Unlike, for example, the roads north of the Thames, which on amalgamation received a common type of milepost, the roads in the Stroud district retained the styles of the dozen or so individual Trusts. Iron plates with cut inscriptions are almost certainly of early date. Thus the two surviving plates of the Nailsworth Trust, at Dee's Garage, Nailsworth (ST 848999) and Tiltup's End (ST 845974), are plain rectangular iron slabs with incised letters. The one surviving example along the Old Painswick Road, down Stepping Stone Lane (SO 864088), consists of two small, thin iron plates; the upper has the mileage in Roman figures, the lower has the legend 'Miles to Glocefter'. But plates with incised letters also appear on the much later Painswick–Cheltenham road of about 1820, while a slightly earlier link of this road with the new Stroud–Gloucester road of about 1818 has stones with cut inscriptions. Lettering incised in an iron plate also appears on the Cirencester–Birdlip road (with the spelling GLOSTER) and on the surviving plate of the Old Bath Road at Cockadilly (SO 797003) near Nympsfield. According to Paterson, this latter stretch was an improved alignment of the 1780s. Thus we find the practice of incising letters into an iron plate on some of the earliest roads turnpiked in the Stroud district and on some of the latest.

The commonest type of milestone plate is of cast iron with letters in relief, but again each Trust tended to adopt an individual style. The new Stroud–Gloucester road has one surviving plate (SO 841108) 12½ in wide by 10½ in high with a well-defined rim; the Lightpill–Birdlip road (1801) has plates 10¾ in wide by 13 in, with a rim; the Stroud–Rodborough–Cirencester road has plates 12 in wide by 19 in high, with the tops arched. This road was turnpiked in the 1750s, but cartographical and other evidence would suggest these are replacements. On the roads from the Severn to Stroud, the earliest in the district to be turnpiked in the 1720s, the stones are tall pillars of oval or circular section and those east of the Bristol Road have plates curved to the pillars (but one site without a pillar had an identical but flat plate). As the stones west of the Bristol Road bear no indication of plates, but on at least one there are remains of incised letters, the plates can be assumed to be later than the stones. The Uley group had plates of a 'venetian window' shape. The one surviving plate of the new Stroud-Chalford road has letters cast in relief on a right-angled plate (SO 866026), but the plates on the Tetbury–Avening–Minchinhampton route are quite smooth, without rim or relief. These are puzzling, as one correspondent informed me that originally the lettering was in relief.

Roman numerals are presumably earlier than Arabic, and these can be found on the stone at Tunley (SO 937046) on the old Cirencester–Bisley road, cut in the plate of the Stepping Stone Lane stone, and at Cockadilly. The upright medial 'f' for 'S' appears also at Tunley and Stepping Stone Lane. Roman figures are also to be seen on a milestone at Bisley (SO 903060), but this stone bears the maker's name of Clissold, and would seem to be a local emplacement rather than belonging to a Trust. They also appear along the Tetbury–Cirencester road.

Alternative spellings of Gloucester appear, as 'Glocefter' on the Stepping Stone Lane plate, as 'GLOSTER' on the Cirencester–Birdlip road and on the Stroud–Gloucester road, as 'GLOCESTER' on the Stonehouse–Standish–Bristol Road route, and as 'GLOUr' at Cockadilly and 'GLOSR' on the plates of the Nailsworth Trust. A plate on the Gloucester–Bristol Road at Hardwicke has 'GLOUCESTER CROSS'. The actual cross at Gloucester was demolished in 1751, but it is not certain that the plate is early: the spelling 'Glocester' is widely used in the second half of the eighteenth century, but 'Gloucester' appears earlier. There would thus seem to have been a considerable overlap in date of styling of stone, letters and figures; and styling is of general assistance only in dating either stones or plates.

Documentary evidence should give a closer dating. There is, unfortunately, a dearth of turnpike records for roads in the Stroud district, but at least the Minute Book of the Nailsworth Trust (1780) survives in its entirety in the Gloucestershire Records Office (GRO). In this we may read that the committee meeting of 10 September 1782 ordered the erection of milestones, but this repeated a similar order of 23 October 1781, thus reminding us that orders are not necessarily conclusive. The plate at Dee's Garage is on a stone inscribed 1784, but this is a private replacement (not in the original position) of a stone removed during road alterations: the date however seems likely.

At least one definite dating was found in the Gloucester Library. In file JF 9.166 we can read that on 22 September 1823 the Trustees of the Berkeley & Dursley Division of Roads ordered that their milestones should have cast-iron plates, with 'common' numerals, painted white, with black letters; 'the Stones will be six feet long one foot thick and eighteen inches wide. The Plate supposed to be one foot wide. The part for the Parish and the letters to be circular'. A further order was for the replacement of earlier stones found to be too narrow for the new plates. The bill, presented in 1823 by Winwood and Company, came to £10 16s for a total of twenty-four plates. Here then is a precise dating, reminding us as Mr Johnson pointed out that stones may have been replaced, further clues to this possibility being found by a comparison of maps. Two of these plates may still be seen in the Stroud District at the top of Frocester Hill (SO 744005) and at the side of Uleybury Camp (ST 787992).

Eighteenth-century maps sometimes number the miles along turnpike roads: one may presume this indicates milestones or mileposts, though this is not certain. On an estate map of Shipton near Cheltenham, dated 1754, appear actual drawings of milestones, depicting rectangular blocks like the Tunley stone, with Roman numerals (GRO D 1930). The earliest clear cartographical evidence found for the Stroud district is on the 2-in preliminary drawings for the Ordnance Survey. These date generally from the end of the first decade of the eighteenth century, the first edition of the 1-in map being published for this area in the late 1820s. Yet these too present problems. Milestones are indicated on the Tetbury–Avening–Minchinhampton road, turnpiked in the 1750s, but on sites quite different from those occupied by the present existing stones. This earlier positioning is also given in the 1-in first edition of the Ordnance Survey, and taken in conjunction with the style of milestones on adjacent roads—that from Avening to Nailsworth, from Nailsworth through Horsley to the Old Bath Road (both roads were authorised in the early 1820s) and the Stroud–Chalford road of shortly before 1820—it would appear that the existing stones do not date from before the 1820s and most likely not before 1825 at the earliest.

This is perhaps positive evidence, but negative evidence (ie the absence of symbols) is not conclusive, for sheet 171 of the preliminary drawings omits the Uley group, some of which must have existed earlier than 1823, nor do we see any milestones marked along the Nailsworth or Old Bath roads. On the other hand, milestones are marked along the ridge-top route from Painswick Castle past Cranham Woods to Birdlip, which must have been superseded by the construction of the Lightpill–Birdlip road in the early 1800s and the Painswick–Cheltenham road in the early 1820s.

The preliminary drawings however show not only the Longstone near Minchinhampton (a relic of a barrow) but also the three tall stones on Minchinhampton and Rodborough Commons which still remain, though the third is now only a fragment built into a wall up Rodborough Hill. They also show a series from Cirencester to Minchinhampton in more or less the actual positions occupied by the existing stones, though one site is given on the opposite corner of a cross-roads to the existing marker. These stones, however, are marked on the map with mileage from London, 100 miles being reached at Minchinhampton, whereas the existing plates bear distances for Cirencester, Stroud and Hampton (ie Minchinhampton). In addition, up to 1818, the road went from Cirencester along the north side of Cirencester Park for over a mile, then cut south-west across the park to join the present alignment near the turning for Coates. Milestones are marked on the Ordnance drawings along this stretch, though no trace of them could be found when looked for. The 1-in first edition gives the current road alignment to the south of the park, and also numbers the miles as from Cirencester.

Therefore these stones were probably replaced between the time the survey for the preliminary drawings was made and the actual publication of the 1-in map. The present milestones on this road have an arch congruous with the plates as far as the next stone before Minchinhampton. This stone, originally the hundredth from London, shows that it too once had a plate of the existing type, but itself is of quite different dimensions from the others (SO 868013). It might of course be a late replacement, but is more worn and far less sophisticated in style than the others, and therefore, is possibly an original stone. The three common stones, indicated without mileage on the preliminary drawings, now show plate recesses of the same type as the rest on this road. So it seems that the plates were fixed to stones already there, and they may originally have served as route-markers across the empty spaces of the open common.

Other difficulties arising from cartographical evidence may be seen on the routes from the Severn crossing at Newnham to Frocester Hill and to Stroud. It has already been mentioned that these stone pillars (resembling in shape the stones on Minchinhampton and Rodborough Commons) can be sub-divided into two groups—those west of the Bristol road, and those eastwards to Stroud. The 6-in map of the 1880s shows on the former group, the mileage to Gloucester and London. They now have no such indication nor show traces of plates being fixed. One at Frampton canal bridge (SO 746085) reveals faint traces of incised directions. Oral tradition suggests they were erected about 1812. Those to the west of the Bristol road have flattish tops; most of those to the east of the Bristol road have domed tops and curved plates. A painting in the Stroud Museum, dated 1903, of the Cainscross milestone shows it then to have had a plate, but also the flattish top characteristic of the western sub-group: this stone has been removed pending road alterations, but previously the top was hidden by a sundial. The road was turnpiked in the 1720s, but the evidence would seem to suggest that while the present stones were erected shortly after the start of the nineteenth century, plates were fixed on the more frequented part considerably later.

The surviving stones and two surviving plates of the original Nailsworth road are of the same style, and may confidently be allocated to the early 1780s. But on one branch road built towards 1790, that from 'The Spout' up to the 'Bear Inn' on Rodborough Common, we find a stone with traces of letters giving a London mileage cut into it. This stands opposite the site of the home of Sir George Onesiphorus Paul, the Gloucestershire prison reformer who was active in the formative years of the Nailsworth Trust and who, moreover, undertook the construction of the branch past his home. It seems therefore possible that he himself had this stone (SO 848026) put up opposite his house. On the branch from Dudbridge past Selsley to the top of Frocester Hill, built about the same time, are two other stones (SO 833032 & 807019), neither with any trace of plate peg-holes, but the latter bears the marks of defacement and some letters of the word 'MILES'.

What appears to be poaching of a milestone is perhaps shown by the first milestone from Stroud on the new Stroud–Gloucester road (c 1818) which is quite definitely of the type of the older road, even to the traces of the dual plate recesses (one early 25-in map gives it as having the mileage 'Painswick 3'). It seems likely that when the newer road was built, the first mileage stone of the older road was hauled a short way down the bank to do duty on the newer road (SO 848068).

Reference might also perhaps be made to milestones along the Thames & Severn Canal which was built in the late 1780s. Between

Wallbridge at the Stroud terminus and Inglesham on the Thames near Lechlade two types of milestones and plates can be seen. The western type, from Wallbridge to near Sapperton, is of the 'gravestone' variety, mostly with a somewhat flattened top, though at least one specimen, near St Mary's Mill (SO 885022), has its arch well rounded. The plates are cast iron with letters of square section in bold relief, similar in casting to milestone plates on several of the turnpike roads. One plate is in the Gloucester Folk Museum, but another *in situ* is to be seen above Chalford (SO 907026). This group extends as far as the stone near Daneway bridge. The eastern type starts actually by the tunnel mouth at Sapperton (SO 944033), and several plates still remain as for example at Trewsbury Bridge (SO 981995) and by the Inglesham Canal round house. These stones are flat-topped, chamfered alongside the plate, which presents a very different appearance from that of the western type, the letters being cast in a low, rounded relief. Other examples of this type of casting of letters may be seen on the milestone plates of the Tetbury–Cirencester road, which are also of a 'venetian window' shape, with numerals in Roman style, though the numerals on the canal plates are Arabic.

Most of the milestone plates were removed, or the milestones themselves defaced, during the second world war. Some have been replaced, and at least one replacement of the 1960s may be seen on the Brookthorpe milestone (SO 837122), different in style and size of letters from the original. The considerable variety of shape and style both in stones and plates may be attributed to the fact that most of the roads in the Stroud district were local and lacked the unifying influence of an engineer like McAdam or an urban centre like London. The problem of dating both stones and plates is complex and difficult to resolve, and it is also complicated by the interplay of different Trusts and highway authorities. There was a move towards regrouping some Trusts or roads in larger or different units towards the middle of the nineteenth century, but this did not proceed very far in the Stroud district. Unified control over main roads was not achieved until the creation in the 1880s of the county highway authority. Discrepancies in the mileage recorded on Ordnance maps of the later nineteenth century and plates actually observed suggest that the county may have replaced some of these, but the writer has not yet investigated the documentary evidence for this. At all events this note shows that the attempt to date milestones in such a diverse area of separate Trusts as that round Stroud is both difficult and lacking in certainties.

Bibliographical Note

A detailed survey of milestones in the Stroud district appears in *Transactions of the Bristol & Gloucestershire Archaeological Society*, vol 83, 1964.

Plates, page 39

CORRECTION

'Technical Innovation in some late Nineteenth-Century Railway Warehouses' by A. J. Pacey, vol 5, no 4 of *Industrial Archaeology* (November 1968).

A scale of feet should have been included in the drawings on pages 368 and 369 in the above article. The drawing on page 368 in fact appeared on the page at a scale of about 7 ft 2 in to the inch ($\frac{1}{86}$). On page 369, the caption under the drawing should have explained that a detail at *second floor level* was represented, and the scale of the drawing, as printed, should have been indicated as 2 ft 8 in to the inch ($\frac{1}{32}$).

It should have been made clear that both drawings represented one of the Micklehurst line buildings mentioned on page 370 and also in note 9.

BARON F. DUCKHAM

Early Application of Steam Power at Scottish Collieries

A Note and Query

THE purpose of the present note is to make a preliminary list of Newcomen-type and other steam engines erected at Scottish collieries in or before 1800. Although I am interested in compiling an accurate list with approximate dates, cylinder size, cost, etc, my chief purpose is to establish a basis from which a rough estimate can be made of the amount of capital invested in steam power by the Scottish coal industry. This will form one facet of capital accumulation on which I wish to comment in my book on the eighteenth-century coal-mining industry of Scotland, now in active preparation. It would be greatly appreciated if any readers able to provide additional information would write direct to me at the Department of Economic History, University of Strathclyde, Glasgow C1. All help received will be duly acknowledged in my book with gratitude.

Note on sources

The list is based mainly on the parish ministers' returns to the *Old Statistical Account* (1791–9), supplemented by information derived from certain legal records, mainly Court of Session papers or Unextracted Processes, and from family muniments in the Scottish Record Office. The following is the chief literature drawn upon: 9th Earl of Dundonald, *Description of the Estate . . . at Culross* (1793); R. Bald, *A General View of the Coal Trade of Scotland* (1808); Matthias Dunn, *View of the Coal Trade* (1844); 'Senex', *Glasgow Past & Present* (1884 ed); R. L. Galloway, *Annals of Coal Mining and the Coal Trade, first series* (1898)—Galloway and Dunn drawing on the famous list made by William Brown in 1769; H. M. Cadell, *The Rocks of West*

Lothian . . . (1925); R. A. Mott, 'The Newcomen Engine in the Eighteenth Century', *Trans Newcomen Soc*, XXXV (1962–3); L. T. C. Rolt, *Thomas Newcomen: the Prehistory of the Steam Engine* (1963); J. Strawhorn, *The New History of Cumnock* (1966); J. R. Harris, 'The Employment of Steam Power in the Eighteenth Century', *History*, LII (1967); J. Butt, *The Industrial Archaeology of Scotland* (1967).

Note on dates etc

Entries in the *Old Statistical Account* [OSA] are frequently vague. In any case the list must be far from complete. Over half the volumes were published by 1794 and parishes not possessing a Newcomen engine by then may well have seen one erected by 1800. Occasionally parish ministers simply mention an 'engine' being used for drainage at a nearby colliery. Sometimes this undoubtedly refers to a waterwheel and pumps. Where I am unsure if steam power is being alluded to I have placed a question mark in the list.

Parish or Colliery	*Number of Engines*	*Source*	*Date and Particulars*
Ayrshire:			
Ayr Coal Co	1	Court/Session	before 1800
Bartonholm	1	Unex Process	before 1798; 30-in cylinder
Caprington	1	Rolt	c 1775
Cumnock	1	Strawhorn	1771
Kaims	1	Court/Session	before 1789
Loudon	1	OSA, III (1792)	
Mauchline	1	OSA, II (1791)	
Newton-upon-Ayr	1	OSA, II (1791)	
Shewalton	1	Unex Process	before 1798 34/36-in cylinder
Stair	2	OSA, VI (1793)	
Stevenston (including Saltcoats)	6–7	OSA, VII (1793) Unex Process; Boulton/Watt MSS; Butt	1719; 1732; c 1778–1800 four engines built: 28-in, 36-in, 52-in, 60-in cylinders. The first may have been a rebuild of 1732. One Boulton/Watt engine (winding) with 36-in cylinder added in 1800–1

Parish or Colliery	*Number of Engines*	*Source*	*Date and Particulars*
Clackmannanshire:			
Alloa (Collyland)	1	OSA, VIII (1793)	1764; 40-in cylinder
Clackmannan	1	OSA, XIV (1795)	
Dumfries-shire:			
Sanquhar	1	OSA, VI (1793)	erected by Symington
East Lothian:			
Pencaitland	1?	OSA, XVII (1796)	'engine'
Fife:			
Carnock	1	OSA, XI (1794)	
Dunfermline (Halbeath)	2	OSA, XIII (1794)	c 1785
Dysart	2	OSA, XII (1794)	
Kilconquhar	1	OSA, IX (1793)	
Kinghorn	1	Boulton/Watt MSS	1800–1; 48-in cylinder. Not certain if supplied to a colliery
Pittenweem	1	OSA, IV (1792)	Dunn states 1764
St Monance	1	OSA, IX (1793)	
Wemyss	2?	OSA, XVI (1795)	'engine'; one certainly steam
Lanarkshire:			
Barrachnie	1 or 2	OSA, VII (1793)	one a steam winder (1792)
Cambuslang	1	OSA, V (1793)	1787
Carmichael	1	OSA, XIII (1794)	
Carntyne	1	Senex	c 1768
Fullarton	1	OSA, VII (1793)	
Govan	2	OSA, V (1793)	one a steam winder
Maryston	1	BC Process	c 1800
Rutherglen	1	OSA, IX (1793)	c 1776; erected by Gabriel Grey of Scotstoun
Shettleston	2	OSA, XII BC Process	1764; c 1791, 'Green Coal Co'
Wilsontown	1	NSA, VI (1845)	c 1788–9
Midlothian:			
Duddingston	2	OSA, XVIII (1796); Dunn; Galloway	1763–4; second engine before 1792. Both had 66-in cylinders
Edmonstone	1	Bald	1725–6, 28-in cylinder (brass)
Loanhead	1	Clerk MSS	1790s
Musselburgh?	1	Dunn	probably the first engine at Duddingston
Newton	2	OSA, XI (1794)	

Parish or Colliery	*Number of Engines*	*Source*	*Date and Particulars*
Perthshire [then]:			
Culross	2	Dundonald	before 1793; 40-in, 50-in cylinders
Renfrewshire:			
Neilston	1	OSA, II (1791)	
Stirlingshire:			
Airth (Elphinstone)	1	OSA, III (1792); Rolt	c 1720
Larbert	1	NSA, VIII (1845)	1760
West Lothian:			
Carriden (including Grange and Kinneil)	4–5	OSA, I (1791); Cadell; various family MSS	one, possibly two, before 1770 (Kinneil). Two steam winders, 1792 and 1794 (on Grange estate)

In addition to the engines listed above, one was almost certainly erected on the Earl of Dunmore's estates in 1769. By the 1790s colliery investment in steam power was clearly advancing at a more rapid pace. In 1794 the minister of Shettleston estimated there were nearly twenty engines at coal mines around Glasgow. Several not here accounted for must have been erected in the Lanarkshire coalfield alone, under the stimulus of better sales offered by the Monkland Canal.

Plate, page 38

W. L. NORMAN

Fall Ings, Wakefield

Some Notes on an Eighteenth-Century Foundry

ALTHOUGH the information regarding the activities of the Fall Ings foundry leaves much to be desired, that which is available is of some interest. In particular, it provides further evidence of the methods by which entrepreneurs financed their enterprises during the early years of the Industrial Revolution. At the same time it indicates the lengths to which some manufacturers would go in order to secure a measure of certainty in respect of raw materials and with regard to inventions which held the promise of profit.

The earliest known reference to an iron foundry at Fall Ings, Wakefield (OS 343198), is to be found in an indenture dated June 1792.[1] In that document mention is made that John Sturgess of Leeds, John Sturgess of Bowling (Bradford), Richard Paley (an iron merchant) of Leeds, William Sturgess of Datchett (Bucks), and John Elwell of Fall Ing had carried on the business of cast-iron founders at Bowling and Fall Ing as co-partners, in accordance with an agreement dated 14 October 1789.

Whilst it is not known when activities commenced at Fall Ings, it would seem that the foundry was established before the Bowling works. Cudworth mentions that in 1784 John Sturgess senior, an iron master of some repute, who resided at Sandal and whose works were at Wakefield, was among the first to recognise the valuable nature of the coal and ironstone deposits in the area of Bowling.[2] Sturgess subsequently joined with the partners listed above to establish the first foundry at Bowling. In December 1787, the following contributions were made to the Bowling enterprise: John Sturgess (senr) £700; John Sturgess (jnr) £1,050; John Elwell £350; Richard Paley £700; in September 1788, William Sturgess contributed £700[3]. Whether such

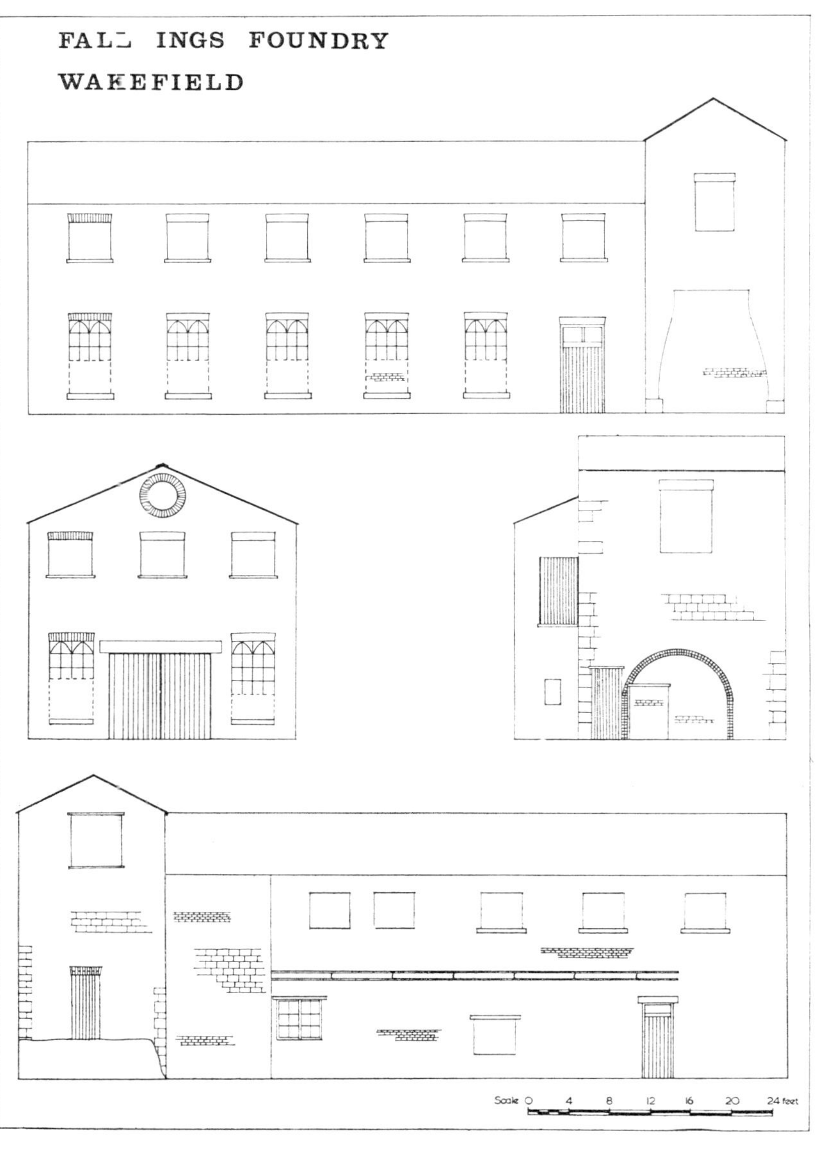
FALL INGS FOUNDRY
WAKEFIELD
Scale 0 4 8 12 16 20 24 feet

payments constituted part of the initial outlay for the enterprise, or whether it merely provided capital for the smelting equipment which was installed there in 1788, is not known. In the years following the establishment of the Bowling works there was '. . . a constant transmission between Fall Ings and Bowling of sad irons (flat or laundry irons), posnets, ovens, boilers, sash and clock weights', whilst from 1788 until 1792 pig iron was sent from Bowling to Fall Ings to be converted into wrought iron.

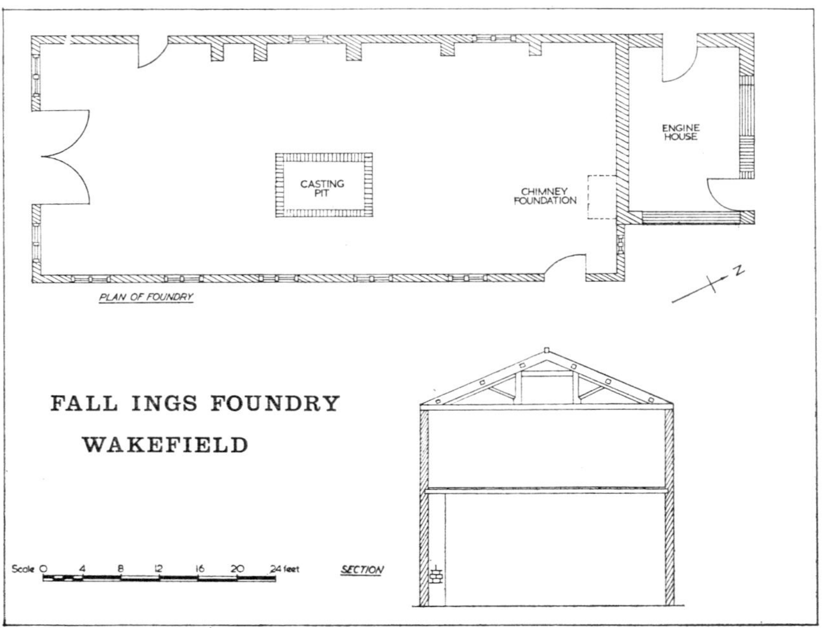

FALL INGS FOUNDRY
WAKEFIELD

Although a previous contributor has stated that the Wakefield works collapsed in 1792,[4] I can find no evidence to endorse this. What is known is that the partnership continued at Fall Ings until 1792, when it was dissolved, Elwell continuing there on his own account and withdrawing his interest in the Bowling works, which his ex-partners continued to operate.[5]

Within five months of the dissolution Elwell was seeking capital from his ex-partners, but the reason for this is unknown. In November, he secured a mortgage of £1,000 from Paley and contracted to pay interest at 5 per cent until such time as the debt was repaid.[6] Apparently, no plans of Elwell's foundry now exist, but some indication of the size of the enterprise is given by the fact that he mortgaged 'Outbuildings, foundry buildings, barns, stables, Engine House, warehouses, smithy, engine and all engine furniture and machinery'. With the exception of the engine house, the early buildings have gone; the style and materials of the present shell of the foundry buildings suggest that it was constructed during the early decades of the nineteenth century. Elwell subsequently redeemed his property in January 1794, when John Crawshaw, a 'gentleman' of Button Hills, Sheffield, bought a half interest in the firm for £2,000.[7] In the same year Elwell reduced his control further when he sold half of his own interest to Samuel Aydon, an ironmaster of Flanshaw.[8]

It would seem that Crawshaw did not have any direct associations with Fall Ings before 1794, but he was known to Elwell before that date. In November 1793 both men, acting in partnership, had contracted with Richard Lumbley Saville, Lord of the Manor of Shelf, for control of:

> All those Beds, veins or seams of Iron Stone lying or being above the Black or Uppermost Bed of Coal in and under the Wasteground within the Manor of Shelf where the same Bed of Coal is already got or shall be got during the Term of 21 years. . . . And also full and free Liberty, Power, and Authority to erect and build upon any part of the said Commons . . . one or more blast Furnaces and all other Buildings necessary for the working of the said Iron Stone or for the Habitations of workmen . . . and to get Stone for the purpose and clay for the making of Bricks, and also making Newcastle Waggon Ways . . . for the purpose of conveying Iron Stone and Coals or any other to and from the said Furnaces. . . .[9]

For these rights the partners contracted to pay an annual rent of £120. Because the agreement did not authorise the mining of coal, the partners at the same time entered into an agreement with Robert and Joseph Woodhead, stuff-makers of Halifax who were then to supply

'. . . saleable coals . . . for the consumption of one Blast Furnace to be erected for the mining of Iron Stone into metal. . . .' The Woodheads, having leased the coal-mining rights from Saville in 1792 for a term of 21 years, had complete control in this respect. By the agreement of 1793 they conceded to Crawshaw and Elwell the right to open and work the old pits to extract the ironstone and also the posts of coal which still remained there. After Aydon was admitted to the Fall Ings partnership he was granted a 25 per cent interest in the Shelf enterprise,[10] but whether he only bought part of Elwell's share is a matter for conjecture.

By the first decade of the nineteenth century Elwell and Aydon had severed their connections with the Fall Ings foundry and had concentrated their activities at Shelf, where they later gained a reputation as iron-bridge builders. Evidence of their activities is provided by Parker who states that Elwell and Aydon were responsible for the building of a 31-yd long bridge over the Aire at Newlay in 1819.[11] Crawshaw continued at Fall Ings and at some time during the first years of the nineteenth century was joined by his brother, William.

That this new partnership was entered into before 1808 is indicated by the fact that the brothers financed a patent for William Roberts in that year. Roberts, an ironfounder of Hull, had secured a fourteen-year patent to manufacture a new type of stove. The Register Stove contained two flues, one in the front arch of the grate and the other under the arch '. . . whereby two Draughts of Air are produced, the one for preventing the Room from smoking, the other for heating the Room with considerably less quantity than usual of coals'. In order to finance the patent, Roberts contracted with Jonathon and William Crawshaw, ironfounders of Fall Ings, who were to meet the cost of the Letters Patent and then subsequently purchase the right from him. As part of the agreement, Roberts was to retain the right during his lifetime to make and sell the stoves, and after his death the brothers were to pay 2½ per cent of the value of the sales to his executors at six-monthly intervals until the patent expired.[12]

The reasons why Roberts, himself an ironfounder, should make such an agreement with the Crawshaws clearly were not simply related to the problems of finance, for the contract also stated that he was to obtain castings from Fall Ings at £1 1s per cwt until such time as he could manufacture his own. The belief that the Crawshaw enterprise was stronger than Roberts's tends to be supported by the fact that the latter insisted upon both parties selling at equal prices, presumably in order to minimise competition. Of course it is arguable whether both these considerations meant that Fall Ings was a foundry of particular importance at that time, but it is interesting to speculate on this possibility.

Acknowledgments

I am indebted to Mr J. Goodchild, Curator, Cusworth Hall Museum, Doncaster, who kindly lent me the Fall Ings Papers upon which this article is based. Thanks are also due to the following students of the Wakefield Technical and Art College who prepared the drawings: R. Coombes, R. Johnson, P. Kittrick, M. North.

Notes

1 Fall Ings Papers.
2 W. Cudworth, *Histories of Bolton and Bowling*, Bradford, 1891, 205.
3 Cudworth, op cit, 206.
4 *See* H. Long, 'The Bowling Ironworks', *Industrial Archaeology*, vol 5, no 2, May 1968.
5 Fall Ings Papers, Indenture, June 1792.
6 Fall Ings Papers, Indenture, 9 November 1792.
7 Fall Ings Papers, Indenture, 7 January 1794.
8 Fall Ings Papers, Indenture, 8 January 1794.
9 Fall Ings Papers, Indenture, 1 May 1794.
10 Ibid.
11 J. Parker, *Illustrated History from Hipperholme to Tong*, 1904, 357.
12 Fall Ings Papers, Articles of Agreement, 8 December 1808 and 10 December 1808.

Plates, page 40

Book Reviews

The Growth of the British Cotton Trade, 1780–1815 by Michael M. Edwards, MANCHESTER UNIVERSITY PRESS, 1967, pp vi + 276, 45s.

Considering the prominence given to cotton in the conventional accounts of British economic history, it is remarkable how little has in fact been published on the subject. Since G. W. Daniels, not much has been contributed by the Manchester economic historians. The cotton industry was only a marginal interest for both Ashton and Redford, and the same is true of the present generation of economic historians there. Important studies have been produced recently, notably by Professor Pollard, Dr Chapman and Mr Fitton but of a specialised nature.

This book comes as near to being a general study as anything published in the last fifty years, although far from being a complete history of the cotton industry in the Industrial Revolution period. The centre of interest is deliberately shifted from technological change to a broader view of the cotton trade as a whole. Successive chapters deal with the supply of raw material and the demand for yarn and cloth and with the provision of fixed and working capital. The changes are dramatic enough even when Hargreaves, Arkwright and Crompton are absent from the stage. Perhaps the most striking effect was the stimulation of growth in the provinces with the displacement of London as the main market for raw material and cloth by Liverpool and Manchester respectively.

The chapter dealing with fixed capital is a remarkable illustration of how little is known of early factory development, other than in a few important mills. The missing information can be supplied, if at all, only by field survey of surviving factory sites and by an intense search for business records. The paucity of the latter is made very clear by the extent to which the author has had to rely on the records of a single firm, McConnel and Kennedy, whose papers are preserved at the University of Manchester.

This is an important book and although about as easy to read as a balance sheet is equally basic to an understanding of the early history of the cotton industry. The available manuscript sources in London and Lancashire have been carefully examined and skilfully used. The chapter on the supply of raw material is interesting on the efforts to stimulate production in India, Brazil, and even Africa in which the Board of Trade was fully involved, but the author is less sure in dealing with the spectacular development of cotton-growing in the lower South of the United States. The effects of war conditions too, would seem to have deserved more detailed treatment than a simple periodisation of the expansion and contraction of the cotton trade during the period under review. Still, these are minor criticisms of an important new study.

In its broad conclusions, the book reaches a position mid-way between the Industrial Revolution or take-off model, as it is perhaps more popularly called nowadays, and the revisionism of the quantitative school who object to such significance being attached to an industry which they assert contributed no more than 4 or 5 per cent to the national income. Consequently, we find a statement on the one hand that 'complete factory production . . . was not a dominant characteristic of this period' and on the other an insistence on the 'very profound effect' of the 'vital commercial changes' on economic development in Britain. The former contention is not really valid for the fact that large numbers of spinners in the early years had recourse to converted corn mills and the like or to rented space rather than erecting their own buildings cannot alter the nature of the production. The rapid growth of supply and demand and the changes in organisation arising from a continuing need for specialisation are all evidence of the effect of technical innovation in producing economic change. The book in fact provides further important evidence to confirm the growing realisation among historians that the Industrial Revolution concept is a reliable tool in the study of economic change, but that the process is infinitely more complicated and delicate than one might realise from the writings of earlier historians.

University of Manchester E. R. R. Green

Industry before the Industrial Revolution incorporating a study of the chartered companies of the Society of Mines Royal and of Mineral and Battery Works, by William Rees, UNIVERSITY OF WALES PRESS, Cardiff, 1968, two volumes, 126s.

Misgivings about the nature of this work are aroused by its title, heightened by the preface and confirmed by a reading of the two volumes. The title itself may well mislead would-be readers since the book does not deal with the general development of industry before the Industrial Revolution but is 'primarily concerned with the mining and smelting of iron, lead and copper' and, it should be added, the mining of coal where the author avowedly relies on Nef's work. Lacking a thesis, the book is essentially a collection of facts. Further it concerns itself with a geographical area which lacks the coherence necessary for regional analysis.

A study of the evolution of industry in a pre-industrial society could be of practical value to those concerned at the present time with problems of underdevelopment but they will gain little from this book. Indeed the whole standpoint of the work lacks sophistication from the point of view of the economic historian. 'Capital', 'wages', 'labour', 'prices', 'profit', 'location' and 'trade' find no place in the index. As for the industrial archaeologist, he will have to wait a little longer for a definitive guide to industry in Britain before the Industrial Revolution.

University of Exeter W. E. Minchinton

The Early Iron Industry of Furness and District, by Alfred Fell, FRANK CASS & CO LTD, London, new impr 1968 of the 1908 edition, 461 pp, ill, maps and plates, 6 gns.

Industrial archaeologists will be very pleasantly surprised by the methodology of Alfred Fell, since he described and mapped sites as well as providing a historical account of ironworking in Furness and in Scotland by men from Furness. This new impression of the 1908 edition should be particularly welcome to a wide range of people, varying from those interested in the history of metallurgy to historical geographers or local historians concerned with or interested in north-west England and the Scottish Highlands.

Fell divides his book into six parts, after an introductory sketch of technical developments in the iron industry before 1800. Part I concerns itself with the mines of Furness—leases, mining methods and problems, costs and profits of production, distribution and marketing. In Part II, Fell describes the timber resources of the region and the problems which the ironmasters encountered in trying to exploit them for charcoal. Significantly enough, the price of charcoal rose substantially in the period 1715–65, encouraging the ironmasters to seek alternative fuel supplies, either of a totally different kind or from outside the Furness region. Several of the iron firms began to take a serious interest in the timber resources of Scotland, both in south-west Scotland and in the Highlands. Descriptions of ironworks—bloomeries and smithies before 1600, furnaces and forges of the next two centuries—form Part III. This section is especially useful since Fell describes the technology employed, the plans and locations of sites and, incidentally, provides a guide to the kinds of documentary material likely to be most useful to present-day archaeologists.

Fell does not neglect the approaches of social history. In Part IV he examines the masters and men, providing a bird's eye view of social conditions in a developing industrial region in the eighteenth century. Perhaps the major problem of the Furness ironmasters was the shipping of metal. It was not merely a question of high transport costs on bulky goods but of unreliable captains, high insurance rates, war risks and the difficulties of providing circulating capital. Part V, on the trade in iron, tells us much on all these topics, providing a rich store of information for comparative studies with other industries in other regions. Part VI gives an account of the Furness ironmasters' activities in Scotland at the furnaces of Invergarry, Furnace and Bonawe, the latter two being outstanding monuments of Scotland's industrial past. Frank Cass & Company are to be congratulated for their enterprise in reprinting this magnificent book in their series of industrial classics.

University of Strathclyde John Butt

Industrial History in Pictures: Scotland, by John Butt, Ian L. Donnachie and John R. Hume, DAVID & CHARLES, Newton Abbot, 1968, 111 pp, ill, 42s.

Readers of *Industrial Archaeology of Scotland* need no longer feel frustrated by the frequently recurring asterisks in the gazetteer which promise but do not reveal. This book has now fulfilled the promise and may indeed be a revelation to many who have not realised that old familiar industrial buildings, either preserved or adapted to modern use, may be of considerable historic interest. Apposite is the fine photograph of the Bishop Mills on the river Kelvin (Glasgow), a mill-steading since medieval times.

Mechanically-minded readers will find much to enthuse over in pictures such as the Albion Motor Company's assembly shop in 1901, the Hurlet Alum Works (c 1850) or the more detailed illustrations of a water-driven tilt hammer and several types of steam-age engines. A particularly attractive section of the book is that dealing with iron smelting, commencing with the charcoal furnace at Bonawe on Loch Etive, a safe site on Campbell territory where operations commenced in 1752, and including Wilsontown, Muirkirk and Carron. The sketch of Muirkirk ironworks is most interesting and informative. In many of the photographs the factory chimney is an incidental if prominent feature but, as an example of the more elegant type still to be seen in Scotland, Cox's Stalk, Camperdown Linen Works, Lochee, was surely worthy of a place.

The authors have ranged Scotland. They explain that the omission of agriculture and rural crafts is deliberate as they consider these subjects worthy of a separate book. Nevertheless water-driven mills and a horse-gin have been included and small towns have not been overlooked. In neither the parent book nor its picturesque offspring are there illustrations of the shale-oil industry, although the latter does depict workers' houses at Addiewell which lack a date to facilitate the comparison invited.

Illustrations in the roads section include Telford's bridge at Craigellachie (rebuilt after the Moray floods of 1829 by Joseph

Mitchell and in recent times rebuilt in steel) and the bridge over the Tay at Aberfeldy usually attributed to General Wade, few historians having troubled to enquire where the eminent soldier acquired his architectural skill. The plans of the Aberfeldy bridge are to be found in William Adam's *Vitruvius Scoticus*, and Wade himself has recorded that 'the best architect in Scotland was employed and master masons and carpenters sent from ye northern Countys of England'.

A salt tang is introduced by pleasing harbour scenes including one of Portpatrick, which in 1874 was superseded by Stranraer as the terminal of the mail steamers on the North of Ireland route. If familiar with the Clyde, the reader will seek in vain for a pictorial record of Greenock's old-established sugar-refining industry or the explosives industry at Ardeer, where the British Dynamite Company was established in 1871. Fortunately, the latter has been attractively recorded in an ICI publication.

In view of the fact that the British Aluminium Company has closed, or is about to close, its original establishment at Foyers (dating from 1895), it is perhaps a pity that it should vanish unrecorded. A picture of the Kinlochleven works, established in 1904, has also been omitted. Hydro-electric pioneer schemes have perhaps not been considered old enough to rank as history but posterity should not be allowed to think of the industry as a gift from a benevolent government. At Kinloch Rannoch, the thoughtfully-designed power station of the Grampian Electricity Supply Company was erected in 1930; the Galloway Water Power Company's power stations at Glenlee and Tongland were in operation by 1935, while the Lanarkshire Hydro-Electric Power Company harnessed the falls of Clyde in 1927. In this connection the name of the late Sir Edward MacColl should not be overlooked by industrial historians.

This Scottish volume of *Industrial History in Pictures*, while completing the original work, is quite capable of standing on its own feet. As it covers a field almost completely overlooked by publishers of the traditional 'Bonnie Scotland' books, it should penetrate into the libraries of photographic art, even if the more punctilious librarians insist that 'Industry and Technology' is its correct classification.

Glasgow John Robertson

Leeds and its Region, M. W. Beresford and G. R. J. Jones (eds), LEEDS LOCAL EXECUTIVE COMMITTEE OF THE BRITISH ASSOCIATION, 1967, 50s (35s paper) plus postage. Available only from Austick's Bookshop, 21 Blenheim Terrace, Leeds 2.

This volume is the latest addition to the row of British Association *Surveys* which provide a sound conspectus for geologists and archaeologists, for geographers, historians and economists, of a growing number of 'regions' of Great Britain. As the editors state, the purpose of this particular volume is 'not only to introduce the region to the visitor but also to give the local reader some food for thought'. Readers of this journal will find most to interest them in Part II, 'The Emergence of Leeds in its Region'. The story of the changing pattern of economic activity in Leeds and its environs is succinctly told, but with little regard for the surviving physical evidence, apart from two splendid plates of the Aire & Calder warehouse of 1827–8 and of back-to-back housing at Hunslet.

Medieval grist mills, cloth making, coal mining, flax spinning, engineering, footwear and other manufactures find their place in the account, and the improvement of transport facilities is also set out with a separate chapter on passenger transport developments (which would have benefited from a map). But the liveliest chapter is Maurice Beresford's essay on 'Prosperity Street and others' in which he asks questions about the visible remnants of the past. In particular, Professor Beresford notes that 'Water Lane, Meadow Lane and Hunslet Lane are still a largely unexplored paradise for the industrial archaeologist, and there is still a good deal of original factory building along the riverside and the Leeds and Liverpool Canal. . . . A full survey of these relics of pioneer industrialisation is still awaited'. Here is a challenge; may the later pages of this journal show it is being met.

University of Exeter W. E. Minchinton

The Life and Adventures of Michael Armstrong, The Factory Boy, by Frances Trollope, FRANK CASS & CO LTD, new impr 1968 of the 1840 edition, pp viii, 387, 24 ill, 95s.

Long before the mid-Victorian novel-reading public learned to enjoy the Barsetshire saga, Anthony Trollope's mother Frances (1780–1863) had maintained her large family by equally prolific writing. Fanny's most celebrated novel was *Michael Armstrong*, originally issued in twelve parts from February 1839 and published as a volume by Henry Colburn in 1840. The book has for many years been difficult to obtain, and its reissue in the new 'Cass Library of Victorian Times' deserves a warm welcome.

When Mrs Trollope decided to write a 'social novel' in support of the generally Tory-Evangelical campaign for factory legislation, she did not approach the task simply as a writer of fiction; in fact she indulged in considerable research. The factory reformers' parliamentary leader, Viscount Ashley, provided her with introductions to the principal Tory and Radical leaders of the northern agitation. With her eldest son, Thomas Adolphus (who recalled the tour in his autobiography *What I Remember* in 1887), Fanny visited the northern textile districts in February and March 1839. They met such men as the Radical trade-union leader John Doherty, the pugnacious Anglican 'Parson Bull', the philanthropic Tory worsted manufacturers John Wood and William Walker, the revolutionary Tory minister Joseph Rayner Stephens and the ultra-Tory 'King of the Factory Children', Richard Oastler. Tom Trollope later recalled their shock at the 'horrors of uncivilised savagery and hopeless abject misery' which they discovered. And the journey influenced the book.

Michael Armstrong combines reform propaganda with typical Victorian sentimentality. Its story of a wretched boy apprenticed to a brutal Derbyshire millowner owes much to the popular 'biography' of Robert Blincoe; its villain, Sir Matthew Dowling, is the archetype of reformers' nightmares; its heroes include Parson Bell of Fairly (Bull of Bierley). The book has a certain charm as a good example of the early Victorian 'condition of England' novel. But it has special interest for social and industrial historians as the best fictionalised account of the factory reformers' case. The reprint maintains the high standards of production to which we are accustomed in the publications of Messrs Cass.

University of Strathclyde J. T. Ward

Art and the Industrial Revolution, MANCHESTER CITY ART GALLERY, 1968, 100 pp, 24 plates, no price.

To coincide with the publication of the second edition of Francis Klingender's *Art and the Industrial Revolution*, Manchester City Art Gallery arranged an exhibition of which this is the catalogue. But there is an important difference between the book and the exhibition. Whereas Klingender ended his survey with the Great Exhibition of 1851, the Manchester exhibition went up to the 1880s. This enabled a new phase of artistic interest to be documented. Before 1850, probably because industrialists were not keen to commission works dealing directly with industrial activity, the art of the Industrial Revolution was almost wholly incidental and workers in most cases occupied a subordinate part of the landscape. But the climate of opinion began to change in the 1840s and the period 1850–80 reveals the growing personal involvement of the artists. Although their interests ranged more widely, the Pre-Raphaelite circle comprised the first group of artists whose paintings were an implicit criticism of city life. This well-documented catalogue has an introduction by Sir Arthur Elton, from whose collection more than a quarter of the exhibits were drawn. The catalogue is well illustrated because some of the plates used in the book are reproduced in it, but, as eleven out of the twenty-four illustrations are not duplicated, it forms a useful supplement to Klingender's *Art and the Industrial Revolution.*

University of Exeter W. E. Minchinton

Notes and News

Editorial

Our first duty and pleasure is to place on formal record our great thanks to Kenneth Hudson. Kenneth has been an active pioneer of industrial archaeology since before the subject was at all recognised. He edited the journal at the most difficult period of its existence and in addition has produced a remarkable output of books and articles. We are most grateful to him and also to Bath University of Technology which supported both the study and the journal.

Our subscribers and readers should not expect any revolutionary changes in policy. We hope to build on the firm base which Kenneth has left us. We would like our readers to send us information from their local area and to provide us with more articles. Before writing articles we would prefer would-be contributors to get in touch with us so that we may send them a sheet of our literary conventions and general information for contributors. We are anxious to know how our readers and subscribers think the journal could be improved and we will, if we can, print queries and letters relating to research projects.

It cannot be stressed enough that any journal of merit depends upon the continued support of its readers. We will try to do our best, and we hope that our readers will co-operate with us. There is a growing and lamentable tendency to split the supporters of *IA* into professionals and amateurs. This is a sign that the discipline is being accepted. But we should declare formally our belief that these divisions are foolish, unwarranted and inimical to the best interests of industrial archaeology. All with enthusiasm have a part to play. If you are not in a society with a local group, join one or form one. Whatever your views, let us know of them.

John Butt
Ian L. Donnachie

Preservation Corner

In each *Notes and News* we hope to feature an individual site or building which is preserved as part of the nation's industrial heritage. The aim will be to capture briefly in word and picture the character of the chosen subject and in so doing to provide as much regional variety as possible. Readers are cordially invited to contribute ideas and illustrations from their own area. In this issue we feature Ballycopeland windmill, Co Down.

Ballycopeland Windmill

This finely preserved windmill is the last of many in Co Down and was saved for posterity through the foresight of its last miller, who gave it to the Northern Ireland government in 1935. Guardianship was assumed by the Ministry of Finance in 1937 and extensive repairs were carried out, particularly to the windcap, fantail and sails. The existence of dry rot and woodworm caused the virtual renewal in 1958 of the main flooring and internal machinery, which was carefully copied from the original in new timber. At the same time an engine-house built for a steam engine was demolished and the exterior of the mill restored to its original finish in modern materials.

Ballycopeland was built sometime after 1788, in the era of extensive corn production and mill reconstruction during the French wars. It is a typical tower windmill of the period, probably built by local craftsmen using designs from the north of England. The tower is 33 ft high with an external ground diameter of 22 ft 3 in, tapering to 17 ft at the top on walls 2 ft thick. The mill has a wooden, boat-shaped revolving cap fitted with an automatic fantail and four great patent sails. Of the under-drift, type the mill has hopper, stone, gear or drive and ground floors all maintained and equipped as they would have been in its working days. There are three sets of millstones including pairs from Derbyshire and Germany.

Ballycopeland exhibits numerous features of a mill constructed at a period when windmill technology had reached its peak. It is certainly the best preserved and most complete windmill of the type once common in northern England, Scotland and Ireland and is an undoubted asset to the heritage of Ulster as well as a delight to industrial archaeologists. For a full and detailed description of Ballycopeland, see *A Guide to Ballycopeland Windmill* by Peter S. Rhodes (HMSO Belfast).

Ballycopeland Windmill, Co Down

The automatic fantail of Ballycopeland Windmill

Conference on 'The Future of Industrial Archaeology'

Dr R. A. Buchanan of Bath University of Technology writes to us as follows:

The Conference was organised by the Centre for the Study of the History of Technology at Bath University of Technology, and was held at Northgate House, Bath, on 1–3 November 1968. It was attended by 65 members from all parts of Great Britain, and also from Sweden, the USA, and Eire.

The main business of the Conference was a discussion of the theme 'The Future of Industrial Archaeology'. This theme was introduced by Dr R. A. Buchanan in his opening address, and was developed by the three main speakers on the Saturday morning, Dr E. R. R. Green, Mr W. K. V. Gale, and Sir David Follett. Each of these speakers made personal statements, but they were also able to represent particular points of view on the subject under discussion. Thus Dr Green spoke about the CBA and the universities, Mr Gale put forward the point of view of the Newcomen Society, and Sir David gave an account of museum policy towards industrial archaeology. There was a wide-ranging discussion of the views expressed by these speakers, and on the following morning Mr L. T. C. Rolt had the task of drawing together the diverse strands of this discussion in his concluding address. In the course of doing so, Mr Rolt presented the case for the formation of a national organisation to promote the interests and objectives of industrial archaeology.

At the final session of the Conference a resolution was formulated and passed unanimously. It read as follows:

> This Conference resolves to elect a steering committee of six members, with power to co-opt further members, to:
> (a) discuss with the CBA and other interested bodies the possibility of strengthening the industrial archaeological functions of the CBA, or:
> (b) consider the formation of a Council for British Industrial Archaeology to promote the interests and objectives of industrial archaeology,
>
> and to refer back to the members of this Conference and to the societies represented here when they have done this.

The Conference proceeded to elect the steering committee by a secret ballot, with Dr Marie Nisser and Mr Robert Vogel acting as tellers. The members elected were: Dr R. A. Buchanan, Mr L. T. C. Rolt, Mr J. K. Major, Mr N. Cossons, Dr P. N. Jarvis, and Professor W. E. Minchinton.

A field party to visit the principal industrial archaeological sites of central Bristol was held on the Saturday afternoon. It was led by Mr Neil Cossons and included the old Temple Meads station, Redcliffe shot tower (in process of demolition), Cumberland Basin, and the storehouse of the City of Bristol Museum Technology Department at Upper York Street. There was also an opportunity in the programme for an exchange of information about current work in industrial archaeology through slides, films, and reports.

Brunel Society

The Brunel Society was formed in February 1968 with the objectives of preserving the works of Isambard Kingdom Brunel, promoting research and study of his life and achievements, and fostering the imaginative spirit of one of the nineteenth-century's greatest engineers. The inaugural lecture on 'Brunel—The Man' was given by Brunel's biographer, L. T. C. Rolt, at Bristol Museum on 20 April 1968. A programme of lectures and other events in the London and Bristol areas has been planned and met with some success. The society intends to publish a regular newsletter, to gather books, photographs and other material, and to organise excursions. Later it is hoped to sponsor research and award prizes for essays and projects about Brunel and his work. The society will also make responsible representations to appropriate authorities where works of Brunel are in danger of being lost or destroyed. Enquiries and support for the society have come from many parts of the country and several overseas countries. Membership is open to everyone interested in Brunel and his work, and the Honorary Secretary, Mr S. A. Urry, can be contacted at Brunel University, Uxbridge.

Flood Loss

The disastrous floods of July, reports the *Bristol IA Society Bulletin 4*, besides causing loss of life and property, resulted in severe damage to industrial buildings. Since it was far from clear how much of industrial archaeological importance had been destroyed, a register of damaged sites was compiled, including bridges and mills. One of the few good things to come out of the havoc created by the floods in the south-west has been at the Charterhouse-on-Mendip leadworks site, where water cut a chasm through the embanked track leading from the field-studies centre. A massive masonry abutment has been revealed, which appears to be part of an old dam with gaps for sluice gates. Downstream from this is a newly uncovered segment of rough stonework, cylindrical in form, which could be the base of a chimney.

New Lanark

The future of the famous New Lanark mills on the River Clyde, scene of the social experiments of Robert Owen, is in the balance. The summer of 1968 saw the closure of the cotton mills by the owners, the Gourock Ropework Company, who have centralised all of their activities at

Detail of the balcony in the school at New Lanark

The school at New Lanark with the balcony for Robert Owen's band which played at his workers' dances

their headquarters in Port Glasgow. The wonderful state of preservation of the mills themselves and of the associated workers' dwellings in the village is due in no small measure to the care bestowed upon them by the 'Gourock'. The last of the machinery has now been removed from the so recently bustling mills, and the tradition of cotton spinning started by David Dale in 1784 has probably been broken for ever. The mill has now been placed on a care and maintenance basis for two years, but efforts to find another tenant or buyer have so far proved unsuccessful.

The good work of the New Lanark Housing Association, which aims to restore and modernise the houses of the village, is still going actively ahead. The completion of the second phase shows clearly that fine modern flats can be created, without damaging the outward appearance of the old buildings. Nearby, Caithness Row is perhaps one of the finest pieces of restoration ever undertaken on nineteenth-century industrial housing. It is hoped eventually to have a permanent museum in the semicircular Counting House at the end of the row. Many individuals and national bodies are fortunately concerned about the future of New Lanark mills and village, which is probably the most impressive and best preserved industrial site in Britain.

Looking down the lade at the oldest cotton mill in New Lanark

Nathaniel Ireson

Graham Higgins, of Wincanton, Somerset, has been investigating the work of a master-mason and potter, Nathaniel Ireson, who was active in the Wincanton area during the middle of the eighteenth century. Ireson worked on many local houses and churches, including Blandford, Bruton and Gillingham. He built Ireson House, near Wincanton, as his headquarters and this still stands. The house formed part of Windmill Farm and had a quarry adjacent to it. The quarry, which Ireson operated, is now, Mr Higgins reports, 'vastly overgrown, the shallow rock faces being only just distinguishable'.

It is probable, however, that Ireson will be best remembered as a potter. He carried on a pottery at Ireson House for many years and there are a number of examples of his work in museums and in private collections. Several fine pieces are in the Conference Room at the Cow & Gate milk factory in Wincanton. The pottery produced Delft ware, in a wide range of colours and shades. The prevailing colour is blue, but many of the smaller pieces are pink.

Mr Higgins has so far been unable to discover the exact spot where the clay was dug.

Labourer 'sold' mill for £200

The *Daily Telegraph* on 12 November 1968 reported that a Bradford labourer had been jailed for eighteen months for selling a mill he did not own for £200. The mill, in fact, belonged to a local firm who had bought it for £25,000 but had not yet put it to use.

IA in Edinburgh

In addition to a full course of lectures on Industrial Archaeology over the coming session, the Department of Adult Education & Extra-Mural Studies at Edinburgh University is holding special conferences on aspects of the study. A forthcoming weekend conference will study and practise surveying techniques for the industrial archaeologist and how these can be applied to surveying of industrial buildings and plant. It is hoped to carry out an actual survey of an old mill. More ambitious is a study tour of Scottish industrial archaeology (Monday to Saturday 7–12 July 1969), visiting important industrial sites including New Lanark, Leadhills, Bonawe ironworks, Crinan Canal, Perth waterworks etc. The fee including accommodation will be about £35 and further details can be obtained from the Department at 11 Buccleuch Place, Edinburgh 8.

Grand Industrial Tour

Industrial archaeologists and historians, particularly those interested in the history of mining, already owe much to Arthur Raistrick, and they are again in his debt for transcribing, editing and introducing *The Hatchett Diary: A Tour Through the Counties of England & Scotland in 1796 visiting their Mines and Manufactories* (published by D. B. Barton Ltd, Truro). This day-to-day account of a four months' journey through England and Scotland by coach and post-chaise, with perceptive comments on the countryside, roads, inns and towns, is in itself a valuable and interesting contemporary document. Yet its author, Charles Hatchett (1766–1847), was no ordinary dilettante 'doing the tour', but an accomplished scientist familiar with continental factories and mines. Leaving London in May 1796 'by the Salisbury coach' en route for Devon, Hatchett stopped off to visit the Portland stone quarries and the Bovey lignite mines. In Cornwall he observed mining and smelting operations and gives detailed accounts and sketches of activities and equipment at many famous mines.

He afterwards travelled to Birmingham via Bath, Bristol and Worcester, and there called on the Boulton & Watt foundry—'a wonderful establishment'—before visiting the great ironworks of Coalbrookdale. After seeing the Etruria pottery, and Arkwright's cotton mills near Matlock, Hatchett gives an interesting description of the Derbyshire lead mines. In Sheffield collieries and steelworks naturally occupied his attention, while in Newcastle he visited a variety of industries including chemical and leadworks. Travelling north by the great post road, Hatchett reached Edinburgh, where he spent two weeks in academic circles. At Carron ironworks he saw five furnaces in full blast and the casting of 'Cannon, Shells, Shot and all sorts of Iron Kettles'. After visiting the Breadalbane lead mines at Tyndrum, he headed south once more, arriving in Glasgow on 22 July. The journey through Clydesdale took him to Clyde ironworks and New Lanark cotton mills, before bringing him to the famous Leadhills mines high in the Lowther Hills. A brief tour of the Lake District brings to a close this immensely valuable account of mines and factories in the early days of the Industrial Revolution.

Aston–Clinton Limeworks

Mr Cyril Tilling of Dunstable has written telling us of the demolition of the Aston–Clinton limeworks, located near the Chiltern Hills, four miles west of Dunstable. The works were built about 1928 and for forty years supplied lime to many parts of the Home Counties. The four kilns at the works produced about 30 tons of lime per week, although fuel consumption was very high.

Detail of one of the lime kilns at Aston–Clinton

Aston–Clinton Limeworks before demolition

A Survey of Victorian Technology

Interest in the history of technology is gradually growing in Great Britain and as readers of this journal will know, industrial archaeology is a key factor in this development. But the fact remains that too many relics of early engineering works, buildings, machines, equipment, tools and records are in danger of disappearing without trace, without being recorded and without at least a representative assortment being preserved.

The Department of History of Science & Technology at Imperial College in London has been commissioned to survey the problem as it affects the technical history of the Victorian period, loosely defined as 1815 to 1914. The survey is directed towards three objectives:

1. Finding out what is already being conserved and how well.
2. Finding out what else should be conserved especially in those branches of engineering where no attention to conservation has yet been given at all.
3. Examining the agencies and procedures which already exist for conserving items of technical significance of the Victorian period.

The subject material of the survey readily divides itself into two categories: the movable and the immovable. The former includes items such as machinery, equipment and tools, and also documentary relics such as plans, drawings, photos, accounts and correspondence. The immovable items comprise such things as bridges, dams, canal works, industrial and agricultural buildings, mills, mines, furnaces, shipyards and so on.

For various organisational reasons the

survey is not intended to last very long—until the middle of 1969 at the latest—and nor is it desirable that it should. Prompt action is vital. There is at present a chronic lack of information about what should be preserved and where examples might be found, and at the same time recognised and immediate procedures for dealing with relevant items need to be established. If the survey can as quickly as possible point the way to deal with these problems, it will have proved very useful. The process of preservation may yet be hastened sufficiently to ensure the survival of many valuable things which would otherwise be lost.

It is not the purpose of the survey to uncover individual items or to take up particular causes, but rather to do an 'information job' in general terms. There must be many readers of *Industrial Archaeology* who can help the Victorian Technology Survey to achieve its purpose, perhaps because they already have experience of what is involved or because they have ideas as to what should be done. Dr Norman A. F. Smith at the Department of History of Science & Technology at 180 Queen's Gate, SW7, is the principal investigator and will be most grateful for any help or advice that readers can offer.

IA Down Under

R. N. Walker, Director of The National Trust of Australia (New South Wales) has written from Sydney telling us about the establishment of an Industrial Archaeology Committee, to carry out research and make recommendations on the preservation of industrial equipment, which can be restored and retained *in situ*. This work is to be undertaken in conjunction with the Museum of Applied Arts & Sciences, which concerns itself with similar equipment that can be removed and shown to best advantage in the museum.

The Irish Society

The Irish Society for Industrial Archaeology has entered its second year with increasing membership and a newly launched Newsletter. It is now embarking on an increasingly full and varied programme of activities to include lectures, field-trips and members' evenings. The society hopes to encourage its members to give preliminary reports on studies which they have recently undertaken. Many members and other individuals are carrying out recording work, and the society aims to coordinate this activity, as well as undertake more systematic, comprehensive surveys. One of the ambitions of the society is to compile a guide to sites, buildings and machinery of industrial archaeological interest in Ireland. Dr Corran of Arthur Guinness & Sons Ltd has started on a bibliography of books, papers and articles relating to all aspects of Irish industrial history and archaeology, which should prove a valuable aid to everyone undertaking research. Dr Louis Cullen, Department of History, Trinity College, Dublin, is interested in locating and preserving business records, and this could become a fruitful source for the Irish industrial archaeologist.

Bauble-making: a Leicestershire speciality

A bauble was a small household object bought more for ornament than for use. In Leicestershire baubles were made from spar, or alabaster, quarried at Chellaston in Derbyshire and turned to shape on a lathe. The main demand came from seaside places in the south of England. The industry flourished during the second half of the nineteenth century, dying away rapidly between 1900 and 1910, mainly as the result of competition from cheap imported souvenirs.

Leicester Museum has a good collection of baubles. It includes watch-stands, powder-pots, inkwells, candlesticks, a tobacco jar, miniature grottoes and a mustard pot. Only one bauble workshop is known to survive, at Shardlow, in Derbyshire.

An illustrated account of the industry has been written by J. A. Daniell. It is available at 2s 6d from the Leicestershire Archaeological & Historical Society, The Guildhall, Leicester.

Highland Coal Mine

One of the oldest continuously worked coal mines in Britain, at Brora in east Sutherland, has been given a new lease of life with the aid of a £100,000 grant from the Highlands & Islands Development Board. Mining of this highly localised coal on the narrow coastal plain by the Moray Firth has been pursued since the sixteenth century. Brora was so important at this time that it was created a burgh of barony by James VI in 1601. In the early nineteenth century the colliery assumed a new importance, with the development of an important salt-making industry. The present shaft was sunk at this period, pumping and haulage being carried out by a double waterwheel. The colliery was linked with the salt pans and harbour by a wagon-way of 20-in gauge. Later a brick and tile works, rows of colliers' houses and workshops were built. The development of herring fishing led to the establishment of other crafts, notably boat-building and coopering. After a period of closure the Brora mine was reopened by the Duke of Sutherland in 1872 and continued to supply a wide market in the Highlands and even as far afield as the Faroe Islands. After several disastrous fires in the workings it looked like the end of the road for the mine in 1961, until the miners decided to buy and work the mine themselves. At present the annual output is around 8000

Brora Colliery

25-ft lathe installed to true up shafting in a Perth factory, c 1868

tons, but test bores made in 1966 have proved the existence of a rich seam of over 8 million tons. This modest little mine, with its classic pithead gear, is an interesting, if somewhat alien feature on the Highland landscape.

Museum of Buildings

Adjoining Avoncroft College, near the village of Stoke Prior in Worcestershire, work has begun on the first Museum of Buildings in England. The purpose of the museum is to preserve—by removal and reconstruction—representative examples of English timber-framed buildings which would otherwise be demolished. Several thousand pounds have already been raised by private appeal and the site at Avoncroft has been generously provided by the Fircroft Trust. The work of reconstructing the museum's first building, a fifteenth-century house from Bromsgrove, is well in hand and others are planned to follow.

Although the phrase 'Museum of Buildings' has an unfamiliar ring to British ears, on the Continent both the concept and the need for such museums have been accepted for many years. In several countries in Europe, representative buildings have been taken down and reconstructed, usually in the form of a 'village'. In this way they form a visual record of lost crafts and skills and show how people lived in earlier centuries. Such museums of buildings have been assembled at Arnhem in Holland, Aarhus in Denmark, Kommern in Germany and at Skansen, Stockholm. With the exception of the Welsh Folk Museum at St Fagan's near Cardiff and the Ulster Folk Museum at Cultra Manor, no projects of this kind exist in Britain. Yet Britain, and especially England, is remarkable for the number of timber-framed buildings which have survived into an age when the potential destructive power of new roads and urban redevelopment far exceeds anything experienced in the past. It is to save at least a few of these irreplaceable buildings that the Avoncroft Museum of Buildings is appealing for support. Further details may be obtained from Avoncroft Museum of Buildings Ltd, Avoncroft College, Stoke Prior, near Bromsgrove, Worcestershire.

The Antioch Woollen Mill

The Merrimack Valley Textile Museum has purchased all the machinery in the Antioch (West Virginia) Woollen Mill. The machinery has been removed from the mill and is now en route to North Andover, Massachusetts, where it will be assembled for display and study. The Director of the Museum, Mr Thomas W. Leavitt, said the purchase is the most important acquisition of machinery made by the museum during the last ten years. Included in the collection are a wool picker, manufactured by M. A. Furbush & Son, Philadelphia; a set of three woollen cards, Bridesburg Manufacturing Company, Bridesburg, Pennsylvania; c 1877, a wooden-framed 100-spindle spinning jack, Bickford & Lombard, Worcester, Massachusetts; c 1864, a wooden warping reel and creel, a throstle twister, A. Jenks & Son, Bridesburg; probably 1850 or before, a broad multi-harness power loom, George Crompton, Worcester; c 1880, a narrow multi-harness power loom, Fairmount Machine Company, Philadelphia; and c 1893, several smaller nineteenth-century machines used in the manufacture of woollen cloth.

The Antioch Woollen Mill was owned by the late Scott Rotruck, who lived a few yards from the mill. Tradition has it that the building was erected as early as 1789; the date '1861' is marked in mortar on the basement wall, which indicates a repair to that part of the structure. Originally a grist mill, and still containing some buckwheat- and corn-grinding equipment, the building was filled with textile machinery in about 1917. The machines passed through many hands before they came to Antioch, having been in mills at Maysville and Martin, West Virginia. Motive power was provided by an overshot waterwheel until a few years before production ceased. The second world war caused the wool supply to be diverted to government contractors; after the war most of the machinery was never used again for commercial production. Blankets and overcoating were two of the chief products of the mill. Until he sold the machinery to the museum, Mr Rotruck wove very distinctive and artistic rugs on his hand loom for sale to occasional visitors.

According to James C. Hippen, the curator, who conducted the negotiations for the Antioch purchase, the addition of these items to the museum will 'substantially strengthen' its collection, now probably the most comprehensive assembly of historic cloth-making equipment in the United States.

Several pieces placed on exhibition immediately include the Jenks throstle twister and the Crompton broad loom.

A Spinning Jenny and the American Peace Corps

In the archives of the Bath & West Society there is a letter, dated 29 November 1777, from John Cook, of Thorncombe, near Chard, to the Secretary of the Society. It described one of Cook's inventions, a new kind of spinning machine. This was, in the words of its inventor, 'one of the Most Simple Construction. It takes up but very little more room than a Common Spinning Wheel. It carries 10 or 12 spindles at pleasure, and is very much like a Common Spinning Wheel in appearance. The Head stands erect: the spindles run in the Head parallel to the Horizon. The Wheel is turned by a winch, and will perform double the work of the Common Jenny with greater ease'.

The Bath & West Society gave prizes for new inventions, but Cook was old, poor and infirm and died before he could send in a model to claim the prize. In 1966, the Curator of the Textile Museum at Helmshore, Lancashire, Mr C. Aspin, was shown Mr Cook's letter. He was much impressed by the invention and considered it would work better than the ordinary jenny. He had been asked by the American Peace Corps to suggest improved spinning methods for places where the one-thread hand wheel is still used, and he recommended Cook's jenny for backward neighbourhoods in Turkey.

John Hall & Son (Dukinfield) Limited

Mr Brian Lamb continues his impressive series of privately produced notebook-monographs on local subjects of importance in the field of industrial archaeology with a report and survey of a firm of fireclay manufacturers established in Dukinfield in 1792, on the east bank of the Peak Forest Canal, although the works was in operation two years before the canal was completed. Until it closed early in 1967, it produced high-quality clayware by hand, with very little machinery. Mr Lamb has made his survey and record while it is still possible to document this early industry and its methods. He has been greatly helped in this by the practical demonstration of the various processes given to him by Mr G. H. Crossley, who was foreman at Dukinfield until 1960. The report is illustrated with Mr Lamb's customary skill and accuracy and gives an extremely thorough account of what went on at the works. It is not for sale, but copies have been deposited at a number of centres, including the Ashton-under-Lyne Library.

Sussex Windmills

Mr David G. Jones has prepared a folding map showing the location of the remaining thirty Sussex windmills. It has been compiled with the help of Mr F. W. Gregory, the expert on Sussex mills, and indicates the type of mill—post, smock or tower—and also shows the number of complete surviving sweeps on each mill. It is available at 2s post free from Mr Jones at 22 Manor Road, Hampden Park, Eastbourne.

Lime Kilns at Merstham, Surrey

Lime is known to have been quarried in the Merstham area in the early sixteenth century, but the real development of the industry dates from the opening of the horse-drawn Croydon, Merstham & Godstone Railway in 1805. The limeworks were controlled for some years by the well-known early nineteenth-century contractors, Jolliffe & Banks. A mysterious circular earth bank on the site was excavated during 1962 by a team directed by Mr E. S. Wood and a report of its findings is published in Vol LXIV of *The Survey Archaeological Collections*. The bank proved to be made up of two contiguous circles, and, by a most interesting process of deduction, Mr Wood arrived at the conclusion that the circles were used for making mortar or cement for lining the first Merstham railway tunnel.

As an appendix Miss Marguerite Gollancz, County Archivist, contributes a note on the records of Merstham limeworks, now deposited in the Surrey Record Office. They extend back in broken series to 1872 and have suffered a good deal from damp during the period up till 1961 when they were kept at the limeworks.

Lime Kilns at Marple, Cheshire

The Marple branch of the Cheshire Federation of Ratepayers & Kindred Associations has revived the campaign to restore and preserve the eighteenth-century lime kilns built by Samuel Oldknow. When his spinning mill at Mellor was opened in 1794, Marple had 600 inhabitants. The employees at the mill were mostly women and children, and to provide employment for men, Oldknow built roads, bridges and a canal and developed a lime-burning industry.

Marple Antiquarian Society cleared the site and began a fund to restore the kilns, but gave up the attempt because they were advised that the cost of preserving the crumbling stonework would be prohibitive, although in 1964 the kilns had been scheduled by the Ministry of Works as an industrial monument. However, the secretary of the Ratepayers' Federation, Dr W. F. Beech, says Oldknow's kilns should be preserved 'because they are a feature of the landscape, and an early example of landscaping to disguise an industrial building'. It appears that the quality of the stonework has caused some people to think that the ruins were those of a monastery.

Durham University

The University now has an Industrial Archaeology Group, with about forty members. The group has had talks from Frank Atkinson and Michael Wheeler, of the Bowes Museum, and during the summer paid a visit to the museum's stored collection of industrial relics. A visit has been made to Seaham Harbour, where the Secretary, Mr J. Harvey Chesshire, reports that members 'were shocked at the very visible signs of depression', and other places to be seen are the lead mines and disused railway tracks of Weardale.

East Riding Agricultural Machinery Preservation Society

The society has been formed to collect and preserve in working order all kinds of farm machinery of any age and to establish a permanent museum of farming history, where the collection will be housed and displayed. There are about one hundred members, nearly all of them working farmers. One has specialised in tractor history and another has built up a small collection of stationary oil engines.

The secretary of the society is Mr H. E. Kirk, of Louvain, Rowley Road, Little Weighton, Hull. He would be glad to hear of any suitable machinery which the society might want to acquire and of any research activities in other areas.

Marconi and the Isle of Wight

Mr Cyril J. Scott, Curator of the Herbert Art Gallery and Museum, Coventry, writes to say that he read Mr Pocock's article on Marconi and the Isle of Wight in Vol 5 No 1 with more than usual interest, as during the winter of 1941–2 he was a member of the crew of a radar station on St Catherine's Point and was billeted in Knowle's Farm. The farmer was very proud of the association with Marconi and he told the radar crew that it was from his farm that the first cross-channel experiments were carried out. They were shown two relics of the station:

1 Some shelves in one of the farm cottages which they were told were installed by Marconi's staff. These were quite uninteresting in themselves, but were much prized by the farmer who went to pains to request us not to damage them.
2 A concrete base which had obviously at some time supported a substantial pole. This lay between the house and the cliff edge and was pointed out as being the base of Marconi's aerial mast.

Miss Kirkpatrick's tablet was not in evidence but was probably removed during the war for security reasons.

Mr Scott mentions that, by coincidence, in 1945 at Cattolica on the coast of the Adriatic he found a 'Marconi lived here' plaque on the wall of the regimental headquarters.

Our Contributors

ANTHONY TRIGGS, a journalist with the *Portsmouth Evening News*, is interested in genealogy, local history and numismatics. He collected the material for his article on Hampshire windmills over three years.

ALAN SMITH is Keeper of Ceramics and Applied Art at the City of Liverpool Museums.

PETER S. RICHARDS is head of the Department of Commerce and Liberal Studies at Wallasey College of Further Education; at present engaged in research on the location of industry at Deeside in Flintshire.

IAN L. DONNACHIE is a lecturer at the Edinburgh College of Commerce and editor of our *Notes and News*; special interest: mills and milling.

CHRISTOPHER COX is head of the History Department at Holland Park School, London; born in Stroud and educated in Gloucester; owes interest in industrial archaeology to Michael Rix of Birmingham Extra-Mural Department and Lionel Walrond of the Stroud Museum; currently engaged in research into the growth and decline of the turnpike system in the Stroud district.

BARON F. DUCKHAM is a lecturer in the Department of Economic History, University of Strathclyde; editor of *Transport History* and currently working on the history of the Scottish coal-mining industry.

W. L. NORMAN is a lecturer in the Liberal Studies Department of Wakefield Technical and Art College where he is currently developing courses in industrial archaeology and local history.

J. D. PORTEOUS

Goole: A Pre-Victorian Company Town

THIS *article, following an earlier one by Baron F. Duckham, 'The Founding of Goole: an early Nineteenth-Century Canal Port'* (INDUSTRIAL ARCHAEOLOGY, *vol 4, no 1*), *helps complete the history of the establishment and growth of a company town about which very little has been written previously. Dr Porteous, who has also published a paper entitled 'A New Canal Port in the Railway Age: Railway Projection to Goole 1830–1914'* (TRANSPORT HISTORY, *vol 2, no 1*), *here concentrates on the buildings of Goole.*

In the early part of the nineteenth century, the Aire & Calder Navigation Company[1] decided to modernise its system by creating the Knottingley–Goole Canal, linking the West Riding with the River Ouse, and thence with the Continent,[2] and at the same time to create a small canal town. This town is unique in character,[3] being the product neither of social experiment nor of industrial philanthropy but more like an early example of what has become known in modern America as 'the company town'.

It is not known when the idea of building a town near their new docks presented itself to the A & CN directors. George Leather, their engineer after Rennie's death (1821), reported in 1822 of Goole:

> The establishment of trade and the consequent rise of a town will . . . enable you to sell off or let building ground, so as to add greatly to the profit of the concern.

Up to this date it seems that no thought had been given to the accommodation of future dockers and watermen, except for the harbourmen and lock-keepers, whose dwellings were to be interspersed among the docks. The next year, however, Leather reported that since the dock contract had been let in May 1822—to Messrs Jolliffe & Banks—the number of applications for building land had been so great that unless something were done to accommodate them, the speculators would be likely to commence construction on adjacent non-company land. Leather therefore recommended the company to produce speedily a uniform building plan to which all builders should be required to conform.

Not having all the adjacent land in their possession,[4] and determined from the first to establish full control over the development, the directors engaged Leather to produce a town plan, which seems to have been ready in 1823. It was probably identical with the 1825 plan shown in the top diagram and was extremely elaborate. An elevation on the original depicts a classical arrangement, consisting of imposing arcaded façades surrounding on three sides an open square and facing towards the waterfront. In form this resembles the common Mediterranean plan, for example that of the Praça do Comercio in Lisbon. No doubt the capital required to establish such an ambitious settlement was not forthcoming in view of the huge expenditure on canals and docks together with the constant revision of proposals for the dock system, a projected elaboration of which can be seen in the bottom diagram. The A & CN Building Committee approved only the eastern third of Leather's plan, which was to be entirely surrounded by water, as befits a town expected to be totally dependent on water-movement. The rest was 'postponed'.

The initial task was to lay out the major streets, the first of which was begun in late 1822 and completed by 1823. Because of the low-lying nature of the area, with a minimum of only 8 ft OD, and its consequent liability to flooding, the streets were built up several feet above the surrounding surface, material for this operation being taken from the concurrent dock excavations and surrounding land. The latter was subsequently relevelled following the construction of warping drains in the traditional Humberhead fashion, the whole process being an admirable, though unusual, example of the technique of 'cut and fill'. Progress was slow at first, and in 1824 the directors were exhorting the Building Committee to hasten in laying out the land at

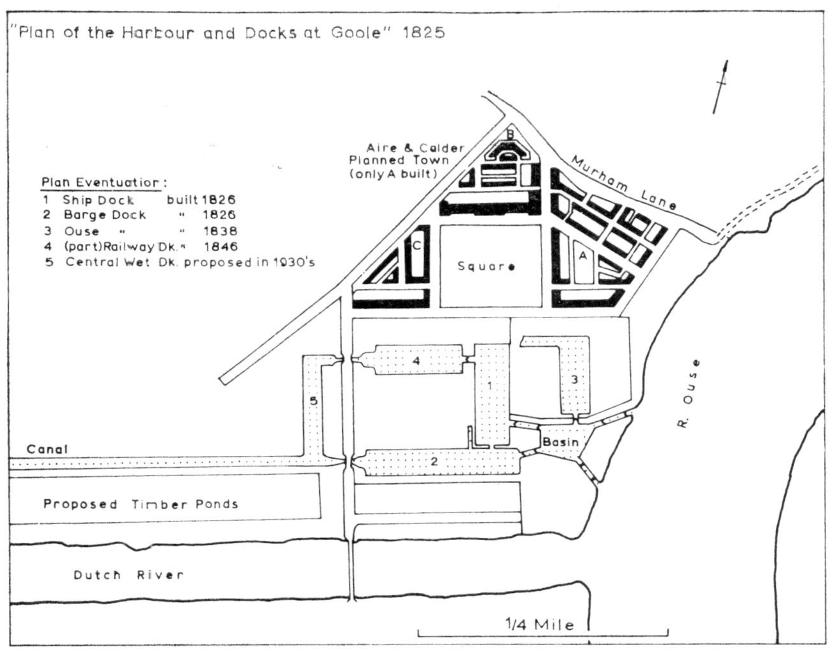

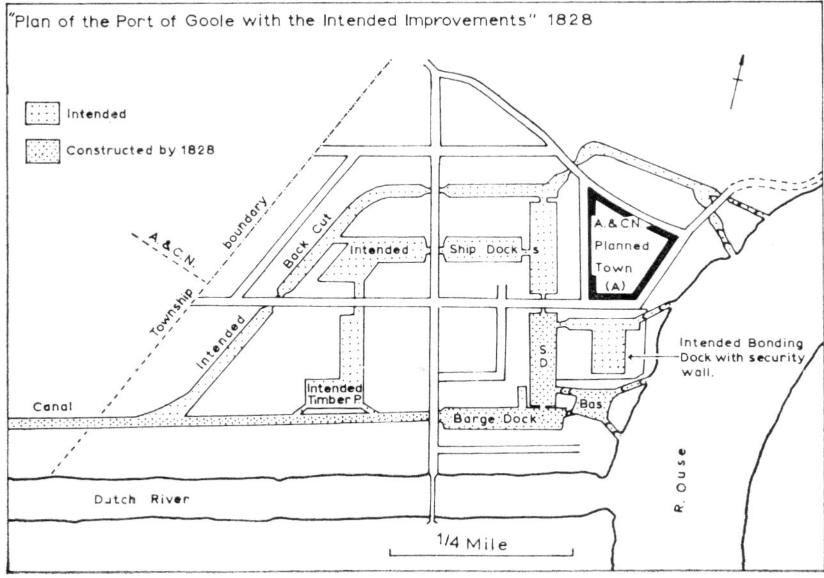

Early company projects for Goole

Goole, in addition to speeding the completion of the docks, which by now was already well behind the original schedule.

Once the streets had been planned, housing was begun. Nothing had been done by 1824, when Leather reported that the building plan had not yet been finalised, although speculators were clamouring for leases: 'The only building yet begun is an Inn, by Sir Edward Banks, which is getting up fast with the second storey'. In common with other canal-created ports, the first permanent building to be completed was a hotel, in this case the 'Banks Arms', renamed c 1835 'The Lowther' (in honour of the A & CN one-time chairman, Sir John Lowther) after being bought in 1827 by the company and integrated into its building pattern.

The A & CN Building Committee soon busied itself, however, and the flood of pent-up constructive energy was released soon after mid-1824; a year later some houses were nearly finished. By 20 July 1826, the date of the official opening of docks and canal, eleven dwelling-houses and two cottages had been completed, and fifty-nine other cottages, a public house and 'a smithery' in 'the Back Streets', together with twelve dwelling-houses in the SE frontage, were in various states of completion for A & CN. Leases to other parties included plots for nine cottages and another smithy, while Sir Edward Banks was believed to be about to erect further houses. Some sections were almost complete, except for pavements. According to a newspaper report, somewhat at variance with Leather's, thirty houses were already inhabited in July 1826, while seventy more were under construction in the NW part of the town.[5] The centre and NE were thus the last areas to be completed, as North Street's irregular façade and the date '1834' on the wall-plaque of the Oddfellows' Lodge demonstrate.

During all this building activity the warping up of land and the raising of streets continued, while a number of 'common sewers' were under construction. To the south of the docks, near Goole Bridge, a secondary detached area of building, in the same style, was also in progress, in conjunction with warping from the Dutch River. This was primarily to provide low-standard cottage accommodation for the inhabitants of a hutted squatters' settlement which had appeared in the area to provide shelter not only for the navvies on construction work but also to house those drawn to the new town for permanent employment.

'New Goole' was built entirely of red bricks, the claylands of the locality furnishing adequate supplies of material for a surge of brickmaking; large brickponds persisted for a number of years. In addition, the spoil from the dock excavations was set aside not only to build up the streets, but also to make bricks when supplies ran low. Although a great deal of stone came by water for the dock works, little was used in the town itself, which may be said to have arisen bodily from the ground on which it stood. This growth was capped entirely with imported slate, still largely intact.

The result of this activity was a singular port town, with over 250 building structures. From the start, each street and quarter was planned to perform some specified function, and building-unit shape and size varied accordingly. Aire Street, one-sided in memory of Leather's original plan, became the major commercial street, containing stores, inns, saloons, and other provision for the wants of the seamen (see p 137). It retains this character today; betting shops and sundry other changes are not out of keeping. Ouse Street, unusually wide in order to accommodate an open market, was the secondary commercial street, with a mixture of shops and dwellings. In both streets dwelling space was located behind or above the commercial premises. East Parade's large structures were built for the middle and professional classes, and thus graduated naturally to the office block of the present day. Behind these sheltering façades the poor were clustered in the small terraced cottages of the centre and north, typified by George Street (see p 137), penetrating towards the SE corner by means of poorer cross-streets. The latter corner, with the largest inn, and with numerous workshops, the 'Public Rooms', 'Commercial Buildings' and the chapel in the immediate vicinity, was the hub of the town, the nearest point to the dock system. This cluster of larger constructions can be seen on the aerial photograph on page 138, which also makes plain many of the points made in the next section.

The aerial view also emphasises Ouse Street as a divide between the areas to the north and south (right and left respectively on the photo). A land-use analysis reveals that 108 of the 132 structures classed as 'cottages' were located north of Ouse Street, while eight of the eleven 'industrial premises and large individual structures' were to be found in the smaller area to the south. The divide is less meaningful for retail premises and the larger 'dwellings',[6] however, because of the transverse nature of Aire Street and East Parade, and the division of Ouse Street itself. Taking these major streets individually, sixteen of East Parade's seventeen structures were 'dwellings and professional quarters', while nineteen of Aire Street's twenty-three were retail premises and inns. Ouse Street's transitional nature appears in its tally of twenty-three cottages, thirty shops and only a single 'dwelling'.

Leather's 1828 plan of Goole (bottom diagram) contains a riverside view of an opulent and well-built town. Its somewhat ideal nature is realised if one compares similar engravings of ports ranging from Hull to Runcorn. The long façades of white, many-windowed buildings, crowned by a forest of masts, with the occasional ship heaving to in the foreground, would seem to be a perfect image of the early nineteenth-century port. Goole's architecture, however, did display considerable and impressive uniformity, a product of the company's rigorous control. The spirit of this control can perhaps best be found in Leather's 1826 report, which stresses the virtue desirable in the A & CN's Goole agent: 'as the town is all your own, much will depend upon his forming the habits and manners of the people'. The instructions in the Lease Book, referring to 'Dwelling-houses being built in a uniform manner' translate this paternalism into substantial reality. Formal terraced uniformity and an outward display of quiet opulence seem to be the keynotes.

The architects, Messrs Woodhead & Hurst of Doncaster, produced a building pattern in no way original, but rare on this scale. The outward appearance of the town was designed from the point of view of the waterman. Facing the harbour, the solid three-storey respectability of East Parade, the professional quarter, was calculated to impress the new arrival by water. In Aire Street appearances are maintained by the uniform Georgian shop-house façade, which in today's pastel shades is still the most impressive street in Goole. In Ouse Street, a long uniform vista of two-storey shops and houses is relieved at the block-corners by three-storey structures designed as large retail shops and inns. The houses of watermen and others were neatly tucked away in the cross-streets between these three major axes, but spread out to the north of Ouse Street, where George Street provided a monotony of grim squat two-storey cottages. The northern façade, fronting North Street, demonstrates its lateness of construction (late 1830s and 40s) by its mixture of styles. This side was remote from the docks, facing bare fields, and thus restrictions could be relaxed.

Tending to reinforce the uniformity of style and brickwork was the insistence on bevelled block-corners. Rounded corners are common in old port areas, probably to assist the cornering of loaded drays, but rarely have they been used on such a scale as the *leitmotif* of a whole planned town. At strategic positions the bevelled corner would accommodate a shop frontage, the one depicted in the photograph of George Street on page 137 bearing the sign 'Rinso saves coal every wash day'. Elsewhere the corner would have a door, or more rarely, a blank wall, but in the northern section the association of corner shops and working-class housing anticipates the characteristics of later bye-law housing.

Perhaps the rear view of the low-class housing best illustrates the A & C's concern with outward show. Here the blank brick walls are relieved by only the smallest of windows, some of which appear to have been put in subsequent to building completion. The lowness of the unmade back alleys relative to the raised streets is a further indication, and also provides a clue to one of the area's peculiarities, quasi-cellared dwellings. Only the streets were raised, housing being constructed on the original level, so that the ground floors, though exposed to daylight at the rear, took on the character of cellars at the front. Thus the houses exhibited the peculiarity of a frontdoor one storey above the backdoor (see p 138).

In Ouse Street the buildings had six rooms; while the street-level front room served as retail premises, the rear and upper rooms housed the family, for a second family frequently occupied the 'ground floor', with light and air only from the dank back alley. In George Street was manifested the strange form best described as 'one up, one down and one quasi-cellar'. These cottages, seemingly two-storeyed at the front, and therefore apparently extremely cramped, revealed a kitchen below front ground-level when viewed from the rear. Rare cases of doubling-up of families occurred even in these three-roomed cottages. In all cases the lower-floor ceilings were uncomfortably low for the average male, while frequent floods and the backing-up of sewers, with the consequent inflow of sewage, must have made life intolerable at times.[7] The court type of building pattern was rare, and occurred only in the northern part of the town, where controls were lax; a number of 'yards', with back-to-backs, existed behind North Street, and a triangular court known as the 'Nine of Diamonds' behind the inn at the NW corner.

The most impressive building of all is the Lowther Hotel, built privately before the A & C pattern had been created (see p 137). Its peculiar character thus stands out against a uniform background; tall, sharp-edged and powerful, with the minimum of decoration, it effectively reflects the austere opulence of the A & CN. Today its rear outbuildings have been partly demolished, and the upper storey is entirely boarded off, while a wall-sized mural of the early Goole docks peels from the wall of the former directors' board room. It is probable that this hotel may be the last remnant of the whole area left standing within a few years, for it is one of Goole's two structures designated as Buildings of Special Historic Interest under the 1962 Town and County Planning Act. It is a fitting memorial to its builder, the famous contractor who began life as an illiterate agricultural labourer.[8]

Since the first world war, the A & CN company town, the nucleus of present Goole, has gradually become little more than the major local example of urban blight. This has been accentuated by the movement of Goole's focus of activity from this area towards the railway station. Until 1965 the town of 1824–40 remained inhabited and almost intact. Last year, however, under the latest urban renewal scheme, demolition began, the first phase designed to level the central core of small cottages, leaving only the external street frontages of Aire Street, East Parade and part of North Street.

At the time of writing much of the central area lies in ruins, exposing the remarkable pattern of raised streets surrounding a series of shallow depressions, representing the original surface, in which the buildings were erected. The rest of the company town, except the public houses at the three corners, is scheduled for demolition within the next two years. It is this urgency, and the lack of initiative shown by the Borough Council in recording a unique piece of industrial archaeology, which has led to the writing of this article, based on a recent land-use and reconstruction survey, a number of house sketches and measurements, and a large number of photographs taken in 1965 and 1966. Very soon this unique company town of 140 years ago will have vanished as though it had never been, its only legacy, besides memories, being a skeletal street pattern.[9]

Notes

1 The substance of the first part of this article is derived from the Aire & Calder Navigation Company Archives, including minutes and engineers' reports, housed at the British Transport Historical Records Department, York.
2 For the industrial archaeology of the port, see B. F. Duckham, 'The Founding of Goole', *Industrial Archaeology*, vol 4, no 1 (1967), 19–28.
3 K. Hudson, *Industrial Archaeology* (1963), 130
4 Land sale deeds, British Waterways, Leeds
5 *Morning Chronicle*, 26 July 1826
6 The A & CN's own classification
7 Late nineteenth-century Reports of the Medical Officer of Health. Other towns in low-lying situations, such as Hull, have no cellars.
8 T. Coleman, *The Railway Navvies* (1965), 54; H. W. Dickinson, Jolliffe & Banks, Contractors, *Trans Newcomen Soc*, xii (1931–2), 1–8
9 Even this pattern could disappear should the area be redeveloped for light industry.

Plates, pages 137–8

CHARLES DODSWORTH

Further Observations on the Bowling Ironworks

THE *article on the Bowling Ironworks, Bradford, by Hilary Long, in the May 1968 issue of this journal, prompted the writer to offer the following observations on the same topic.*

H. J. Maltby, a local historian of the area, writing in 1924,[1] stated that the original partnership at Bowling was made between John Sturges, ironmaster of Sandal near Wakefield, and Richard Paley, ironmaster of Leeds. However, no smelting was carried out until 1788, when Sturges and Paley were joined by William Sturges of Datchett, Bucks, and John Sewell of Wakefield, with a capital of £3,500. They contracted to work the coal, iron and other minerals of Sir Francis Lindley Wood's Bolling (or Bowling) estate.

A few years later came the incident in which the partners ran foul of Messrs James Watt the younger and Matthew Robinson Boulton, son of the founder of the famous Soho firm, who, in 1796, filed a suit against Sturges for the abrogation of patent rights in the construction of Watt-type engines. The patents were almost due to expire and a number of evasions had been made, particularly by Bateman and Sheratt of Manchester. Boulton and Watt set up quite an effective system of industrial espionage, in which they were assisted by, in the present instance, Benjamin Gott, the famous Leeds industrialist and talented textile technologist. He had purchased an engine from Soho, had installed some of their gas-making plant in his three mills, and maintained close business relations with the partners.[2] Apparently it was he who learned of the illegal engine construction at Bowling, and passed the information to Boulton and Watt. Using Gott's office as a base, Lawson, one of their agents, was able to visit the Bradford ironworks under an assumed name. He obtained first-hand information, and this led to the successful claim for royalties.

A new partnership at Bowling was made in 1804, and during the period of the war with France the firm broke into the lucrative trade in iron guns. As a result the partners were able to purchase the Bowling estate lands for £20,000 in 1816, and the mineral rights in 1821.[3] Trading was carried on under the name of John Sturges & Co from 1804 to 1849. Between 1849 and 1870 the firm was known as the Bowling Iron Co, and advantage was taken of the Acts of 1862 and 1865 which simplified company law; Bowling therefore became a limited liability company.

After 1870 the rate of expansion of industrial production in Britain slowed, and Bowling Ironworks was adversely affected. The company continued to make high-grade wrought-iron products using the antique cold-blast process, coupled with the historic hand-puddling method of refining. This was originally developed by Henry Cort in 1782–4. However, the demand for wrought iron made by traditional methods was being reduced by competition from mild steel. Increasingly, after 1862, this was available cheaply and in quantity by the Bessemer and the later Siemens-Martin and Gilchrist-Thomas processes. Steel's increasing supremacy helped force Bowling to go into receivership in 1898, but parts of the plant area continued to be occupied by firms trading in iron goods, such as Messrs Tanks & Drums Ltd. Another part of the area became a Corporation tram depot.[4]

One factor in the decline of Bowling was the impending exhaustion of the company's coal reserves in the Bierley–Hunsworth areas for, unlike the nearby Low Moor Co, Bowling had not greatly extended its supply lines for coking coal and iron ore. Sturges' enterprise was only one of several iron-making firms that sprang up in the area south-west of Bradford in the 1780s and of these, Shelf and Bierley works were absorbed by Low Moor in 1824 and 1854 respectively. Bierley works was close to the Bowling area and this acquisition, taken with the other lands owned by Low Moor, limited the expansion of Bowling works. When the small Birkenshaw works closed in 1815, the stock of

4,000 tons of iron ore was purchased jointly by Bowling and Low Moor.

A few years earlier the Birkenshaw works had temporarily closed, and with the blowing out of the single furnace the engineers had found re-employment at Bowling. It is worth recording that the Birkenshaw ironworks had received its ore not by a railway, but by a short and little-known canal, some half a mile long, which was still marked on the six-inch OS map of 1847 as 'The Navigation Bank', near GR 200280.[5]

The local 'black bed' and 'better bed' seams of the lower coal measures, which were the basis of the Bradford industry, were of particularly low sulphur and phosphorus content and were of excellent coking quality. Coke making was done in beehive ovens, or in open piles. None of the coal was wasted, and even 'smalls' were carefully collected for use. The Bowling Co quoted sulphur contents of 0·42 per cent and 0·45 per cent for 'better bed' coal from 'F' Pit, Tong, and Holme Pit, Bowling. Beehive ovens survived in use in Yorkshire well into the twentieth century in spite of their low productivity of coke as this was believed to be of superior metallurgical quality.

Unfortunately, the thickness of the 'black bed' seam was only 22–34 in, while the 'better bed' was 14–24 in thick. The clay-ironstone bed that overlay the 'black bed' seam was never thicker than 2 ft, and had an iron content of 29 per cent.[6] The pits were sited up to four miles away from the plant and were of small size, sometimes only 'dayholes' or adits, and they were worked by the inefficient and outdated 'room and pillar' system of mining. All the 'better bed' pits had closed by 1896, while those working the 'black bed' had closed by 1913. The Bradford coalfield had shrunk from forty-nine working pits in 1871 to three that were still functioning in 1924.

Perhaps the most interesting feature of the Bowling ironworks was the evolution of its transport network. The writer is at present engaged in the study of the development of early wagonways in this area, which is as yet incomplete. The plant was served by a series of narrow-gauge railways which almost certainly started as wooden-edge railways, since these are recorded as having been constructed on nearby Wibsey Slack in or about 1780, to supply the Bradford, Horton, and Low Moor districts with coal.[7]

The year 1790 is a reasonable provisional date for the first lines at Bowling, since the original coal and iron pits were situated within a few hundred yards of the works and the expansion of production accompanying the war with France would have required the opening of new mines at a somewhat greater distance. The pits at this time were very small, employing only a few men. However, none of the large-scale maps of the district that the writer has examined shows any railways at Bowling before 1822. The first one to give any indications was Joshua Thorp's Map of Leeds, surveyed in 1819–21, and published in 1822. It shows a railroad as two parallel dotted lines linking the works with a point on the Leeds road near the present East Brook Lane (GR 170330). This was almost certainly an iron tramroad whose plates would have been cast at the works, and it ran along the north-eastern side of the present Hamerton Street. It served a coalyard behind the one-time Golden Lion in Leeds Road, where coal unsuitable for iron making (ie coal from seams other than the 'black' and 'better bed' seams) was sold to the public. Thorp's map is equally vague about certain other Yorkshire railways then in existence, and its failure therefore to mark wooden wagonways is not surprising. The early lines at Bowling would have fed the works from small coal and ironstone pits in the area north of the present B6148 (Rooley Lane). The use of iron rails at Bowling was briefly referred to in Priestley's classic book of 1830.[8]

C. Greenwood's map of Yorkshire on the scale of 10 miles to $7\frac{1}{4}$ in, based on Mudge and Colby's survey in 1817 for the Board of Ordnance, failed to record any of the contemporary wagonways at Bowling. Henry Teesdale's reissue of this survey (on a slightly altered scale) in 1828 was a slight improvement, in that the Bowling–Hamerton Street line and part of the Low Moor system were shown, using the symbol of two full parallel lines with cross marks.[9]

In 1831 appeared S. D. Martin's revised version of Greenwood's map of the Leeds area.[10] This is an excellent map, about 2½ in to 1 mile, and showed very clearly the growth of railways in the Bowling area, linking pits on the Bolling Hall estate to the works (see Figure 1). There were three main branches, the one down from Bradford already mentioned, one running south to coal pits near Bierley Chapel at 177305, and one running south-west, about 2 miles, to a point on the Bradford–Huddersfield road at 159310. These lines were marked 'Railway' or 'Rail Road', and it is almost certain that they were iron tram-

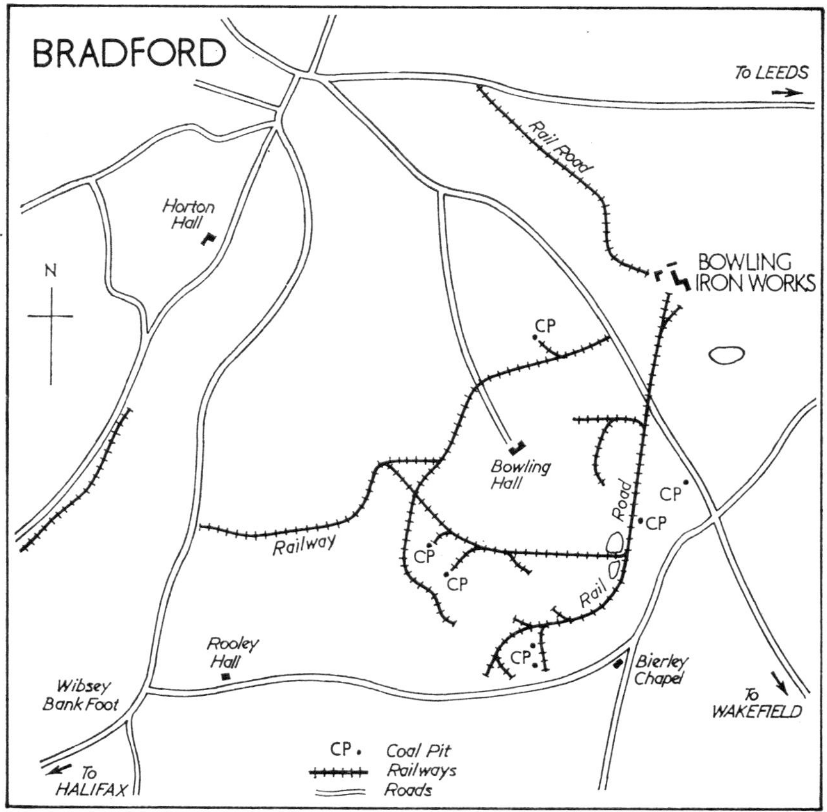

Fig 1 Tramroads serving Bowling Ironworks, 1831 (from Martin's Map of Leeds)

roads. Even so, the map is known to be incomplete, at least as far as railways are concerned.

Another excellent map which helps to trace the course of transport development at Bowling is Thomas Dixon's map of Bradford, surveyed in 1844–6, and corrected up to 1856. This was a 10 in to 1 mile plan, and showed full details of the Bowling network. The first point to be noticed is that the lines were labelled as tramroads. The next is that by 1846 the company had extended the Bierley branch across Rooley Lane, B6148, and begun the incline down towards Toftshaw Bottom, North Bierley. Traffic was heavy on this incline for a sizeable building housed Burras stationary engine (GR 176310) which hauled loaded wagons up from Bierley and controlled the descent of loads to Bowling works and also down to a new coalyard near the Lancashire & Yorkshire station in the centre of Bradford. There were six sets of parallel tracks at this point to accommodate trains waiting to negotiate the various inclines. Dixon's map shows signs of revision at the ends of the tramroads, and there were some reasons for thinking that the details are best regarded as showing the situation a few years earlier than 1844, since it differs in some ways from the first edition, the six-inch OS of 1847, which must be regarded as authentic. However, Dixon's map shows that the third main branch, that shown on Martin's map as following a south-westerly course to GR 159310 on Manchester Road, had been dismantled. Only an isolated fragment of it remained, situated across the cutting of the L & YR. The line that looped round to this branch from Burras engine on the 1831 map, had now been extended down to the above-mentioned coalyard in Duncan Street, Bradford. This line is clearly labelled 'Bowling Iron Works Cos. Tram Road'.

The network ending in the works yard was supplied with plenty of reception sidings since coal and ore were coming down the other branches from the mines at Dudley Hill. The tracks ended at the calcination kilns for the carbonate ore, and the coking kilns and coking heaps for the coal. Another set of tramroads served to take coke and processed ore to the furnaces.

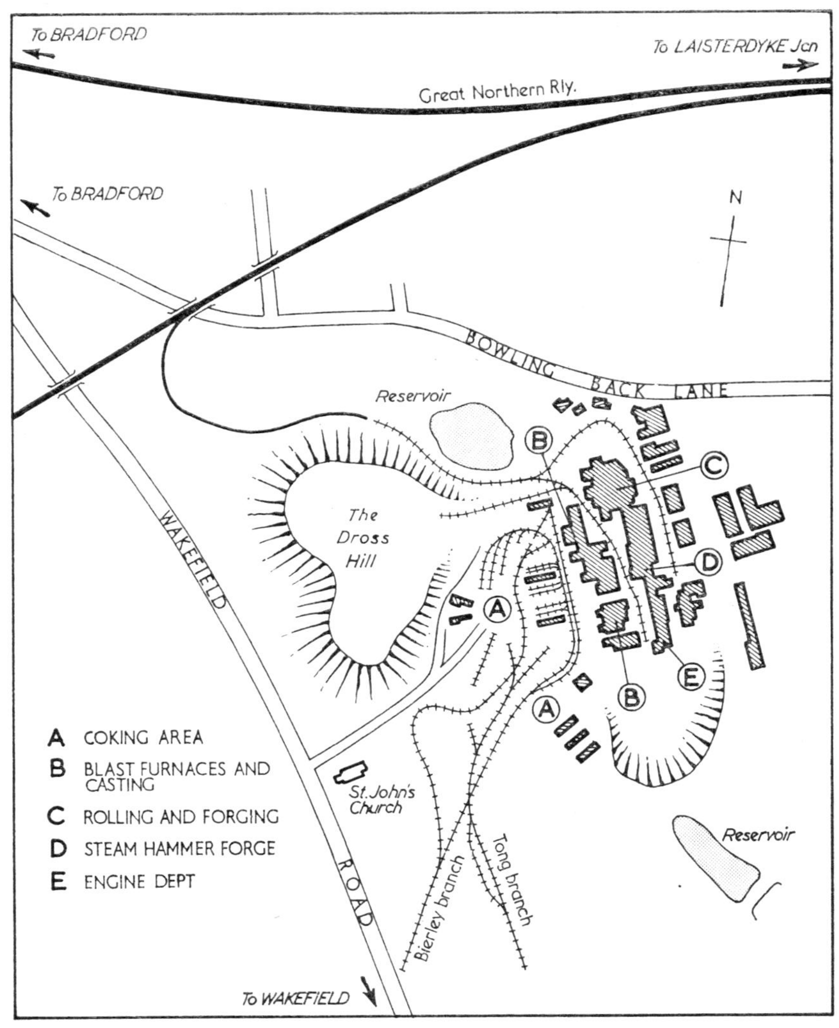

Fig 2 The Bowling Ironworks, 1871 (after Dixon and Hindle)

It seems at the moment that the Bowling Co abandoned tramroads just before 1847 and relaid their lines with edge rails. The six-inch Ordnance map clearly distinguished between tramroads and edge rail lines. The extensive tramroad network built by Henry Leah & Co to serve its Bierley coal staith (today traceable in Bierley as Staithgate Lane) was clearly detailed. But the lines leading from Bowling to Bradford, Dudley Hill, and the Bierley–Hunsworth mining areas were labelled 'Railway to Bowling Iron Works', and were shown with a single crossed-line symbol, while the tramroads were shown with two parallel lines. This symbol was still used to indicate the tramroads serving the coke-making area, and to show the incline down Hamerton Street entitled 'The Waggon Road'.

Although Bradford had been connected to the canal system since 1774, it had to wait till nearly 1850 for a main-line railway. The L & YR line from Halifax was opened to Low Moor in 1849, and to Bradford in 1850. The Laisterdyke & Bowling junction spur line was built in 1854, and in the course of making excavations for the cuttings at Bowling an old mine gallery was uncovered. In this were found primitive mining tools, made of wood but tipped with wrought iron.

By the time that Dixon & Hindle's map of Bradford appeared in 1871, Bowling works had gained a connection to the Great Northern Railway. A double-track branch of the Bowling junction line ran along an embankment to the works from Bowling station. This became a single line by the large dross hill (or slag heap), but split again with one siding running down between the block housing the plate and rod mill and casting departments, and the other main block which housed the forging departments. The other siding ran down the eastern side of the latter building. Thus iron ore and coal entered the works on the western or raw material preparation side, while finished products left the works via the standard-gauge lines on the eastern side.

According to a correspondent, the ironworks had four 0-4-0 saddle-tank locomotives, supplied by Black, Hawthorn & Co, one of which was new in 1892. There were two standard-gauge shunters, a Hudswell

Clarke obtained in 1872, and a Black, Hawthorn engine obtained in 1879.

Dixon & Hindle's 1871 survey showed that the narrow-gauge railway network had undergone some changes, since in the works yard the lines serving the pits in the Sticker Lane area of Dudley Hill had been removed. Also the 'Waggon Road' down to Bradford had gone out of use. The long incline from Burras engine (Bierley), down past the Bowling dyeworks to the Duncan Street coalstaith in Bradford, had also ceased operation and been dismantled. The changes in availability of coal which led to the decline of the narrow-gauge system in the Rooley Lane area caused the company to extend the lines elsewhere. In 1839 it had purchased the mineral rights of the Earl of Scarborough's estates in the Hunsworth area, providing a mining field of some 1,200 acres. To reach this area the Bierley branch of the network was extended south-eastwards. By 1847 the coal and ironstone pits around GR 185295 were reached by the mile-long Victoria Incline. This ran from a stationary engine at GR 181306 down to Toftshaw Bottom, GR 184293, some 200 ft below, where its course was near to pits supplying the Bierley coalstaith (via tramroads), and close to others supplying the Low Moor ironworks.

From here two narrow-gauge inclines ascended the sides of the little valley. One was the gravity-worked Wheel Incline which rose about 170 ft in half a mile. The other was the engine-worked Eight Horse Incline, which rose as much as 50 ft in half a mile to an ironstone pit overlooking the village of Oakenshaw. Although the tracks were laid with edge rails, some pits were connected to the railhead by short tramroads. This suggests that tramplates were used for underground haulage, and that wheeled corves were run down from the pit bank and tipped into narrow-gauge wagons.

By 1892, the date of the second six-inch Ordnance Survey of Yorkshire, some new extensions had been built. One was to Hunsworth pit, a mile from the Eight Horse Incline, while the other was a continuation of the surviving Dudley Hill branch, which now ran from near Dudley Hill station to Charles pit, Holme. From here a narrower-gauge track, for mine cars, ran to GR 219315 at Tong, and then rose to Far Tong pit (GR 230311) via the Alexandra Incline. Fieldwork suggests that tub lines fanned out from here to serve small pits on the slopes of Cockersdale, a one-time heavily industrialised valley which is now once more entirely rural in character. In 1966 some opencast fireclay working made temporary use of the Alexandra Incline as a lorry road.

Few traces of Bowling Iron Co Ltd can be seen today. At the site of the works the flattened dross hills remain, and the old-time operations are recalled in the sign for Foundry Lane, which led up to the coking area. No trace of the Waggon Road exists, and the lines around North Bierley are buried beneath housing developments. Yet at Toftshaw Bottom and at Cockersdale some of the tracks can be traced, and much is still as it was a hundred years ago.

Notes

1 H. J. Maltby, *The BMA Book of Bradford*, Bradford (1924), 99 & 111
2 H. Heaton, 'Benjamin Gott and the Industrial Revolution in Yorkshire', *Economic History Review*, iii (1931), 45–66 and especially 53; A. E. Musson and E. Robinson, 'The Early Growth of Steam Power', ibid, xi (1958–9), 418; cf also 'The Leeds Woollen Industry', *Transactions of Thoresby Society* (1929), 190
3 Maltby, op cit, 99
4 Communication from C. Scholey, Bradford, 1967
5 1st edn 6-in OS (Yorkshire), 1854
6 'Memoirs of the Geological Survey', *The Yorkshire Coalfield* (1878)
7 Maltby, op cit, 111
8 J. Priestley, *Historical Account of the Navigable Rivers, Canals and Railways throughout Great Britain* (1831)
9 Map of Yorkshire, Henry Teesdale & Co (1828)
10 Thorp's Map of Leeds, resurveyed and corrected by S. D. Martin (1831)

RICHARD KING

Joseph Paxton and the Crystal Palace

BY the nineteenth century the Industrial Revolution had achieved a technology which emancipated artistic expression from ancient forms and permitted an unparalleled creative boldness.

The architectural creativity, a manifestation of the maturation of industrial technology, is best reflected in the international exhibitions of the century. These exhibitions, embodying a synthesis of the yet unformulated goals of the Industrial Revolution, represented the march of industry and served a vital function in its expansion. In an era of increasingly free trade, the product of economic liberalism, they promoted the spirit of creative competition, not only among the manufacturers who displayed their products, but also among the architects who designed the buildings in which these products were exhibited. Since these exhibition halls were meant to be only temporary structures, architects were encouraged to experiment with new techniques which industrial technology made possible. By mid-century the triumph of the Industrial Revolution was complete. The wonders which technology had wrought were the glittering product of a century of patient experiment, brilliant invention, and ceaseless toil, of which the penalties were the slums, the new serfdom, and Messrs Engels and Marx. No single event more appropriately reflects the triumph of the Industrial Revolution than the Great Exhibition of the Works of Industry of All Nations, held in London in 1851.

The gospel of work was the philosophy underlying Victorian morality. The belief that the quality of human life would ultimately be enriched by the works of industry both inspired and justified the new order. The machine which the Industrial Revolution had brought was consequently regarded as a major element in the new moral system being erected in Victorian England. The displays of machinery attracted by far the most interest at the exhibition. The steam engine had become the most outstanding factor in British life. In a mere two decades, the face of the country had been transformed; the lives of millions had been made wider and brighter by the railways, of which there were more than five thousand miles in 1850. Steam was a living thing, a wild romance.

What more fitting tribute to the philosophy of the virtue of honest toil could there be than an industrial exhibition which would serve, not to amuse, but rather to edify all mankind? As envisaged by Prince Albert, such an exhibition would unite and uplift mankind. Similarly, the queen, confiding to her diary, referred to the exhibition as a Peace Festival. And William Thackeray, celebrating the event in the *May-Day Ode*, wrote:

> From Mississippi and from Nile—
> From Baltic, Ganges, Bosphorus,
> In England's ark assembled thus
> Are friend and guest.
>
> Look down the mighty sunlit aisle,
> And see the sumptuous banquet set,
> The brotherhood of nations met
> Around the feast!

That in fact the exhibition did both amuse and edify cannot be denied. The seventeen thousand exhibitors provided a seemingly endless collection of machinery, art manufactures, objets d'art, industrial models and the like. Among the more curious exhibits were products made from the new material india-rubber, shown by the Goodyear Rubber Company; a machine which manufactured envelopes at the rate of forty-five a minute; a variety of lighthouse lenses, reflectors and lights recently patented by Thomas Stevenson, the father of Robert Louis; a model of the half-mile long suspension bridge being built across the Dnieper at Kiev, by far the longest iron bridge then built; and a prophetic model of a proposed canal across the isthmus at Suez. Over six million persons came to gaze at the wonders on exhibit; the queen herself was an almost daily visitor. 'All the world', wrote Lord

Charles Greville in his *Mémoires*, 'has been flocking to the Crystal Palace, and we hear nothing but expressions of wonder and admiration.' Although the Duke of Wellington questioned the usefulness of the 'Show', he foresaw its success.

But the importance of the exhibition itself was overshadowed by the significance of the masterful fusion of aesthetics and industrial technology represented in the great hall which housed the exhibits, the fabulous Crystal Palace, as well as of the career of its designer, Sir Joseph Paxton, which exemplified the values held important in Victorian England.

Paxton is an appropriate symbol of the industrial age, and of nineteenth-century England in particular. His career indicates the unusual opportunities for creative potential which the Industrial Revolution provided. A farmer's son, Paxton was first employed as a gardener at the Horticultural Society's gardens at Chiswick. Here he met William Spencer, sixth Duke of Devonshire, who was so impressed with the young man's intelligence and ability that he took him off to be head gardener on his estate at Chatsworth. At Chatsworth Paxton worked wonders: he built a gigantic rockery; a 300-ft fountain in honour of the Tsar Nicholas, who never came to see it; and the model village of Edensor. He sent expeditions to America and India in search of rare plants which had never before been grown in England, and to house them he built an enormous arboretum and the Great Conservatory, an acre in extent, which the Victorians considered one of the wonders of the world.

Paxton soon rose far above the status of a gardener. He was the duke's companion, philosopher and life-long friend, managing his affairs as well as his estates. The duke had extensive railway interests which Paxton managed, becoming a director of many companies. Investing in land and railways himself, Paxton established a considerable personal fortune. But his primary personal interests remained botanical: he launched and edited several horticultural journals, wrote an authoritative *Treatise on the Dahlia*, and imported and successfully grew on the duke's estates over eighty varieties of orchids. A public figure, a Member of Parliament, a monument of self-help, Paxton was a representative man of the steam age whom Victorians could admire and emulate.

It was the Prince Consort's scheme for an industrial exhibition which was to give Joseph Paxton his greatest opportunity. Albert was an enthusiastic patron of industry and the fine arts. The Royal Academy, the Royal Society and a thousand lesser bodies down to provincial polytechnics and philosophical clubs sought the prince's support. Of one of these, the London Society of Arts, he became president in 1843, enjoining the society 'to wed mechanical skill with high art'.

In 1849 the prince conceived the idea of transforming the society's next exhibition of art manufactures, scheduled for 1851, into an exhibition of British industry. In the same year, the eleventh quinquennial exposition was held in Paris, to which one of the visitors was Mr Henry Cole, the indefatigable benefactor of English industry and a member of the Council of the Society of Arts. With his wide technical knowledge, Cole immediately perceived the superior excellence of French manufactures in many departments of industry. A staunch advocate of free trade, he recognised the benefits to be derived from an exhibition which placed French and English manufactures side by side. Upon his return from Paris, he proposed the idea of an international exhibition to Prince Albert, who enthusiastically agreed that 'particular advantage to British industry might be derived from placing it in fair competition with that of other nations'.[1]

Such was the inception of the scheme for the first international industrial exposition. The major responsibility of the distinguished Royal Commission appointed in January 1850, was providing for the housing of the exhibition. Upon the commission's invitation, 245 plans were submitted from all over the world. All were rejected and the Commission's Building Committee, having picked the brains of the unfortunate 245, submitted a plan of its own. Not only was their method of procedure of very doubtful honesty, but the outcome of it all was a monstrosity which raised a storm of opposition to the entire undertaking. The proposed building looked like an immense railway station: all roof and veranda, with colossal false arches of horrible proportions. Perched upon this squat shed was a hideous sheet-iron dome; of all the wonders of industry to be exhibited, the committee thought that none would be more wonderful than this! Besides the aesthetic objections to the building, it would cost as much to remove as to build it, and the materials had no salvage value worth mentioning, two considerations of compelling importance to the commission.

The opposition to the exhibition scheme coalesced around the colourful person of Colonel Charles de Laet Waldo Sibthorp, Member of Parliament for Lincoln. He was one of those narrow-visioned persons who regard all the world in terms of one great evil. For Sibthorp that evil was Free Trade: political conceptions chased through his mind in glorious confusion, but in the end they all resolved themselves into so many aspects of the country's downfall through free trade. In a series of parliamentary outbursts, he envisioned thieves and anarchists flocking to London from all over the world, the latter for the purpose of assassinating the queen; an influx of Papists, bringing with them idolatry, schism, bubonic plague, and venereal disease; and aliens hiring houses in Kensington for the establishment of brothels.

Vigorous opposition also came from the occupants of the houses which had recently been built facing Hyde Park, the proposed site of the exhibition, and from the inhabitants of the adjacent residential areas who foresaw a ceaseless procession of tourists passing through their exclusive avenues. The radicals took pleasure in denying the right of the Crown to erect buildings in the royal parks, and the protectionists feared that the country would be flooded with cheap foreign products, driving British manufacturers into bankruptcy.

But the very moment at which the whole enterprise, to which the name of the Prince Consort was irrevocably tied, was on the verge of a fiasco, Joseph Paxton rescued the Commissioners and saved the exhibition with a bold and startling plan for a building 'more curious than anything that could be seen in it'.[2]

The building Paxton proposed to the Royal Commission was 1,851 ft long, encompassing 800,000 sq ft—four times the area of St Peter's in Rome. It rose in three tiers, like an immense Babylonian ziggurat, being crowned with a central transept of awesome dimension. What lent the building both novelty and aesthetic merit was the fact that it was to be constructed of plate glass and iron, an artistic expression ideally suited as an exhibition technique.

The traditionalists had denied the possibility of beauty and form in a ferro-vitreous building. They went further in maintaining that modular construction could not be a work of art, believing that an organic whole could not be added to without destroying its architectural unity. But by 1850 Paxton was a master without equal in designing prefabricated glass and iron buildings of considerable beauty.

The aesthetic conception of the Crystal Palace is thought to have been inspired by Paxton's study of the structure of the water lily *Victoria Regia*. In 1837, an English traveller in British Guiana had been startled by the sight of a giant water lily, the seeds of which had been brought back to England where they germinated; but the plants had not flowered. In 1849, Paxton secured a plant for Chatsworth, placing it in a special heated tank stirred by waterwheels of his own design. In three months' time it flowered: eleven leaves 5 ft in diameter lay about the gigantic bud. *Victoria Regia* attained a stupendous growth. One day Paxton set his small daughter to stand on one of the lily's great leaves; it easily bore her weight. Impressed by the plant's slender strength, he studied its structure; strong ribs radiated outwards, being held tautly by delicate cross-ribs. It was a marvel of natural economy. Faced with the necessity of rehousing the growing lily, he built the lily-house, itself a marvel of economy and delicate strength capable of withstanding both wind and hail.

The construction of the Great Conservatory and the lily-house convinced Paxton that not only were large ferro-vitreous buildings a practical possibility, but also that industrial technology permitted aesthetic conceptions in architecture, the ultimate potential of which was not yet clearly realised. This is the lasting significance of Paxton's design for the Crystal Palace.

As the achievement of English industry and as an application of the simplest system of manufacture—serial production in which the parts of the building were pre-fabricated in different workshops throughout the nation—the Crystal Palace was the realisation of a new conception of architecture, one for which there was no precedent. Indeed, the grandeur of its conception far out-distanced the technical possibilities of its time. It was, as Lothar Bucher remarked, a revolution in architecture from which a new style would date, 'a Midsummer Night's Dream seen in the clear light of midday'.

The novel construction employing glass and iron demanded a new aesthetic response. The structural equilibrium between load and support had always been apparent in architecture at a glance, but in the Crystal Palace a poised equilibrium of all parts of the structure had been achieved. To the beholder regarding it from the interior, it was difficult to perceive just how the weight of the building was supported. The building was ethereal; it stimulated the imagination to wander freely about the enormous, apparently unbounded, structure. The translucent quality of the palace was reinforced by the fact that since there were no shadows cast inside the building, the eye had no perspective as to the size or relative dimensions of the structure. All one saw was a delicate network of lines (the girders) which provided no clue by which the eye could judge distance or size. The side walls were too far apart to be embraced in a single glance, and the ends of the building simply faded into the horizon beyond. The effect was one of grandeur and insubstantiality; the building simply blended into the atmosphere. It was the architectural counterpart of the sea and landscapes of the Romantic painter, J. M. W. Turner. Like Turner's *Simplon Pass* or *Ulysses Deriding Polyphemus*, Paxton's Crystal Palace took the beholder into the world of imagination, into limitless light-filled space enveloping forms which were without structure or solidarity. Paxton achieved an exquisite union of the aesthetic concept of the delicate English hot-house with industrial technology, a curious association of gentleness with an unmistakable majesty in a prophetic artistic conception. It did not pass without notice that industry, after all the blight and chaos it had created in England, was capable of erecting a fairy-like temple of great beauty.

Although the Crystal Palace had much in common with Romantic artistic conceptions, the building represented a complete break with past architectural traditions. As an appropriate symbol of nineteenth-century society, it reflected the values that industrial society cherished: functionalism and practicality, the importance of intrinsic merit, simplicity and honesty of expression. Embodying the courage and vitality of the Victorian age, the palace was the most perfect example of functionalism in architecture; but then few buildings of a comparable importance had the purpose for which they were designed so clearly specified. The frankness with which it expressed its materials and construction, rather than concealing them behind a non-structural façade, and the suppression of structurally irrelevant ornamentation are characteristic of the artistic conception of the machine age. In so far as the Crystal Palace expressed utility, revealed rather than concealed its structure, and maximised the potential of the material of its construction, it was indeed the precursor of a new style of architecture inspired by the industrial age it was designed to promote. But as an artistic conception, the Crystal Palace was perhaps the finest, and certainly the last, expression of an architectural tradition which combined the aesthetic concepts of Romantic art with values characteristic of the machine age, through the use of newly invented technology, a tradition which the industrial age was soon to discard.

Notes

1 Christopher Hobhouse, *1851 and the Crystal Palace*, London: John Murray, 1950, 9.

2 Letter dated 23 July 1850 from the Duke of Wellington to Mary, Marquise of Salisbury.

I. C. AND LL. DE S. WALKER

McDougall's Clay Pipe Factory, Glasgow

In November 1967 the last firm of Glasgow pipemakers, D. McDougall & Co Ltd (latterly known as C. B. & McDougall Ltd) of 18 Charles Street, St Rollox, Glasgow, closed, its factory being scheduled for demolition as part of a major roadway construction programme. The writers visited the factory in September 1967 and were able to observe and photograph the last batches of pipes being made.

J. Arnold Fleming—whose account of Glasgow pipemakers is by no means accurate—asserts[1] that the firm of McDougall was founded in 1810 by a Duncan McDougall ('a fine type of Highlander' according to Fleming) but such records of the firm that do exist (two fires this century having destroyed most of them) indicate that the firm was founded in 1846. In the Glasgow Post Office Directory for 1846–7, appearing in 1846, Duncan McDougall appears in the general alphabetical section as the manager of Murray's Caledonian Pipe Works, a firm first recorded as making pipes in 1830 (though the associated pottery firm, under a number of names, goes back to at least 1801 and possibly to 1790).[2] In the directory for the following year McDougall appears for the first time in the classified trades section as a pipemaker at 87 King Street, Calton, Glasgow—the Calton had been a pottery area since the seventeenth century and many nineteenth-century pipemakers worked there. In the next directory McDougall appears twice in the classified section—once under the above address (probably in error) and once at 74 North Hanover Street—and in 1849 the firm's title changes to the Glasgow Pipe Manufactory, an entry repeated in 1850, but the address continues as North Hanover Street. Under the general alphabetical section in 1847 and 1849 a note beside McDougall's name requests that orders be left at 11 Argyle Street—this was the address of an ironmonger, J. Stewart & Co, and some distance from North Hanover Street. In 1851 the title was unchanged, but the address was now 277 Parliamentary Road, where the firm was to remain for almost forty years. In 1852 and in most subsequent years until the beginning of this century it is given under both McDougall and the Glasgow Pipe Manufactory. In 1889 the firm is listed at the site it was to occupy until its closure; its administrative address then became 51 Hobden Street but this office has now (summer 1968) been closed, and McDougall's is being wound up. (According to Mr M. F. Rodger, a director, the appearance of the city coat-of-arms on its notepaper was said to be a privilege granted because the firm was among the first hundred incorporated in the city.)

When not called the Glasgow Pipe Manufactory, it originally appears to have been called simply Duncan McDougall, but in March 1871 Donald McDougall—presumably a son—and a Campbell Rodger (1840–1924) went into partnership as D. McDougall & Co. (The alphabetical section of the directories suggests Duncan McDougall died c 1869.) Subsequently, Rodger bought Donald McDougall out. In 1909 the firm was turned into a limited company—D. McDougall & Co Ltd—and in 1965 a merger with a non-pipemaking firm resulted in the name being changed to C. B. & McDougall Ltd. By the time Fleming was writing in 1923 the proprietor was Patrick Wylie Rodger (1879–1940), a son of Campbell and father of Mr M. F. Rodger.

The clay latterly used by McDougall's came in powdered form from the firm of Watts, Blake, Bearne & Co, Newton Abbot, Devon, though until about ten years before their closing, unprocessed clay was bought and worked by McDougall's. Kaolin was used for the better-quality pipes as it gave a purer white than the ball clay used for ordinary pipes; the poorest clays were kept to be made into small blocks for whitening doorsteps. The powdered clay was 'milled'—soaked in water and put through a machine which mixed the clay and cut it into 'balls' or slabs. The correct texture of the material was judged by experience rather than by any scientific measurement. Six of these balls weighed approximately a hundredweight. From this wet clay the pipemaker took in each hand the correct amount for a pipe (the amount being judged by experience, as different pipes require different quantities) and made roughly-shaped blanks known as 'rolls' by rolling and pressing the clay on a board with the greater pressure on the outside edge of the hand. The pressure was increased as the piece of clay lengthened, to form the stem, leaving the head of the piece for the bowl (see p 139). When making pipes with heels a 'hand board'—a small piece of flat wood—was used for rolling, as, by using hands only, there was a tendency for the roll to be too thick at the neck, in which case the heels apparently tended to come off. A skilled worker could run off a dozen medium-sized rolls, each about 5 in long, in approximately a minute (the workers were paid by piecework). At one time McDougall's made sixteen rolls to a pipemaker's dozen, but latterly only twelve.

The rolls were then placed on a 'bench' or 'dozening board' (a small wooden board) and dried on racks in a hot-air room. Next they were wetted and again experience was the criterion for judging how dry and then how moistened they should be. When the rolls were fairly pliable but still firm, the ends of what were to be the stems were cut off with a 'knife'—a blade set in a handle—and the 'wire' inserted almost, but not quite, as far as the head of the roll to make the bore. The wire used (see p 139) was a metal knitting needle modified by having its end blunted and slightly widened in cross-section by hammering, which facilitated its penetration of the clay and allowed a clean hole to be made where it entered the bowl. The worker demonstrated with a pointed 'finishing wire' that it was extremely difficult to push a pointed wire through the stem. The blunted wire was lubricated in a mixture of paraffin and whale oil, as were the mould and 'stopper' (the piece which makes the bowl). This mixture had no specific proportions in its composition.

Once the wire was in position, the roll was laid in the desired mould, the two halves of which were then placed in the 'chest' (the metal frame which contains the vice) and tightened into position (see p 140). The two halves of the mould, which were held to each other by pinions, bore any lettering and decoration which was to be transferred to the pipe. The recent practice has been to eliminate words on stems as much as possible, as the letters wear down and need resetting, whereas last century makers in Glasgow and many other places had their name on one side and that of the town on the other, invariably with the lettering in opposite directions on the two sides. Certain export pipes, including the famous TD pipes,[3] have SCOTLAND on the stem to comply with Customs regulations; in 1891 the United States made it mandatory that all imports be marked with their country of origin.[4]

Each mould had its own stopper for forming the bowl, and this was fitted, by means of a bolt, to a lever attached to a block of wood beside the chest. The stopper swung freely and pushed into the mould in a continuously perpendicular position, the mould having been suitably positioned. The handle was pulled down sharply once or twice to push the stopper fully into the mould, and the wire then pushed into the bowl, thus finishing the bore. The mould was then removed from the chest, and the top of the bowl formed by trimming it, through the slot near the top of the mould, with the knife. The pipe was then taken from the mould, the wire withdrawn, and the still-moist pipe carefully stacked with the rest. Trimmings from stem ends and bowl tops were dropped through a hole in the floor and collected underneath to be mixed with the prepared clay.

By the time the quota of pipes had been moulded, those done first were dry enough to be finished. This process required a 'finisher's knife', a 'smoother' and a 'finisher's wire' (see p 140). When in full production one finisher would work to two moulders. The finisher's knife had two curved notches on its blade side, and these came in various sizes for trimming differently-sized pipes. The larger notch was for trimming the bowl, the smaller for the stem. However, on the pipes being made at the time of the visit it was the back of the knife that was being used to trim off the excess clay along the mould lines because correctly-notched knives were rarely available. The smoothers, made from a small bar of metal, similarly came with two differently-shaped curves on the lower side and were used to rub smooth the areas scraped by the knife (see p 140). The finisher's wire was used to make certain that the bore ran through to the bowl and to poke free the 'dottle'—the bit of clay pushed into the bowl ahead of the piercer.

Following this part of the work, the pipes were placed in racks and taken for 'potting'—packing in fireclay 'saggars' (pronounced 'seggers' by the workers) preparatory to firing. McDougall's did not place the pipes round a central cone in the saggars, as was the older practice, but laid them with the mouthpieces to the centre and the bowls downwards in carefully overlapping circles (see p 141). The saggars were then taken to the kiln, a circular brick structure (see p 141) reinforced with iron bands, where they were stacked ten or eleven high—a kiln of the size used by McDougall's could take approximately 300 saggars (see p 140). The top saggar was covered either with a lid or an empty saggar to prevent the flames' gases damaging the pipes. The kiln had six coal fires round it fired from the outside, a flue in the floor and a vent on the roof which was opened if a rapid cooling was desired. Coal was used simply because it was the cheapest fuel. In 1920 four such kilns were being used by the firm.

The complete firing process took the better part of a week, the firing itself usually being done on a Wednesday. On Tuesday evening the kiln door was bricked up, and the fires were lit at 5.0 or 6.0 the next morning. Generally by noon the temperature was approaching that desired—approximately 940° C—though the length of time could vary considerably with wind conditions and other problems such as an incompletely cleaned flue. It has been known to take over twelve hours to work up the temperature to the desired range. However, generally about 3.0 pm the furnace was allowed to cool naturally (though it could be cooled a great deal faster without harming the pipes) and the pipes removed on the Friday.

Shattering of pipes could occur if the last-made pipes to be put in the kiln had not been dry enough. The kilns had their particular idiosyncrasies, certain parts being 'softer' (cooler) than others. Pipes destined for export were placed in the hotter parts as this made them stronger and less liable to break in shipping; however, pipes fired thus smoke hotter than the others because they are less porous. Any

Aire Street from the docks: sheds and railway lines face a unilateral frontage of cafés and public houses. In the foreground is the Lowther Hotel (formerly the Banks Arms), which was the first public building erected in Goole

George Street: two-storey workers' housing. A large cellar gives three levels in all. In the foreground is a typical chamfered corner shop

See 'Goole: A Pre-Victorian Company Town', pp 105–13

Rear view of North Street. Note the small windows, rounded corners and sunken back lanes in a landscape of brick and slate, typical of Aire & Calder Goole

The Aire & Calder planned town in relation to the dock system. East Parade faces the camera with Aire Street at the rear. Later settlement lacks the order and regularity of this nucleus. North is to the right. (*Courtesy:* Yorkshire Post)

See 'Goole: A Pre-Victorian Company Town', pp 105–13

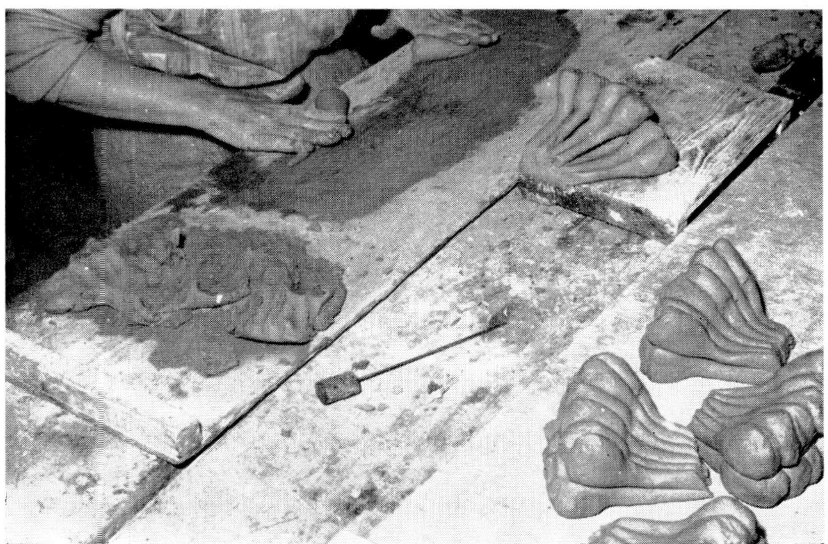

Rolling and pressing the clay

Inserting the wire to make a bore in the pipe

See 'McDougall's Clay Pipe Factory, Glasgow', pp 132–46

The 'chest', a metal frame which contains a vice for tightening the pipe moulds (Courtesy: City of Birmingham Museum)

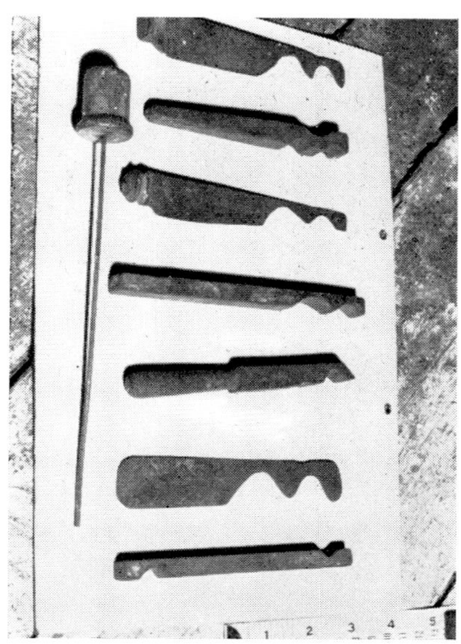

The finisher's tools. Note the measure at the bottom which gives some indication of sizes

Trimming and smoothing a pipe

Pipes ready for firing

The pipe kiln

Saggars in the kiln

See 'McDougall's Clay Pipe Factory, Glasgow', pp 132–46, for all plates on these two pages

Engraving of Crystal Palace (*Courtesy: Radio Times Hulton Picture Library*)

See 'Joseph Paxton and the Crystal Palace', pp 124–31

The Abbey Mill at about the time it closed in 1930. South aspect, taken from the northern outfall sewer embankment. The Channel Sea is to the right

See 'Aids to Recording (3): Surveying an Industrial Ruin—The Abbey Mill, West Ham', pp 147–56

An aerial view of Jennings Pottery. Note the round kilns

See 'Jennings South Western Pottery, Parkstone', pp 164–71

The last kilns in use at the time of closure (Courtesy: Photo Nicol, Bournemouth)

A selection of the acid-resisting ware made at the pottery during the 1914–18 war
See 'Jennings South Western Pottery, Parkstone', pp 164–71

which had been underfired were set aside to be refired the next time. After the removal of the pipes the kiln was prepared for the next firing and the pipes taken to be packed in wood shavings in cardboard boxes. (By this stage a pipemaker's gross was the standard 144, but in early parts of the process 192—sixteen dozen—was a pipemaker's gross to allow for breakages and rejects.)

Higher-quality pipes, such as those made with bowls shaped as heads, were made of kaolin. These pipes were given a thick upwardly-curved stem stub to which a downwardly-curved vulcanite mouthpiece was attached. As the bore of the stem stub had to be wide at the stub end in order to take the vulcanite part, it was made not with a wire but with a curved and pointed metal 'poker' placed in the mould. The pressure from the stopper inserted into the bowl forced clay around the poker, thus forming the stub stem. The moulds used for these pipes were tripartite, the third part containing the facial features. The mould lines are thus not down the middle of the face but down either side at the ears and were carefully trimmed so that the joins were invisible to the casual glance. The most delicate part of the process was the 'scouring' (cleaning with a sponge) of the face without marring the subtleties of the cheekbone modelling or the eyes, preparatory to varnishing the outer surfaces with shellac. The 'common clays', as the cheaper pipes were called, were not varnished.

In September 1967 McDougall's were finishing off their last batches of pipes, with two pipemakers both moulding and trimming. The potting, firing, and packing were each done by another person. In 1914, according to Miss Mary Johnston, who had been with the firm since that date, 50 men and 100 women were employed; during the second half of last century there were probably about 250–300 workers employed, according to Mr M. F. Rodger.

In 1961, McDougall's still had between 30 and 40 moulds in use,[5] for although the market was not large, 60 gross a week were still being produced, and smokers in Glasgow, Edinburgh, Aberdeenshire, and Ireland, for example, have different preferences as to shape and size. At one time McDougall's had between 800 and 900 moulds. In 1961 one shipment a year was being sent to each of the West Indies, the United States, and Canada. Before the second world war pipes were still being shipped to West Africa and the East. Throughout the 1950s production remained steady, and the above statistics also applied into the mid-1960s until the final run-down. The decline of the clay pipe-making industry is perhaps caused as much by rising costs and a lack of skilled labour as the decrease in the use of the pipe itself.

With the demise of this firm, some moulds have gone to John Pollock & Co of Manchester, now the sole pipemaking firm in Britain. It would be appropriate if Glasgow were to follow the example of Edinburgh, York, and Leeds in establishing a pipemaker's workshop in a museum as a memorial to a trade which gave Glasgow last century a very large export market all over the world.

Notes

1 J. A. Fleming, *Scottish Pottery*, Glasgow (1923), 243
2 Ibid, 221
3 I. C. Walker, 'TD Pipes—A Preliminary Study', *Quarterly Bulletin of the Archeological Society of Virginia*, vol 20, no 4 (June 1966), 86–102
4 B. L. Fontana et al, 'Johnny Ward's Ranch: A Study in Historic Archaeology', *The Kiva* (Journal of the Arizona Archaeological Society), vol 28, no 1–2 (October–December 1962), 93
5 I. Knight, 'The Auld Clay Pipe', *Scotland's Magazine*, vol 57, no 5 (May 1961), 34

Acknowledgments

The authors would like to thank one of the directors of McDougall's, Mr R. G. A. Hemming, Miss Mary Johnston and the rest of the staff for all their help and information. Their thanks also go to Mr M. F. Rodger of Montreal, another director, for his reminiscences of the firm earlier this century.

Plates, pages 139–41

ALAN L. THOMAS

Aids to Recording (3)

Surveying an Industrial Ruin: The Abbey Mill, West Ham

TONGE ISLAND, in the Channel Sea River: nowadays probably not one local citizen in a thousand would know the spot by its ancient name, but for nine centuries at least it was an important place in the neighbourhood, and it is certainly one of the oldest industrial sites in the London area. The Channel Sea is one of the network of streams which form, in effect, a delta for the River Lea for the last few miles before it joins the Thames. Nearly all of these waterways pass through West Ham, now part of the London Borough of Newham, and they have played an important part in the evolution of the area.

Water- and windmills flourished on the Lea marshes from Saxon times until well into this century. About twenty were listed in Domesday, and there seems to be little doubt that one of them straddled the Channel Sea stream at Tonge Island. There certainly was a well-established mill on the site in the early years of the twelfth century for Queen Maud, who died in 1118, bought it as an endowment for the upkeep of a Roman causeway across the marsh. Less than twenty years later the Cistercian abbey of Stratford Langthorne was founded, not a stone's throw away, and the mill was duly absorbed into the estate. From that day to this it has been known, naturally enough, as the Abbey Mill.

Following the dissolution in 1538 the mill passed into secular hands, and a variety of owners used it. Rape and linseed were milled there, in addition to flour, and at one time it seems that a blacksmith was in occupation. By the late nineteenth century the last of many rebuildings on the same site produced a grim-looking brick structure of a kind common enough in most industrial areas. So it remained, even after the last sack of corn was ground in 1930, until the old mill took fire one night during the war and was razed to the ground.

During the seminar held late in 1966 which inaugurated the Lea Valley industrial archaeology survey, Denis Smith, who had organised the meeting, showed some photographs of the mill. These looked interesting, and I went to see for myself what was left of this ancient industrial site. There seemed to be very little still standing. The bases of a few heavily built walls, with doorways and window openings bricked up; a single pair of lock-gates, out of use; and the waterwheel pit, with its roller-shutter type sluice-gate almost complete. The head- and tailraces were both completely choked with every kind of filth, and turf and bushes covered the site generally. In addition the Channel Sea was at its lowest level, exposing acres of black mud and rubbish. The whole was most unprepossessing.

There was something undeniably intriguing about the remains of the Abbey Mill. While meditating idly one day it dawned upon me that since the Channel Sea is basically a creek fed by the Thames, and that only a trickle of water flows downstream at low water, this was not just another watermill, no matter how ancient: it had been a *tide* mill, a rarity in such an inland situation. Further, it could only have worked on the ebb tide.

The place warranted more investigation and following a consultation with Denis Smith, a visit to the local library produced a number of superficial references and two photographs. Copies of the latter, considered carefully on site, explained several of the more enigmatic remains. Another item in the library archives was a small photocopy of a site survey apparently made in 1819. Under a magnifying glass several almost invisible details showed up, including the most exciting legends 'windmill over this building', and 'house for steam engine'. Since the waterwheel pit was also clearly shown, in its correct position, here was further food for thought: not many industrial plants used three forms of motive power simultaneously, and steam engines of this period cannot fail to be of interest.

By this time 1966 had turned into 1967 and, since we had evidence that Abbey Lane was to be widened in the near future, it was decided that the wisest course to adopt would be to ignore pure historical research temporarily and concentrate upon recording the ruins as they stood. With an accurately surveyed ground plan as a working foundation we thought it likely that later researches would be to some extent eased and so far this has proved to be the case. With our restricted resources, not least in the amount of time that could be devoted to the job, we had to adopt some unconventional methods.

We reduced working kit to the absolute minimum. Our choice of clothing was governed by the biting winds and rain of February and March, but the urge to keep warm was tempered by the need to scramble about without getting snagged on projections. This was an important point, for we later proved a 10-ft depth of soft ooze in the races, and to fall 20 ft into that yielding filth would have been a serious business. In the end we found that corduroy trousers (which do not tear easily) tucked into gumboots provided a fair measure of protection for the lower half, while a heavy waterproof jacket over a thick jersey combined adequate warmth with sufficient pockets.

A major deviation from accepted land-surveying practice lay in taking our drawing-board with us. By making an accurate drawing on site and plotting each dimension as it was measured, we reasoned, errors would show up at once. Few things are more frustrating than to take masses of dimensions and rough sketches on site and at a later date try to turn them into an intelligible drawing. Inevitably, they refuse to tie in properly, and more often than not a key measurement is missing. We had no time to spare for such diversions.

Another item that proved most useful was a foolscap-sized board with a built-in spring clip, which was much used for detail sketching. It is worth mentioning that to maintain a standard sheet size for one's paperwork is a worthwhile practice in any kind of research or recording activity. At first sight it seems a trivial detail, but the benefits of being able to file papers easily in commercially available folders and binders without unnecessary folding or cutting, are very real. Drawings, which must often exceed the chosen standard size, can easily be arranged so that they fold down to size with the minimum number of creases. And, of course, a completed research project looks very well when the story is written or typed neatly and included with photographs and drawings in a tidily bound booklet.

The number of drawing instruments taken on to site was kept to the minimum, but included several pencils. Pencils are elusive things, and it is well to have at least one in each jacket pocket. Most were kept round-pointed, but a couple were of the hardest grade the drawing-paper would stand, and they were kept chisel-pointed for drawing fine lines. An indispensable item was the beam compass, or trammels. Ours had a chisel-pointed pencil lead carried in one head and a needle in the other.

Working in close conjunction with the beam compass were two standard draughtsman's scale rulers. We were fortunate in possessing a suitable scale 18 in in length, for these are not common items, but since it proved unwieldy in marking small dimensions a 6-in scale was also pressed into service. A roll of common adhesive tape came in handy for holding down odd papers, pencils, scales, and other items that threatened to blow away.

Added to these items was a reel of thin string; a packet of chalk; a fairly heavy hammer; a pound of 2-in nails; and a rough tree-saw for odd bushes that were in the way. A borrowed pickaxe and an ordinary garden spade had obvious applications. After a couple of moderately uncomfortable sessions it dawned on us that a folding table of the camping variety together with a matching chair would make the work of draughting in the open air much easier. Finally all of our equipment was entered upon a checklist and ticked off before and after each session: it was used for the last time in making this catalogue.

With a site of this complexity we felt it best to start from one internal corner of the oldest part of the main building, and work out from there. We chose the fairly large scale, for this kind of work, of $\frac{1}{4}$ in to the foot, or $\frac{1}{48}$ full size. In order to minimise errors in measuring we tried wherever possible to take 'chain' dimensions (Figure 1), by which method all of the measurements along a wall are taken from one point.

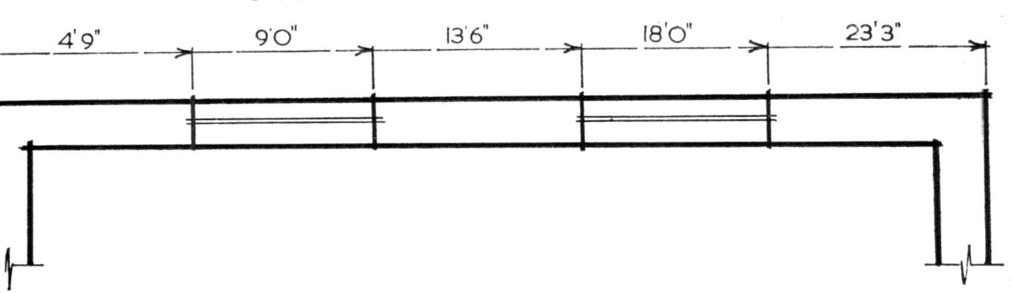

Fig 1 Chain dimensions: by taking as many dimensions as possible from one point, errors are minimised

Doors, windows and any other details are all included, and by adopting this plan the position on paper of any item is plotted quite independently of its neighbouring details. It is surprisingly difficult to decide to the nearest inch what a dimension should be in an old building, and it is all too easy, when positioning items in the usual step-by-step way, to be several inches out on the overall dimension.

Our first wall was obviously straight, and its overall inside length was taken off the scale with the beam compass. Again, it is easy to be (scale) inches out if dimensions are taken directly from the rule on to the paper, but both points of the trammels can be positioned precisely in the rule graduations. The first wall was then plotted on paper, and the overall length of an adjacent wall taken. Since the included angle was not a right-angle the beam compass was used to describe an arc in approximately the correct position. A dimension taken diagonally across the open ends of the angle positioned the outer end of the second wall precisely (Figure 2). From this base it was an easy matter to repeat the triangling process and locate the rest of the enclosure, and a final check corner-to-corner measurement showed an error of something like 1 in in 35 ft: this, we thought, good enough.

Encouraged by this satisfactory beginning we pressed on, and quite soon the main part of the mill structure had been recorded. Almost every position was triangulated in this manner, and many minor errors were brought to light. At first we worked two-handed, in the conven-

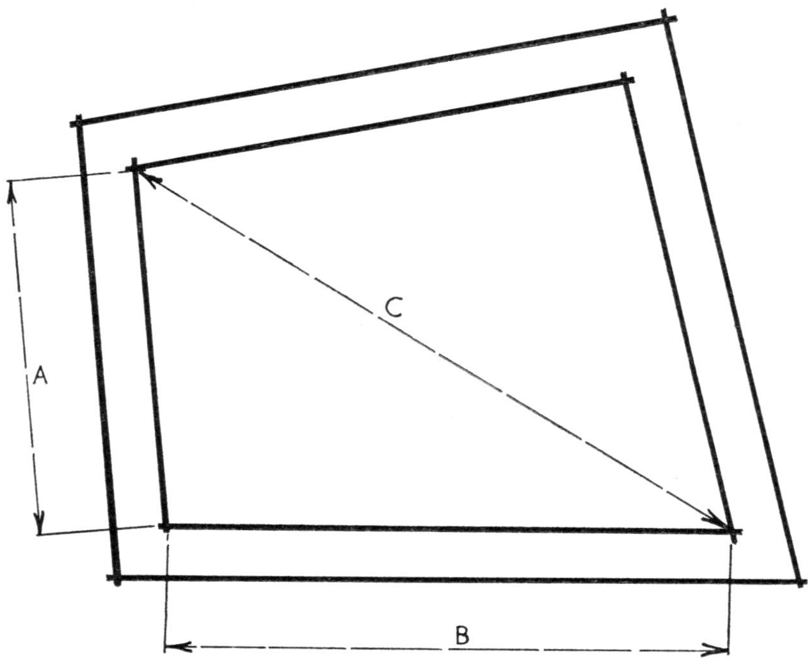

Fig 2 Triangulation: dimension C establishes the angle between A and B

tional way, but we discovered during the first week of February that work on the new road was scheduled to begin before the end of March. If there was to be any prospect of recording the site adequately before it was obliterated, output had to be increased and from this time onward virtually all dimensions, even the longest, were made single-handed.

This apparent impossibility was actually surprisingly easy: a nail was hammered into a wall at a convenient spot and its position plotted. With the tape-measure ring hooked over the nail one person simply walked along the survey line calling out dimensions of details on the way—all of which were, of course, related to the nail. It even proved quite possible to plot the shape of two large and irregular arches single-handed: points were marked off at 2-ft intervals around their peripheries in chalk and radial dimensions taken from a nail placed at random in a convenient spot (Figure 3). Working single-handed in this manner meant that the draughtsman could keep progress under control, and tell at once which dimensions were required next.

With time drawing short we turned to the more complex task of measuring the vertical remains of the mill and its surrounding buildings. The only adequate answer was a surveyor's level, and we were lucky to be able to borrow a 'quickset dumpy' from a well-disposed friend. If all else fails, such devices may be hired. A dumpy is essentially a small telescope, which is arranged to rotate in a perfectly level

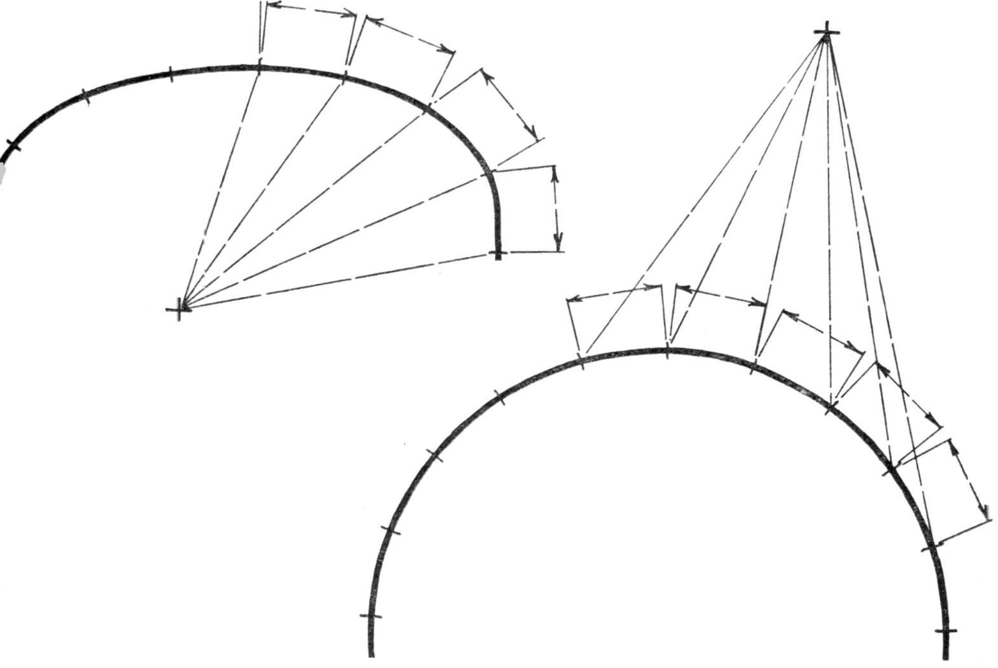

Fig 3 Regular and irregular curves can be plotted by combining radial and tangental measurements

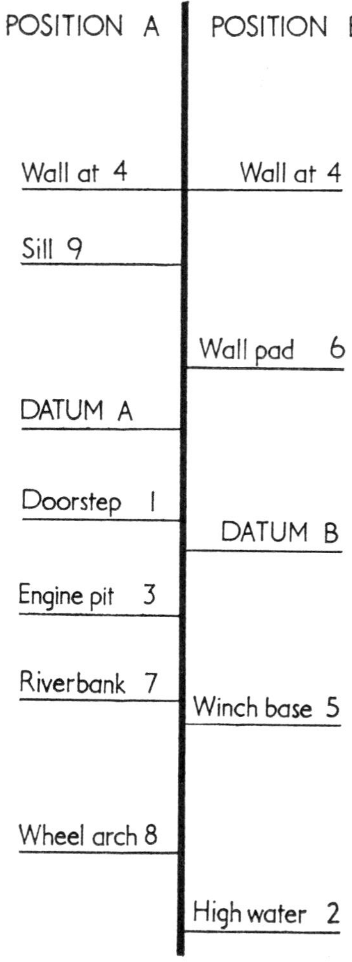

Fig 4 Levels plotted to scale are easily checked and ready for use. Each number is keyed to a position marked on a ground plan

plane about a mounting carried on top of the familiar surveyor's tripod. The telescope has a fine graticule marked on the lens, and it follows that any heights in sight above or below the datum formed by the graticule, can be measured. Professional surveyors use a somewhat complicated sighting staff when levelling but this, we felt, was unnecessary for our purpose. In fact, we found that our long tape showed up admirably through the dumpy sights and kept measuring complications to a minimum. Dimensions were taken from two positions and plotted to scale in an unconventional but effective manner, which showed up individual relationships at once (Figure 4), one item being measured from both positions to establish a link between the two sighting positions.

String solved two types of measuring problem. The steam engine pit, which had an asymmetrical shape and lay awkwardly in relation to neighbouring walls, could have been measured well enough in the conventional way but it would have taken time—and time we did not have. But by hammering in a nail at the head and tail of the pit and stretching string between them the shape was plotted by offsets and became a single-handed job (Figure 5). Secondly, measuring the batter, or slope, of the river banks was done by tying a weight to the string and using it as a plumbline. With a 6-ft tape extended down the bank and the plumb bob hanging so as to just touch the end, the offset from string to bank top could easily be measured.

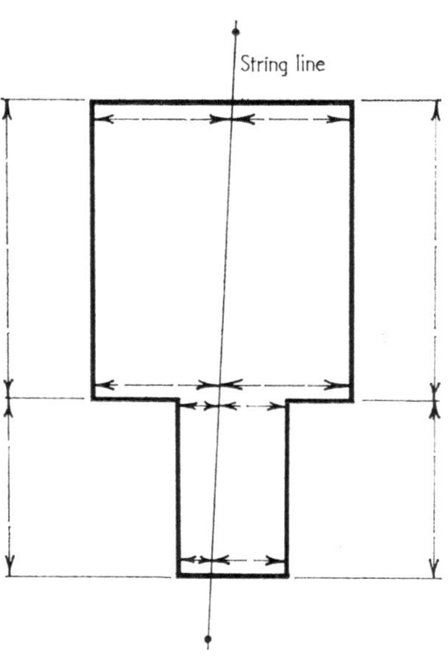

Fig 5 String can be used to form an artificial datum line in measuring irregular outlines

After rather more low-tide wading about in the Channel Sea River than either of us relished, we felt that although the contractors were imminent we had done fairly well. Most things visible had been recorded together with several, originally hidden, that pickaxe and spade had brought to light. There were still some mysteries of course, but when the contractors moved on site just before Easter they brought with them a 30-ton excavator and sundry other machinery. These made light work of utterly destroying the remains of the mill and also, to our greater satisfaction, of clearing out the choked waterways and rubble-filled foundations. Friendly relationships were established with the men on site, and also that important person the resident engineer. He was most intrigued with our discoveries, and held up proceedings on several occasions while details were recorded. This helpfulness was not entirely a one-way traffic: copies of our drawings were welcomed by the quantity surveyors on the job as superior to their own!

This survey of the Abbey Mill is only the first, and quite possibly a minor, instalment in what seems likely to be a lengthy detective story. The primary objective in describing the ways and means by which it was carried out is to encourage others to go and do likewise: a modicum of common sense is quite as effective as all the equipment and systems of the professional surveyor in achievinguseful results.

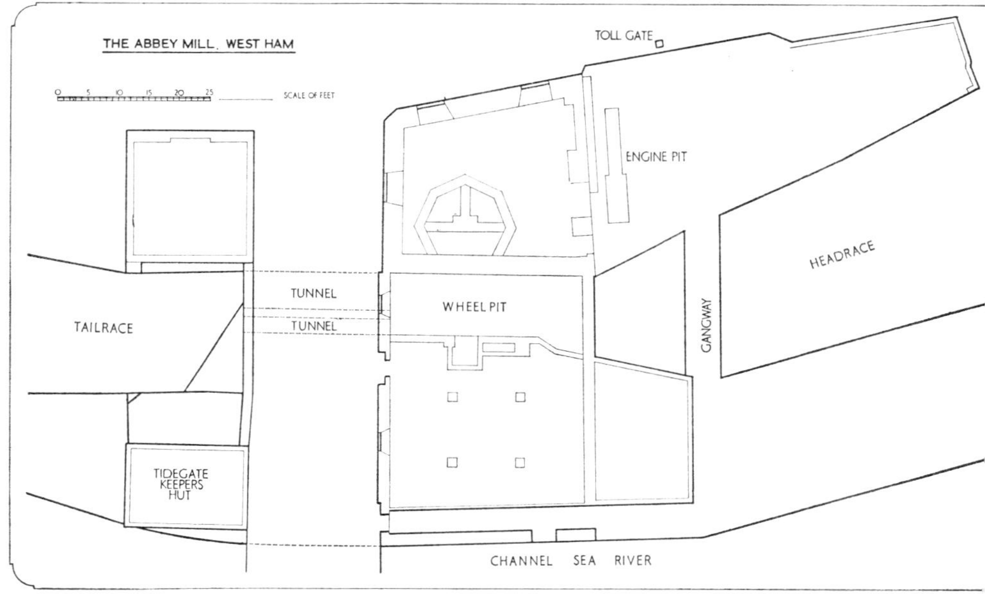

Fig 6 Plan of general layout of the Abbey Mill, West Ham

Plate, page 143

SUMMER COURSE IN HISTORY

The University of Hull Department of Adult Education is holding a summer course in history from 25 July to 2 August 1969 at Saffron Walden College of Education, Saffron Walden, Essex. There is a variety of study groups including one on the techniques of industrial archaeology. Application forms are available from the Department at 195 Cottingham Road, Hull, Yorkshire. The total cost for the course, including excursions, is £18.

RICHARD STOREY

Aids to Recording (4)

Industrial Sites

THIS article is not concerned with individual buildings or the machines in them, but with the sites of single productive enterprises or of multi-occupied industrial estates. It is a field of research which borders on and at times overlaps that of the business historian. Thus, the siting of a factory may be determined largely by the motives of the owner of a particular plot of land who is willing to sell at a certain time to a buyer who may be an industrialist. This motivation will probably only be traceable, if at all, in written or printed material, which is mainly, although not entirely, the province of the business or economic historian. Peculiarities of siting noted in the field and confirmed by a map can, however, lead to the search for this documentary evidence and the 'rediscovery' of the history of the site in question.

It is a legitimate concern of the industrial archaeologist by his observations to become aware of such peculiarities of industrial sites, with a view to discovering what local factors, such as land-holding or previous industrial use, affected their development. Particularly fruitful subjects for this kind of enquiry are what town-planners term 'non-conforming users'—industries situated in predominantly residential or rural areas, for example. There are usually special factors affecting their relationship with neighbouring development of a different kind. An attempted classification of these and other types of industrial site is given below, based on observation in the field and reading.

There is another side to the question, the reverse procedure of rediscovering former industrial sites on which other development, in urban areas usually residential, has subsequently taken place. This is particularly characteristic of aerodromes, whether simply airfields or the sites of aircraft manufacture; often only the name of a road remains to serve as a reminder, as in the case of Mollison Way and De Havilland Road off Stag Lane, Hendon, on the site of the DH works and airfield from 1920 to 1930.[1] With the steadily growing pressure on housing in London and all big cities, one can expect to see this trend accentuated, as some of the last policy statements of the London County Council with regard, for example, to Woolwich Arsenal and Croydon Aerodrome indicated.[2]

CLASSIFICATION

1. FORMER EXTRACTIVE INDUSTRY SITES

(i) When worked out, quarries or gravel pits, if not reinstated to the general surface level, sometimes provide conveniently unobtrusive sites for manufacturing industry or commercial undertakings.
Example: former chalk pits on south side of Ware Road, Hertford, close to eastern boundary of town. These now house a transport depot, the County Council Highways depot, a vegetable wholesaler and a large service garage and motor repair works. (Probably the site of the Barrow Field lime kiln of Henry Norris, builder, Hertford, 1860s.)
(ii) If left derelict, the true nature of the original extractive/processing activity may not be readily recognisable. *Example:* Brickfields, Ware, Herts, now covered by smallholdings and allotments.[3]

An example of derelict extractive sites having recreational value, and one very much in the public eye at the time of writing, is the Lea Valley park project. One of its proposed features is the use of the flooded gravel pits in the valley for aquatic activities of various kinds.[4]
(iii) The surface of the site may be reinstated and revert to agricultural use, or be used for residential or manufacturing purposes or as open space. Professor L. Dudley Stamp made some interesting points about the restoration of this type of industrial wasteland in his book *Applied Geography*.[5]

2. SITES MAINLY INFLUENCED BY FACTORS OF LOCAL LAND-OWNING

In one sense this heading could apply in some way to all the aspects of this survey, but under this heading it will be restricted to those instances in which the influence of local landowners appears to have been dominant in affecting a particular industrial development. Local influence is probably most commonly seen in the effects of landowners' opposition to, or promotion of, railway schemes, which was often strong enough to determine the course the projected lines would take. An example from the small area of east Hertfordshire on which I am currently working is the 'Ware, Hadham & Buntingford Railway' (closed under the Beeching Plan at the end of 1964). Landowners' objections to this line, construction of which commenced in 1859, resulted in its junction with the Hertford (East)–London line being at St Margarets (Stanstead Abbots), not Ware.[6]

An example of industrial-estate siting due to a great extent to land-owning enterprise is the Caxton Hill Industrial Estate, Hertford.[7] This had its origin in the purchase in 1901 of 50 acres of the Balls Park Estate by Mr Herbert Brazier, a sand and gravel pit-owner. Gravel extraction commenced and continued on part of the site until after the second world war. In 1954 a well-known local printing firm, Stephen Austin & Sons Ltd, moved into new premises on the Caxton Hill site. In 1959 Hertford Industrial Estates Ltd was formed to develop an industrial estate there. This company became public in April 1962 and in March 1965 made application to the Birmingham Stock Exchange for permission to deal in the ordinary shares of the company.[8]

3. INDUSTRIAL SITES BASED ON FORMER MILITARY INSTALLATIONS

The outstanding examples of this category are, of course, Slough and Park Royal. These, in particular the latter, are examined by P. G. Hall in *The Industries of London Since 1861*[9] to which those interested in this and other aspects of industrial siting in the Greater London area should refer. On a less spectacular, but none the less important, scale this class of industrial sites is extremely widespread, and most readers will probably know examples in areas familiar to them. The examples which follow are merely intended as typical illustrations of this kind of site:

Hertfordshire	Buntingford	depot of J. Sainsbury Ltd, provision merchants, in former RAOC depot, London Road.[10]
	Hertford	according to the *Hertfordshire Mercury*, 7 April 1933, the works of Messrs Addis Ltd, brush manufacturers, in Ware Road, absorbed buildings used by the Herts Militia. (The firm moved to Hertford from Clerkenwell in 1920.)
	Hunsdon	depot of Robert Dixon, land equipment engineers, and Hunsdon Laboratories of Smith & Nephew Research Ltd on former service aerodrome.
Norfolk		Lotus Cars Ltd have transferred their works from Cheshunt, Herts to a former RAF airfield near Norwich.[11]
Suffolk	Rougham	near Bury St Edmunds: Eastern Counties Farmers Ltd depot on former service airfield.

4. SUBSEQUENT USE OF FORMER INDUSTRIAL SITES

A general treatment of the subject is given in the *Times Review of Industry and Technology* for January 1965.[12]

(i) *Extractive industry sites* have already been referred to under (1) and (2).

(ii) *Communications*

(a) *Airfields* have already been mentioned. Non-military ones are both quite numerous and difficult to trace, since the trend increasingly is for housing to cover these valuable open spaces in urban areas. *Examples:* in London, in addition to Croydon and Stag Lane there are Hendon, Heston, and Cricklewood. In the provinces, Christchurch, Hants, the former de Havilland (Airspeed) airfield, is another example of a site of aircraft manufacture which is to be developed residentially.

A less important, municipal airfield at Bury St Edmunds which was developed in the heyday of light aircraft and private flying in the 1930s was given over to service uses during the war (including flying), and in recent years the site has been redeveloped as the Westley Housing

Estate, with nothing to indicate its former use.[13] The site of a small club aerodrome in Essex—the Herts & Essex Aero Club at Nazeing, near Broxbourne—has in recent years been given over to sand and gravel extraction.[14]

(b) *Canals* have recently been mentioned in connection with proposed hovercraft 'tracks' in inner London. A more conventional example of a change from one type of communication to another is the purchase of the Derby Canal by the Corporation for use as part of the new Derby inner ring road.

(c) *Railways* were a development mentioned in my article on industrial archaeology in the South-East generally (*Industrial Archaeology*, vol 2, no 1).

(iii) *Manufacturing Sites*

The use of buildings constructed for one industry by undertakings in a different sphere of manufacturing calls for a separate survey, and I indicated some examples (the maltings of Ware, Herts) in the article referred to above. A larger industry in northern England—cotton textile manufacture—may be expected to provide many more examples. Two were given in the *Guardian* in December 1964.[15]

Industrial sites may occasionally be taken over by public services of various kinds. An instance of this, recorded in the *Camden & St Pancras Chronicle* (5 March 1965) is the demolition of the former Idris factory, Pratt Street and St Pancras Way, London NW1, which has been redeveloped to provide a site for the new headquarters of the North-West London District Post Office. An earlier example is given in Richard Smith's paper *Walthamstow in the Nineteenth Century* (Walthamstow Antiquarian Society, Occasional Publications no 2, 1938). He describes the history of the copper rolling mills of the British Copper Co with a detail which is perhaps unusual for a local historian before industrial archaeology as we know it had crystallised, and, significantly for this survey, he mentions the acquisition of the remains of the old buildings by the East London Waterworks Co after the mills ceased working in 1857. In passing, it may be noted that the mills, before their purchase by the British Copper Co, had had an interesting history, in connection with which Smith mentions powder grinding, linseed crushing and paper making.

The determination of the LCC and its successor, the Greater London Council, to tackle London's enormous housing problem with greater vigour is resulting in the residential development of a number of important industrial sites. As well as Woolwich Arsenal, these include Stuart's Granolithic Works, Poplar,[16] and the Crown Works site of Messrs Higgs & Hill Ltd, civil engineers, in Kennington.[17] This latter example is of especial interest, in that the firm intends to concentrate at Wellingborough, Northants, one of the Greater London Council's expanding towns.

Residential redevelopment of industrial sites is not, of course, restricted to the metropolis, nor to large towns. As this article was concluded, in April 1965, demolition of most of Canons Maltings, Ware, which stood beside the A10 at the north end of the town, was going on in an atmosphere of controversy.[18] It was vainly hoped that a sixteenth-century section of the buildings would be preserved; further Tudor brickwork was encapsulated in the main nineteenth-century portion, some of it visible at the base of the outside wall. This disappeared with redevelopment, although it may be assumed that the interest shown in the site as it was about to be cleared resulted in some gaps in its apparently ill-recorded history being filled. Until more money and more enlightened attitudes are brought to bear on the raw materials of industrial archaeology at local levels, where many of the decisions which activate bulldozers are still taken, we can hope for little more than this.

Notes

1 C. M. Sharp, *D.H.: An Outline of de Havilland History* (1960)

2 *Guardian*, 19 March 1965

3 *Hertfordshire Mercury*, 2 June 1933: letter of Wm Trory re brick production in late nineteenth century

4 Amongst numerous examples in the national and local press, see *Hertfordshire Mercury*, 19 March 1965, 9; 'London Letter', *Guardian*, 25 March 1965, 10

5 L. Dudley Stamp, *Applied Geography* (1960), 136–8. See also *Guardian*, 20 April 1965, for a description of a new project in the North-East

6 *Hertfordshire Countryside*, vol 19, no 73 (summer 1964), 20
7 *Hertfordshire Mercury*, 22 January 1965, 8
8 *Hertfordshire Mercury*, 19 March 1965, Company Notices
9 P. G. Hall, *The Industries of London Since 1861* (1962)
10 See, for example, *Hertfordshire Mercury*, 19 February 1965 and 18 May 1967. Also *Commercial Motor*, 28 July 1967, 96–101
11 *Guardian*, 21 November 1964. This firm began in Hornsey and has thus moved from an inner to an outer suburb and thence beyond the Metropolis. This type of industrial migration might well be termed 'ricochet' movement.
12 'Reclaiming Swansea's Wasteland', *Times Review of Industry & Technology*, vol 3, no 1 (January 1965), 44–5
13 For this information I am indebted to Mr L. E. Payne, Secretary to the Mayor of Bury St Edmunds, and to Mr M. P. Statham, West Suffolk County Archivist.
14 *Essex Journal*, vol 3, no 1, 56
15 'New For Old', *Guardian*, 14 December 1964, (financial columns)
16 *Guardian*, 12 March 1965
17 *Guardian*, 19 March 1965
18 *Hertfordshire Mercury*, 9 April 1965. W. Branch Johnson, *Industrial Monuments in Hertfordshire*, Herts CC (1967), 7

General note: this article does not now represent the full extent of the author's views on industrial sites, but may serve as an introduction to a complex subject.

A. J. A. COOKSEY

Jennings South Western Pottery, Parkstone

A Preliminary Survey Report

DURING *February and March 1967 twenty members of the Poole (WEA) Industrial Archaeology Group, under the leadership of Mr Cooksey, carried out a survey of the installations and records of this old-established pottery, which was closed at very short notice. Mr Cooksey's report is illustrated on pp 143–4 with photographs taken by the secretary of the group, Mr D. Caddick.*

The History of the Pottery

George Jennings was born in the New Forest area, and before starting the Parkstone works, he had a pottery in Lambeth. The South Western Pottery was founded in 1856 (although another pottery was already in existence on the site at Blake Dene nearby), where there was a seam of Dorset ball clay. The bricks for the buildings were probably made at the brickworks in the Lilliput Road area.

From 1860 onwards the company specialised in terracotta work, examples of which are still to be seen locally, including the eagles on the gateways to Poole Park, which were priced at £5 5s each. It also produced bricks on an adjacent site using the Hoffmann continuous process. George Jennings had many patents, mostly covering various types of sanitary pipework. He was the chief sanitary engineer for the 1851 Crystal Palace Exhibition and supervised the moving to the Sydenham site. His success at the 1851 exhibition led to contracts and exhibits in London 1862, Dublin 1865, Paris 1867 (where he won a silver medal), Philadelphia 1876, Paris 1878, Sydney 1873, Melbourne 1880 and Adelaide 1881. Soon after the outbreak of the Russian war, he constructed sanitary fittings for the British hospitals at Varna and Scutari in the Crimea, where they were fixed by a staff of his own workmen from the Lambeth works. Sanitary pipeware was to become the staple product of the company for the rest of its life. At the turn of the century the firm also specialised in the manufacture of acid-resisting stoneware, some of which was eventually used in the naval cordite factory at Holton Heath in 1914 (see p 144). In 1903 Thomas Wragg of Swadlincote took over the Jennings company, but the Parkstone works continued to trade under the name of Jennings until its closure recently.

In the early thirties work was started on the construction and development of the first continuous salt-glazing pipe-producing tunnel kiln to be built in Britain. This produced large quantities of sanitary pipeware, much of it for export, until the outbreak of the 1939–45 war, after which the plant was not brought back into use again. The shed that housed the kiln was over 400 ft in length and was demolished soon after the survey was completed.

During 1966–7 some of the machinery, which at the beginning was steam-driven, was made automatic by modifying the electrically-driven plant installed in the early 1920s.

Production Methods

The clay was originally dug by hand, but in 1922 a type-B Erie steam shovel was purchased from the Ball Engine Co, of Erie, Pennsylvania. The clay was, at first, brought into the drying sheds by horse and cart, but after the 1914–18 war an ex-WD petrol locomotive hauled trucks on a 24-in gauge railway. The locomotive had seen service in France towing tanks and had shrapnel marks on its side. The company had possessed three 0-4-0 standard-gauge saddle-tank steam locomotives, the last of which, *George Jenning*, a 25-ton outside-cylinder saddle tank supplied by Pecket & Sons of Bristol in 1902, worked until 1963. This was used for the transport of coal from Parkstone railway station to the pottery and for taking finished goods back for shipment to customers. Salterns Pier, made from old bricks and

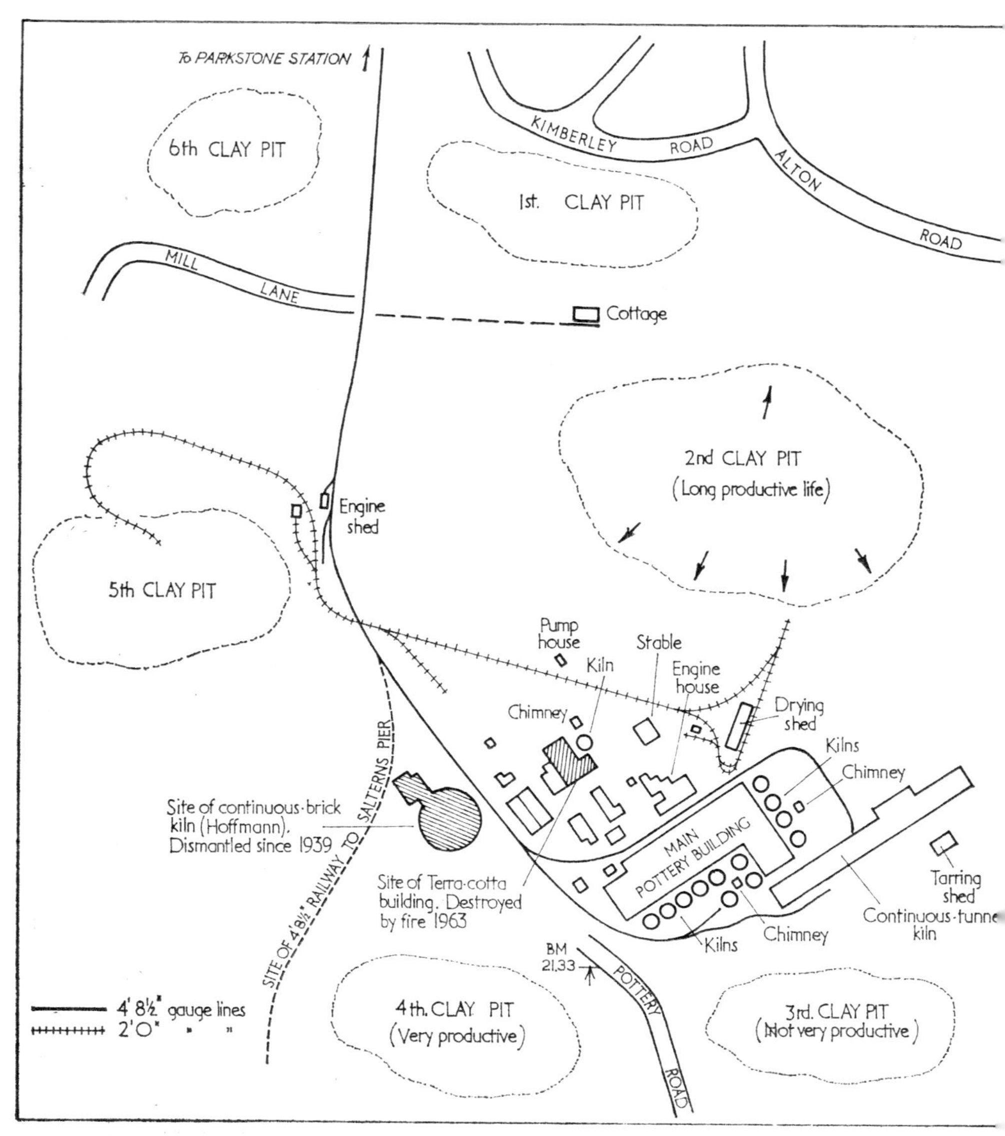

Outline of site of South Western Pottery

pipe rubble from the pottery, was used in the early days to ship the pipeware to customers all over the world in sailing ships. Another railway, which was standard-gauge, also ran round the back of Lilliput cemetery across the main road to the Blue Lagoon and followed the course of Sandbanks Road to the old firm of Alban Richards & Co Ltd which repaired LNER wagons after the first world war.

All the machinery at the pottery was driven by steam plant originally. The steam engine was a 600-hp single-cylinder Thornewall and Warham (Burton-on-Trent) engine installed in 1922. The cylinder was 2 ft in diameter and had a 3 ft 6 in stroke, with Corliss-type valve gear. Its flywheel was 12 ft in diameter on a 1-ft diameter shaft. Belt drive was by means of twenty-two 1½-in diameter cotton ropes, which also drove a 125 kw AC alternator made by Newtons of Derby. In 1930 a 50-hp Belliss & Morcom two-cylinder vertical engine was installed with a direct-coupled 75-kw AC alternator by Crompton Parkinson of Chelmsford. This supplied lighting at night and power to the tunnel kiln twenty-four hours a day.

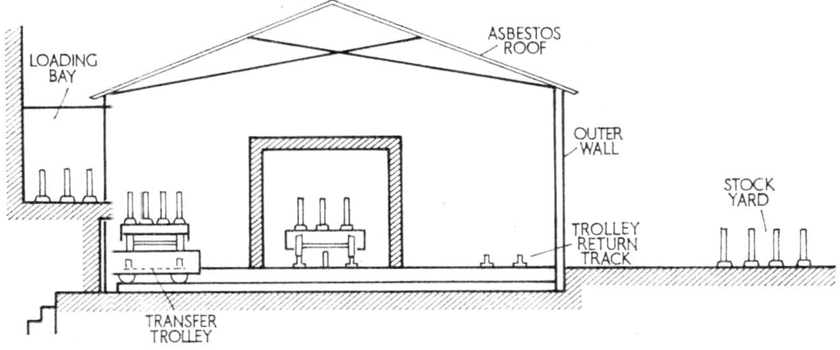

Section through loading bay showing method of transfer

From the drying-sheds, the clay was passed to an edge-running grinding mill, built by Schofield of Keighley, which was originally belt-driven. Broken fired pottery was also fed into a grinding mill to produce 'grog', which was used to help eliminate expansion problems during firing. The products of these two mills were then fed upstairs to a single-shafted clay pre-mixer, with a coupled pug mill, also built by Schofields and belt-driven originally. This process was eventually superseded by shredding the dried clay in a large rotating machine and passing it on to a box feeder, and crushing rolls, and finally, through a pug mill.

The 'pugs' were then elevated to the next floor on a conveyor, ready for use. The 'grog' was introduced at the crushing rolls stage which performed a kind of kneading action and ensured an even distribution throughout the wet clay ready for the moulders and pipe-extruding machines. These produced the straight pipe sections, a pug of the grog-clay mixture being extruded through a die forming the 'socket' section of the pipe, and the body being formed by lowering the bottom half of the die to extrude the clay over a central mandrel. Originally, pipes were produced as straight sections, and coupling pieces in two halves joined the 'butts' together (a Jennings' patent device). The butt was made by a steam-operated ram over which the clay was extruded and the socket halves were produced in a steam-operated press. This was then superseded by a straight butt with a hand-finished socket, the serrations which form the key in the joint being put on by kitchen knives ground to shape, or wooden templates. All the other sections were hand-moulded right up till 1967, exactly as they were at the start of the pottery in 1856. Firstly a plaster-of-paris male master mould was produced by the model shop, while the two female halves were fitted together at the most convenient centre line, depending on the shape. The inside faces were scraped smooth so as to give an even surface to the finished pipe.

The moulder cut a slice of mixed clay and pressed it into the half-mould, which had been dusted with dry powdered clay by means of a 'sock'. A skilled moulder could ensure an even thickness all over the mould and tested this by pressing his fingers against the clay. He then fitted the two halves together and sealed the faces of the joint by using a wooden tool to push them into close contact.

The 'green' pipes were removed from the mould and left to dry prior to firing. Hot steam pipes were passed under all the floors, which were slatted with about $\frac{3}{8}$-in gap between the slats. The downdraught kilns, originally inside the main building, were coal-fired from points around the base. As the sealed-in pipes were heated up, they were held at around 800° C until they were free from moisture. The temperature was then raised to 1,100° C, and salt was added to the fires. When vaporised the salt was drawn down through the kiln and over the white-hot pipes by the draught sucked through the flues in the floor, thus glazing the surface of the pipes. The amount and quality of the salt glaze was not under any measured control; thus many pipes were scrapped and used as grog. The kiln temperature was measured by means of a pyrometer, which was monitored by a recorder that was originally clockwork-operated but in 1967 was electrically-operated twenty-four hours a day. (Two of the Mark I recorders have been given to the group.) The pipes were finally graded, by the quality of the glaze and by hydraulic pressure testing, all to a British Standard Specification.

The Survey Methods

The situation was unusual, since the last employees left their tools, pipes, etc, all in position. It was therefore possible for members of the group to walk round and select items for their museum and to take photographs on the site. Apart from discussions with the management and sorting through the firm's books, catalogues and printer's blocks, the main job was that of selecting topics for photographing to enable a good cross-section of the pottery's work to be recorded.

One of our greatest disappointments was the fact that the first-ever salt-glazing continuous pipe-producing tunnel kiln, built by Shaws in 1930, had been dismantled just two weeks before our survey. Only the shell remained, but we were able to record details of the process and photograph what remained of the building, which gave us some idea of the size of the plant and documented a true piece of pioneering in the automation of this industry, a development that was some thirty years ahead of its time.

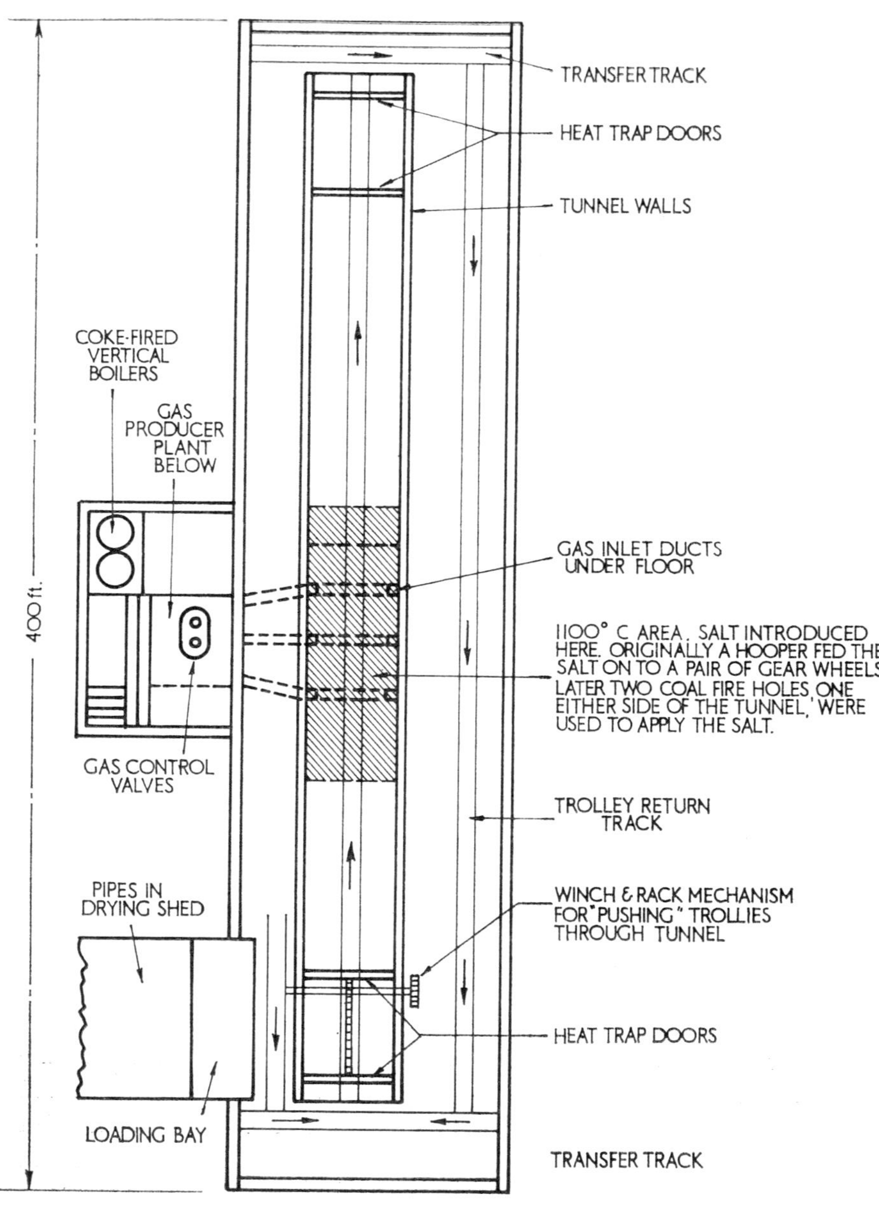

Details of the first-ever continuous salt-glazing pipe-producing tunnel kiln, built in 1930 by Williamson of Shaws at Parkstone

Another interesting little facet of the company's history was the fact that a certificate from the National Savings Group showed the existence of a savings group at the works for fifty years.

Among the small trolleys, known as 'dandies', used for handling the heavy green pipes on their steel base plates, we discovered what was obviously the forerunner of the modern fork-lift truck. In the old terracotta works, the pipes were transferred from one floor to another by means of a hydraulic lift, which consisted of a 3-ft diameter shaft between ground and top floors. The pipes were loaded on to a steel drum inside the shaft which was then pumped by water to the first floor above. Although no recent employee knows the exact operation, efforts will be made to contact retired employees to ascertain details of the system used.

Acknowledgments

Much of the valuable information on the plant and machinery was supplied by Mr Tom Dunford who was chief engineer and has long family connections with this pottery.

The group wishes to thank all members of the South Western Pottery for their willingness to help and make the survey possible, especially Mr & Mrs T. Harrison, Mr Hampshaw (now in Australia), Mr Dean, Mr H. R. Pearce, and a former employee of the company and member of our group, Miss K. Viney.

Plates, pages 143–4

ARTHUR E. J. WENT

The Ovoca, Ireland's First Motor Fishing Boat

When, in 1902, the Rev W. Spotswood Green, then Chief Inspector of Irish Fisheries, wrote his article on the sea fisheries of Ireland in *Ireland, Agricultural and Industrial,*[1] only sailing boats were used inshore in Irish waters. Steam power had been introduced, it is true, some years earlier as regards large vessels but, because of the bulk of the apparatus needed, steam propulsion was never successful in the smaller inshore units. I remember myself seeing in the west of Ireland in about 1937 the remains of a small fishing vessel (about 30 ft in overall length) furnished with a steam engine and an upright boiler, and I wondered how any crew could have operated her successfully.

Early this century the internal combustion engine seemed to offer the best prospects for mechanising smaller fishing craft and in Ireland, as elsewhere, experiments were made by installing such engines in existing sailing boats. As Green and Holt[2] pointed out in their report on the sea and inland fisheries of Ireland for the year 1907, sailing vessels were then having difficulty in 'competing with steamers in all branches of the fishing industry' and because of the financial risks involved in investing in steam vessels by fishermen working from home ports, it was thought desirable to experiment with a paraffin motor.

Earlier Michael Tyrrell of the firm of John Tyrrell & Sons, Arklow, Co Wicklow, had designed and built a model for a motor fishing boat which Tyrrell claimed could face any competition from steam drifters.[3] It had a cruiser stern and the hull was designed especially for the internal combustion engine. As a result of the prevailing interest in the introduction of internal combustion engines into fishing vessels the Department of Agriculture & Technical Instruction for Ireland decided to have a boat built to Tyrrell's new design and issued to a carefully selected crew, Charles and Richard Toole of 26 Harbour Road, Arklow, Co Wicklow.[4] The vessel, a 25-tonner, subsequently named *Ovoca*, was fully rigged for sailing and had the following dimensions:

Length	48·4 ft
Breadth	14·4 ft
Depth	7·2 ft (depth of hold from tonnage deck to the ceiling amidship)
	7·8 ft in the engine room.

The *Ovoca* was propelled by a 20-hp Danish *Dan* two-cylinder engine of the hot bulb type by P. Jörgonsen of Copenhagen and a variable pitch propellor. She had her engine room forward and the cabin aft. Fears were expressed that with this type of installation the length of the shaft might give trouble. An intermediate shaft, with universal joints, was introduced but these fears of trouble were unfounded.[5] She was constructed of pitch-pine and oak and was ketch-rigged.

On her trials the *Ovoca* did six knots, without the use of sails. She was registered in Dublin on 13 February 1908.[4] Tyrrell[3] states that after her first year experience showed that the large sail was not required so both of the original masts were shortened and the bowspit and mizzen boom were removed.

Such was the success of the *Ovoca* (her gross earnings in her first year were said to have nearly equalled her first cost, other than for fishing gear) that there were demands from fishermen for similarly propelled vessels. She had taken part in the seasonal Donegal and east coast herring fisheries and the rest of the year had worked a Danish seine net.[6] In 1907 the Department of Agriculture & Technical Instruction for Ireland also issued a loan to another crew of fishermen on the northern coast of Ireland to put a paraffin motor into a 25-ton boat named *Monico*.[2] This policy of putting paraffin engines into boats proceeded apace after 1907 so that by the year 1910 twenty-one such engines had been installed, eight in existing sailing vessels and thirteen into boats especially designed and built for the purpose.[5]

Re-engined, with a new winch and wheelhouse installed, the *Ovoca* was operated from Balbriggan, Co Dublin, until a few years ago. Since then she has been lying up in Balbriggan and, as she had become unseaworthy, her registry was closed in August 1966. A model of the *Ovoca*, constructed by John Tyrrell & Sons, Arklow, is now preserved in the Irish Maritime Museum collections.

The *Ovoca* was a pioneer venture. She was amongst the first fishing vessels anywhere to be designed especially for propulsion by an internal combustion engine. It is, therefore, worth recording her career while acknowledging the Rev William Spotswood Green, who was largely responsible for the interest taken by the Department of Agriculture & Technical Instruction for Ireland in the construction of the *Ovoca*.[7]

Notes

1 This volume was an expansion of the official handbook produced for the Glasgow International Exhibition of 1901.
2 Green & Holt, *Rep Sea and Inland Fish Ire* (1907)
3 *Fishing Boats of the World*, ed Oaf Traung, *Fishing News* (1955), 203–10
4 Information from Mr Lonigan, Custom House, Dublin
5 *Rep Sea and Inland Fish Ire* (1910)
6 *Rep Sea and Inland Fish Ire* (1908)
7 *Sci Proc R Dublin Soc* ser B ii, no 3, 32

L. D. W. SMITH

The Fireproof Floors of Witley Court

When Witley Court in north-west Worcestershire was extensively rebuilt about 1860 under the direction of Samuel Dawkes, a large number of fireproof floors were installed. A few can still be found in the ruins, despite a disastrous fire in 1937 and three decades of abandonment. It is now only possible to examine the ruins at basement level. This is shown on the sketch-plan (Figure 1) on which the positions of all surviving evidence of fireproof floor construction are marked. A plan of a particularly interesting survival is shown in Figure 2: in this instance half served as a flat roof and half as the floor of a corridor. Two brickwork walls were also carried.

A reconstruction of typical details is given in Figure 3. Rolled iron joists (AA) are used with dimensions and spacing varying from floor to floor. Their ends are built deep into the walls. Oak battens about 3 in × 1 in (BB) are laid flat, with their ends resting on the lower flanges of the joists, and carry a layer of brick-rubble concrete (C). The surface of the concrete is in all cases badly decayed and it is impossible to ascertain either its overall thickness or what type of floor-finish it carried. Below the battens are fixed 1½ in × 1 in counterbattens (D) and laths (E) of Baltic Redwood[1] for a ¾-in three-coat plaster ceiling.

The entrance-hall floor is the only one in which the joists are given intermediate support. Two 16¾ in × 10 in rivetted beams formed of angles and plate reduce the joist span to about 9 ft. The joists are not fixed in any way to the beams but merely rest on ledger angles. Each beam is supported by a 10-in diameter cast-iron column.

To establish the date of these floors, it is only necessary to observe that every floor in the parts of the building added in Dawkes' reconstruction appears to have been of this fireproof type. The reconstruc-

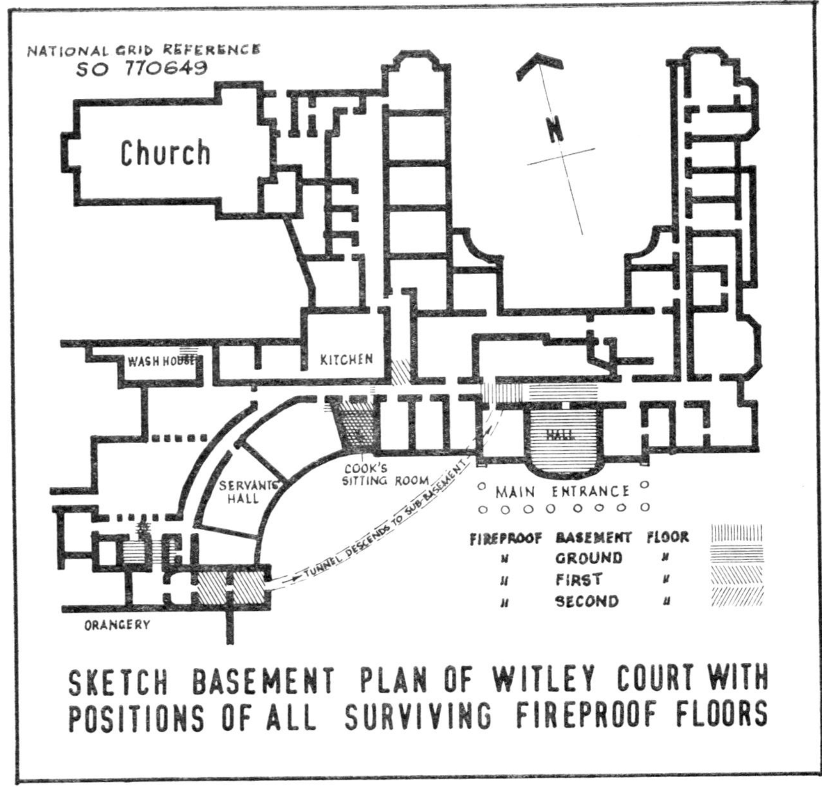

Fig 1

tion took place in 1859–61, which is a perfectly reasonable date for the floors. The three in the entrance area and the one near the kitchen are of identical design and are presumably of the same date.

The design of the fireproof floors shows them to be a variant of a patent floor known as the Fox & Barratt type, of which standard details are given in Figure 4. The reasons for the architect's choice of Fox & Barratt construction are fairly clear, as it offered all the advantages of fireproof construction while avoiding most of the disadvantages which had prevented the earlier brickwork arch fireproof con-

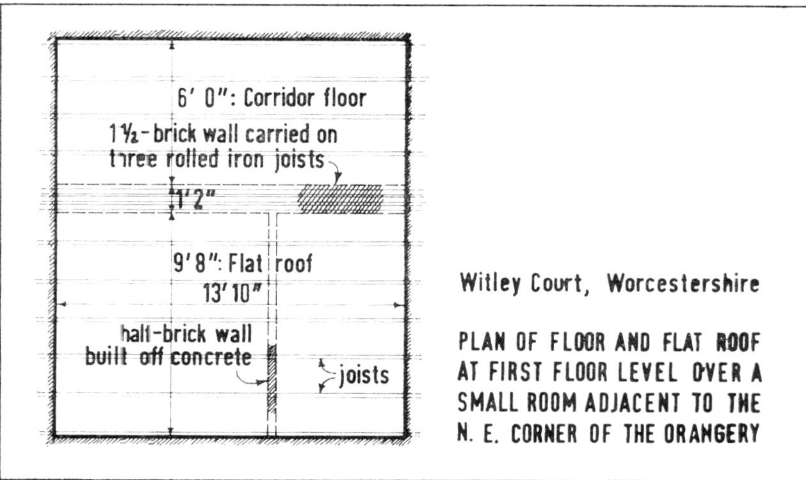

Fig 2 above; Fig 3 below

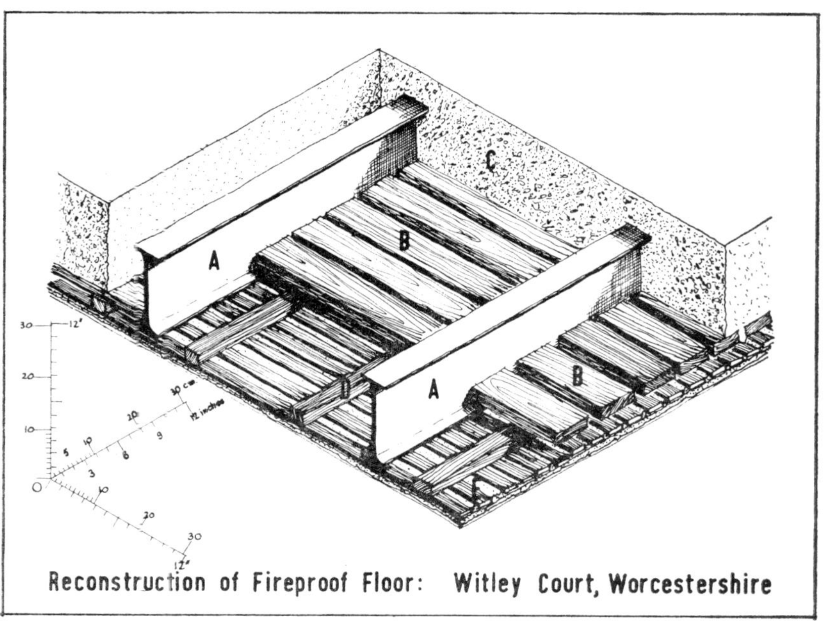

struction from being introduced into domestic use. The Fox & Barratt construction was said (by the patentee, admittedly) to be as inexpensive as traditional timber joist flooring.[2] It was much more soundproof, less subject to beetle attack and dry rot (particularly as no timber was built into the walls), and it was vastly stronger. Its strength meant that it could carry brickwork walls, as shown in Figure 2, and that the floor was rigid enough to carry finishes such as stone which would not tolerate the deflection inevitable with a traditional floor.

The last-mentioned advantage would account for the presence of a Fox & Barratt floor in the entrance hall, if Dawkes decided to pave it for the first time in stone. The portico of the main entrance dates from the early nineteenth century, and it might be thought that an earlier date could be claimed for the floors in the vicinity of the entrance. They could not, however, be early nineteenth-century as rolled wrought iron was not then available.

In short, Fox & Barratt construction seems to have had similar advantages to reinforced concrete, and a word in passing is called for to dispel the idea that it represents a primitive form of that particular structural innovation. The joists were so designed as to bear the floor-load without any help from the concrete. 'Before they are fixed, they are proved, under a pressure exceeding the greatest load that can ever be brought upon them.'[3] This was specifically a test for bending, not a tensile test, as is shown by the fact that 'it is done by means of a lever, at a very trifling cost'. It was, however, clearly recognised that the floor was stronger with the presence of the concrete than with the joists alone, although 'the extent of addition, to the original strength of the joists, by firmly fixing the ends, and then by the perfect union and combination, obtained in the process of construction, has not been ascertained'. It was clearly recognised also that the manner in which the concrete gave additional strength to the original strength of the joists was by preventing the joists from buckling:

> The strips, or pipes [ie the battens], form the groundwork of a continuous strut, which is completed by the subsequent application of the mortar and concrete: the latter completely imbedding the whole of the ironwork, which

is pressed equally on both sides, as the concrete is well trodden under the upper flanges of the joists. Thus it will be seen that the force of compression acts upon the joists, only through the medium of the concrete, and this material is well known to be one of the best for resisting that force.

The Witley Court floors are not strictly in accordance with the patent as the ceilings were constructed differently. According to the patent a layer of render should precede the concrete and be forced down between the battens to create a key for the ceiling plaster. In this way there would be no ceiling cavity. Smaller battens, about 1 in × 1 in should have been used, on which 'is spread, about $\frac{3}{4}$ in thick, the sort of mortar used by plasterers for what is called rendering, composed of one part of lime to three parts coal ashes, which, protruding through and from between . . . serves as a key to hold up the plastering of the ceiling below'.[4]

The patent required the ceiling to be formed in this manner in order that 'such portions of the materials as are in themselves combustible shall be completely covered by and embedded in such other portions of the materials as are not combustible'.[5] Timber, a combustible material, had not before been introduced into fireproof construction, and the precaution of embedding it was considered necessary. The Witley Court ceilings represent a descent from this standard: they contain an unnecessary amount of combustible material arranged in such a way that when the plaster is once breached a fire can spread over the entire ceiling. It may be of little consequence in a fire whether or not a ceiling is burned away, but it is much more serious if this exposes the joist flanges to be softened by the heat so that the floor collapses.

The departure from the patent specification is not to be explained as a later alteration of the ceilings. The unusually wide battens would give a very poor key for plastering, and since they are obviously original, so must have been the intention to provide a separate ceiling.

In work where a good standard of finish was required, there were good reasons for the variation. The patent design may be criticised because plaster has poor adhesion to iron and it must be applied ex-

Fig. 1.

Fig. 2 is a section between and in the direction of the joists, with a boarded surface, the iron joist being broken off, to show the construction of the floor.

Fig. 2.

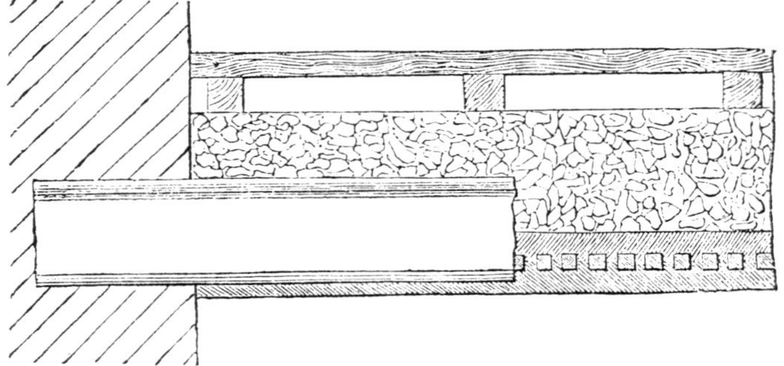

THE FOX AND BARRATT PATENT FLOOR

TAKEN FROM "THE CONSTRUCTION OF FIREPROOF BUILDINGS" BY JAMES BARRATT Assoc. Inst. C.E. 1853

Fig 4

cessively thickly to give adequate cover to the joist flanges. There is great likelihood of cracks appearing on the ceilings along the joist lines, which would be unacceptable in an expensive house. A more unsightly defect would be pattern staining, due to differences in thermal conductivity between the joists' positions and elsewhere, which would appear on the face of any decorations. This defect must have been familiar with earlier Fox & Barratt floors and a correct remedy has been found.

The fireproof floors of Witley Court were put to the test on the evening of 7 September 1937. ' "Unhappily, practically the whole of the building has been affected", said a member of the Witley Court Staff', according to *Berrows Worcester Journal.*[6] 'The fire started in the region of the servants' quarter . . . the east wing, tower, and middle are gutted', and 'the greater part of the east wing was gutted but much of the west wing was saved.' The fireproof parts do not seem to have distinguished themselves: they are now in worse ruins than any other part.

The ruins of Witley Court have now been exposed to the elements for over thirty years. The roof has gone and no timber floors whatever have survived. The basement floor is now buried several feet deep in rubble and prospective visitors should be warned that the building is in such dangerous condition that they enter at their peril. Even the remaining fireproof floors are no longer really to be trusted.

Notes

1 Timber species kindly identified by the Forest Products Research Laboratory
2 James Barratt, 'On the Construction of Fire-proof Buildings', *Proc Inst Civ Engrs* (1853), vol 12, 244
3 Barratt, op cit, all quotations in this paragraph
4 Patent 10,047 (1844)
5 Preamble of Patent
6 *Berrows Worcester Journal*, 11 September 1937

Book Reviews

Brindley at Wet Earth Colliery: An Engineering Study by A. G. Banks and R. B. Schofield, DAVID & CHARLES, Newton Abbot, 1968, 156 pp, ill, maps and diagrams, 35s.

James Brindley's fame rests mainly on his achievements in building the Worsley, Bridgewater, Grand Trunk and other canals, but before he embarked on these great schemes he had acquired considerable experience in millwright work, including the construction of watermills and provision of water supplies for their operation. Probably the most outstanding example of his early engineering activities was his work at the 'Wet Earth' Colliery, on the River Irwell, near Salford, where he was called in to solve drainage problems beyond the capacity of adits and horse-gins.

Water-powered pumping, which had long been utilised in mine drainage, was an obvious possibility, but the River Irwell—the only available source of such power at this colliery—was well below pithead level at its nearest approach, about 400 yd away. Brindley provided a brilliant engineering solution, by constructing a weir across the river at a higher point, to provide a head of water, which was conducted through a tunnel about 800 yd long, into an inverted siphon tunnelled under the river, and then into an open millrace, some 1,100 yd in length, leading to a waterwheel placed in a subterranean chamber at the pithead and operating drainage pumps; the water then passed, together with water pumped from the pit, into a narrow tailrace tunnel back into the Irwell.

This great engineering feat proved remarkably long-lasting. Brindley's original wheel remained in operation until the 1860s, and the turbine which then replaced it continued to be operated by the same water supply until it was finally displaced by steam in 1924. Unfortunately, however, documentary evidence relating to Brindley's scheme has entirely disappeared: all the colliery records appear to have been destroyed. The authors of this book, therefore, had to carry out a purely archaeological investigation, by a detailed examination of the site, including measured surveys and subterranean research. Inevitably, as they admit, some of their findings are conjectural, but they are 'based on engineering logic and it is hoped that the study will not be dismissed as mere guesswork'. Their book is most informatively and attractively illustrated with photographs, drawings, plans and maps, which explain the whole scheme with clarity and authority based on engineering knowledge and experience.

Where the authors make conjectures about the constructional problems involved, they are careful and convincing, but unfortunately they go beyond such matters into dubious surmising about 'the economics of mining production at Wet Earth' in Chapter 6, which is full of such phrases as 'it is assumed', 'it is believed', 'it may be supposed', etc. In the total absence of business records, these conjectures are almost worthless. On a matter of engineering history, too, they are in error. Brindley, they state (p 36), was wise to choose water power in preference to 'the ponderous and vastly uneconomic Newcomen engine that was then [in the early 1750s] proving unsuitable and obsolescent for the increasing demands of the manufacturing industries and deep mine pumping'. Brindley was undoubtedly successful with his water-powered pumping scheme, but it is by no means certain that a Newcomen engine would not have proved technically successful and perhaps more economic. The truth is that the Newcomen engine—far from being 'vastly uneconomic' and 'obsolescent'—was at this time coming into rapidly increasing use for mine drainage and other pumping operations, and was invaluable in saving deeper mines from flooding; even after Watt produced his improved engines, the older type continued to be built and used in large numbers for many years.

These criticisms, however, do not detract from Brindley's remarkable engineering achievements at this colliery, or from the authors' extremely skilful and interesting literary reconstruction thereof. This book is undoubtedly one of the best products of recent researches in industrial archaeology.

University of Manchester A. E. Musson

Industrial Archaeology in Devon, by W. E. Minchinton, Kate Havinden and Michael Dower (available from Devon County Planning Office, County Hall, Exeter, 5s 6d post free).

This splendid booklet, written by W. E. Minchinton and edited by Michael Dower, is based on fieldwork and research by Kate Havinden under the guidance of the Devon Industrial Archaeology Survey Committee. Its aim is to give 'a brief glimpse of the county's richness in industrial archaeology', and within the spatial limitations of thirty-four pages it succeeds in this in a most pleasing manner. Essentially a propaganda medium, sponsored by the Dartington Amenity Research Trust, Devon County Council Planning Committee, Exeter City Council and the Department of Economic History, University of Exeter, this popular booklet was designed 'to stimulate public interest and encourage support for a long term effort of recording and conservation'.

The material is presented in a series of inventories. There are ten main sections and each starts with a succinct summary of its general theme. A systematic coverage is provided by sections on: water, wind and tidal power; tollhouses, milestones and bridges; canals; steam power, tramways and railways; ports, harbours and warehouses; limekilns, mines and quarries; textiles; and housing. Two regional case studies examine briefly the industrial heritage of Dartmoor and the Tamar Valley, both now covered in depth by separate volumes.

Each site (and there are more than 130) is numbered and easily located on a clear, centre-page map or on small regional maps on other pages. An introductory note gives some good advice on access. The descriptions (with grid reference) are short and factual, often giving additional details of other sites in Devon where similar examples can be found. There are some fascinating entries: the famous 30-ft Dawlish waterwheel; the short-lived Bideford, Westward Ho! & Appledore Railway; and the Finch Brothers' Foundry, Sticklepath, now restored as a Museum of Rural Industry. Details of the Devon IA Survey and a useful bibliography are given.

The booklet is beautifully produced with seven line drawings and maps and twenty-one superb plates. Eric de Mare's photograph of the tumbling weir at Ottery St Mary (from *The Functional Tradition in Early Industrial Buildings*), Bideford harbour in 1879, and the engine house at Wheel Betsy mine are only three of the truly delightful illustrations. If this fascinating little publication fails to inspire the latent industrial archaeologist into activity, then nothing will.

Edinburgh College of Commerce Ian Donnachie

Old Nottingham, by Malcolm I. Thomis, DAVID & CHARLES, Newton Abbot, 1968, xii + 200 pp, ill, 40s.

Nottingham is a town that has received an unusual amount of attention from historians. The Victorian forefathers were energetic chroniclers of local happenings and their Edwardian successors proved to be tireless genealogists. In more recent years the infectious enthusiasm of Professor Chambers has established a tradition of regional research at the university that is still bearing fruit. There is no argument that the town is not worthy of this attention; it was one of the cradles of the factory system of production in cotton, and its staple hosiery and lace trades, presenting stark contrasts to each other, epitomised the energy and lassitude, the sudden prosperity and the harrowing poverty that accompanied the Industrial Revolution. Nottingham was at one and the same time one of the most radical, most religious and most overcrowded towns of the last century. All this is rich material for the economic and social historian and Malcolm Thomis sets out, in twelve short readable chapters, to present some of the popular themes that a century of local historical research has thrown up.

Dr Thomis does not attempt to write a continuous history of the town, but contents himself with a number of romantic and dramatic events from the history of the last two centuries, making constant reference to the disappearing physical relics of Nottingham's past. The Luddite attacks on stocking frames in 1811–16, the burning down of the castle in the Reform Bill riots of 1831, the turbulent and corrupt election of 1802, the contest between the freeholders and burgesses over the enclosure of the common fields, anecdotes of the annual Goose Fair, the celebrated public houses of the town, and a famous local school are affectionately handled in turn. There is some entertaining material based on perambulations of the market, old streets, and what were once the common fields of the town. The only sustained reference to history from documentary sources is made on an apologetic note.

The limitations of this book are twofold. The first arises from the publisher's conception of the series to which this work belongs, which is to present popular local histories based on surviving physical evidence. Though Nottingham has, as Dr Thomis remarks, almost a thousand years of recorded history, precious little of it can be found in surviving buildings. Secondly, the author's original research has been heavily concentrated on radical political movements in Nottingham in the period 1780–1830, and the industrial, commercial and religious life of the town are neglected, while there is no attempt to review some of the fascinating material on medieval, Tudor and Stuart Nottingham. Where the author makes a reference to these other facets of local history, he misses the significance of some of the more original contributions to the topics he develops, for instance the published calculations of population growth in eighteenth-century Nottingham and of school attendance in the town in the early nineteenth century. Characteristically, he tells us about Thomas North's tombstone in Basford churchyard without explaining the importance of North's enterprise as a capitalist in the coal industry. In other words, Dr Thomis's snapshots, while entertaining, present an incomplete and unrepresentative view of Nottingham's recent history.

University of Nottingham S. D. Chapman

The Tanat Valley: Its Railways and Industrial Archaeology, by W. J. Wren, DAVID & CHARLES, Newton Abbot, 1968, 192 pp, maps and ill, 42s.

Students of local history, archaeology, and geography will find much to interest them in W. J. Wren's account of the growth of industry and communications in the Tanat Valley. This little-known region in the mountainous heart of Montgomeryshire presents a very different picture today from the intensive industrial scene of a century ago. Although this is not a high-powered academic work, the author vividly recaptures the processes that gave rise to earlier economic activities of which much evidence remains in the present landscape.

The first section of the work deals in considerable detail with the construction and working life of the Tanat Valley Light Railway. The line was opened in 1904 and, after absorption into the GWR in 1923 and later into BR, finally closed in 1960. The author is to be complimented on his handling of the material which is enhanced by the inclusion of a series of excellent photographs. The second section traces the history of mining and quarrying in the valley and an attempt is made, with some degree of success, to bridge the gap between pre-historic exploitation and the nineteenth-century scene.

Each section is preceded by a short introductory chapter which seeks to place these economic activities in their regional settings. It is here that the work is open to some criticism. The introductions consist of a motley assemblage of geographical, historical, and archaeological statements, many of which are over-generalised to the point of being misleading. The River Dee is not a 'rift' valley, neither is it accepted that the Bronze Age marked the arrival of the Celtic peoples in Wales. One wonders, too, whether information on the derivation of local Welsh place names and references to social customs of earlier years is really necessary in a book of this nature.

The text is interspersed with thirty-three line diagrams and maps. These are clear and basic to the text, but it is unfortunate that all are freehand drawings. The general appearance of this work would have been greatly improved had these illustrations been prepared at a higher cartographical level. The absence of any form of scale on many of the drawings is also a disadvantage.

This is an enjoyable book, but one wonders whether its appeal will be other than local.

University of Strathclyde T. R. B. Dicks

Local Society Publications: A Critique

The continued growth of local industrial archaeology societies or groups within existing history or archaeology societies has brought about a happy proliferation of local and regional publications. The main role of such publications is well expressed in *CBA Group 9 Bulletin* no 6 (reviewed below) as 'reporting IA activities so that through a greater awareness of what is being done, more people may take an active part in IA'. They can obviously illustrate various aspects of the subject at a local level and provide a guideline to others tackling similar projects elsewhere, but perhaps most important of all is the opportunity they afford local researchers to publish their findings as a preliminary to submission to this or other journals.

A number of problems beset the local publication: method and cost of production; format and presentation; and scale and primary function. The first almost certainly determines the second, though cost is probably the most critical. Undoubtedly the most useful format is A4, which is large enough for the reproduction of maps and diagrams without loss of detail. Offset printing allows the use of photographs (often with splendid results) although this is more expensive than duplicating. Often the most difficult decision is the scale and function of the society publication. At one extreme is the humble newsletter and at the other the expensively produced journal. The local publications reviewed below present examples of the varied approaches to these problems. Some have successfully married the dual functions of newsletter and journal, while others effectively fill only one of these roles.

Portsmouth College of Technology IA Society has already produced a successful first number of its *Journal*, reviewed in vol 5 no 4 of

Industrial Archaeology. The society *Newsletter* which appears monthly and circulates among nearly forty members, is a quarto-size duplicated publication containing short articles and news of the society's activities. 'The Retort Houses of Hilsea Gasworks' by R. C. Ridley describes 'the last major industrial relic of the nineteenth century on Portsea Island', and is only one of many interesting notes in *Newsletter*, no 3 (November 1968). D. R. Hall's brief account of 'Housing for the Workers' in *Newsletter*, no 4 (December 1968) could well provide the basis for a study of this subject drawing on local examples. These newsletters certainly reflect the enthusiasm and energy of this society.

The *Bulletin of IA in CBA Group 9* has recently been enlarged and is now produced in A4 format. The editor is Geoffrey H. Starmer and enquiries about subscriptions (10s for four quarterly issues) should be made to J. Kenneth Major, 2 Eldon Road, Reading. No 6 (October 1968) is an excellent eighteen-page publication, containing four main articles and numerous other short features. John Gray's 'An Industrialised Farm in Berkshire' tells of the ill-fated schemes of Robert 'Tertius' Campbell, an ex-Australian gold prospector with money to burn. 'Hayes Boat-Yard, Stony Stratford' by R. J. Ayers provides an extended source list on the history of a most unusual boat-building concern. 'An IA Tour in Northamptonshire' by Geoffrey H. Starmer is a useful and detailed guide to local sites, essentially designed for the motorist but clearly demanding the use of boots as well. John Carter reports on 'The Banbury Steam Engine Fair', an event of national interest to enthusiasts. There are detailed reports of activities, research, lectures and publications in IA in each of the five counties within CBA Group 9: Bedfordshire, Berkshire, Bucks, Northants and Oxfordshire.

Lincolnshire Local History Society IA Group's *Industrial Archaeology Newsletter* is soon to change its title to become *Lincolnshire Industrial Archaeology*. The group hopes to 'improve the quality and appearance of the Newsletter' and have taken a first step towards this aim by changing the format and increasing the number of pages. Vol 3 no 4 (October 1968) is a sixteen-page, duplicated booklet ($6\frac{1}{2}$ in $\times$ 8 in) with an illustrated card cover. It contains two main articles (both illustrated with maps and plans) and three short features recording details of group fieldwork and excursions. The first article, 'The Great Northern Locomotive Dept, Boston' by Neil Wright, is a thorough and well-documented field report on the remains of a railway workshop using mid-nineteenth-century plans as a starting point. 'The Riverhead at Grimsby' by P. R. White describes the first dock works and the industrial buildings associated with them. Many of the features mentioned have been permanently recorded by means of a photographic survey and sketch plans. Brian Loughbrough's account of a boat trip on the Lower Witham by group members shows how much can be gained from an organised field excursion of this type.

The publication of a bulletin containing articles is the aim of the Sussex IA Study Group, and the original idea that its *Newsletter* should have this function has been abandoned. *Newsletter* no 2 (October 1968) is an eight-page quarto-size multilith booklet containing details of progress on nine field surveys being carried out in Sussex by the society: natural power; fuel power; tollhouses and milestones; railway architecture; warehouses; breweries; kilns; Brighton and Hove; and Shoreham harbour. Two useful aids are the short bibliography of Sussex newspapers giving dates and locations in local libraries, and a list of names and addresses of individual society members and corporate bodies. Offset printing has allowed the reproduction of two fine photographs (a tilt hammer at Dunnings Mill, East Grinstead, and a horse-gin at Patching, near Arundel), which for some reason have been placed on the back page.

Bristol Industrial Archaeological Society sets itself a high standard in the publication of *BIAS Bulletin* and this is more than matched in *BIAS Journal*, no 1 (1968), priced to non-members of the society at 7s 6d and available from the Secretary, BIAS, Bristol City Museum, Queen's Road, Bristol. This appeared at the close of the year and is a fine thirty-six-page publication printed on A4-size paper. For the technically-minded, the text was typed on the IBM Executive machine with Mid-Century typeface and the contents printed offset litho on

Recorder Cartridge 117 gem paper using a Rotaprint 30/90 machine. The presentation, from the cover inwards, is superb, although one has to admit that the space available for textual matter might have been used more economically. The cover itself, designed by F. Howarth, is based on an old tollboard from Bagstone Gate now in Bristol City Museum. There are five articles, besides notes, reports and book reviews. The main feature, 'Turnpike Roads of the Bristol Region', is an excellent summary by Neil Cossons of the survey of turnpike trust relics carried out by BIAS members in the summer of 1967. The methodology could well be followed by any industrial archaeologist studying turnpikes. 'A Note on the Bath Roads' by Angus Buchanan and Don Browning provides regional detail on the same theme. Joan Day in 'The Language of Bristol Brass' provides a unique record of technical terms used in the wire and rolling mills on the River Avon at Saltford and Keynsham, which closed in the 1920s. 'The Port of Bristol Workshops at the Underfall Yard' by F. D. C. Jeffery details machinery and equipment discovered during surveys for the National Record of Industrial Monuments. Excellent photographs or line drawings accompany most of the articles and the journal is a credit to editor, contributors, designer and printer.

The aim of any individual, group or organised society actively pursuing industrial archaeology fieldwork or research ought to be to record what is found not only on a card index, but also in some more permanent form. This important medium of co-ordination, the local society or regional publication, will have an increasingly significant part to play in industrial archaeology in the future. The local society newsletter or journal, no matter how it is produced, can do much to encourage its members to publish their findings and thus create a record of their own local activities in the national task of recording. All such publications are vital for the future of industrial archaeology.

Edinburgh College of Commerce Ian Donnachie

Our Contributors

DR J. D. PORTEOUS is a geographer from Howden Dyke near Goole, Yorkshire; educated at Cambridge with postgraduate research at Hull University. He is spending 1968–9 in the Department of City & Regional Planning at Massachusetts Institute of Technology.

I. C. DODSWORTH, BSc, Colour Chem, MSc, Polymer Chem, ex-University of Leeds. Industrial chemist, 1959–66. Presently, senior chemistry teacher, Magdalen College School, Oxford. Organises there a small group interested in industrial archaeology and associated topics. Main interests: coal and metal mines, and especially, early wagonways and their trackwork. Present research interest—the Low Moor Co, Bradford (ironworks).

RICHARD LOUIS KING is head of the Circulation Department of the Business Administration Library at the University of California, Los Angeles, with special responsibility for the Robert E. Gross Collection of Rare Books in the History of Business and Economics; active also in California politics.

IAIN C. WALKER studied prehistoric European archaeology at the University of Edinburgh, and since 1962 has excavated colonial sites in Canada. He has specialised in studying clay tobacco pipes and is at present on educational leave from the National Historic Sites Service, Canada, with a Canada Council Doctoral Fellowship to study clay tobacco pipes at the University of Bath, with special reference to the Bristol pipe industry.

LL. DE S. WALKER has excavated Amerindian and colonial sites in Canada and has also done museum work and artefact research.

ALAN L. THOMAS is currently plant editor of the weekly civil engineering newspaper *Construction News*.

RICHARD A. STOREY read History at Cambridge (Downing College) 1956–9. After National Service and one and a half years in local government (mainly town planning administration) he joined the staff of the Historical Manuscripts Commission in February 1963, where he is now Chief Assistant Registrar, National Register of Archives. Recently appointed editor of *Business Archives*, he also contributes a quarterly column to *Veteran Car*.

ALFRED J. A. COOKSEY is currently lecturer in Mechanical Engineering at Poole Technical College; studied at Bournemouth and Kingston-upon-Thames Technical Colleges, AMIW, AMISM; became interested in IA through WEA course in 1966. He is making a personal study of the clay industry in East Dorset, from Roman times to the present day.

DR ARTHUR E. J. WENT has a doctorate in zoology. He is scientific adviser to the Fisheries Division, Department of Agriculture & Fisheries, Dublin, and an expert on the past and present of the Irish fishing industry.

L. D. W. SMITH, ARIBA, is an architect living in Birmingham.

Notes and News

Active Correspondents

The response to our request for active correspondents has been good and has greatly helped to extend the coverage of *Notes and News*. We welcome letters from readers on all aspects of industrial archaeology. Suggestions for new features to be included in these columns, photographs, regional, society, institutional or museum news should be sent to the *Notes and News* Editor (see front inside cover).

Intending contributors are invited to write for a copy of *Information for Contributors*, which details preferred styles for *Industrial Archaeology* and gives useful tips on presentation. If you have an article for us please write to the Editors for your copy of this useful guide.

Preservation Corner

In each issue we feature a notable industrial site or piece of equipment preserved as part of the nation's heritage. Readers are invited to contribute to this. News of preservation activities will also be most welcome, particularly if they are accompanied by photographs for illustration. In this issue we feature a notable early Scottish ironworks recently taken into guardianship and restored by the Ministry of Public Building & Works.

Bonawe Ironworks, Argyll

Shortly after his appointment as an adviser on industrial monuments to the Ministry of Public Building & Works, Rex Wailes visited the eighteenth-century ironworks complex at Bonawe, near Taynuilt, Argyll, and described them as 'the most important things to do with iron production history in Scotland'. He added the caveat that despite the remarkable state of preservation of the works, they would soon fall apart if nothing was done to arrest decay. Over five years have since elapsed and during that time the charcoal iron furnace and its associated buildings have been designated an ancient monument and a comprehensive scheme of restoration has been undertaken by the MPB & W.

The significance of Bonawe derives from the fact that they are perhaps the most complete charcoal ironworks surviving in Britain. They date from the period before the technique of using coal to smelt iron had been fully developed. English forests had been stripped bare of timber for charcoal making and ironmasters were prepared to go to any lengths to get supplies. They were even prepared to go to the Scottish Highlands, in the eighteenth century still a remote and isolated region. Prior to the erection of Bonawe two other ironworks were

Cast-iron lintel on the furnace dated 1753

built in the Highlands: one at Abernethy on Speyside c 1730, which used local high-grade ores; the other at Invergarry c 1727 in the Great Glen. Both were short-lived, being hampered by technical difficulties and transport costs.

Bonawe was much more favourably located on the west coast, easily accessible by sea. Perhaps more important, north Argyll was endowed with extensive stands of natural woodland. The Lorn Furnace Co, a partnership of ironmasters from the Furness district, leased Duncan Campbell of Lochiel's woods in 1752 and proceeded to build their furnace near the shores of Loch Etive. Skilled labour and materials were imported from the south and despite initial difficulties Bonawe was soon producing good-quality iron. For over 100 years it continued in operation, until 1866 when the furnace was blown out for the last time.

The furnace itself is a massive square structure of local stone set into a steep bank. Under the roof a charging platform runs round three sides of the furnace, a few feet below the uppermost windows indicated in the accompanying illustrations. Ore and charcoal from the storehouses on the hill behind were wheeled in barrows to the furnace top for direct loading. Blast was supplied by two sets of bellows powered by a waterwheel at the side. The furnace has an interesting lintel bearing the date 1753. In front of the furnace stood the casting house, but not much of it is left standing. Here the molten iron was run into the pig bed when the furnace was tapped. Bonawe had a capacity of about 750 tons per annum and the quality of its iron was very high.

Beyond the furnace are three large slated sheds, two being used for storing charcoal and the other for ore. A row of tenements, built on L-plan c 1795, provided housing for company workers. Although damaged

Ancient Monument staff of the MPB & W examine progress during reconstruction of the furnace at Bonawe

Jetty on Loch Etive used for import of ore and export of pig iron

by fire in 1966 the houses survive in good order. On the Loch Etive shore, about a quarter mile from the works, is a small jetty, known as Kelly's Pier, built to accommodate the sloops which transported ore and supplies from the south and loaded pig iron for the return voyage.

The restoration of this interesting site has set an excellent standard for the future and preserved a unique ironworks as part of the national heritage.

Copper Mining on Alderley Edge

L. V. Grinsell of The City Museum, Queens Road, Bristol 8, writes:

The occurrence of numerous grooved stone-mining implements at this site has been known since the middle of last century. Some authorities, including Sir William Boyd Dawkins, attributed them to the Bronze Age, on the strength of the presence of flint flakes and implements, and earthworks then considered to belong to that period, in the immediate vicinity. They did in fact claim that the copper workings themselves date from the Bronze Age, but their reasons for that belief were altogether inadequate.

It is now known that copper was being mined at Alderley Edge in 1698 and the years following (*Trans Bristol and Glos Archaeol Society*, vol 63 (1943), 150). If any industrial archaeologist can supply adequate information concerning post-medieval copper mining in this area, it would assist in the much-needed task of making a reassessment of the evidence (if any) for its exploitation in prehistoric times. References known to the writer are *J Royal Anth Inst*, vol 5 (1876), *Trans Lancs and Cheshire Ant Soc*, vol 23 (1905), and P. Ireland, *Prehistoric Properties of the National Trust* (1967), 11–12.

Aerated Water: The Pop Industry

Mr Harold Gregory, Cold Arbour House, Buckley, Flintshire, has written telling us of his interest in the history of the aerated water industry and allied trades. Glass and stoneware bottles, he says, form an integral part of this history, and a bottle or piece of bottle often gives evidence that a particular firm operated in a particular area. Mr Gregory has an interesting collection of pop bottles, which were mostly rescued before the demolition of a local aerated water factory founded by his grandfather in 1888.

Information about this industry is limited, though it seems to have been in existence since the eighteenth century. Dr

Joseph Priestly (who married a daughter of Wilkinson the ironmaster) is credited with the invention of soda water c 1772 as a cure for scurvy. Many of the early engineers such as Bramah and Watt, writes Mr Gregory, were directly concerned with the manufacture and installation of aerated water machinery and bottling plant. Actual manufacture, bottling and distribution was apparently carried on by many small firms up and down the country. One particular bottle still intrigues Mr Gregory—a grey, vitrified stoneware bottle with an extended lip, marked 'Blackwood and Co Patent Syphon Bottle London', the nominal capacity of which is a mere 4½ fluid oz. Mr Gregory would welcome any information about this interesting industry, particularly from readers who know of small local works which are still operating.

(Aerated water manufacture, like brewing, seems to have been a widely dispersed activity until the end of the last century, but it has since become increasingly concentrated, and at present large firms covering a wide area seem to be common. *Editor*)

Excavations at Chingley, Kent

The Bill to dam the River Bewl near Old Forge Farm, Lamberhurst, in order to create a reservoir for the provision of water for the Medway towns has recently become law. Two iron-working sites are threatened: the late sixteenth-century blast furnace at grid ref TQ/684327 and the seventeenth-century finery forge at 682335.

Preliminary excavations began in August 1968 with the aid of a grant from the Ministry of Public Building & Works made through the Society for Post-Medieval Archaeology.

Bottling machinery and plant in a mineral waterworks, Buckley, Flintshire, c 1920

Another excavation is planned for summer 1969, the dates being 18 July to 11 August. Volunteers will be most welcome, and full details of access, accommodation and subsistence allowances may be obtained from: D. W. Crossley, Department of Economic History, The University, Sheffield S10 ITN.

A French Weaver and Wilton

Mr W. R. Hicks, 6 Pewsey Place, Southampton SO1 2RX, writes as follows:

For some time past I have been trying to trace the history of an immigrant French weaver who, under his anglicised name of Anthony Dufosee, settled at Wilton before the middle of the eighteenth century and there took an active part in the local carpet industry. For over 150 years it has been repeatedly stated in print, with varying detail and without documentation, that he was brought to Wilton by, or at the instigation of, the ninth Earl of Pembroke, either before or after the latter's accession to his title in 1733. There is nothing improbable in this story, nor in the assumption that (together with a compatriot named Pierre Jemaule) he had to be brought to this country surreptitiously; equally, there is so far no direct evidence to substantiate it. I have established that he was married at Wilton in 1742, that he settled down there and eventually had a house of his own, and that he died there in 1785; what is more important, two samples of his work have survived and are still in the possession of one of his descendants. There, at present, firm information ceases.

Unfortunately, details of the early Wilton carpet industry are hard to come by, despite the Couran patent of 1741, which seems to have been for a type of velvet loom, but with which Dufosee does not appear to have been associated. (The three patentees were Ignatius Couran, a London merchant, and John Barford and William Moody, both of Wilton.) His national status may have been a factor here; I do not yet know at what date he became a property owner, and have not found his name in the lists of denizations. In 1769 the Wilton factory was destroyed by fire, and there are, so far as is known, no surviving records.

It might be possible to add to our knowledge of an obscure period of Wilton history (say, roughly, 1720–60) if technical information about machinery and equipment came to light. It is a fair assumption that our Frenchman brought with him experience of the pile-cutting process already in use at the Savonnerie in Paris and soon to become the hall-mark of Wilton carpeting, and that he helped to introduce it. If we could discover when and where the pile-cutting equipment was made, we should be on surer ground in the matter of dates, and that alone would be a great step forward. It could have been quite simple and made locally by hand, in which case nothing is now likely to be discovered. But it might have been machine-made, perhaps as far away as Sheffield, and in that case it may be that records still survive. Can any readers of *Industrial Archaeology* suggest a possible source of information?

'Iron Mad' Wilkinson's Boat

Mr Charles Clarke, Lindley House, Lindley, Nuneaton, Warwickshire, has brought to our notice a reference in *The Tarns of Lakeland* by W. Heaton Cooper (Frederick Warne & Co, 1960) which links together Helton Tarn and John Wilkinson, the iron-mad ironmaster. Wilkinson had local connections with this part of the Lake District and is believed to have launched the first iron boat on Helton Tarn. According to tradition this boat still lies there in deep mud, but whether in fact this is true is not known for certain. But, says Mr Clarke, in view of the present comments on the *Great Britain* one feels that something further ought to be done to investigate the existence of Wilkinson's boat.

Print taken from an old block found at Jennings Pottery c 1870. Line engravings often form a useful source for the industrial archaeologist

Pictorial Sources

Following Kenneth Lindley's article 'Wood Engraving & Industrial History' (vol 5 no 4), Mr C. J. Hunt, The Library, University of Manchester, has written to us as follows:

Last year I wrote to a number of record offices, libraries and museums to enquire whether they had any nineteenth-century photographs of the lead-mining industry of the Northern Pennines. I had no success, perhaps not surprisingly, although I knew that a photographic survey of surface features in the area had been commissioned by a mining agent as early as 1860. What I found more surprising was the absence of any national policy towards the searching out, preservation and indexing of *old* photographs of industrial scenes.

The value of 'pictures' to the industrial archaeologist is so obvious as not to need stressing. For example, the magnificent series of photographs in the Leicester Museum showing the building of the Great Central Railway in the 1890s is a more vivid portrayal of what happened than any documentary evidence. Such a series of photographs as this is rare, if not unique, but isolated prints dating from the last century of industrial structures and of the people connected with them do survive in comparatively large numbers. These prints may appear in published material such as guide books and Blue Books, and in semi-published brochures and books of views. They may be in family albums or the archives of firms and public and local authorities or they may be buried in the collections of plates, negatives and prints by famous and forgotten photographers. But the economic historian or industrial archaeologist seeking visual source material must do a considerable amount of searching and also be very lucky to discover whether old photographs of a particular industry or a particular geographical location survive, and if so, where. Some record offices and public libraries have built up good subject/place indexes to their local pictorial collections, but many depositories have no such indexes, and there is certainly no attempt on a national scale to produce a union list of the photographs held by the various institutions. Even a guide listing these institutions, with an indication of the nature and scope of their holdings, would be a tremendous help, and is something that could be compiled with relatively little effort.

It would appear that there is a real bibliographical void here—a void that commercial undertakings are attempting, not very successfully but maybe profitably, to fill. The scale of the indexing problem is large, but not insurmountably so, particularly with the help of the mechanised indexing systems being developed today. The real problem is the persuasion of the institutions concerned that there is a demand for such a service and that public money in one form or another might legitimately be spent in providing it. I have emphasised photographs here, but they are, of course, only one pictorial form. Oil and water-colour paintings, prints and drawings have long been important sources for historians of other disciplines than fine art. Yet there has been no effort on the part of art galleries to index their collections in a way useful to anyone other than art historians. Even the catalogue (reviewed in vol 6 no 1) of the splendid exhibition *Art and the Industrial Revolution* (shown in the Manchester City Art Gallery 31 May to 14 July 1968) is arranged by artist, the only index being of individuals and institutions who had lent exhibits.

The purpose of this note is to enquire of readers of *Industrial Archaeology* whether they agree that the present situation with regard to pictorial sources of information for industrial archaeology is unsatisfactory and, more important, whether there are any practical ways of improving matters. Individuals (and subsequently publishers) could do something by indexing such rich sources of pictures as the *Illustrated London News* and the *Graphic*. But the organisation of the larger task of persuading institutions to index adequately their pictorial holdings and the construction of a national index must be a job for a national body.

A selection of the Grand Central Railway photographs is reproduced in the Leicester Museum booklet—*The Last Main Line* (Leicester, 1963), ed R. D. Abbott, photographs by S. W. A. Newton.

The industrial archaeologist wishing to become acquainted with the scope of the pictorial material available can start by looking in two surveys of the field: F. D. Klingender, *Art and the Industrial Revolution* (London, 1947); 2nd edn, ed Sir Arthur Elton (London, 1968). W. H. Chaloner & A. E. Musson, *Industry and technology*. 'A Visual History of Modern Britain' series (London, 1963). Neither of these two excellent works sets out to record comprehensively all sources of illustration.

Buckinghamshire Restoration

Notes and News for August 1968 contained details of a watermill restoration at Ford End Farm, Ivinghoe, Buckinghamshire, and Mr K. A. Larking, 23 Brampton Rise, Dunstable, who has made a special study of the mill, has sent us some fine photographs of the building and its associated features. The existing mill dates from the late eighteenth century, although there has undoubtedly been one on the site since medieval times. It is a three-storey wooden structure on brick foundations with an interesting mansard roof and is built into an earthen bank which also serves as a dam for the mill pond, a common feature in areas where water supply is seasonal. The overshot, wooden and cast-iron waterwheel is located in a lean-to at the side of the building. Repair work during restoration was

Ford End Mill, showing the extensive mill-pond and lean-to enclosing waterwheel

Mill tools from Ford End

Meal bins and chain hoist, Ford End

Millstone casing and hopper, Ford End Mill

carried out on the wheel by a local carpenter, while members of the Pitstone Local History Society fitted a new sluice-gate and overhauled the grinding equipment. As the accompanying photographs clearly show, a most worthwhile project has restored to working life a fine country mill.

Wiltshire Conference

The first steps towards the establishment of a society for IA in Wiltshire were taken at a conference in Devizes in December 1968. The conference, sponsored by Wiltshire Archaeological Society and the Salisbury & South Wiltshire IA Society, aimed at encouraging a closer liaison between county organisations interested in industrial archaeology and also in achieving greater publicity for the urgent task of recording and possibly preserving Wiltshire's industrial relics. Representatives from Wiltshire Archaeological Society, Devizes and Salisbury Museums, Wiltshire County Council, Ministry of Public Building & Works, Society for Preservation of Ancient Buildings and other organisations expressed support and interest. An ad hoc committee to consider the establishment of a society was appointed and anyone interested should contact Mr D. A. E. Cross, Wyndham, Shrewton, Wilts.

Business Archives Council

The Business Archives Council, now under the chairmanship of Professor Peter Mathias, has recently appointed Richard Storey (whose work will be familiar to readers of *Industrial Archaeology*) as editor of its twice-yearly Bulletin *Business Archives*, which is published in June and December. The council's objects are to preserve business archives and encourage interest in business history. *Business Archives* records the council's activities, but also aims to record other relevant developments in the fields of business archives and history, and to publish shorter papers on these and other sources of business history. From time to time it is hoped to include in *Business Archives* material of direct relevance to the industrial archaeologist. Those interested in learning more about the Business Archives Council, membership of which is open to individuals as well as institutions, are invited to write to its office at Ormond House, 63 Queen Victoria Street, London, EC4.

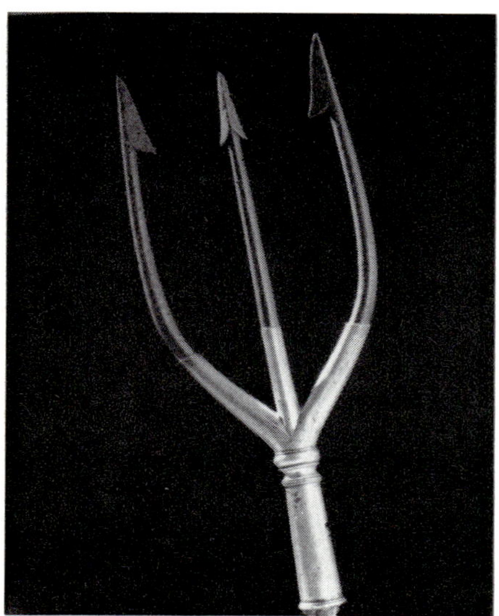

The trident from a public house in Cowes, Isle of Wight

Scheduling First

Fred, a Yorkshire terrier, whose owner lives at Hillam Hall, Monk Fryston, near Selby, Yorkshire, is probably the best-housed dog in Britain. He is certainly tenant of the most stately dog home in the country. His early nineteenth-century kennel has a gabled roof and a Gothic doorway, and has been listed by the Ministry of Housing & Local Government as a building of historic interest.

Neil Cossons Moves

Readers will welcome the news that Neil Cossons, former Technical Editor of *Industrial Archaeology*, has been appointed Deputy Director of Liverpool City Museums. For the past four years Neil has been Curator in Technology at the Bristol City Museum and has been responsible for building up the very remarkable collection of technological and industrial material at Upper York Street. Neil Cossons has also been a vigorous pioneer of the study of industrial archaeology in the Bristol region and has worked for Bristol IA Society (of which he was Secretary) since its formation, with great enterprise and enthusiasm.

A Trident

Mr G. D. Peach, 48 Primrose Gardens, London, NW3, writes as follows:

I wonder if readers of *Industrial Archaeology* can identify and possibly explain the use of this trident (illustrated) found under the floorboards of a public house in Cowes, Isle of Wight? The item has since been hanging on the wall of the pub for a number of years and is polished regularly, which accounts for the obvious shine! The prongs are made of iron or steel and the shoulder is made of brass. The haft is also of brass but has copper beaten into it. I have taken the trident to the British Museum and sent photographs to the Victoria & Albert Museum and Museum of English Rural Life. The V & A thinks it was a fishing spear, but the others disagree. I would be most grateful for any further information.

Dating Worcester Porcelain

For nearly a year Mr Henry Sandon, curator of the Dyson Perrins Museum of Worcester, has been organising, supervising and taking part in an archaeological dig on the Warmstry House site where the original factory of the Worcester Royal Porcelain Company was founded in 1751. About one million fragments of pottery, as well as kiln furniture, moulds and tools have been unearthed, all of which greatly add to knowledge of pottery manufacture in the mid-eighteenth century. Although there is a great deal of work to be done on the finds yet, it is already obvious that much eighteenth-century pottery, whose origin was in doubt, was made at Worcester and nowhere else. Marks long thought to belong to other factories can now be proved to be from Worcester. Because of the careful recording of each phase of the dig, and of the stratified levels, definite dating of fragments is possible. Study of the glazed and unglazed pieces and of the tools found has also thrown light on the detail of the pottery craft. Preliminary cleaning and analysis of this important material has been completed and an exhibition of these unique finds has been staged at the Dyson Perrins Museum.

Littleborough, Lancs

Returning to this area after fourteen years, Mr Keith Parry, 5 Hare Hill Road, Littleborough, is surprised by the wealth of early industrial remains and works still intact. His surprise is, however, only exceeded by his amazement at the lack of awareness

Old Townhouse Mill, Littleborough, formerly water-powered

Lydgate Mill, Littleborough, situated near the old Blackstonedge turnpike road

shown locally. There are ten scheduled buildings and roughly the same number which failed to get listed, one of which was a superb three-storey weaver's house. Nearly the whole distance of 300 yd to the main square is solid pre-Victorian property, but the square has only three Victorian frontages and one modern shop-front. The rest is eighteenth-century and includes three 'mint' cottages, two fine inns and a fascinating group of early nineteenth-century shops. Even the church is unusual, a spartan Gothic structure with a gallery supported by cast-iron columns. The centre of the town is comparatively new, although only a handful of buildings are post-1900.

Most of the industrial features are higher up the hills where the whole range of the industrial revolution can be traced. The Fothergill and Harvey mills date from the very beginning and Shore mills are of similar date. Lydgate mill, which incorporates a much-altered farmhouse and is located high on Blackstonedge, was used by Granada TV for *Inheritance*. Old Townhouse is an interesting three-storey mill which was water-powered and never converted to steam. Littleborough also has the works for the Manchester & Leeds Railway (Summit Tunnel) and the Rochdale Canal. Mr Parry thinks that 'a fairly isolated area like this offers examples of industrial archaeology in "original" condition' and is most anxious to see this heritage recorded before it vanishes completely.

The Cow & Gate Milk Factory, Wincanton

The Cow & Gate Co began operations in Wincanton in 1890, in a small factory at the back of the White Horse Hotel. The business expanded rapidly and in 1893 a new factory was built to the south of the town. By 1916 demand for the company's products, especially its Infant Milk Foods, had grown to such an extent, writes Graham Higgins, that an old roller-skating rink was bought and converted into a packing department. The old factory was demolished in 1932 and a new creamery built on the site. In 1936 this was extended to include the packing department.

Cow & Gate was a most faithful customer of the Somerset & Dorset Railway, which closed in 1966. The Cow & Gate premises were adjacent to the railway and a siding took milk wagons directly into the factory. The track has now been removed, but the site of the old lines can still be clearly seen, as a reminder of the original reason for choosing this site for the factory.

Forthcoming Conferences 1969

A one-day conference, to which representatives of industrial archaeology societies will be invited, is being organised jointly by the CBA and the Bath Conference Steering Committee. It will be held on Saturday, 11 October 1969, with the aim of considering closer integration with the CBA. The 1969 Bath Conference will itself be held from 31 October to 2 November 1969.

International Exhibition

Sussex IA Study Group accepted an offer to exhibit industrial archaeology at the fourth Franco-British Industrial Exhibition held in Brighton from 7 to 15 September 1968. Here the group occupied a complete stand, which created a great deal of interest. Mr K. C. Leslie, Hon Secretary of the group, says that it gave them a tremendous opportunity to present industrial archaeology to a wide cross-section of the public, including engineers and industrialists who so much need to be approached about the claims and interests of the study. Although the French were interested, writes Mr Leslie, they did not seem to understand what the subject was about, but a most useful bi-lingual handout prepared by the group helped to put them in the picture. The Sussex Group have been asked if they would be interested in taking their display to France during this year, and certainly must have set a precedent by being probably the first to present industrial archaeology at a trade fair.

Welsh Cornish Engine Restored

The good work of the Industrial Steam Preservation Group (formerly the Hodbarrow Preservation Group) extended during last winter to the care and maintenance of the only surviving Cornish engine in Wales at the Dorothea slate quarries, Tal-y-sarn near Caernarvon. Mr C. D. Topp, chairman of the preservation group, writes that this Holmans engine dates from 1904 and is not only the last in Wales, but also one of the last big, truly Cornish engines to be built. The engine has a cylinder diameter of 68 in and is installed in a three-storey, slate engine house.

The overall condition of the engine is not

Horse-gin at Patching, near Arundel, Sussex (from Sussex IA Study Group Newsletter 2). See Local Society Publications: A Critique, *p 188*

bad, says Mr Topp, for the building has been used to house electric pumps which operate on the same shaft. The brightwork is very tarnished in places, the paint on the house and engine valve-boxes needs replacement and one of the safety governors has fallen away and been damaged. The engine was last used c 1958, when it was stopped because of the state of the boilers. The boilerhouse has fallen into disrepair and it is proposed to remove what little remains of its roof and tidy it up until something more permanent can be done.

Mr Topp, Gurney House, Leazes Terrace, Newcastle-upon-Tyne 1, will be especially glad to hear from industrial archaeologists in North Wales who would be willing to continue the work of refurbishing this fine old engine. The Industrial Steam Preservation Group hopes to diversify its activities to other aspects of preservation work in the future.

Greater London

A Greater London Industrial Archaeology Society has been formed. It will carry on the good work started by the Thames Basin Archaeological Observers' Group in the field of industrial archaeology. The new society aims to co-ordinate the work of individuals and groups, and produce a regular bulletin keeping members informed of activities in the region. It hopes too to prevent duplication of effort, to direct attention to areas of priority, and present a considered and informed approach to industry and local authorities in matters of preservation. The Thames Basin Group has published a most interesting booklet entitled *Industrial Monuments of Greater London*, which is available from Paul Carter, 20 Chestnut Grove, Sudbury, Wembley, Middlesex, at 7s 6d plus postage.

Layout Planning

Richard Muther & Associates, Consultants in Industrial Management, 6155 Oak Street, Kansas City, Mo 64113, have written telling us of their interest in the history of layout planning as it relates to early industrial operations. This topic seems an extremely interesting one particularly for the industrial archaeologist, who is so much concerned with the physical arrangements of industrial works and plant. Perhaps interested readers might care to take up this line of enquiry in their own area.

Beam engine and engine house, Dorothea slate quarries, near Caernarvon

Cambridge WEA Summer School

The fifty-fifth Summer School held at King's College from 19 July to 2 August 1969 includes a course on industrial archaeology, which will be concerned with two particular themes—railways and windmills. The first, including such aspects as earthworks, stations and other buildings, urban growth, industrial siting and the visible remains of early history and operation will afford numerous insights and starting points for further development. The second will permit more detailed study of a single aspect of the subject. Visits to local sites will be an integral part of the course. Further details of this course can be obtained from The Secretary, Stuart House, Mill Lane, Cambridge CB2 1RY.

New Home for Scottish Railway Records

The British Railways Board has handed over to the Secretary of State for Scotland the official documents, minute books and other historical records concerning the former railway companies in Scotland. These will be lodged in the Scottish Record Office, HM General Register House, Edinburgh—just over 100 yd from their present home at 23 Waterloo Place, Edinburgh.

The transfer, which took place in January 1969, had been arranged with the consent of the Minister of Transport under the provisions of the Transport Act, 1968.

Several thousand documents are involved, covering the period from 1840 to 1948—the year of railway nationalisation. They include official records of the former North British, Caledonian, Highland, Glasgow & South Western, Great North of Scotland, and other Scottish companies, and of the LMSR and LNER in Scotland; groups of records on railway subjects; and a specialised library and sets of periodicals. The collection contains a vast amount of valuable information for railway historians and also for social and economic historians.

Stereo Photography

Neal DuBrey of Port Elizabeth, South Africa, has written to us to say that he is applying his hobby of stereo-photography to industrial archaeology in two ways—by preserving existing examples in vivid modern colour stereo, and by collecting old stereo 'cards' many of which are most fascinating. This enables him to examine sites at his leisure 'in the solid, since no planar photograph can approach such realism'.

G & SWR Relic

One reader has sent his explanation of the 'unknown object' illustrated on p 308 of *Notes and News* (vol 5 no 3). Mr S. R. Arnold, Norwood, May Hill, Ramsey, Isle of Man, says that the object is a coal-levelling trolley. Mr Arnold says East Lothian coal had to be stacked and levelled in 2-ft layers, otherwise fire from spontaneous combustion would result. Expensive ventilating ducts could be laid in the running shed or coal dump but usually running sheds had four or five of the trolleys. Any other explanations?

M. J. T. LEWIS, W. N. SLATCHER
AND P. N. JARVIS

Flashlocks on English Waterways

A Survey

THE flashlock is a thing of the past, but much of the river commerce of England once depended on navigations which employed the device. Whereas a pound lock has two sets of gates to pass boats from one level of a waterway to another, a flashlock has but one. Only a century ago there were still about sixty-three examples in use, fifty years ago about twenty-one. Now there is none.

This paper presents the results of our survey of flashlock remains. A list that we drew up of sites where remains might reasonably be expected ended in the surprisingly large total of seventy-three, each of which has been inspected from the bank and a fair number from the water. Everything measurable has been measured, although only a selection of drawings can be published here. Of the fifty flashlocks where some trace survives, only four retain the major part of their gates, but twenty-four have their masonry or brickwork more or less intact. We hope, but cannot guarantee, that the survey is complete. It is, however, a survey only, not a history of flashlocks. To assist in understanding them, we have described their working and, briefly, the history of each navigation involved; but the very extensive fieldwork has precluded much documentary research.

There were several functions that a flashlock could perform. These were to help to ease vessels over shallows below by releasing a 'flash' or flush of water, enable boats to pass through a weir, and assist them through the reach above. Although the release of flashes was an integral part of the system, it had its drawbacks. The resulting torrents might provide motive power for boats passing downstream, but they proved a hindrance to upward traffic and by eroding the banks they often worsened the shoals and reduced the already inadequate depth.

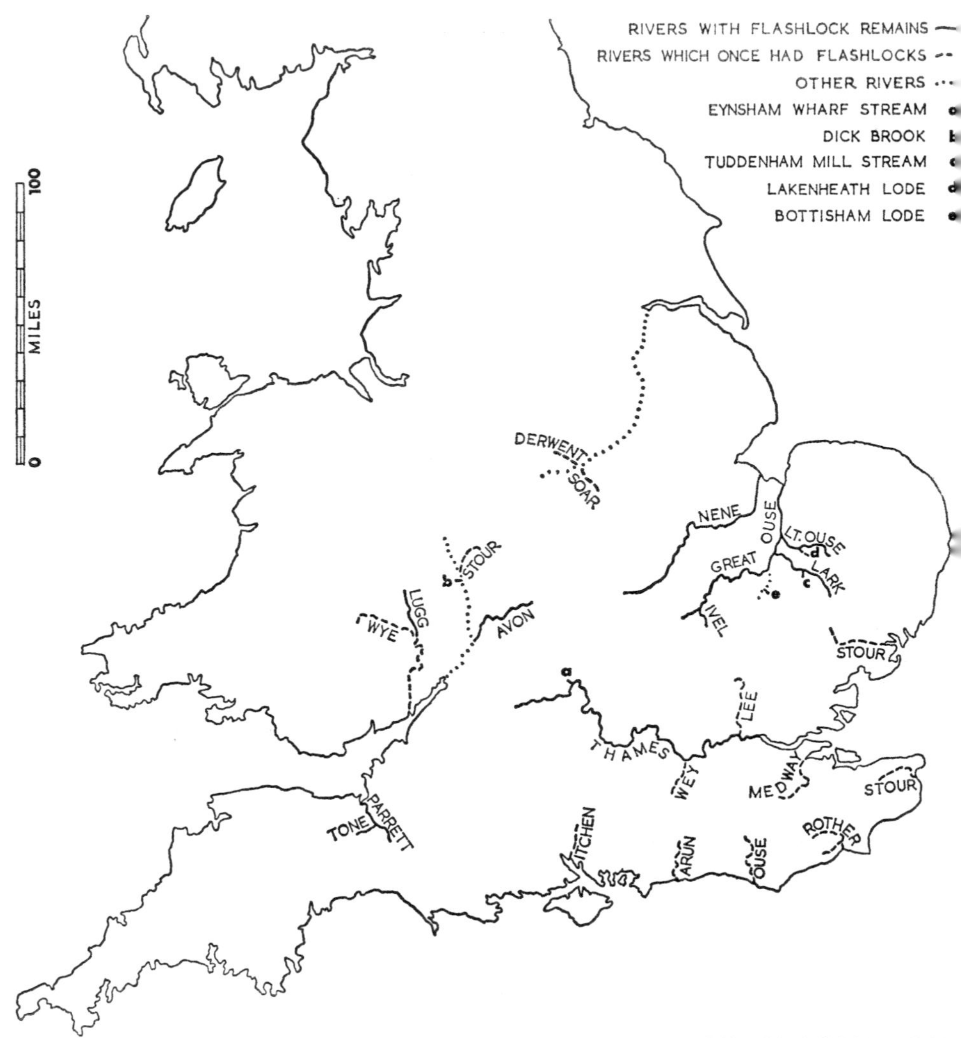

DISTRIBUTION OF FLASHLOCK

Fig 1

The wastage of water at each operation, moreover, was enormous, and boats tended to congregate in groups to pass the flashlocks, in order to save water. Even so, it often ran short in dry seasons, which led to disputes between the various users. With flashes, a river could rarely be worked economically and it is no surprise that, wherever traffic justified it, the pound lock and a stable river regime ultimately prevailed. On the Thames and other rivers so improved, little survives of the flashlocks. In contrast, most remains are to be seen on the lesser Fenland rivers, where the mid-nineteenth-century structures lasted until the demise of the navigations.

Flashlocks were used in three main areas of the country—the Thames basin, some tributaries of the Severn, and the rivers fringing the Fens. Though their use had occasionally been suggested there, they are noticeably absent from the Yorkshire Ouse basin and from other northern rivers. There was none in Scotland nor in Wales, and the few in Ireland we have not investigated. Regional variations are reflected in the terms used to describe these gates. Though 'flashlock' is a name generally applicable, it is particularly used of the primitive type best known on the Thames, where 'flashweir' and simply 'weir' were equally common. The later type with gates is sometimes called 'navigation weir' or 'navigation gates', while 'watergate' and 'halflock' appear in the West Country and West Midlands. In East Anglia the normal term is 'staunch' or 'stanch'. We have distinguished two basic breeds of flashlock. One, the beam and paddle type, was usually kept closed; the other, which we call by the generic name of staunch, normally stood open, and embraced three different types of gate.

Beam and Paddle Weirs

The principle of the flashlock dates back to the middle ages, the earliest and most elementary type being usually the result of a compromise between the navigation and milling interests on a river. Since time immemorial, water for mills had been impounded by weirs thrown across the river, and some device was needed to pass boats through these weirs if navigation was to be carried on. In between mills, too, weirs were often necessary to bank up the water deeply enough for boats to surmount shallows. So a portion of the weir was made removable, with a wooden cill across the river bed and a horizontal swinging beam directly over the cill above water level. At intervals against these timbers were set vertical baulks or 'rimers', against which in turn were set square planks with handles attached—the paddles—to hold up the water. The top ends of the paddle and rimer handles were kept under control by a detachable horizontal guide bar, and the main beam often had a handrail attached. The rest of the weir was a fixture, where only the paddles could be moved to regulate the flow of water. In early days the materials and workmanship were crude, but in the end the structures had become quite neat, even if complicated. Timber cladding gave way to stone abutment walls, and wooden pivots for the beams to cast-iron ones.

When such a flashlock was to be opened for boats, the guide bar, the paddles and the rimers were removed individually, and then the main beam was swung horizontally on its pivot to open the gap. A great cascade of water resulted. Boats going down simply shot the rapids, but those going up had to wait for the worst of the torrent to subside before being hauled through the lock by brute force assisted by fixed winches. They then waited again until the weir was closed and the river above had risen enough to allow them to proceed. In dry seasons when there was little water in the river and the full fall of the weir, up to 4 ft, was employed, there might be a wait of several days before the reach above was sufficiently full. On the other hand, in time of flood when the fall was negligible and the water banked up from below, the gate might be left open.

Locks of this type were once to be found on many rivers. The best known, and the longest lived, were those on the Thames, where the last survival was demolished only in 1937. Here, the few remains are disappointing, but a nearly complete example can be seen on Eynsham Wharf Stream. In many cases these flashlocks were early replaced by pound locks, for they were highly dangerous, and wasteful of time and water. For the latter reason they were the cause of much acrimony between boatmen and millers. The millers often had prior rights to river water, and frequently delayed boatmen for weeks when water was short, before allowing them to open the weirs and proceed. Hence, it is said, the bad language traditionally ascribed to bargees.

Staunches

More sophisticated flashlocks appeared in course of time. Rarely, as at Thorney on the Parrett, they were built alongside watermills; but at such places the pound lock became the norm. In between mills, however, pound locks were sometimes undesirable because they reduced the length of river on which the mill next downstream depended for its supply, and because, by permanently banking the water up the tailrace of the mill above, they reduced the efficacy and power of its wheel. So single gates were installed in these places, which, normally standing open, were closed only when boats had to pass. The *raison d'être* of many surviving staunches can be traced to this consideration. Elsewhere, a staunch served to raise the river above it to carry boats over a ford—Tempsford on the Great Ouse is a good example. Here too the gates normally stood open, leaving the ford shallow for traffic on the Great North Road. Indeed the staunch was generally used only by evening or night, when there were few road travellers to be incommoded.

With these locks, navigation was still more tedious than with the old weirs. The whole reach of water between two staunches had to be treated as one huge pound lock. When boats were going down, a man was sent ahead to shut the next staunch and allow enough water to build up for the boats to reach it. The man went on again to close the next staunch down, the weir was opened, and the boats waited above the staunch until the reaches above and below were level and the gate could be opened to let the boats through. The same thing in reverse happened on the way up. As reaches were anything up to 4 miles long, all this took time. If traffic were light and water plentiful, this delay mattered less, but unless staunches were demanded by the presence of mills or fords, they were rarely to be found on rivers once the pound lock had been introduced. Where such staunches did exist—on the Little Ouse for example—the reason was no doubt simply one of relative cost. On canals, with a generally precarious water supply, flashlocks were unknown.

Gate Staunches

Apart from the beam and paddle type, staunches fall into three categories. By far the largest group was formed by those with an ordinary gate or pair of mitre gates like those on any pound lock. This design goes back to the seventeenth century if not before, and continued in favour to the very end—the last one was built in Suffolk c 1890, and the last to be usable was demolished on the Warwick Avon in 1961. At these staunches, a short wall was built against each bank, and the river was generally divided into two or three channels by small artificial islands. Across one channel was the staunch; across the others the weirs. Sometimes the weir might be on the river proper, the staunch by itself on an artificial cut; and on small streams such as the upper Lark the weir was dispensed with altogether, surplus water simply flowing over the gates. The fall of water at a staunch varied with the season. In average conditions it was usually within the range of 2–4 ft, though Thorney halflock on the Parrett was quite exceptional with a 10-ft fall, and involved a chamber with a top cill, like a pound lock (see plate on p 226).

In most cases the walls of a staunch were roughly parallel for 20 or 30 ft, splaying out at the ends in wing walls that merged with the natural bank, although a few western rivers had much longer 'chambers', up to 100 ft or more. The height of the walls depended on the draught of the navigation and the drop in water level. The water has usually proved too deep, muddy or swift to allow inspection of the floors, but they were probably more often planked on a timber framework than solid masonry or brick. Single-leaf gates were found only on the Avon; otherwise they were double-leafed, meeting in a mitre at a sharp angle. Where it can be checked from the mitre-cill against which the gates closed, this angle was commonly 90 degrees, as in many early river locks but in contrast to the 120 or 130 degrees of canals and more modern river locks.

The gates were mostly hung in the usual way, the heel-post (the vertical member nearest the lock wall) pivoting in a socket on the floor and held at the top in an iron anchor or loop set into the lock wall. Between pivot and anchor, the heel-post rotated in a hollow quoin, usually of wood but occasionally carved in the masonry. The Lark and Ivel, however, were unusual in perpetuating the pintle hinge, like any farm-gate hinge but several sizes larger. In this, as in other matters, they resembled the Suffolk Stour, which likewise once had many staunches. Another similarity between the Lark and the Stour was the use of the stride, or horizontal beam, across the lock carried by the very tall gateposts some 7 or 8 ft above the water. The purpose of these strides would appear to be more to resist lateral thrusts from the soil or the gates than, as Thacker suggests, to prevent boats entering the locks with sails set. On the Lark and Tuddenham Mill Stream there were strides over staunches, to which Thacker's explanation is not fully applicable (see plate on p 229).

The Tone was one of the few rivers where the gates were opened and closed with balance beams alone. Winches mounted on the lockside were the norm; indeed they were the only means of opening gates against a head of water before a level was made. They were to be found alone on many rivers, though Woodston on the Nene had balance beams as well, and the Avon watergates also had short beams weighted with stones. To open the Lark and the Ivel gates (again like the Suffolk Stour), one had to lean perilously over the water and pull a chain linking the mitre-post to the wall. Gates normally opened into recesses in the wall, either straight or curved. It is not clear whether a curved recess implies a curved gate.

Water was emptied from the higher reach by opening paddles in the gates or, much more quickly, by lowering the weir. The Avon gates once had four paddles apiece, Woodston on the Nene two. Elsewhere, one may find small secondary recesses inside the gate recesses, to accommodate single projecting paddles. But paddles were not universal, for the Great Ouse gates were innocent of them. Only one set of staunch gate paddles survives, on Tuddenham Mill Stream, with ordinary rack and pinion gear for raising them (see plate on p 230).

Guillotine Staunches

Much less common than the ordinary gate was the shutter or clow raised vertically out of the water by chains. Its use in flashlocks was confined, it seems, to East Anglia: the Little Ouse, Nene, and Bottisham Lode. On the first of these, two transverse rollers were mounted on two massive wooden uprights fixed into the staunch walls. The lower roller was rotated by a large spoked wheel, up to 13 ft in diameter, fixed to one end, or by crank handle and a train of gears. At the other end, it was geared to the upper roller which wound up two chains and the gate attached to them. The gate was guided vertically in slots adjoining the main uprights. The whole contraption had to be lofty to raise the gate high enough for boats to pass under. A light footbridge allowed access to the weir and operation of the big wheel. Remains on the Little Ouse are now negligible, but an almost identical staunch, complete except for the big wheel, survives in sad decay on Bottisham Lode. The Nene staunches were originally of much the same design, but were raised by crank handle, had only one roller, and were later rebuilt with steel frames. Unlike mitre gates, guillotine gates could be opened against a head of water, and down-going boats could shoot the rapids (see plates on pp 231 & 232).

Plank Staunches

This, the simplest version of the staunch, had been known in China for a thousand years, and was not uncommon in France. It is identical with the stop-plank arrangement regularly used to dam off pound locks for repair: a vertical slot in each wall, into which planks are dropped horizontally one on top of another to form a simple dam. To refill the waterway below, the top plank is removed, the water cascades over, and when the levels are equal, and the pressure released, the other planks are lifted. Apparently no staunches were built to this design; but several on the Lark were adapted to it in the reconstruction of 1890, the gateposts simply being replaced by slots (see p. 228).

. . . . .

The survey has included flashlocks only, that is to say single barriers which enabled boats to pass from one level of a waterway to another. We have, therefore, excluded single tidal gates which hold up the water at low tide, sea doors that keep out the tide at high water, and single stop and flood gates. Although Dutton Stop at the western end of the Trent & Mersey Canal is to all intents and purposes operated as a gate staunch, it is merely the relic of a pound lock. The clows on the underground canal at Worsley near Manchester also fall outside our scope, for their purpose was to provide motive power for the boats. They banked the water up only a few inches, and being opened on the approach of a boat produced enough current to waft it along.[1]

The influence of flashlocks on the early development of pound locks can perhaps be seen in the turf-sided locks on the Kennet and the Wey, which treat the chamber as a section of river; in the odd circular and diamond-shaped chambers on the Avon; and in the former use of paddles and rimers instead of gates on the Avon and (allegedly) the Ivel. Indeed, the borderline between staunches and pound locks cannot be accurately defined. Two staunches set close together make a pound lock, and we have had to draw an arbitrary distinction. The Lark is the river most involved. The two Mildenhall West staunches were set 360 ft apart, and the two Mill Heath ones 283 ft apart, the 'chamber' between being up to 50 ft wide with unwalled banks. These gates were called staunches when in use, not a lock, and their difference from the standard Lark pound lock, a rectangular brick chamber 88 ft × 11 ft 6 in, is our justification in counting them as staunches. Lackford lock, with a long crescent-shaped chamber, may well have begun life as two staunches, but since the chamber is walled we have considered it as a pound lock. One has to draw a line somewhere, but Mildenhall staunch illustrates how essentially meaningless such a line is, for it was converted about 1890 into a pound lock by the addition of lower gates. An irregular and unwalled oval chamber 125 ft long was thus formed, with the staunch itself, untouched, providing the top gates (see plate on p 229).

Another borderline case can be found in the occasional double locks on rivers, where an extra gate is added below the pound lock for use if water is so low that boats cannot get over the cill of the middle gates. The resulting lower chamber is sometimes long and curved, as at Thames lock on the Wey and Stamford Bridge on the Yorkshire Derwent. These lower gates thus have much in common with staunches, but are perhaps best considered as part of a staircase or two-rise lock.

What of the future? Though many flashlocks will no doubt moulder peacefully for years, more are at the mercy of floods, river authorities and even restoration societies, as the case of the lower Avon shows. In most instances, preservation would be quite unrealistic; but it is to be hoped that when the rest of the Great Ouse is reopened, Castle Mills staunch will not be swept away. It might also be desirable to safeguard the remains of the upper Eynsham Wharf Stream weir. Bottisham staunch is perhaps too decayed for preservation *in situ*, but its essentials could easily be removed for re-erection in a suitable museum as a memento of an inefficient but long-lived stage in the development of inland navigation.

SURVEY

(Widths of staunches are the minimum, measured inside the masonry)

River Thames[2]

Navigation up to Oxford began in the twelfth century, and flashlocks had appeared by the thirteenth. Many of them, though by no means all, were at mills, consisting simply of movable sections of the weir. The river was later made navigable from Oxford to Cricklade. It is one of the strange facts of waterway history that these primitive, dangerous and wasteful weirs survived so long on a major river. The first three pound locks were built between 1624 and 1632, with a fourth soon after; but it was not until the last thirty years of the eighteenth century that any more appeared: a large series that gradually extended up the river. A few more followed early last century, but the last big batch, above Oxford, was not built until the 1890s. Between 1868 and 1880 all surviving flashweirs were removed, except for four which lasted well into this century: King's, replaced by a new lock in the 1920s; Medley, abolished in 1931; Eynsham, replaced by a lock about the same time; and Hart's, which was removed only in 1937, the last of a long line. King's had a pair of mitre gates; so did Medley for a time. But all the rest were of the classic beam and paddle type, often with wooden walls and therefore leaving no tangible remains behind them, bar the pool that was formed below the weir by erosion. Of about seventy flashlocks that have adorned the Thames, we investigated the sites only of those where the estimable Thacker reported remains in 1910.

Blackford weir (SU 165960). Removed 1869. Now no trace.

Hart's or Eaton weir (SU 246985). On left bank just above modern footbridge, cruciform wrought-iron clamp fixed to top of wooden post, with broken-off cast-iron beam pivot bolted to its centre. No other remains. (See Fig 2.)

Tadpole or Rudge's or Kent's weir (SP 335004). Removed 1869. Now a few shapeless masonry fragments and timber stumps on right bank.

Limbre's or Langley's weir (SP 394012). Removed 1872. Now only c 35 ft of featureless drystone walling on left bank.

Ark weir (SP 437032). Fell into decay in 1850s, gradually collapsed. Curved wall c 30 ft long, partly of very large blocks up to 4 ft 6 in long, partly of small rough masonry, on left bank (illustrated on p 225).

Eynsham or Bolde's weir (SP 444087). No trace—obliterated by lock.

King's weir (SP 480104). No trace—obliterated by modern weir.

Medley or Binsey weir (SP 498074). No sign of navigation weir. Cast-iron cill of fixed weir (in left-hand channel) still visible.

Swiftditch weir (SU 508965). No trace—covered by abutments of modern bridge.

Hurley weir (SU 820843). Although the flashlock was superseded by a pound lock in 1773, the winch used for hauling barges up through the weir still survives, rotten and garlanded with wild vines. The drum, with five of the original six capstan bars, stands 6 ft high, but its base, where the rope was wound, is now buried. The lower bearing is quite invisible, and of the upper only the wooden framework can be seen. The winch stands in private grounds on the left bank, just above the weir end (see Fig 2).

Eynsham Wharf Stream[3]

A small tributary of the Thames just below Eynsham lock (see Fig 2). The shallow half-mile navigation up to Eynsham wharf was assisted by a beam and paddle flashlock built before 1791 some 200 yd above the confluence (SP 446089). Although traffic ceased in 1925, the beam survives (illustrated on p 226), bolted to the stop-post and now supporting a footbridge and handrail alongside. It is not the original, for it dates from 1911 (cost £8 10s). The length is 31 ft, the section increasing from 8½ in × 8 in to 19 in × 17½ in. The pivot consists of a circular convex plate nailed to the top of a post, a similar plate on the underside of the beam, and a pin through their centres. No trace of paddles or rimers remains, though two iron-plated wooden blocks fixed to the upstream edge of the beam may have held the bar that retained the tops of the paddles and rimers. Behind the lock on the right bank is a circular pen of four concrete posts and iron hoops, a cage to prevent loose weir paddles being swept away by floods. The posts are marked OCC—the Oxford Canal Co owned the stream for a century. The limestone walls, patched with brick, are 13 ft 8 in apart.

When the Thames was dredged in 1913, the water level was lowered, and boats could not clear the weir cill. So a second flashlock was installed about 30 yd up from the confluence (SP 448088), the last to be built in the country and, ironically, of the most primitive sort. It cost £105. The curved concrete walls remain, with the cast-iron beam pivot and another paddle pen on the right bank, and two wooden posts (a stop and a rest for the beam end) on the left bank. The width is 14 ft.

EYNSHAM WHARF STREAM
9.7.68
upper flashlock
plan
elevation
WATER LEVEL
0 1 FEET 10
beam pivots
0 1 2 FT
EYNSHAM UPPER 9.7.68
THAMES: HART'S 12.5.68
EYNSHAM LOWER 9.7.68
River Thames: HURLEY WINCH 27.8.68

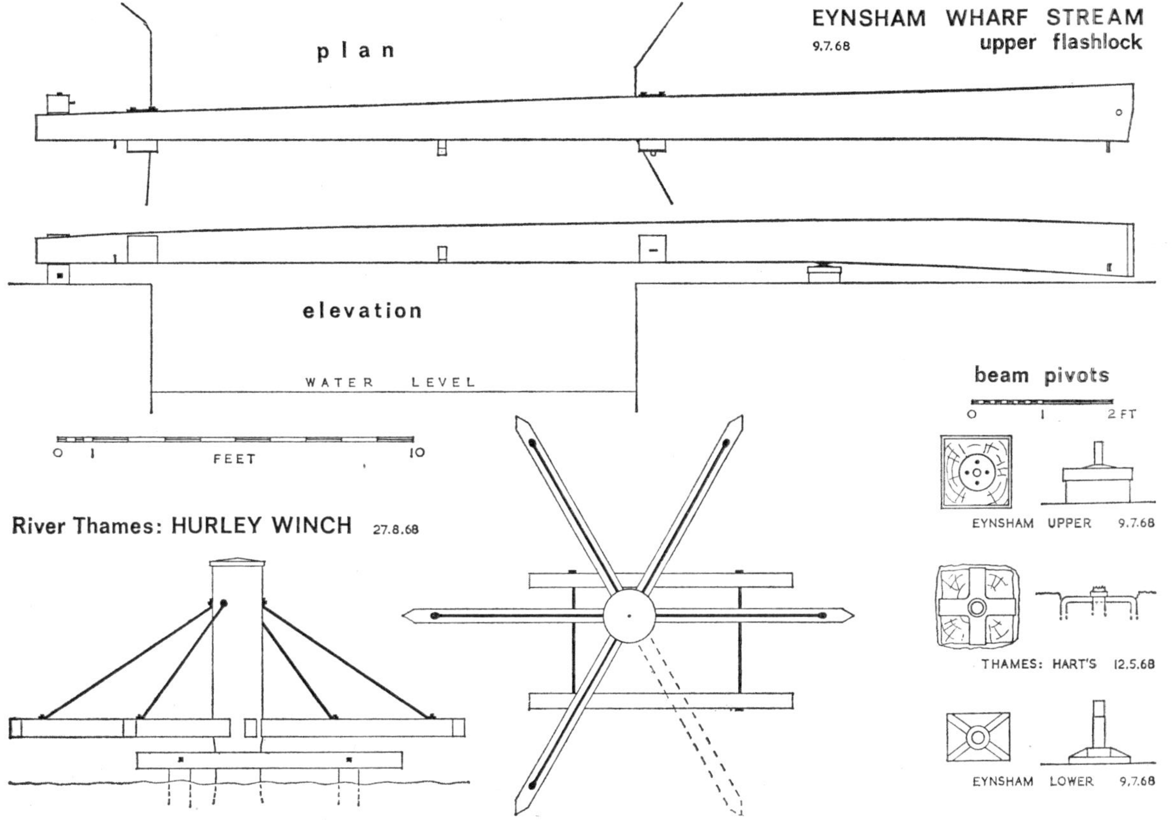

Fig 2

Sussex Ouse

A map of 1724 marks a lock (probably a flashlock) on a small nameless tributary that was navigable up to Maresfield Forge near Shortbridge.[4] It has been out of use for at least a century. The lower part of the stream has been diverted, and an incomprehensible pattern of stakes and timbers in its soggy bed marks the site of the lock (TQ 443207).

Dick Brook[5]

This small stream (see Fig 3) was made navigable for half a mile above its confluence with the Severn three miles below Stourport. As not a single contemporary reference to the navigation has yet been found, we can only deduce its history from archaeological evidence and the little that is recorded of industry in the valley. The results are inconclusive, and much more work needs to be done.

A mile and a half above the Severn, on a tributary of the Dick Brook, stands a charcoal blast furnace which can probably be identified with that built in 1652–3 by Andrew Yarranton (1619–84?). A mile below, on the Dick Brook, is the 'Forge', a site which has had a varied history. In 1713 and 1720 it was a fulling mill, in 1728 and 1739 a paper mill, later in the century a flint mill, around the beginning of the nineteenth century a forge, and finally a bobbin mill. It marks the upper end of navigation on the Brook, which had two gate-type staunches or halflocks. One is some 300 yd, the other about 30 yd, above the Severn. Both are built of large sandstone blocks up to 2 ft 6 in square and 1 ft thick, closely similar to a massive retaining wall between the forge site and the Brook. Previous writers have always ascribed these three features—furnace, forge site and navigation—as a connected scheme to Andrew Yarranton. For this there is no clear evidence. He was, however, an early protagonist of inland waterways, who was responsible from 1655 onwards for much work on the Salwarpe, the Worcestershire Stour (which had several halflocks) and the Warwick Avon, and who produced schemes for many other navigations.

0 10 20 30 40 50 60 70 80 FEET
WASHED OUT
River
Lugg
MORDIFORD HALFLOCK
7.7.68
ANCHOR
LOWER HALFLOCK
27.4.68
Dick Brook
BRICK PATCH
MAINLY BRICK
Dick Brook
UPPER HALFLOCK
27.4.68
1715

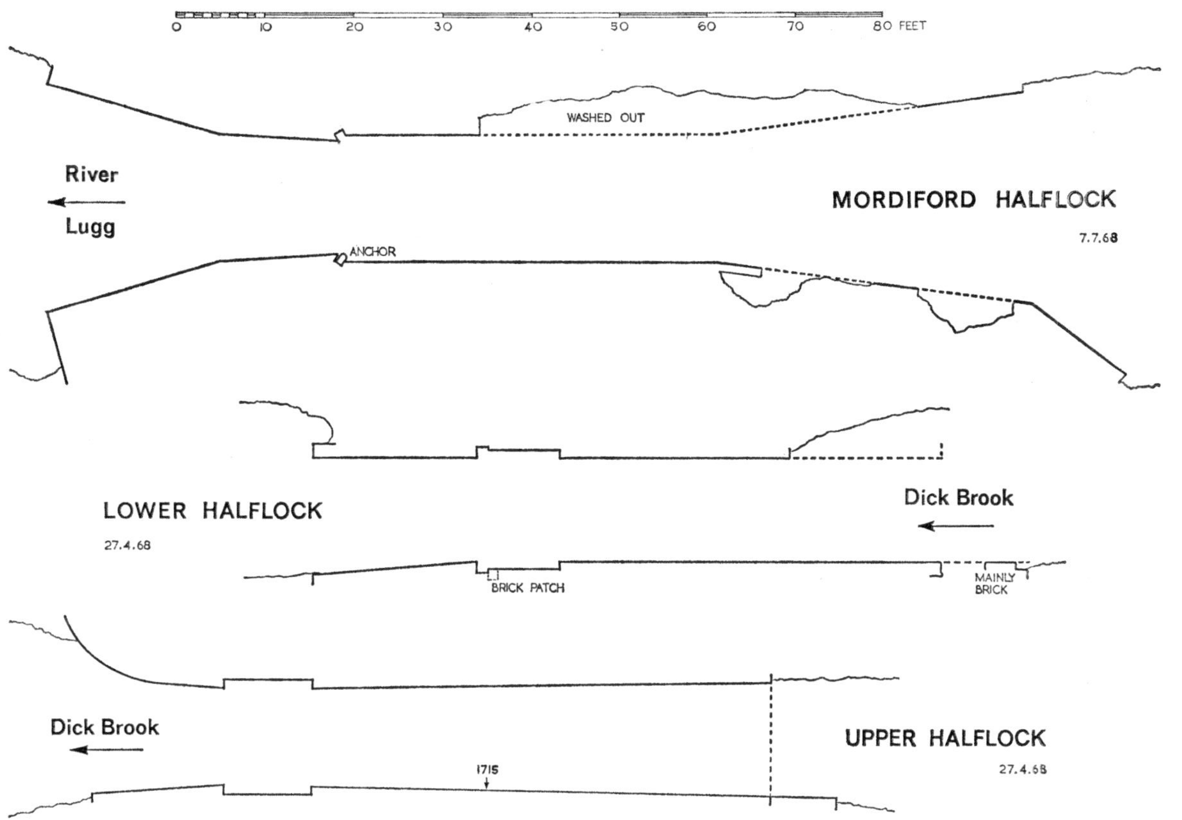

Fig 3

But two features of the upper lock have not previously been noticed: one is the date 1715 carved in crude 1¼-in figures on the face of the top surviving course (illustrated on p 230), and the other is that the stone blocks have been packed with fragments of roof-tiles and pottery saggars to hold them level. This was certainly done at the time of building, or of a very extensive rebuilding, since the sherds are to be found even in the highest joints where they could not have arrived naturally, and some are immovably wedged in. The saggars raise problems. Fragments of them from the forge site certainly antedate the forge and so belong to the eighteenth century. Those from the lock have been used at least once in biscuit firing, and though the flint grinding at the forge site may have been carried out for the Royal Worcester Porcelain Co (founded in 1751), there is no evidence for actual pottery making there, either in the form of wasters or of a kiln. To make confusion confounded, the saggar fragments from the lock have been tentatively dated to the nineteenth century.[6] Finally, the lower lock shows obvious signs of repair. One wall was extended, mainly with rather crude red hand-made brick, and one gate recess was patched with it. It seems most likely that the navigation dates wholly to the eighteenth century, with a long enough life to need repair. A Yarranton origin is not, however, impossible. But Yarranton's furnace lasted only a few years. Thereafter, none of the industries of the forge site, on so small a scale, would warrant a special waterway. The purpose of the navigation remains as obscure as its date.

Lower halflock (SO 812667). No weir. Masonry varies in height from water level to five courses (5 ft). Upper end of right wall washed away since 1929. Left wall 71 ft 6 in long, with later extension at top end largely of brick and much ruined by tree roots. Width of lock 11 ft 6 in. Straight gate recesses with small extra insets for wooden gate-posts.

Upper halflock (SO 810666). No weir. Much more ruinous, especially on right side, though part of left wall still 6 ft high. Date 1715 cut on top course halfway along. Rough masonry floor, ending in straight line at top of lock, and falling perhaps 2 ft over length of lock. Wall

River Thames: a punt shooting Ark Weir in the 1850s

River Thames: flashweir paddles and rimers

Eynsham Wharf Stream: upper flashlock beam, looking downstream. The footbridge is modern

River Parrett: Thorney halflock (left), *with modern weir falling into the chamber*

Great Ouse: Castle Mills staunch (right), *looking downstream, with fixed weir* (left) *and adjustable weir* (centre)

Great Ouse: Castle Mills staunch left gate and arched culvert for chain from winch

(Above), *River Lark: King's staunch, looking upstream. One quoin post is visible under the left of the modern footbridge. Weir, with transverse beam, on right*

(Right), *River Lark: Bury St Edmunds staunch with slot for planks and framework of timber floor. The large stones come from the coping*

(Below), *River Lark: initials T.G.C. 1832 on coping of Mildenhall staunch*

River Lark: Mildenhall staunch from below

River Lark: Mill Heath upper staunch. Note paddle recess on left, and gate-cum-stride post with hinges. Mill Heath lower staunch in distance

Dick Brook: upper halflock, date 1715 on wall

Tuddenham Mill Stream staunch, looking downstream. The footbridge is modern

River Nene: Alwalton staunch on right and weir, looking downstream

River Nene: Stanwick staunch, looking downstream. Demolished 1938
(Courtesy: Welland & Nene River Authority)

Bottisham Lode staunch: rollers, gearing and gate chain

Bottisham Lode staunch, looking downstream. The great spoked wheel was once on the right-hand end of the lower roller

77 ft long, later lengthened upwards on left side only. Butt joint between main wall and extension. Lock 10 ft 9 in wide at minimum. Straight gate recesses. Accurate measurement difficult.

Warwickshire Avon[7]

William Sandys made the river navigable from Tewkesbury to Stratford in 1636–9, building a number of locks, weirs and floodgates. The weirs were apparently flashlocks of beam and paddle type, the floodgates (usually called watergates here) of the gate type. Some were converted to locks later in the century by Yarranton, and more in the 1820s. By 1828 only Bidford (beam and paddle) was left on the upper Avon, and Cropthorne and Pershore (gate) on the lower river. The upper Avon was abandoned in 1875, and the lower Avon fell into bad repair, becoming unnavigable above Pershore during the second war. The upper river still remains derelict, though restoration plans are afoot. The Lower Avon Navigation Trust has reopened the river up to Evesham, sweeping away Pershore and Cropthorne watergates in the process. The basic *raison d'être* of Cropthorne is the ford immediately above, on the site of Jubilee Bridge; that of Pershore is the shallows above the watergate. In both cases there are mills which would have suffered from pound locks.

Bidford weir (SP 098517). Removed 1955. No trace.

Cropthorne watergate (SP 000455). Both weirs, both islands and gate removed 1961. Weir wall on left bank of rough masonry and brick. Masonry watergate wall on right bank, with rebate (but no gate recess as such). Fall once 2 ft.

Pershore watergate (SO 950447). Both weirs, both islands and gate removed 1956. Weir wall on left bank, mostly of blue brick, survives. Only stumps of wing walls of watergate survive on right bank, with coping stones resited in two rough courses to retain bank. Fall once 3 ft.

River Lugg[8] (see Fig 3)

Its history is obscure. Some work, soon destroyed by floods, was done under an Act of 1695, and more under an Act of 1727 which made the river navigable to Leominster. Some time early in the century one Chinn is said to have built halflocks of the gate type, instead of pound locks, and to have absconded with the difference in price. Above Lugg Bridge, navigation was abandoned in the second half of the eighteenth century; below, it continued intermittently until the mid-nineteenth century. Three halflocks still existed, long out of use, in 1906, and there may once have been others between Lugg Bridge and Leominster.

Lugg Bridge halflock (SO 531418). Apparently under a now-demolished wing of mill that spanned the river. Soggy island may mark its site.

Longworth halflock (SO 552240). Island and weir wall gone. On left bank, halflock wall 96 ft long, mostly large masonry with brick at top end. Near lower end, single rebate with hollow quoin carved in coping stone only—wooden quoin underneath has gone. Triangular groove for iron gate anchor. Stones here much displaced by tree roots (see Fig 11).

Mordiford halflock (SO 568374). On leftmost of several channels below bridge—weirs evidently on right-hand streams. Converging rough masonry walls 124 ft long, 12 ft 6 in apart at minimum, much washed away. No gate recesses as such—single angular rebates for wooden hollow quoins. Left one has wrought-iron anchor fastened into wall below coping. (See Fig 3.)

River Tone

After earlier efforts to improve the river, it was made navigable up to Taunton in 1717, with one lock and at least two halflocks. These were increased to four locks and four halflocks by the end of the century. Commercial traffic above Ham ceased about 1878, and up to Ham about 1929. Navigation rights were extinguished in 1967, and flood prevention and bank strengthening works by the Somerset River Authority in the past three years have obliterated the locks. All the halflocks had mitre gates.

Bathpool and *Ham halflocks* (ST 249257 and 290255). Now no trace.

Newbridge halflock (ST 317269). Obliterated by flood sluices now being built (August 1968).

Curry Moor halflock (ST 317269). Barely 100 yd below Newbridge. The same work has removed the whole structure except stumps of wing walls in right bank. On left bank, pile of rubble including cast-iron socket of gate pivot.

River Parrett (see Fig 4)

There has always been a natural navigation, beset with obstacles, from Bridgwater up to Thorney, and it was not until 1836 that the Parrett Navigation Co was incorporated to improve the river. Four locks, one halflock and the artificial Westport Canal were completed in 1840. The upper limit of navigation was probably Kingsbury Episcopi. But in 1875 the locks were abandoned, and traffic ceased on the upper reaches.

Thorney halflock (ST 428227). A most unusual example (illustrated on p 226). On left bank, cornmill and millhouse. River divided into three channels: left one contains high breast wheel, about 14 ft 6 in wide with 11-ft diameter; centre one has sluice weir (sluices fairly modern); right one is halflock. Small limestone masonry, rougher than that of mill (of 1842) and millhouse. Chamber 11 ft 6 in wide, 51 ft 5 in long from top cill to bottom of gate recesses. Chamber ends in stone cill, 5 ft high above lower water level and 5 ft below upper level. Straight gate recesses with small paddle recesses. New footbridge across. With its huge fall of 10 ft and a top cill, it is a compromise between a halflock and a pound lock. In operation, with a boat coming up, the upper river must have been emptied via the weir to the top cill level, and the chamber emptied by the gate paddles. The gates would then be opened to admit the boat, and closed behind it. With weir and gate paddles closed, the river would build up again, filling the chamber by spilling over the top cill. It seems an extraordinary arrangement, since top gates could so easily be provided, but history, and the masonry itself, shows that they never were. It is possible that stop planks were used instead—any trace of the slots would be obliterated by a more recent wall—but in this case would the navigation company have referred to Thorney as a halflock? With the end of traffic and the re-

0
10
20
30
40
50
FEET
8.7.68
THORNEY
HALFLOCK
CILL
MODERN OVERFALL WEIR
WEIR
BRIDGE
SLUICES
River Parrett
ROOF OF
WHEEL HOUSE
PENSTOCKS
BRIDGE
MILL
MILLHOUSE
Little Ouse
CROSSWATER
STAUNCH
2.8.68
River
Ivel
WEIR BEAM
TEMPSFORD
LITTLE
STAUNCH
10.7.68
STONE
ISLAND
BRICK
PLANK
FLOOR

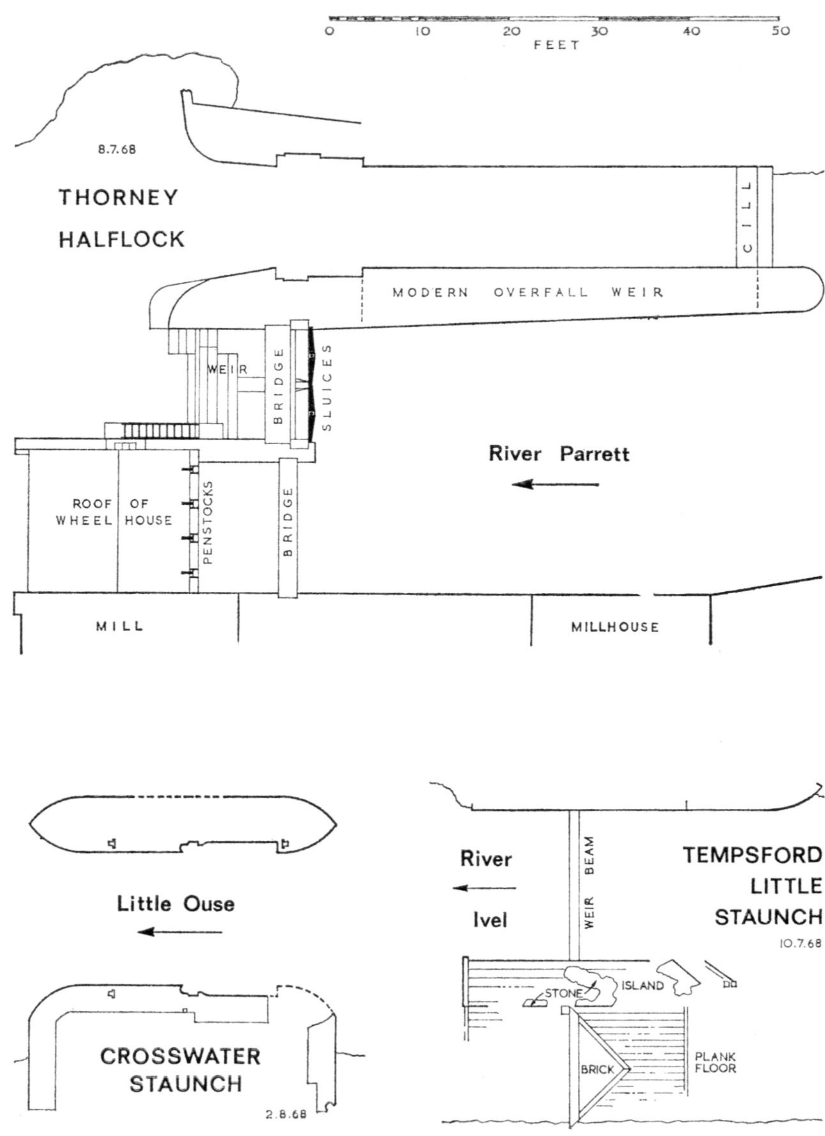

Fig 4

moval of the gates, the top of the chamber was blocked by a stop wall built on the cill, and the top two courses were removed from most of the island, to form a new overfall weir from the existing weir channel into the chamber (see Fig 4).

Great Ouse[9]

Between 1618 and 1630 Arnold Spencer built a series of sluices (perhaps pound locks) up to Eaton Socon, and from 1674 to 1689 Henry Ashley senior extended the navigation up to Bedford with more sluices and staunches. These staunches were certainly of the beam and paddle type until, between 1832 and 1845, they were rebuilt along with the sluices by Sir Thomas Gery Cullum (Bedford to Barford) and by Cullum and John Francklin (below Barford). The previous four staunches were replaced by three—two of them on new sites—of the gate type. Traffic ceased above Tempsford in 1876, above Eaton Socon in 1878, and by 1890 little was moving above Godmanchester. Leonard Simpson, the new owner, repaired and reopened the navigation in 1894, but three years later, after protracted lawsuits, it was abandoned. It is now restored up to Tempsford, and the top two locks have been reopened by the Great Ouse River Board, supported by the efforts of the Great Ouse Restoration Society.

Castle Mills staunch (TL 094509). One of the most complete remaining examples (illustrated on p 227). Brickwork complete—basically yellow (c 1840), much repaired with red (1894). Brick fixed weir separated from sluice weir by second small island. Weir raising gear survives. Straight gate recesses. Gates, very decrepit, meeting at 110 degrees. No gate paddles. Long anchors. Wooden hollow quoins. Gates opened by chains which pass upwards through arched and inclined culverts to winches beside the staunch. Winches have triangular cast-iron frames marked BAYLISS & THACKRAY ENGINEERS HUNTINGDON. Stop plank slots above and below gates. Wooden footbridge to island now gone. 12 ft 1 in wide, water once 3 ft 3 in deep. Staunch to deepen shallows below Castle Mills lock 300 yd above. (See Fig 5).

Tempsford staunch (TL 161542). Yellow brickwork complete, with

0 1 2 3 4 5 6 7 8 9 10 11 12 FEET
ELEVATIONS OF WINCH
WINCH
PIT
ANCHOR
plan
BACK EDGE OF BRICKWORK
HOLLOW QUOIN
STAUNCH TOP
elevation
GATE RETAINING CHAIN
right
gate
CHAIN
CULVERT ARCH
WATER LEVEL
Great Ouse
SLUICE RAISING GEAR
SLUICE
WEIR
general plan
0 10 20 30
FEET
FIXED
WEIR
CASTLE MILLS
STAUNCH
12.11.67 & 7.9.68

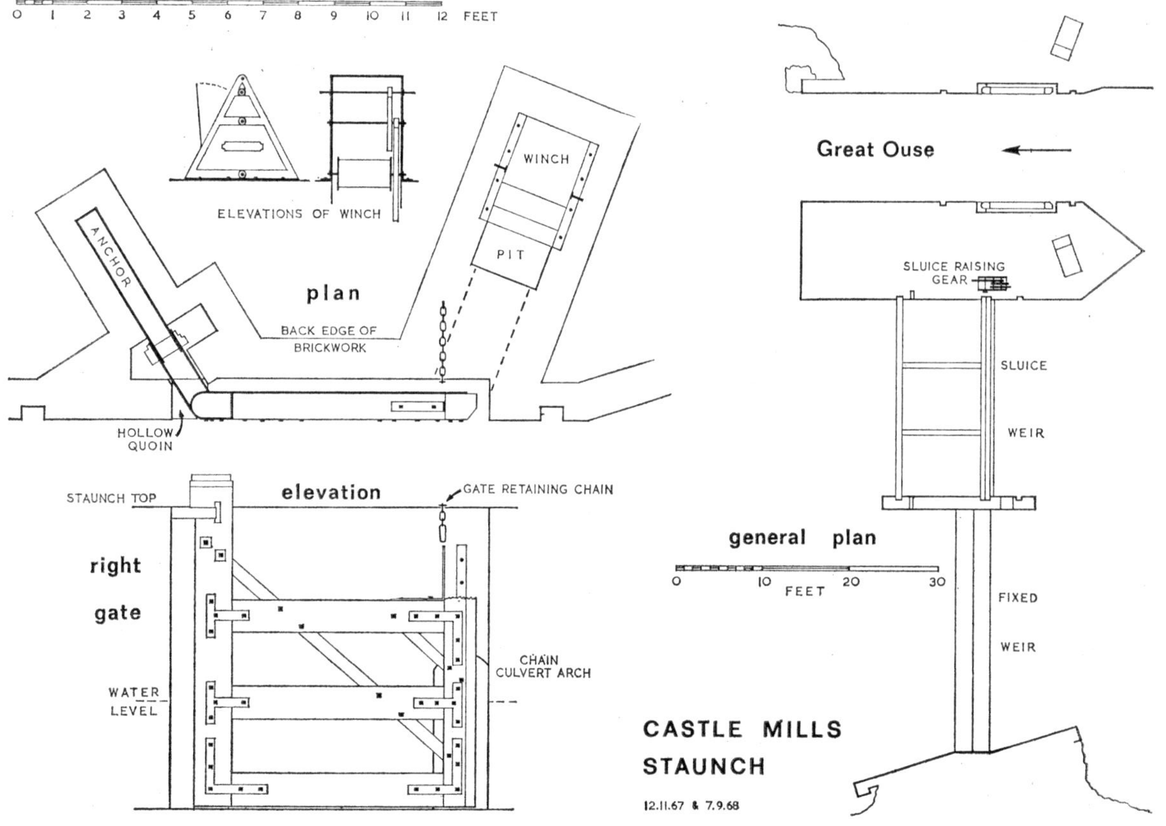

Fig 5

island (cemented over). Weir removed. Curved gate recesses. Fragments of wooden hollow quoins. Brick seating of right gate winch over chain culvert. Stop plank slots above and below gates. Modern footbridge over staunch and weir. 12 ft 3 in wide, water once 3 ft 1 in deep. Staunch to raise level over Tempsford ford, where Great North Road crossed before bridge was built. (See Fig 11).

Belford or St Neots staunch (TL 192621). Island and weir wall removed. Only left staunch wall, buff brick repaired with red. Slightly curved gate recess. Depression marks site of gate winch. At bottom end of chain culvert, a vertical roller is mounted in wall to reduce friction of the chain. Once 12 ft 4 in wide, water 4 ft 6 in deep. To lift boats over shallows below St Neots lock. (See Fig 11).

River Ivel[10]

Made navigable from Biggleswade to Tempsford on the Great Ouse in 1758, with five locks and three gate staunches. Commercial traffic ceased by 1876. We could find no trace of the beam and paddle type of staunch mentioned by Priestley. Practically nothing of the staunches now survives above water, their plans being recoverable only by underwater archaeology.

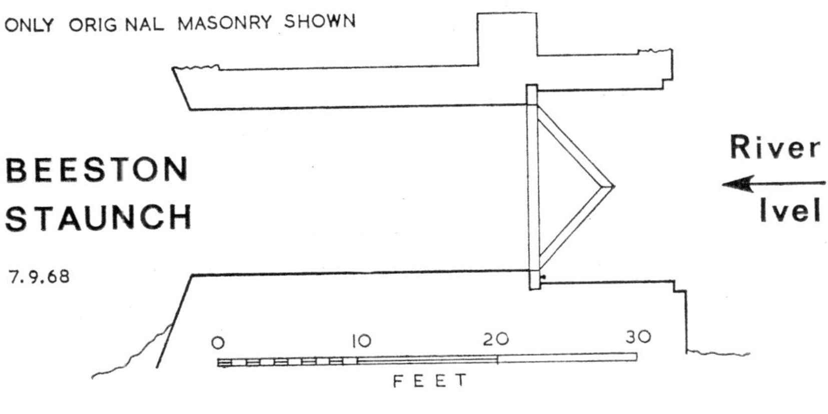

Fig 6

Beeston staunch (TL 183471). Weir on separate channel. Sandstone masonry. Gates, unusually, at upstream end of staunch. Straight recesses with no upper return. Stumps of gateposts survive, with one hinge. Mitre-cill, angle of gates 95 degrees. 12 ft wide. On abandonment, all masonry removed to below water level, and river widened leaving foundations of right wall in mid-stream. Stones re-used in abutments of new bridge over staunch (see Fig 6).

Sandy Doors (TL 170487). With Sandy lock, on artificial cut bypassing Sandy mill. Similar in structure and design to Beeston, but shorter. Most of masonry removed to below water level. Gatepost stumps survive. Immediately below gateposts, footbridge across staunch—modern deck on original abutments. 11 ft 9 in wide.

Tempsford Little staunch (TL 161534). Only the weir wall (brick and masonry) on right bank still stands; but weir cill and foundations of island (sleeper beams and a few stones) can be traced underwater. Plank floor. Mitre-cill, angle of gates 90 degrees. Width 12 ft. Paved ford 70 yd upstream was reason for staunch. (See Fig 4).

River Lark and Tuddenham Mill Stream (see Fig 7)

The first major work to make the Lark fully navigable up to Bury St Edmunds was done under an Act of 1700 by Henry Ashley junior. The river remained in the same ownership as the Great Ouse for nearly two centuries. Probably all the eleven locks and fourteen staunches dated in their final form to the 1830s and 1840s, when Sir Thomas Gery Cullum had an extensive rebuilding programme. West Row staunch, however, may be later, as may the fifteenth staunch, Isleham, which was controlled by the South Level Drainage & Navigation Commissioners. The thirteen miles from Mildenhall to Bury had fallen out of use by 1889, when the Eastern Counties Navigation & Transport Co Ltd was formed to restore the navigation. Repairs were completed, and even the small tributary of Tuddenham Mill Stream made navigable, by 1894, but at such cost that the company went into receivership, and the river above Icklingham was abandoned. Traffic ceased altogether at the end of the first war. Cullum's staunches were of standard pattern with few variations. The buff brick walls were divided into slightly concave bays by three vertical timbers, of which the centre pair were the gateposts and the top pair held stop-plank slots. Sometimes the gateposts were extended upwards to carry a stride. Floors were of planking laid on three main transverse beams, with a mitre-cell fixed on top. The Eastern Counties Co abolished three staunches, converted one into a pound lock, and repaired all the rest—often extensively—with red brick. But in at least three cases, presumably to save expense, they did not restore the gates but installed stop-planks instead, either using the existing slots or moving them to the sites of the gateposts. Some staunches were necessitated by mills, a few by fords; but in many cases their *raison d'être* is not clear.

Bury St Edmunds staunch (TL 849665). (Illustrated on p 228.) No weir—river too small. Brickwork ruinous, stone copings lying in river. 11 ft 3 in wide. No mitre-cill. Apparently converted c 1890 from gate to plank type. Cottage on main road by terminal basin dated T.G.C. 1839. (See Fig 7.)

Fornham staunch (TL 845674). No trace—area disturbed by gas main works.

West Stow staunch (TL 811707). No weir. Brickwork largely complete. Stone copings. 11 ft 6 in wide. Mitre-cill gone. Rotting fragments of gateposts (not plank slots). Modern accommodation bridge over.

Lackford staunch (TL 800711). No weir. Brickwork complete. 11 ft 6 in wide. Straight gate recesses with paddle recesses. Part of left gatepost with hinge. Cottage a little below staunch dated T.G.C. 1842. (See Fig 11.)

Mill Heath staunches (TL 782714). Two almost identical, 283 ft apart. Both by-passed by large meander of river. Brickwork nearly complete. Upper staunch 11 ft 6 in wide, lower 12 ft. (Illustrated on p 229.) Mitre-cills, angle of gates 90 degrees. Part of left gatepost with hinge in lower staunch; in upper staunch left gatepost complete with hinges, extended upwards to support stride. Stride survives, much rotted, on ground. (See Fig 7.)

PLANK FLOOR
T.G.C. ...
PLANK FLOOR
KING'S
14.4.68
WEIR BEAM ABOVE WATER
COPING
CILL
T.G.C. 1832
MILDENHALL 18.2.68
MILL HEATH UPPER
1.8.68
b
PLANK
FLOOR
a
a SECTION b
31.7.68
BURY St EDMUNDS
11"
PLANK SLOT
BRICK
STONE
STRAKE
0
10
20
30
40
50
FEET
RIVER LARK STAUNCHES

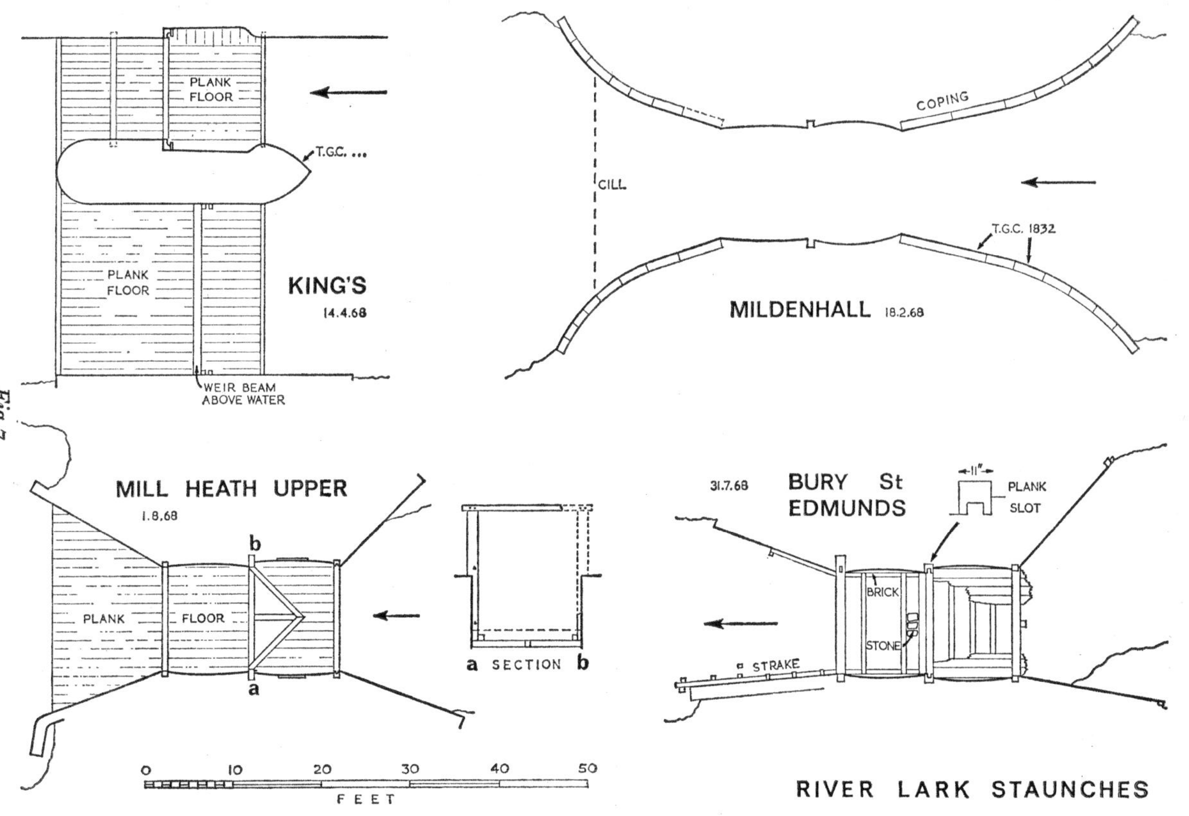

Fig 7

Temple Bridge staunch (TL 757729). Replaced in 1960 by gauging weir, except for small fragment of wing wall.
Jack Tree staunch (TL 754733). Weir only cut c 1890—weir side of island not walled. Most of brickwork survives. 11 ft 6 in wide. Much rebuilt c 1890, mitre-cill removed, converted to plank type with slots at head of staunch. Once 4 ft deep; 4-ft fall.
Barton Hall staunch (TL 720740). Recently demolished and river widened. Only dry weir channel survives.
Mildenhall staunch (TL 709743). By-passed by mill-stream, so no weir. Brickwork almost complete. 11 ft 5 in wide. Stone coping inscribed T.G.C. 1832 twice (illustrated on p 228); c 1890, on abolition of Mildenhall West staunches and dredging of river between, lower gates added, converting staunch into pound lock to enable boats to surmount staunch cill. Later top gates and mitre-cill removed. Staunch now served as weir; lower gates replaced by steel guillotine sluice. Once 3 ft 9 in deep. (See Fig 7.)
Mildenhall West staunches (TL 701744 and 702744). Two staunches 360 ft apart, abolished c 1890 and river widened. Now only a few shapeless stumps of brickwork.
King's or Cow Gravel staunch (TL 691744). (Illustrated on p 228.) Practically complete. Heavy beam across weir. Straight gate recesses. Gates and mitre-cill evidently removed c 1890, and hollow quoins converted into stop-plank slots. Stone coping inscribed T.G.C. (date illegible), but staunch cottage dated T.G.C. 1842. 11 ft 4 in wide, once 4 ft deep; 3-ft fall. (See Fig 7.)
West Row or New staunch (TL 671749). Island removed. Right weir wall and left staunch wall remain. Non-standard—wall not divided into bays, and gate recesses straight. This, and its title of 'New' staunch, suggest that it may post-date the 1830s' rebuilding, though it existed by 1881. Part of gatepost and one hinge. Once 12 ft 6 in wide, 4 ft deep; 3-ft fall. (See Fig 11.)
Isleham staunch (TL 649757). Superseded by Isleham lock (still in use), and obliterated by modern weir.
Tuddenham Mill Stream staunch (TL 732729). (Illustrated on p 230.)

Stream straightened and dredged, and staunch built, c 1890. No brickwork or masonry—sides of plank cladding. 10 ft 8 in wide. Left gatepost complete, with hinges, extended upwards to carry stride, which is missing. Gates almost complete; each has three horizontal panels, the top one being open. Single paddle in each, raised by rack and pinion gear of standard Lark pattern. Gates met at 90 degrees. Mitre-cill survives. Whole staunch, though almost all there, in advanced state of decrepitude, with a rickety footbridge laid across gate tops (see Fig 8).

Little Ouse[11]

The river has long been navigable up to Thetford, and has never had any pound locks. In the mid-eighteenth century, however, Thetford Corporation built seven staunches, and completely rebuilt them between 1827 and 1835. By the first war traffic had ceased and the staunches gradually decayed. Most of them were almost entirely removed after 1930 by the Great Ouse River Board. The Little Ouse guillotine staunches form the only series that has been described in detail, so little will be said of them here. At each site the river was divided by two islands into three channels: one with the staunch, one with a clow or adjustable weir, and one with a fixed weir. The gate was raised by a large wheel, or at two staunches by a crank handle. The width varied from 12 ft 1 in to 13 ft 4 in. On the lower part of the river, which used to be maintained by the South Level Drainage & Navigation Commissioners, was the eighth staunch, Crosswater, of uncertain age but quite different pattern. A three-mile tributary, Lakenheath Lode, was also navigable, with one staunch built and maintained by a Lakenheath gravel firm. Below Thetford there are no mills and very few fords: presumably staunches were preferred as being cheaper than pound locks.

Thetford staunch (TL 861832). Adapted for steel sluice. Both land walls and island between fixed and clow weirs survive, much disguised by concrete.

TUDDENHAM MILL STREAM STAUNCH 2.8.68

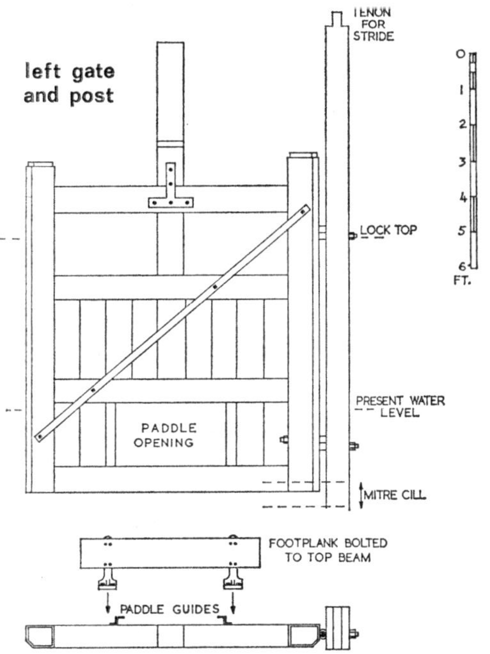

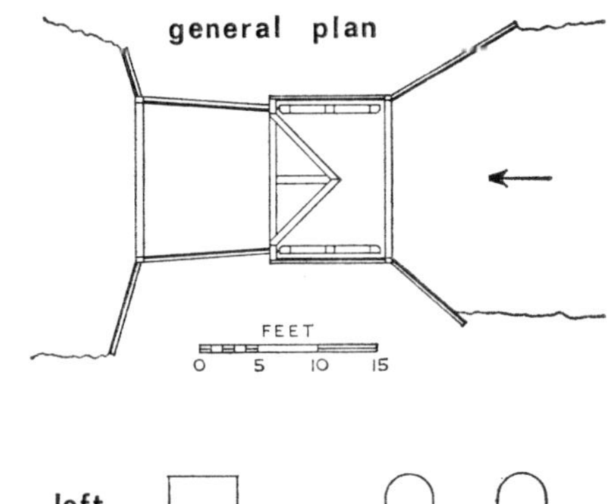

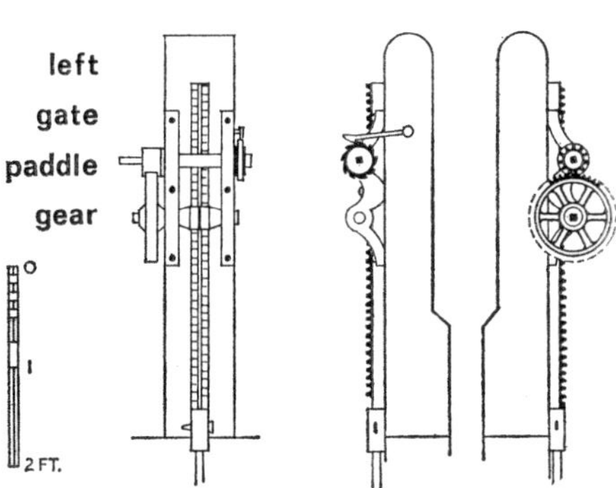

Fig 8

Thetford Middle staunch (TL 851844). Obliterated by 1961 gauging weir.

Turfpool staunch (TL 854856). Both islands gone. Fixed weir wall on left bank, and staunch wall on right bank with slot for upright.

Croxton staunch (TL 846870). Fixed weir wall on left bank only.

Santon staunch (TL 826873). Staunch wall on left bank only. Stumps of main upright and gate guide survive.

Brandon staunch (TL 777867). Obliterated by 1955 sluice.

Sheepwash staunch (TL 758870). Both islands gone. Stumps only of staunch wall on right bank. Fixed weir wall on left bank double-sided and shaped like island.

Crosswater staunch (TL 677858). Buff bricks capped with massive granite coping stones up to 6 ft × 3 ft × 14 in, joined by leaded cramps. Masonry nearly complete, though coping on island much disturbed by tree roots. Built with gates: straight recesses and stone hollow quoins. Another coping stone carved with a hollow quoin survives in one wing wall, either a reject or the relic of an earlier staunch. Before 1908 converted to standard Little Ouse guillotine type, worked by crank handle, with main uprights set in hollow quoins. Depressions in coping stones mark site of struts to support uprights. 14 ft 11 in wide, once 4 ft deep; 3-ft fall. (See Fig 4.)

Lakenheath Lode: High Bridge staunch (TL 702834). No trace—may be buried by recent road embankment. Lode now dry.

Bottisham Lode[12] (see Fig 9)

The history of this waterway is obscure. It is one of several small tributaries of the Cam, part natural and part artificial, and once used both for drainage and navigation. An Act of 1767 appointed the Swaffham and Bottisham Drainage Commissioners and empowered them to levy tolls and to build staunches; but the existing staunch probably dates from after a further Act of 1819. It was certainly in existence by 1886. Traffic, which had never been heavy, ceased by about 1900.

C
A
B
elevation
looking
up stream
GREAT
SPOKED
WHFFI
ONCE ON
THIS END
OF LOWER
ROLLER
A
B
C
side elevations and sections
BOTTISHAM
LODE
STAUNCH
2.6.65
STAUNCH TOP
0 1 2 3 4 5 6 7 8 9 10
FEET
0 10 20 FT.
WATER LEVEL
general plan

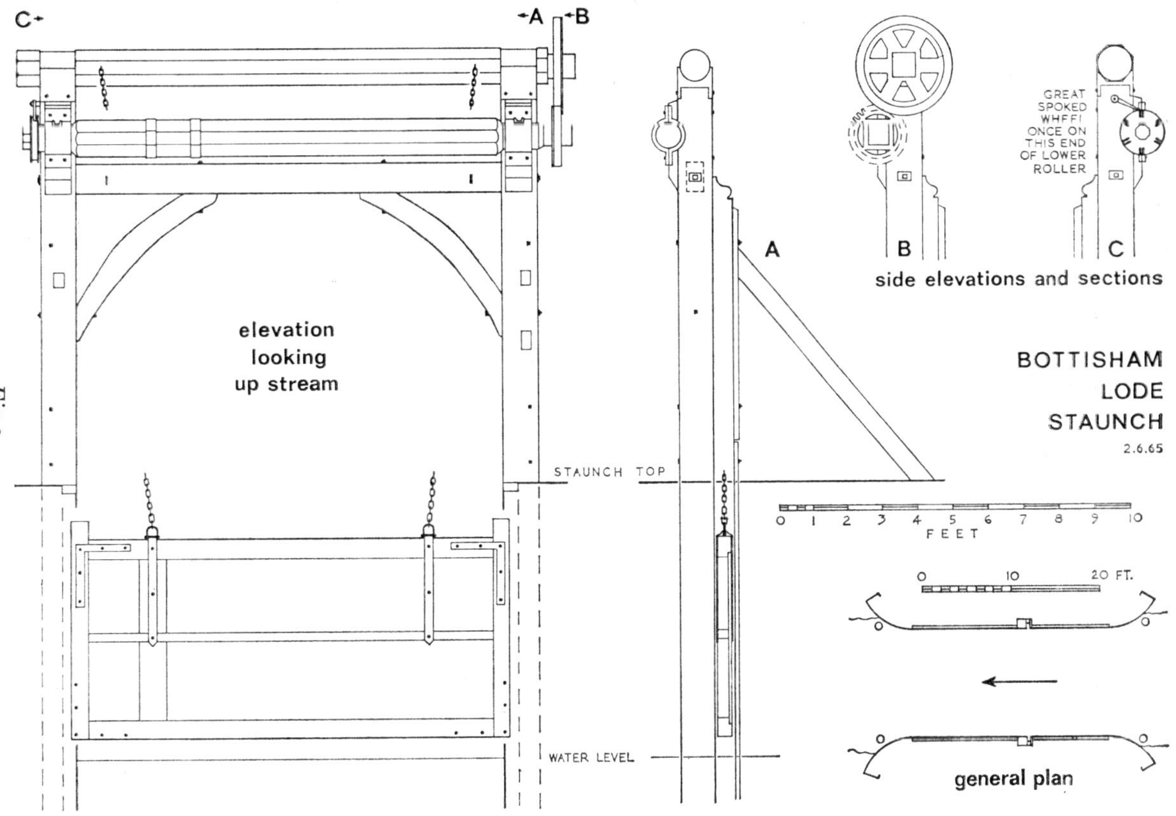

Fig 9

Bottisham staunch (TL 516651). (Illustrated on p 232). Almost identical to the former Little Ouse examples which dated from 1827–35. Intact except for great spoked wheel for lifting gate, for boards of gate, and for footbridge. In so rotten a condition that it cannot last for long. Yellow brick walls 12 ft apart. (See Fig 9.)

River Nene[13] (see Fig 10)

Made navigable from Peterborough to Oundle in 1730, to Thrapston after 1736, and to Northampton in 1761, with 34 locks and 12 staunches. All the staunches were probably rebuilt in the 1830s by Thomas Atkinson of Peterborough, and improved later in the century, when two were converted to locks. They were of the guillotine type with a wooden framework, and several survived until the 1930s. During the early years of this century, however, most of the staunches had their timber main frame replaced by rolled steel joists, with new steel-framed guillotine gates sliding against the upstream side of the main uprights. In 1936–41, under the new Nene Catchment Board, the navigation was extensively modernised. Seven of the staunches were eliminated by deepening the cills of the next locks upstream, and three were converted to locks. The fall at the staunches varied from 1·4 ft at Alwalton to 2·4 ft at Orton; at Woodston the drop depended on the tide, but did not exceed 1·6 ft. Most staunches were built of large well-dressed masonry, unusual in that the side walls fell away from a summit at the gate down to the ends of the wing walls. Woodston, built of blue brick, was a later structure and had mitre gates until they were replaced by a steel guillotine. Some staunches were necessitated by mills, others by fords.

Wellingborough staunch (SP 909671). Obliterated by Wellingborough Upper lock, but weir still in use with new gear.

Stanwick staunch (SP 967723). (Illustrated on p 231.) Steel guillotine demolished 1938. River widened, no remains.

Thorpe or Aldwincle staunch (TL 021814). No weir—not on main channel. Right wall replaced by sheet piling. Left wall in three slightly concave bays serves as pier for rebuilt road bridge on site of older one.

River
Nene
T.A. 1837
0
1 FT.
CONCRETE
STONE
STONE
MATRIX OF RSJ
STEEL
GATE
FRAME
detail of right gate slot
ALWALTON STAUNCH
7.4.68
WEIR
WEIR
0
10
20
30
40
50
FEET
PERIO STAUNCH
15.4.68
MODERN
BRIDGE
T.A. 1838
River
Nene
ANGLES
FILLED IN
Thorpe staunch:
left RSJ
0
1
FOOT
15.4.68
CEMENT
COPING

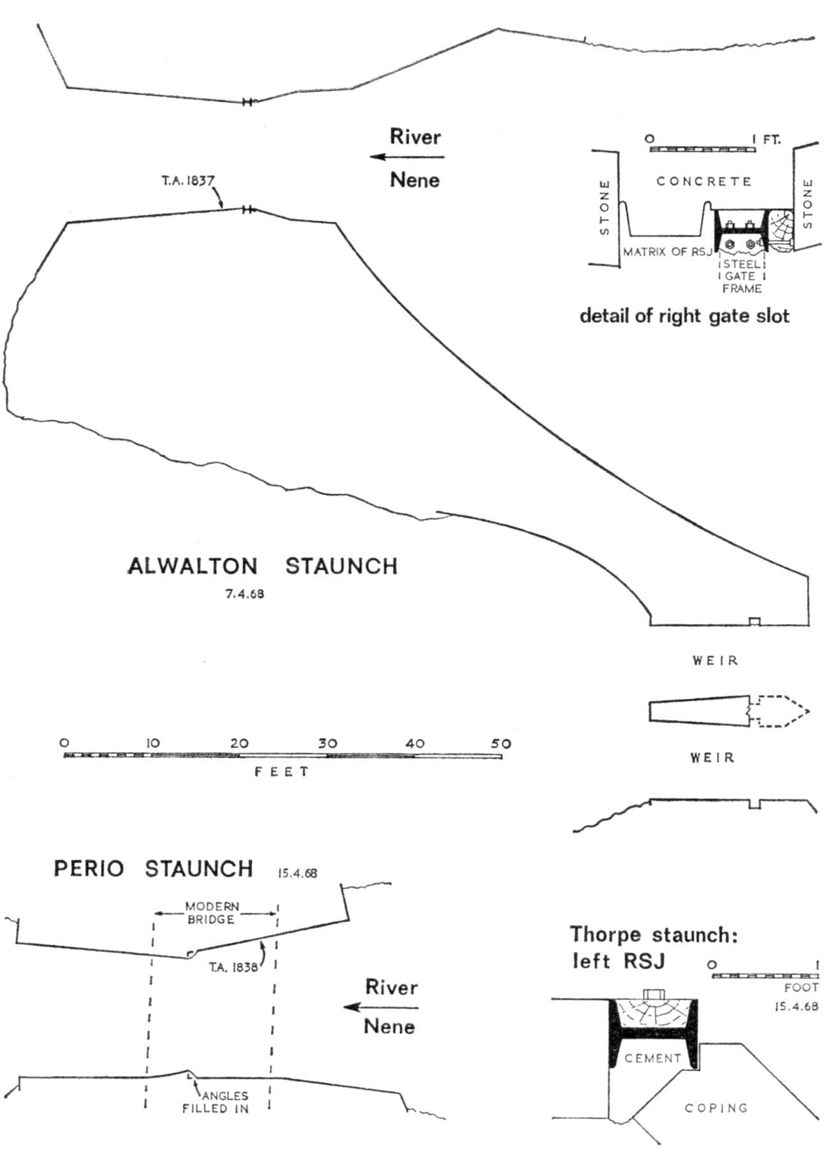

Fig 10

Large well-dressed masonry, rebuilt with smaller stone at top end. Wooden staunch, still there in 1895, stood at junction of upper and middle bays; later steel-framed gate stood at head of upper bay, where RSJ may be seen. This last was demolished in 1940. (See Fig 10.)

Barnwell staunch (TL 042874). Wooden structure remained until blown down in gale in 1940. Site now obliterated by Barnwell Lower lock.

Perio staunch (TL 047927). Wooden framed until its demolition in 1940. Masonry almost intact. Bridge laid across staunch in 1967, wing walls extended in concrete, and weir filled in, as a new cut has left staunch on a superseded loop. In right wall, date-stone T.A. 1838. Angles where the wooden uprights stood are covered by bridge, and are cemented over. Channel 13 ft wide. (See Fig 10.)

Elton staunch (TL 084950). Wooden framed in 1897. River widened, no trace.

Wansford staunch (TL 077995). Steel-framed guillotine and two islands removed in 1941. On left bank, masonry and blue brick weir wall. On right bank, staunch wall, evidently rebuilt drastically. Downstream end of very large fine masonry with date-stone T.A. 1840; middle section starts with double rebate (one angle of which once held the vertical RSJ, now gone) forming a straight 'recess' which may once have been for a gate, and built of smaller blocks; upstream end is a rough wing wall. On top angle of wall are a number of grooves caused by rope wear, but at right angles to the river. 'The staunch could be closed only to pass craft up and down stream. The head of water retained was liable to flood land upstream.'[14]

Alwalton or Knabb staunch (TL 139970). On loop of river by-passed in 1936–9 by new cut. Masonry almost complete. Weir in two channels, with modern footbridge over. Very large island. Staunch bears date-stone T.A. 1837. In each wall, vertical slot with concrete impression of 10½-in RSJ upright. Immediately upstream, 6-in RSJ bearing remains of cross members, the framework of the gate. 12 ft 3 in wide. (See Fig 10.)

Orton or Goldiford staunch (TL 166972). Obliterated by modern lock, 1939.

PIT FOR WINCH CHAIN
TEMPSFORD
STAUNCH
12.11.67
SITE OF WEIR
Great Ouse
0 10 20 30 40
FEET
Lark
WEST ROW
18.2.68
Lark
LACKFORD
31.7.68
RSJ IN HOLLOW QUOIN
Nene
ANCHOR STUBS
RECESS LATER FILLED
STONE
ORIGINAL BRICK COPING TO RECESS
STONE
WOODSTON
15.4.68
Lugg
ANCHOR GROOVE
LONGWORTH
7.7.68
Great Ouse
ROLLER
BELFORD
13.4.68
rivers flow right to left
0 1 2 3 4 5 6 7 8 9 10 11 12
FEET
GATE RECESSES

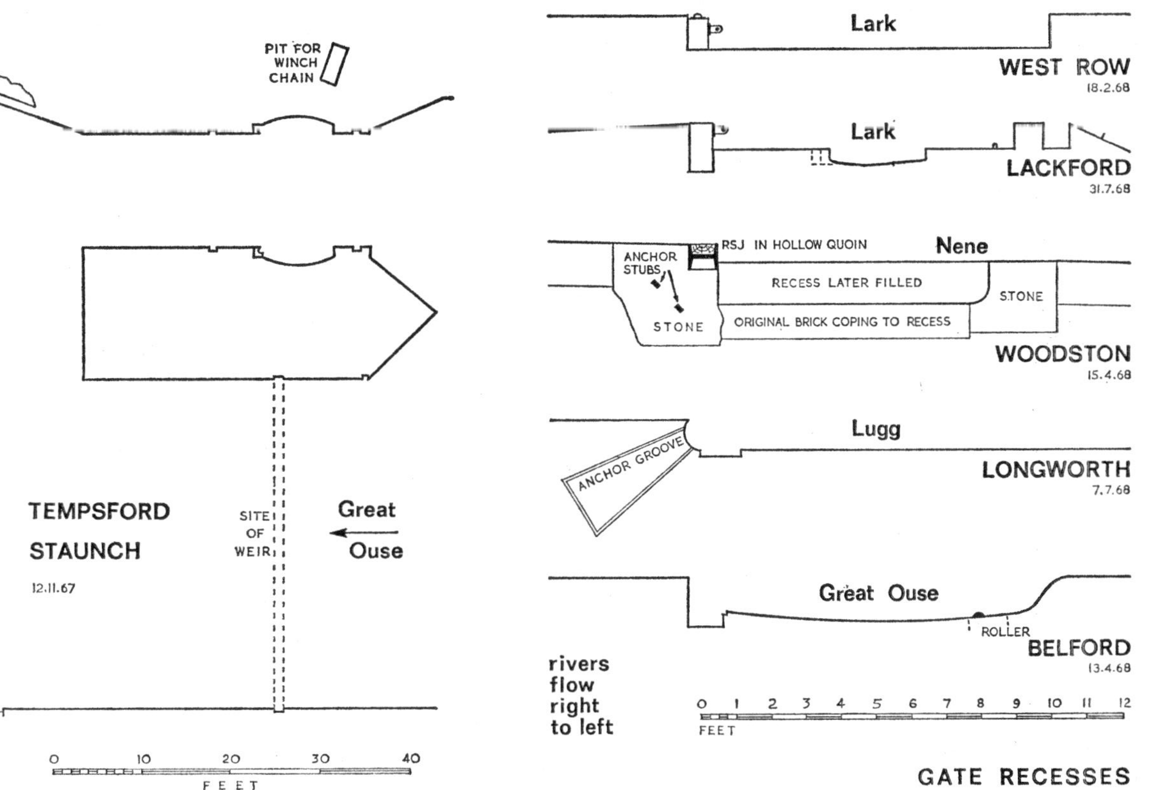

Fig 11

Woodston staunch (TL 183981). Weir, island and steel guillotine demolished 1938. Left bank staunch wall entirely of blue bricks except for two stones, at each end of straight gate recess. Lower stone shows two iron stumps of gate anchor. Recess filled in with blue brick after 1897, and RSJ upright let into anchor stone at site of hollow quoin. Before the construction of Dog-in-a-Doublet lock in 1937, 'on the ebb tide a barge could not pass up through Woodston staunch until the level from Woodston to Orton was lowered. On passing Woodston, the gates were closed and a head (some ½ mile of river) had to build up for the passage to Orton, and similarly at Alwalton. In drought conditions the process was tedious. . . . The reverse process was rather like "shooting the rapids" to pass through a staunch with a minimum waste of water'.[14] (See Fig 11.)

Several possible sites on the Derbyshire Derwent, the Suffolk Stour, and the Wye at Symond's Yat have also been inspected, but in vain.

Acknowledgments

We are grateful to H. W. Clark, Chief Engineer of the Welland and Nene River Authority, Charles Hadfield and H. C. Weatherhead for information; to A. R. Mountford, Director of Hanley Museum, for expert advice on saggars; to Dr Jennifer Tann and Michael Seymour for help in fieldwork; and to the Manchester Public Libraries for assistance in preparing the photographs.

References

The following works have been extensively used: the volumes of the *British Canals* series edited by Charles Hadfield; H. R. de Salis, *Bradshaw's Canals and Navigable Rivers of England and Wales* (1904 and 1928 editions); the Reports of the Royal Commission on Canals and Waterways (1906–9); and Ordnance Survey large-scale maps of all editions.

1 F. Mullineux, 'The Duke of Bridgewater's Underground Canals at Worsley', *Trans Lancs & Cheshire Ant Soc*, vol lxxi (1961), 157.

2 F. S. Thacker, *The Thames Highway*, 2 vols (1920, reprint 1968), passim; H. W. Taunt, *A New Map of the River Thames*, Oxford (5th edn 1886), passim.

3 K. Belsten and H. Compton, 'Eynsham Wharf, Oxfordshire', *Jnl of Railway & Canal Hist Soc*, vol xiv, no 3 (1968), 45–51.

4 E. Straker, *Wealden Iron* (1931), 401.

5 T. C. Cantrill and Margery Wight, 'Yarranton's Works at Astley', *Trans Worcs Arch Soc*, ns vi (1929), 92–115; J. M. Palmer and M. I. Berrill, 'Andrew Yarranton and the Navigation Works at Astley', *Jnl of Railway & Canal Hist Soc*, vol iv, no 3 (1958), 41–6.

6 Mr A. R. Mountford of Hanley Museum, who has kindly examined them, says that the composition of the clay is more similar to nineteenth- than eighteenth-century specimens in his care, but he emphasises the extreme difficulty of dating saggars.

7 Taunt, op cit, 185–8; Charles Showell, *Shakespeare's Avon from Source to Severn*, Birmingham (1901), 146–9, 160.

8 I. Cohen, 'The Non-Tidal Wye and its Navigation', *Trans Woolhope Naturalists' Field Club*, vol xxxv (1956), 84 ff.

9 T. S. Willan, 'The Navigation of the Great Ouse . . . in the Seventeenth Century', *Pub Beds Hist Rec Soc*, vol xxiv, Luton (1946), passim; *The Lock Gate* (journal of the Great Ouse Restoration Society), passim; W. A. Provis, 'On the Locks Commonly Used for River & Canal Navigations', *Trans Inst Civil Engineers*, vol i (1836), 53–4; F. A. Marindin, 'Report on the River Ouse Navigation', *Blue Books*, vol lxxiii (1890–1), 497ff.

10 M. C. Ewans, 'A Brief History of the River Ivel Navigation', *The Lock Gate*, vol i (1962–3), 30–2, 61–4, 80–3, 91–6, 114; J. Priestley, *Historical Account of the Navigable Rivers, Canals & Railways throughout Great Britain* (1831), 379.

11 R. H. Clark, 'The Staunches and Navigation of the Little Ouse River', *Trans Newcomen Soc*, vol xxx (1955–7), 207–19.

12 7 Geo III c 53; 59 Geo III (L & P) c 78.

13 Hugh McKnight, 'Dragon Fly on the Nene', *Motor Boat & Yachting* (19 April 1968), 55–7.

14 H. W. Clark, personal communication (1968).

ARTHUR E. J. WENT

The Ancient 'Sprat' Fishing Weirs in the South of Ireland

IN the past century many ancient and interesting methods of fishing have disappeared from various parts of Europe. The reasons for this are often obvious: many of the older traditional methods have become uneconomic with the rapid rise in the cost of living. An account of some of the 'fixed engines', as they are called, for salmon fishing in Ireland has already been given in this journal[1] (the term 'fixed engine' in this sense means any form of fishing gear, so the angler's rod is an engine also). The present paper deals with the little-known fixed fishing devices, called 'sprat weirs', used in the estuaries of the Rivers Suir, Nore, Barrow (Waterford Harbour) and Cork Blackwater in the south of Ireland. The term 'sprat weir' is something of a misnomer because besides sprats these weirs may take herring, mackerel, whiting, codling, pollock, coalfish, flounders, plaice, dabs, soles, bass, mullet, as well as a few other commercial and some non-commercial species. Apparently these weirs were originally operated mainly for the sprats, which were used for human consumption, but nowadays, when sprats are eaten more rarely, they are used chiefly for eel fishing with baskets. The catches of fish naturally vary from day to day and month to month but taking the year as a whole the fishing appears to be worthwhile to the fishermen engaged therein.

Sprat weirs are of ancient lineage and there is evidence that some have been used for long periods on the same sites. Their ancient origin was fully recognised by the Fisheries (Consolidation) Act of 1959, Section 128 of which permitted their use in the annual close season for salmon.

Large numbers of sprat weirs were used last century in the Waterford Harbour area but by 1949 many of them had gone out of existence.

In that year between Passage East and Ballyhack on the south and Little Island, just east of Waterford City, there were only sixteen (see Fig 1 for their situations), although there were also a great many derelict ones. By 1968 the number of sprat weirs had diminished still further.

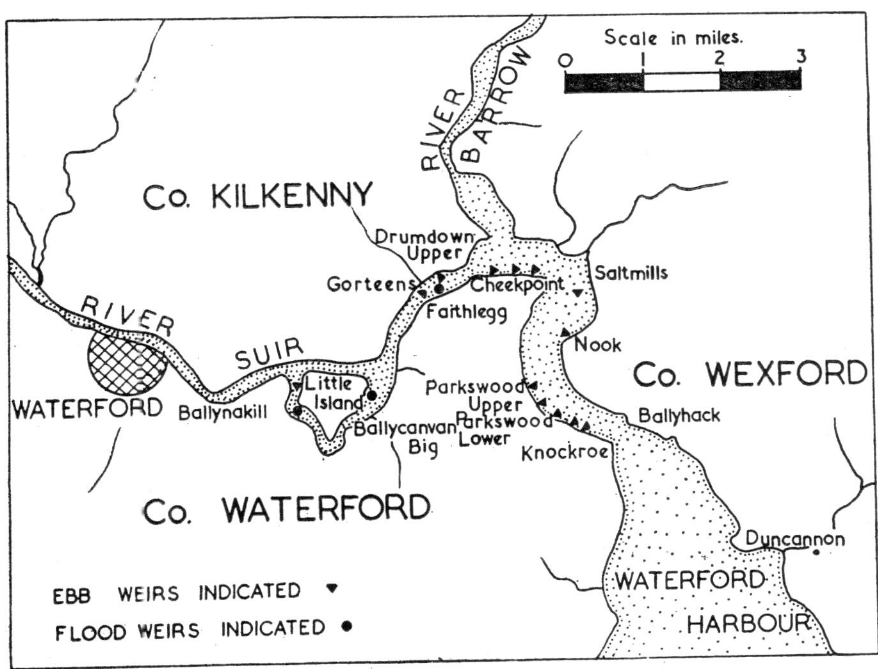

Fig 1 Sketch map showing the situation of serviceable sprat weirs in Waterford Harbour in 1949

Two types of weirs existed in 1949 in the Waterford Harbour area, namely ebb weirs and flood weirs, the former being more numerous than the latter (Fig 1). The only difference in construction is that the ebb weir is directed downstream, whereas the flood weir is directed upstream.

For the most part the bed of Waterford Harbour is deep soft mud and into this at suitable places long poles, similar to the old-fashioned scaffold poles, are driven in vertically in two lines which run across the current. A gap about 6 ft wide (this varies from weir to weir) is left where the poles approach one another closest and over the gap a platform is constructed. To the lower part of the poles, which are usually 1 to 2 ft apart in portions of the arms remote from the gap, netting or wire mesh or twigs may be attached. A long conical net is fished in the gap (illustrated on p 273).

It is well-known that with a rising tide many kinds of fish tend to move onshore or up an estuary and when the tide turns the fish drop downsteam again. The so-called sprat weirs of this type take advantage of this so that at the falling tide, the shoals are caught between the converging walls of the weir and do not usually attempt to swim out of the space between the two arms. Eventually they find their way into the conical net and once there they seldom leave it. The weir is usually fished from a row-boat by the tail- or cod-end of the net being taken aboard and the net emptied. As this type of weir works automatically during the ebb tide, the operation takes little time. It is the construction and maintenance which require long hours of arduous labour. Flood weirs are similar in character except that being directed upstream they only take fish on the flood tide. Naturally the most favourable time for fishing the net is the turn of the tide, ie at dead low water for ebb weirs and high tide for flood weirs.

Perhaps the most interesting of these sprat weirs is that shown off the townland of Nook (Fig 1). This weir is known as Buttermilk Castle Weir from its proximity to Buttermilk Castle erected to guard a small quay on the east side of the harbour originally used by the monks of Dunbrody Abbey to land dairy produce brought over from their farms at Faithlegg on the west or Waterford side of the harbour. Buttermilk Castle Weir was one of the fishing weirs owned by Dunbrody Abbey which at the dissolution were amongst its most valuable possessions available for distribution by the Crown. It was the subject of an inquiry in 1864 when the Special Commissioners of Irish Fisheries declared it to be a legal structure and gave its owner a certificate authorising its use for salmon. Indeed it is the only such weir in Waterford Harbour which can be used for salmon as well as sprats, all the remainder being unlawful for salmon fishing.

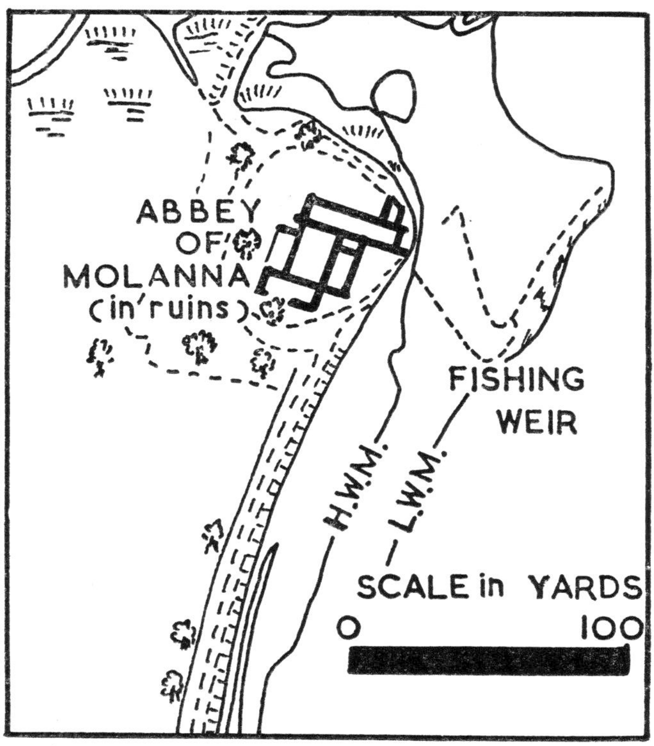

Fig 2 Sketch map showing the situation of the ruined Molana Abbey and the Abbey Weir off Ballynatray in the estuary of the Cork Blackwater

Sprat weirs of the above-mentioned type were apparently used in the estuary of the Cork Blackwater up to the beginning of this century. They have now disappeared but a completely different type of sprat weir of a very old design is still used at Ballynatray on the west bank of the estuary some distance upstream of the holiday resort of Youghal. This is the Abbey Weir so called from its situation adjacent to the ruined abbey of Molana (Fig 2). Formerly this abbey was situated on an island in the west side of the estuary of the Blackwater but some time ago, probably in the eighteenth century, the channel on the west of the island was reclaimed and now forms part of the lands of Ballynatray. The predecessor of the present Abbey Weir may be one of the fishing weirs mentioned in a number of records from the time of the dissolution of the monasteries until the year 1654 when the so-called *Civil Survey* was made. In this survey there is a reference to fishing weirs as follows: 'Temple Michaell and Ballinatray. Old weirs called Curragheguale in Ballynatray, also in T. there is a small castle and fishing weares'.[2]

The layout of this weir may be illustrated most conveniently in the form of a diagrammatic sketch (Fig 3). Two long walls of wattling are placed between the tide marks. One wall, called the 'flood wing' is erected parallel to the contours of the shore line. A second wall, the 'shore wing', is erected at an angle of about 45 degrees to the flood wing on the shore side, a gap of about 9 to 12 in being left between

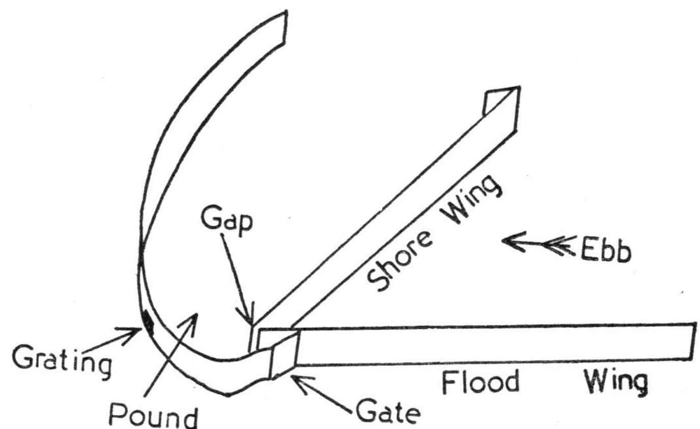

Fig 3 Diagram showing construction of the Abbey Weir (not to scale)

their adjacent ends. The inner end of the shore wing is close to high-water mark and has attached to it a short wall almost parallel to the shore but directed downstream. Another wing is erected downstream of the shore wing, the outer end of this being carried round in almost a semi-circle to meet a structure known as the gate to form the pound. A grating is provided in the wall of the pound, the function of which will be described later. The flood and shore wings are approximately 75 and 48 yd long, respectively. Adjacent to the gap, the shore wing is about 7 ft high but gradually diminishes in height towards high-water mark, being about 4 ft at its inner or shore end. The height of the flood wing is about 7 ft throughout its length.

Each wall is constructed by driving stakes vertically into the muddy sand at intervals of about 2 ft and entwining small sticks between the stakes in such a way as to form close basket-work. In order to make the weir 'fish tight' in its lower part some small meshed wire-netting is frequently attached to the stakes. The gate consists of an oblong frame to which wire-netting of small mesh is suitably attached. A small grating made of small meshed wire-netting on a wooden frame provides a method of cleaning the pound of weeds, sticks and other debris and is also a free passage for fish at certain times. To strengthen the wattle or basket-work walls, which naturally offer great wind and water resistance, and to hold them in place, large stones are piled at the base of the stakes. In addition other stakes called 'gellogs' placed at angles of about 45 degrees to the horizontal are attached to the vertical stakes at one end, the other end being fixed into the ground by means of large stones.

The Abbey Weir operates automatically with the ebb tide. Fish move upstream with the flood tide and as soon as the tide ebbs they tend to return downstream. In doing so they come between the flood and shore wings and then proceed through the gap into the pound from which theoretically they could escape, but in fact they seldom do so. When the tide recedes sufficiently the fish can be moved from the pound.

The Abbey Weir at Ballynatray, the sole survivor of the sprat weirs in the estuary of the Blackwater, is kept in operation because its present owner has, and his late father had, an interest in fish and fishing. Moreover there is a plentiful supply of material on the Ballynatray estate for its maintenance. This weir is certainly one of the oldest fishing engines existing in Ireland today and, even if the erection of similar weirs were permitted by law, the expense of preparing a suitable site and providing the necessary material and labour would be likely to preclude anyone from attempting to erect and operate similar structures today.

References

1 Went, Arthur E. J., 'Some Ancient Irish Salmon Fishing Weirs', *Industrial Archaeology*, vol 3 no 3 (1966), 153–160.

2 *Civil Survey*, VI, 20–21.

Acknowledgments

I wish to thank the Royal Society of Antiquaries of Ireland for the use of the blocks to illustrate this paper.

Plates, page 273

BBC 'Chronicle' Industrial Archaeology Programme

The BBC proposes to offer an Industrial Archaeology Prize open for competition to all engaged in this field. The prize would be of equipment to the value of £250 suited to the special needs of the successful entrant, and runners-up awards of £25 worth of equipment to all those short-listed. These would be presented during a studio programme which would include a film of the finalists engaged in their various kinds of fieldwork.

All current work would be open for consideration and the intention is not to institute special projects but to review recording, restoration, fieldwork, filming activity and plain 'crusading'. If you wish to offer your activities for consideration or to know more about the competition, please contact 'Chronicle', Room 2069, BBC Television, Richmond Way, London W14.

P. T. L. REES

Aids to Recording (5)

The East Lancashire Railway—I: The Accrington to Stubbins Line

THE first plans for a railway to serve Accrington and district were drawn up in 1844 by a group of landowners and businessmen who stated:

> The district has much traffic with Manchester, Liverpool and the rest of the kingdom for which at present there is no means of transit save by hilly and inconvenient roads and by very circuitous canal navigation. Each year increases the extent of this traffic. . . .[1]

So on 3 June 1845, the Blackburn, Burnley, Accrington & Colne Extension Railway was founded. However, it was soon realised that amalgamation with the Manchester, Bury & Rossendale Railway of 4 July 1844 was required to give access to the south; this took place on 3 August 1846 and the East Lancashire Railway was formed.[2] The line was opened on 17 August 1848. In August 1850 the ELR was amalgamated with the Lancashire & Yorkshire Railway by which it was operated until 1922. For the next year it came under the wing of the London & North Western Railway, which in turn became part of the London, Midland & Scottish Railway in 1923.

British Railways took control in 1946 and on 10 September 1951 closed Baxenden for passenger traffic. On 5 November 1960, Haslingden closed for passenger traffic; all goods traffic on the line was withdrawn in the following spring but Helmshore station survived in use until 3 December 1966. In the summer of 1967 the line was rendered useless by the removal of track between Haslingden Tunnel and Hud Hey Bridge. It is only a question of time before the rest is lifted and the property sold.

This history is neither unusual nor unexpected. Developed in a period before road transport was feasible in the hilly Lancashire

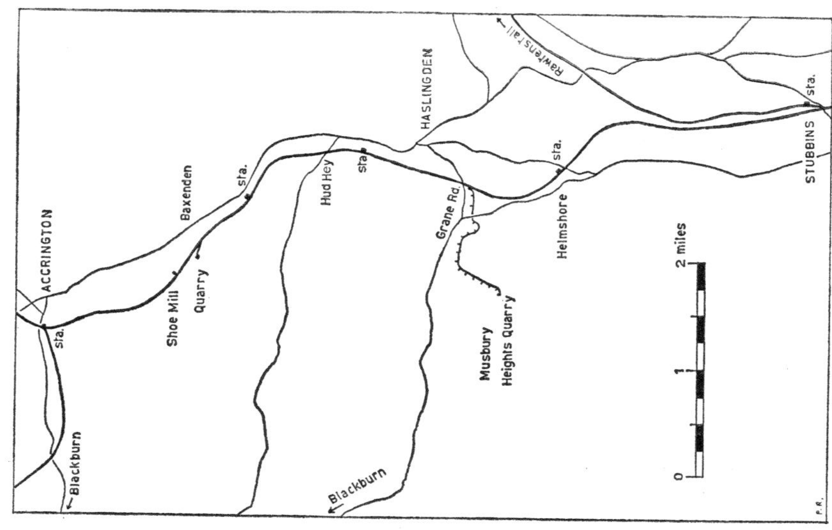

Fig 1

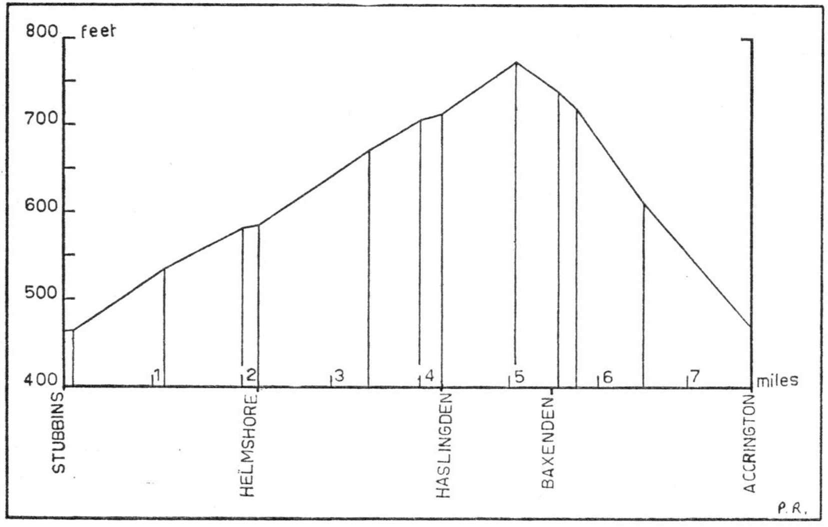

Fig 2 Gradient profile of the Stubbins to Accrington section of the East Lancashire Railway

countryside, reaching a hey-day in the prosperous latter years of the Victorian era, and declining even before British Railways took over, the line showed signs of a deep-seated malady. Road transport won the trade, both the local cotton trade, which was in any case in decline, and the through traffic, which was uneconomic because of the difficult gradients. Passenger traffic succumbed to the onslaught of the bus; inconveniently situated stations did nothing to regain traffic, despite quicker trains and the multiple diesel unit.

The original plans of the Extension Railway had included gradients of 1 in 33 and stationary engines with rope haulage; but this was abandoned for longer, easier gradients worked throughout by locomotive power.

Nevertheless, the line leaving the 1 in 200 gradient at Stubbins soon mounts the two-mile rise up to Helmshore, on which the gradient is never less than 1 in 85. A short stretch of 1 in 97 before Helmshore (584 ft) gives way to a 1 in 78 pull up to Grane Road: from there to Haslingden tunnel the rate of climb is 1 in 81. A short stretch of 1 in 100 carries the line to the station (711 ft), and on to the final 1 in 68 rise to the summit. This is 771 ft above sea level; from it to Baxenden (747 ft) the line drops at 1 in 103. A 100-yd stretch of 1 in 61 makes the transition on to the Baxenden Bank dropping to Accrington at 1 in 38 to Shoe Mill Box, and 1 in 40 for the last mile.

A difficult line to work in both directions, the hard gradient out of Accrington almost always meant banking assistance; the 10-mph speed limit through the station meant absolute control of all down trains, especially those without continuous brakes. The advent of the diesel did away with banking engines; but by then the through traffic was being worked to East Lancashire via Bolton and Blackburn, a longer but easier route.

All the stations of the East Lancashire Railway, apart from the junction station at Accrington and the main station at Bury, were built to a common design of Mr Perring, the resident engineer. They were built of 'white hard handsome stone' quarried locally. Harrison & Sales's guide to the line of 1848 describes the difference between the second and third class as 'the former of stone and the latter of brick and wood or of timber'. The plan aims at simplicity and economy, but as will be shown it was to prove inadequate in handling the traffic of later years.

Even in the early days of L & YR control, extensions were being made; these were in the ELR style. By the 1880s the need for more building was still there; reconstructions of this period followed the usual L & YR pattern. Features of the original design are the windows, with their curved tops, and the moulded corner stones. Where the raising of the platforms, as at Summerseat,[3] has not buried it, the moulded plinth stone is a useful indication of the original design.

The plan (as illustrated after a sketch in the 1848 *Guide to the ELR* by Harrison & Sale) of a central open-air waiting area flanked by the ladies' room and the booking hall, is evident at the three stations to be described as well as at most other stations on the ELR. In fact the best example of the ELR style is at Summerseat where the failure to attract more traffic has caused the minimum of extension. The L & YR rebuilding is easy to distinguish because of the smaller size of stone used, the square windows and the excessive ornate ironwork.

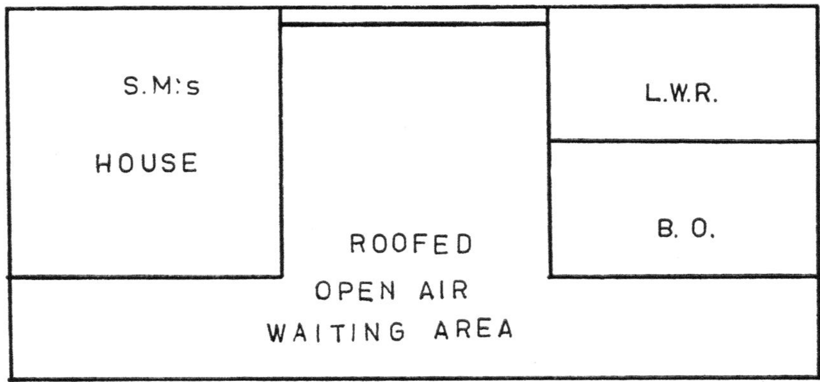

Plan 1 General plan of Mr Perring's ELR stations after Harrison & Sales Guide of 1848

Stubbins to Helmshore

The line divides from the Rossendale Valley branch by a half-mile radius curve just before Stubbins station, and immediately begins the climb to Helmshore. The two lines run almost parallel, though at differing heights, as far as Lumb where the Rossendale line curves away to the east. The Accrington line runs on through a short cutting to a stone and iron viaduct at Alderbottom. The 'elegant viaduct consisting of bays or openings composed of timber framing resting on stone piers'[4] has left no trace. There is no evidence for a date of the present structure, but a note in the L & YR Minute Book of 1882 refers to a 'repairing of the Alderbottom viaduct'. Could this be a rebuilding in iron? In any case its construction of iron plates resting on girders is similar to the occupation bridge just north of Baxenden colliery. Another quarter of a mile further on, the line again crosses the River Irwell, this time on a stone viaduct of nine arches, each of 40-ft span, carrying the line over the river at a height of 70 ft. The second southernmost pier is a later rebuild, but otherwise the structure is typical of all those on the line. Well-built, of the local stone, it is unspectacular and without a visible foundation stone.

The line then runs on an embankment to the high grounds on the side of the valley, which it finally leaves by a deep cutting. Immediately after this is the Ravenshore Viaduct which crosses the 'brawling but useful stream, called the Ogden' at a skew on three arches of 50-ft span each. 'The viaduct is a striking structure from the peculiarity of its romantic position, stretching across so as to fill up completely the chasm between the rocky sides of the river',[5] a description fraught with neo-gothic mysticism. The railway right-of-way was defined by the L & YR by a line of stones, 3 ft high, engraved $\substack{\text{LY,}\\\text{R}}$ running across the valley bottom.

Finally a shallow cutting carries the line into Helmshore station on the other side of the Helmshore to Haslingden turnpike road built in 1827.

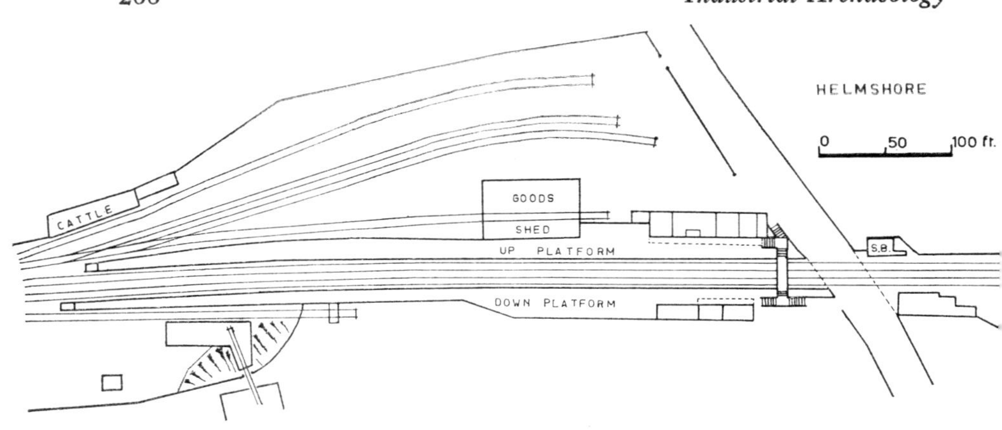

Plan 2

Helmshore Station

The up-side buildings of this station (illustrated on p 274) accord well with Mr Perring's general plan, except that the booking hall is situated at the end in order to provide easier access to the road, which crosses the line at the south end of the platform. The open-air waiting area has been rebuilt into an inside general waiting room; the keying of the new stonework and the wooden framing is easily recognised. The date of this is possibly 1884, unless the entry in the L & YR Minute Book for July of that year refers only to the building of the structures on the down side. Certainly, these are larger than those at Haslingden which in all other respects was a larger station. The toilet facilities are a late edition, also perhaps of 1884.

Houses, built in the ELR style, accommodated the station master and other employees. These still stand on the south side of the level crossing. Full-size level-crossing gates seem to have been in use since the opening of the line; in 1849 they were run into! The footbridge is not typical L & YR style and is probably of LMS date; the signal box is as yet undated. It seems most probable that it was built in the twentieth century before regrouping occurred.

The extensive goods yard is now derelict, with weeds growing between the cobbles. Of the yard crane there is no trace, but there are remains of modern cattle docks, indicating the nature of the traffic in latter years. The goods shed itself is of wood, standing on a brick base, the date of which has not been obtained as yet. There is no reason for its not being of original date.

The platforms are of flag-stones and are a rebuild of 1884, being raised up to 2 ft 9 in, five years before this became compulsory. The lamp standards are of LMS pattern, although there is one in the goods yard which is not of this type and will be discussed later.

An interesting high-level siding was constructed in 1896 from the down sidings into Porrit's mill, running from the track level into the fourth storey of the mill across a brick and timber bridge.

Helmshore to Haslingden

From Helmshore the line runs through a shallow cutting on to the Helmshore Viaduct, which carries it northwards for some 400 yd.

> The line is carried on a retaining wall of stone, 530 feet long, about 18 feet high, and 6 feet thick. To this succeeds a series of 7 arches of 30 feet span each, 9 feet rise and 26 feet high. The line is carried through the plantation between retaining walls 260 feet long and 20 feet high: thence on another series of 7 arches across a mill lodge, 36 feet high, the last of which spans the River Ogden. . . . The whole is built of stone from the quarries of John Hoyle and contains upwards of 300,000 cubic feet of masonry.

The quotation is from the *Preston Guardian* of June 1847, describing the laying of the foundation stone on 21st of that month. An inscribed plate and a bottle of messages and coins are described, but they were enclosed inside the structure and will not be seen until the viaduct is demolished.

The line then continues its rise on an embankment up to the goods yard at Grane Road, the trackbed of the branch to the old gas works running parallel on the down side for some quarter of a mile before that.

The yard was completely closed after 1965; one local goods train was scheduled to stop there in the working timetable of that year. But its main traffic was the quarry trade from Musbury Heights, access to which was made via a private tramway and an interchange yard just behind the goods yard proper. The exchange platforms are still easily visible, crumbling away under grass and weeds. In the yard itself there is nothing except the overgrown cobbling, the lines where the track once was, the foundations of a crane (similar to that at Haslingden), and the brick base of the wooden goods shed. This lasted until the 1950s but was long in disuse before that.

Immediately north of the yard is the bridge over the Haslingden to Blackburn road, a steel girder structure of modern construction. Of the tubular girder bridge, constructed by W. Fairburn in 1847, on the same principle as those at Conway and Menai, but with the track supported between the girder by timber and iron, there is no sign. The present bridge may date from 1881, when the L & YR Minute Book records an 'extension of Grane Road bridge'. Then the line runs straight on an embankment towards Prinny Hill Bridge. This bridge is of similar construction to the Hud Hey Bridge, which will be described in detail. In less than a quarter of a mile the line passes under another bridge, which carries Commerce Street. This iron girder bridge is of fairly modern date, only the stonework dating back to the opening of the line. After another 50 yd the line enters the Haslingden Tunnel, 146 yd long. The tunnel mouths are monumental and unexciting; the inside built of the usual engineers' blue brick and with three refuges on each side. It was constructed by Messrs Cooper & Nowell, and finished on 2 February 1848.

Haslingden Station

Today only the goods buildings are standing, the passenger facilities being demolished in 1966, one month after my photographs were taken (see p 275). Comparison between the drawing from Harrison & Sale's guide of 1848 and these photographs shows clearly the phases of construction. The original building was as in the drawing, and conforms well with Mr Perring's general plan. The typical windows, the worked corner stones, and the roofed waiting area are all easily identifiable. By 1860 however, one year after the L & YR had taken over, this building had proved inadequate for the quantity of traffic which had to be carried, and an order was placed with Patrick Farrell of Salford to extend the passenger accommodation. This extension is what now constitutes the booking hall, the booking office and the ladies' waiting room, and was no doubt accompanied by a complete reconstruction of the roof and the building of the wooden gable ends. The new extension, costing £250, was in the ELR style and most probably was designed by Mr Perring himself. The down-side structures were of wood and were certainly never rebuilt in stone, although rebuilding in wood is possible. At the present only a concrete base can be seen. In 1884 the whole station was repainted, and in 1889 the platforms were raised in accordance with the new law. When this was done, the kerb stone, so much of a feature of the original design, was buried, and only the top of it is visible in the remains to be seen today. At this time the footbridge was erected. This is typical of L & YR design, the close latticing and overhead hoops being features easily recognisable throughout the region. In 1896 extended toilet facilities were added.

The potato shed is of ELR origin, this being clearly shown by the style of windows. The large worked corner stones elsewhere and the roof joists visible at the top of the walls from the outside are other features of the original design. The shed is now but a stone shell, with a collapsed roof, and the timber staging completely rotted away. Adjacent to the shed are the stables, erected in 1896 for the parcel-van horses.

Whether the potato shed was built as such is doubtful; it may originally have been the goods shed. The structure now known as the goods shed seems to be of later date but as yet no written evidence has been found to prove this theory. No other potato shed exists so far as I know on the L & YR system; certainly not on the ELR. In any case the goods shed building was there c 1900 when it appears on a photograph.[7] It is better built than the ELR shed, and has inside joists, different windows and no worked corner stones. It seems typical of a

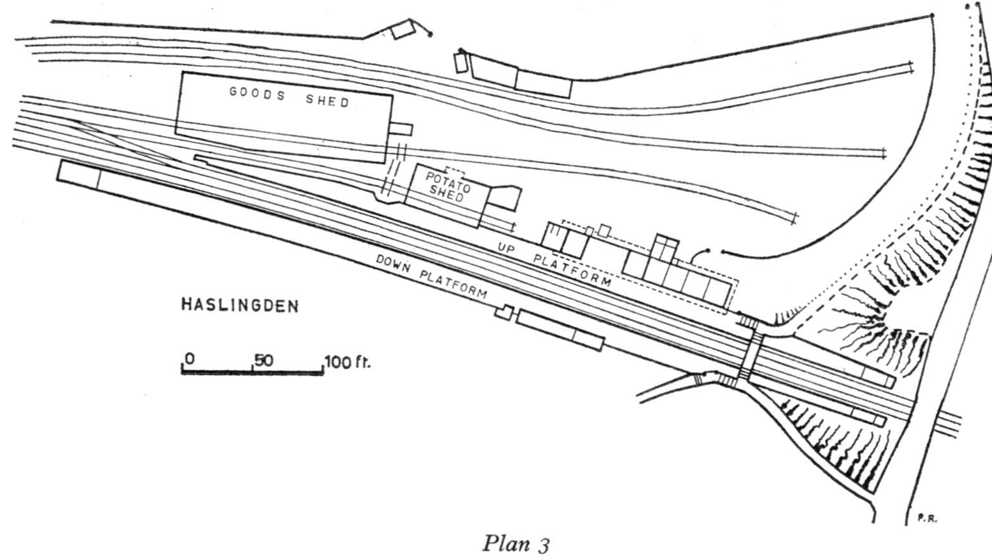

Plan 3

design common to the L & YR of later years; the 1880s would be a fair date.

The goods yard is cobbled and overgrown. Of the stage marked 'in ruins' on the LMS rating plan, there is no trace. The yard crane has left only its base, which is an embedded square of concrete, 6 ft × 6 ft. In this is still bolted the iron base. The cattle docks are stone-topped and wooden-sided, standing next to the shell of the yard master's office.

On the top of the cattle dock stands a lamp-post of the type already noted at Helmshore. It is without inscription—10 in thick up to a collar at 4 ft, and 6 in in diameter from there to full height of 10 ft 6 in. There was in 1960, at the south end of the down platform, a post inscribed 'E.L.R. Co.', but this has now disappeared. (An ELR Co lamp-post has been found on the Rossendale branch line, lighting the Rawtenstall station level crossing: this seems to be the last.) The posts in use at the closure of the line seem likely to be of LMS pattern, the one in the cattle dock probably being L & YR, perhaps dating to 1883 when Baxenden got new lamps. Work was done in the yard in 1866 and 1895, but these dates seem less likely.

The entrance to the yard is guarded by a L & YR notice of 1884, the LMS and BR ones noted in 1964 having since disappeared.

Haslingden to Baxenden

North of the station buildings the line passes through the goods yard pointwork and by the site of the Haslingden signal box. This stood on the down side, 200 yd north of the platform, and was most probably of twentieth-century date. Indeed it may well have replaced the structure shown opposite its site on the photograph taken c 1900. Next to the concrete base which is all that remains, is a stone plate-layers' cabin, built in the late L & YR style. At the site of the Co-operative Societies cabin, as shown on the LMS rating plan, there is another concrete foundation, and adjacent to it a lamp-post of the type found on the cattle dock. No trace exists at all of the wagon repair workshop. The occupation level crossing at Carr Hill Street is signposted by a L & YR notice, 'Beware of the trains'.

Hud Hey Bridge comes next, carrying the main road from Haslingden to Blackburn. The *Blackburn Standard* 22 December 1852 says of it:

> . . . two of the iron girders gave way and came down with a tremendous crash; the iron, soil and stones blocking up both lines of rails underneath. . . . The bridge is still passable for conveyances, one half being safe, and three of the girders still remaining. . . . It is considered by many persons that there was too great a weight of soil, paving, and other stones on the bridge for the length of the span.

Examination of the bridge shows girders of two types, one of curved pattern, the three others straight. The straight girders, on the south side, harmonise with the rest of the iron work—that is the sides of the bridge—and are without the originals. They are identical to those on drawings, initialled by Mr Perring, for bridges on the Accrington to Burnley section.[8] The curved girder then is the replacement of 1853. Needless to say there are weight restrictions theoretically in force, according to a diamond-shaped notice of 1904. This L & YR restriction is of fairly common type, both on the ELR lines and elsewhere. There is also, on the south side of the bridge, another notice of restriction, which although undated is of interest because of its language:

> Lancashire and Yorkshire Railway Company. Take notice that this bridge (which is a bridge of the Lancashire and Yorkshire Railway Company) is insufficient to carry weights beyond the ordinary traffic of the district and that the owners and person in charge of locomotive traction engines or other ponderous carriages or other unusually heavy traffic will be held responsible for any damage. Hunts Bank, Manchester.

Does it date to 1853?

After the bridge there begins immediately the summit cutting of the line, in which the line runs as far as the village of Rising Bridge. An occupation bridge crosses the cutting 100 yd north of Hud Hey Bridge and is constructed of brick piers and straight iron girders stamped APPLEBY-FRODINGHAM 1887. These are undoubtedly the reconstruction of an earlier timber bridge, for which the original standard plans are still extant. Another 100 yd on is the summit, indicated by the usual gradient signs, and an L & YR notice which reads 'Notice. Goods trains must stop here to pin down brakes'. It faces the up line and is 5 ft × 3 ft, maroon, with cast-iron letters, most of which have now disappeared. Two hundred yards north of the summit the line runs under a shallow three-arched skew bridge, carrying the Rising Bridge to Blackburn road over the line. There is a weight restriction similar to the earlier type noted at Hud Hey. Next is an occupation bridge without any restriction. Just north of this bridge is a wooden 10 ft × 6 ft hut, in type and condition similar to that at Helmshore. The Minute Book of 1894 notes the construction of 'cabins costing £10'. Could this be the one at Baxenden?

The Baxenden box comes next, built some quarter of a mile north of the station to control the pointwork into the goods yard and the brick company's yard as well as the crossover between the main running lines. It was here that the banking engines sent up from Accrington were detached, crossed over and run back. The present box was in

Views of sprat weirs in the neighbourhood of Cheekpoint, Co Waterford, in 1949. In both cases the net is not in a fishing position

See 'The Ancient "Sprat" Fishing Weirs in the South of Ireland', pp 254–60

Helmshore station up-side buildings. Note the curved windows and the filled-in open-air waiting area, indicated by the worked corner stones

A view of Haslingden station up-side buildings. Note the narrow curved top windows, the open-air waiting area and the worked corner stones. The goods shed and the potato shed are evidently of different date

See 'Aids to Recording (5): East Lancashire Railway—The Accrington to Stubbins Line', pp 261–80

Houses in Cronkbourne Village, Kirk Braddan, Isle of Man (Courtesy: Manx Press Pictures)

See 'Cronkbourne Village, Kirk Braddan, Isle of Man', pp 281–5

use in 1963, but without doubt there was a structure of some sort here even in 1848. The present structure sports a sign board in the L & YR style, and its condition and general appearance suggest an early date. It must predate the boxes at Haslingden and Helmshore, but a close dating is as yet impossible.

Baxenden Station

The station was closed in 1951 for passengers and in 1961 for goods traffic. Since then it has been demolished and the yard turned into a caravan park. There remains only the skeleton of a footbridge, put up in 1888, and a porter's wooden hut noted on the LMS rating plan. The platforms remain as they were when raised in 1888.

The goods shed is now a caravan repair shop, but still shows evidence of its ELR origin—the joists can be seen from outside, the corner stones are well worked, and the windows are simple rectangles as noted at other sheds on the ELR system. This shed was noted as a 'new warehouse' in the 1859 Minutes, when Mr Perring, asked to design it, estimated a cost of £2,350. Was there an earlier structure here, perhaps

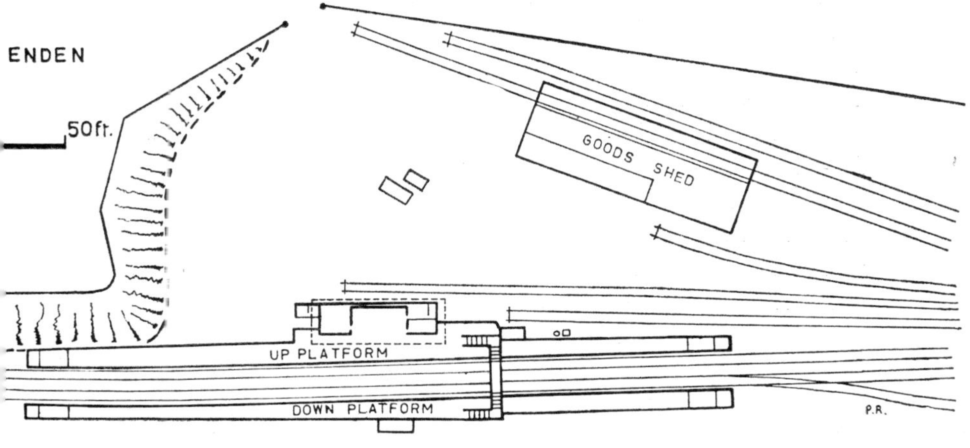

Plan 4

a wooden shed as at Helmshore? No remains of the staging exist; all except the main road doors are blocked. There is no sign of the weighing machine installed in 1894, but the base of a crane exists as at Haslingden.

Baxenden to Accrington

Immediately north of the platform end is a gradient sign 100/47: from here to Accrington the line drops without ceasing. It first runs on a viaduct and skirts a mill lodge on the up side, then comes another occupation bridge, just north of which is the down-side notice to goods trains to pin down their brakes. It is identical to the one at the summit. At the 20-miles post is the site of the old Baxenden quarry sidings. These are indicated by a setting back of the retaining wall on the down side, and a gently rising trackbed running parallel to the line for some 300 yd before it runs into the quarry site. The whole is heavily overgrown.

Next comes an iron occupation bridge, similar in construction to the Alderbottom Viaduct, carrying the line over a farm track. It takes the form of girders slung between two upright stone pillars; the sides are high, constructed from iron plates made rigid by angled bracing spares. Dating is difficult, possibly an L & YR rebuild of c 1882. Then the line runs through a shallow valley and on to a viaduct that carries it over the Woodnook Water, which runs in the bottom of a 75-yd-wide valley. This viaduct is completely different from any other in the East Lancashire area. It may well be a replacement of an earlier timber structure. There are seven arches in all, but there is no stone used, it being totally built of engineer's blue brick. The remains of the iron fence on top of the low parapet still exist; there is a drop of some 50 ft to the river below. Again, a date of c 1880 seems most likely.

At the north end of the viaduct is a sign of L & YR pattern warning those using the occupation footpath there to beware of the trains. Of the Shoe Hill signal box, demolished in 1961, there is only a pile of rubble. There is another cutting and a single-arched bridge, next to which is a trespass notice of 1884: then comes a set of sand drags and a modern PW hut. There follows a girder bridge built, without doubt, under BR management and an iron viaduct which carried the line into Accrington station. This viaduct is built on seven pairs of circular piers which support a framework of girders and latticing above the mill lodge 20 ft beneath. On top of these is the track-bed. The whole looks like an iron copy of a timber design and it may in fact replace a timber predecessor. Can it be dated to the 1880s when the viaduct at Alderbottom was probably replaced?

The line then runs on to the pointwork leading to the goods yard or the platform faces. These are built on a tight curve which necessitates a speed restriction of 10 mph through them. It can have been no easy task to bring a train down to this speed after the long drop from Baxenden summit, especially in the days before the continuous brake.

The original Accrington station building still stands on the up Manchester platform, and although not designed by Mr Perring himself, the typical ELR style is easily evident. There are the moulded corner stones, small bay windows as at Rawtenstall, and the moulded kerb stone. The extensions at Accrington are all in the typical L & YR style and date in the main to the 1880s when much reconstruction was done throughout the whole region. These, of course, are too extensive for the needs of today.

These notes can be no more than an interim report. Much more work needs to be done, both out on the track and with the official records. Some structures are as yet undated; those of what appear to be twentieth-century date have not been considered at all. Apart from details such as these there is need of comparison with the rest of the ELR system and indeed that of the L & YR. Fieldwork is vital, especially now, as British Rail in its search for economy is destroying and demolishing so much so quickly.

References

1 Quotations in the text are from contemporary newspaper sources and are collected in *Haslingden 1800–1900*.

2 9 and 10 Vict c ccclxxviii.
3 Summerseat, a typical ELR station two miles north of Bury. I hope to be able to describe it and the other stations of the ELR system at a later date.
4 & 5 Harrison & Sale's *Guide to the ELR*.
6 Harrison & Sale's woodcut is in *Haslingden 1800–1900*.
7 Reproduced in *Haslingden 1800–1900*.
8 At the BR archives, as yet unclassified.

Bibliography

Official material:

The minutes of the East Lancashire Railway and the Lancashire & Yorkshire Railway are in the BR Archives in London. Sundry timetables and other publications are there and at the public libraries at Haslingden and Bury.

Other material:

Harrison & Sale's *Guide to the East Lancashire Railway* of 1848. A copy is in Bury Library.

Illustrated London News, 30 September 1848, gives a short description of the line.

C. Aspin, *Haslingden 1800–1900* (Haslingden 1963) collects relevant newspaper material and two useful photographs.

E. Mason, *The Lancashire & Yorkshire Railway in the Twentieth Century* (Ian Allen, 1956) gives a brief description of the line; cf also John Marshall, *The Lancashire & Yorkshire Railway*, vol 1 (David & Charles, 1969).

Plates, pages 274–5

LARCH S. GARRAD

Cronkbourne Village, Kirk Braddan, Isle of Man

A Note

CRONKBOURNE Village (SC 373777) is almost the only example in the Isle of Man of housing (illustrated on p 276) erected by a firm for its employees. It was built, probably between 1846 and 1850,[1] by the Moore family for the workers in their sail-cloth mill which was situated a little higher up the river, about a mile from Douglas, the island capital. From their regulations, published 1 January 1850, it is apparent that control was strict but the rents were reasonable, sixpence a week within living memory. By the turn of the century the tenants had benefits such as a reading room for the winter and a cricket club for the summer and this was the first Manx community to have electric street lights.

The mill is now a laundry while the dwellings have recently been bought, and modernised, by the Braddan Parish Commissioners. With their permission, and his own, the plans prepared by their architect, Mr S. F. O'Hanlon, FRICS, for their alterations have been used in writing this note. The forty-two houses were arranged in two parallel terraces at right-angles to the river (see plan 1). The rear terrace had a runnel, down which fresh water flowed, along its front; failing to keep this clear was one of the offences for which tenants were fined. The front terrace lies along what became a main road. The plans were fitted throughout to the variations in ground level. Since no contemporary description has yet been found, the original external finish is uncertain. The roofs are hung with imported slates, as they probably always were. The walls have been painted deep pink but it is likely that when first built the roughly-coursed walling of local slate was exposed.

CRONKBOURNE VILLAGE, Braddan, Isle of Man
24
42
WATER CHANNEL
n
RIVER
CHURCH HALL
PRIVIES
21
8
18
11
12
17
23
22
1
7
0
100'
feet

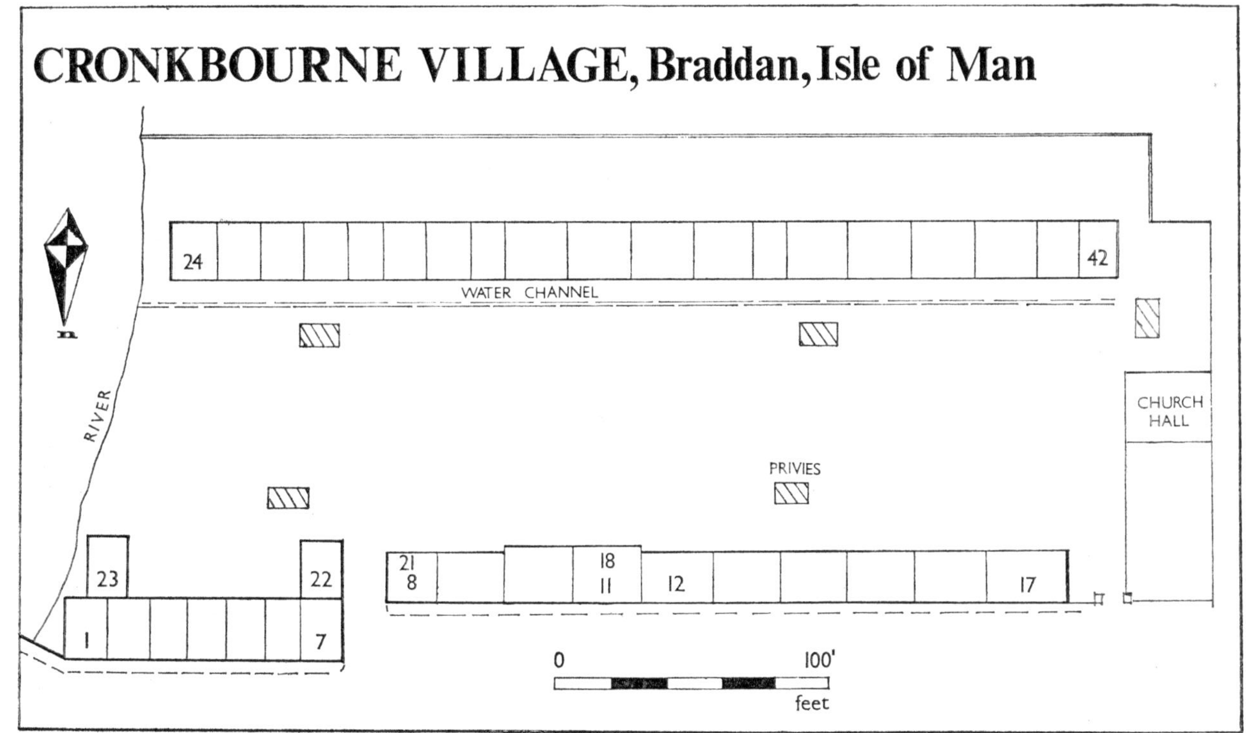

Plan 1

Despite varied dimensions and arrangements there were only two basic ground-floor plans consisting of two (living room and rear scullery), or three, rooms. Except for numbers 8–17 (see plan 4) the houses are two-storey. The single-storey dwellings, total internal measurements being 18 ft × 21 ft or 15 ft × 26 ft, were divided longitudinally into a living room, the full depth of the building, and a scullery with bedroom behind. The larger three-roomed houses have a similar plan (see plan 3), with access to the centrally-placed stairs from the living room. In the two-up, two-down front terrace (see plan 2) the stairs, along the party wall, are reached from the scullery while in the smaller rear-terrace houses—where the third room was merely a pantry sharing a window with the scullery, both lying behind the living room—they start from beside the front door (see plan 5). With the exception mentioned, the window pattern consists of one per room in the outside walls, normally the front and back.

The main structural alterations have been the addition of kitchen-bathroom wings and the demolition of 8 (20) and 9 (21) to improve road access. The outside privies and shared stand-pipes, originally only one tap for all the houses, have thus been replaced by modern plumbing. The surroundings have been tidied and, perhaps regrettably, the water channel covered. However, the final result of the modernisation is a group of attractive small homes in a pleasant setting instead of the demolition which a less sensitive body might have advocated.

Since the two- and three-roomed houses are mixed, the following table may help in interpreting the plans:

Front Terrace 1–7 & 22, 23 at rear: two-up, two-down; c 16 ft × 28 ft deep, internally (plan 2). 18–21, below and behind 8–11: two-up, three-down; c 21 ft × 18 ft deep, internally (plan 3). 8–17: single-storey, three rooms; c 26 ft × 15 ft deep, internally (plan 4)

Rear Terrace 24 & 25, 26 & 27, 28 & 30: two-up, two-down; stairs at front, living room NOT full depth;

Living room	c 8 ft	× 10 ft 10 in	deep, internally
Scullery	7 ft 6 in	× 9 ft	
Pantry	7 ft 6 in	× 6 ft 2 in	

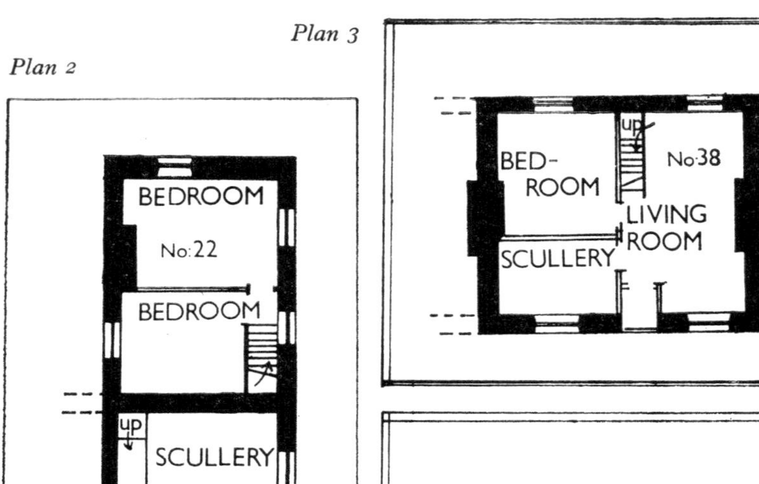

Plan 2

Plan 3

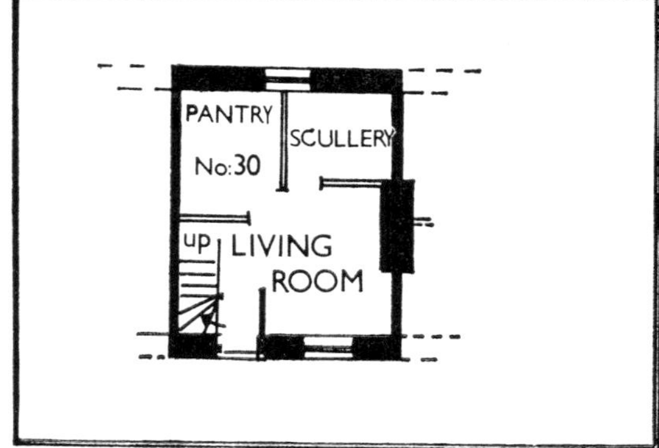

Plan 4

Plan 5

28, 31, 36, 41, 42: two-up, two-down;

Living room	c 14 ft 2 in × 10 ft 5 in	deep, internally
Scullery	6 ft 8 in	

32–35, 37–40: two-up, three-down;

Living room	c 10 ft 7 in × 17 ft 5 in	deep, internally
Scullery	10 ft × 6 ft 5 in	
Bedroom/ Sitting room	10 ft × 10 ft 7 in	

The 1851 Census provides valuable evidence as to the occupancy of the houses. Two millwrights—one with his son as apprentice—a mechanic and a boiler-maker are among the skilled craftsmen. The trades more obviously connected with the mill are as follows:

Hecklers 4
Flax-dressers 6
Spinners 17
Quillers 2
Spoolers 2
Reelers of sail-cloth yarn 2
Warpers 1
'*Workers*' 4 boys, 1 man, 10 girls under twenty and 13 women
Weavers 19
Bleachers 2
Overlooker Samuel Craig

It is noticeable that, although a school was provided, much younger children (eg boy hecklers twelve to fourteen) were working than in the contemporary mining communities. Of the eighty or so workers listed, about thirty gave their birthplace as Ireland. It is clear from the Census returns that the recruitment from the Irish linen trade was fairly steady, rather than occurring only when the firm was first set up, which again may indicate that the strict discipline of the textile factory did not attract the Manx. Nevertheless, by 1861 William Moore was employing a total of 150 hands, the majority housed in the village.

Reference

1 Manx newspapers are indexed to the first date and the building presumably took place before the publication of the regulations for tenants although it could be slightly later.

Book Reviews

The History of the Twelve Great Livery Companies of London, by William Herbert, DAVID & CHARLES, Newton Abbot, 1968 [1st edn, 1834 & 1837]; 2 volumes: xv, 498; xv, 684; ill, 80s and 100s.

The sixties, it seems, are the Great Age of Reprints. Occasionally a sneaking doubt assails one, a horrid prick of conscience: do we reprint so many old books simply because we are too lazy to write new ones? How much easier to reissue a Victorian volume, mistakes and all—even to the mysterious signature of Mr W. Jones, who appears unexplained on the title page of this edition—than to think out afresh all the formidable problems and answers (let alone undertake the research) on the history of London's twelve great livery companies. At £9 for the two volumes, moreover, and no author's royalties to pay, it seems a nice proposition for Messrs David & Charles. And *their* prices (to be fair) compare pretty favourably with those of a number of other reprinting publishers, whose charges are little less than extortionate.

Reprints of old editions of standard works like William Herbert's, first issued in 1834 and 1837, require three things. First, a good critical introduction; secondly, a thorough bibliography of subsequent works relevant to the subject; and thirdly, a sound modern index. No attempt whatever is made to fulfil any of these needs in the present case. There is no introduction and no bibliography. The index is Herbert's own, good enough for its time, but sadly deficient by modern standards. Take the letter F: it comprises only ten headings. True, these are elaborately subdivided; but an index to volumes of this scale which includes under F only feasts, fish, fish markets, fishmongers, frank pledge, funerals, funeral-palls, and furs is surely an oddity in the year of grace 1968. At any rate it will not be much help, it is to be feared, to industrial archaeologists.

However, let us not be ungrateful for—well, not exactly small mercies, but, shall we say, imperfect and voluminous ones to the extent of 1,200 pages. William Herbert was the librarian of the Corporation of London. The blurb is right in saying that his two volumes have remained an important quarry of fact, though some may find it surprising to learn that they have been 'read with enjoyment through the generations'. Actually few things are more dreary to read—except regimental histories and theology—than the story of an institution divorced from the community of people who formed it and for whom it existed. Institutions studied for their own sake are not as a rule specially edifying to the modern mind. At their best they are, like Carlyle's wife, a necessary evil.

In the institutional emphasis lies the strength and the weakness of Herbert's own work. As a librarian and a Victorian he had the insatiable interest in facts which has maintained the value of his two volumes, within their intellectual limits, for more than 130 years after their appearance. But in his day, for good or ill, sociology—or to put it less pretentiously, the study of human societies—had not as yet come to birth, or at any rate not to the baptismal font. After a general 'Historical Essay' on the livery companies as a whole, Herbert proceeds to a detailed description of each company under identical headings: 'origin and history', 'constitution and government', 'dress and observances', 'hall and buildings', 'trust estates and charities', and 'charters'. These are useful and important topics, though no doubt on all of them a great deal more ought now to be said than Herbert informs us of. There is little enough, however, on the story of the companies as living and evolving organisms. There is no systematic study of the changing composition of their personnel over the centuries, which would surely provide an enthralling story, and a most important one too, in the history of both London and the kingdom.

What the industrial archaeologist can get out of these two severely institutional volumes it would be presumptuous for the mere historian to say; but, one suspects, somewhat little beyond the occasional stray fact, and that, with the index as it is, may not be very easy to track down. Nevertheless the reprint is welcome. It is nicely produced and commendably well-bound. If one cannot say that no gentleman's library will be complete without it, one can say that no university library will be.

University of Leicester Alan Everitt

James Brindley, Engineer, 1716–1772, by Cyril T. G. Boucher, GOOSE & SON, Norwich, 1968, 130 pp, ill, maps and diagrams, 35s.

James Brindley is one of the outstanding figures of the Industrial Revolution about whom an almost legendary aura has been fabricated. Dr Boucher, in this book, is concerned to provide more authentic and precise knowledge about him, especially about his engineering constructions, by using his memoranda books, the records of canal companies, etc, and by studying the surviving remains of his numerous works. It is from the latter particularly and from Dr Boucher's illustrative line drawings that readers will derive some interesting new insights into Brindley's technical achievements.

On the whole, however, it must be regretfully stated that this is a disappointing book. Dr Boucher relies very heavily indeed on Smiles's famous life of Brindley, to which he does not make many significant additions. At the same time, he makes no reference to the modern researches on Bridgewater and Brindley by Mr Mallet and Dr Chaloner. The book suffers from a poor chronological arrangement: chapters 2 and 3, for instance, dealing with Brindley's death and his descendants, would have been more appropriately placed at the end. It is also padded out with much irrelevant material: chapter 3, on Brindley's descendants, particularly Arnold Bennett, the novelist, is largely irrelevant; chapter 8 contains a great deal of tedious material on the later history of the canals which Brindley originally built or planned; while there are also a number of 'chatty' interjections. The literary style is rather clumsy and disjointed and compares unfavourably with Smiles.

It also appears that Dr Boucher, while helping to destroy some of the myths which have gathered about Brindley, has fabricated another of his own: that the network of canals linking the four main river estuaries of the Trent, Mersey, Severn, and Thames, and often referred to as the 'Grand Cross', was 'envisaged from the beginning' by Brindley as one great integrated scheme. Of this Dr Boucher provides no real evidence. It is true that Brindley was engaged in surveying for a proposed Trent–Mersey canal as early as 1758, but this scheme was dropped and he became involved in building first the Worsley–Manchester Canal, then the Bridgewater (Manchester–Runcorn) Canal, and afterwards the Grand Trunk. Not until the later sixties is there really firm evidence, in surveys and plans, of Brindley's wider scheme, which appears to have developed gradually rather than to have been visualised from the start of his canal-building activities.

University of Manchester A. E. Musson

Roads and Vehicles, by Anthony Bird, LONGMANS, 1969, pp x + 250, ill, 45s.

This is the third volume in the long-awaited and welcome industrial archaeology series edited for Longmans by L. T. C. Rolt. It is a lively and readable account of the development of the British road system in the last 200 years, and of the tremendous variety of vehicles which have used the roads in this period. It is directed at the general reader, being 'popular' in style and content rather than scholarly: the author is better on historical generalisations than on the detailed exposition of historical events. About a third of the book is concerned with the roads, tracing their administration and the changes in constructional techniques, and the following two thirds deals with the vehicles. The book is pleasantly illustrated, although it would have been useful to have had some line drawings explaining technical words such as those designating parts of wheels and coaches.

The reader is left with the impression that Mr Bird was glad to reach the second part of his narrative, although there is probably less industrial archaeology involved in the vehicles than in the successive relics of the road system. Indeed, a major criticism of the work is that there is not much attention to industrial archaeology in it, apart from a brief discussion of the term on the first page of text. The remnants of obsolete road systems in the form of milestones, turnpike houses, road signs, and stretches of abandoned road, are dealt with only incidentally and almost brusquely, even though these are the real grist to the industrial archaeologist's mill. As a single example of this weakness, General Wade's military roads in Scotland are briefly mentioned (although wrongly dated), but none of the remaining sections are located, either in the text or in the inadequate gazetteer, and there is not a map in the book. Despite this, the book has many good qualities, and as a background study to a complicated subject it deserves to be widely read.

Bath University of Technology Angus Buchanan

John Dalton and the Progress of Science, edited by D. S. L. Cardwell, MANCHESTER UNIVERSITY PRESS, Manchester, 1968, pp xxii + 352, ill, 55s.

This volume, a collection of papers presented to a conference of historians of science held in Manchester in September 1966 to mark the bicentenary of Dalton's birth, represents a notable addition to the literature on this enigmatic figure. The contributions cover the whole field of Dalton's interests—his background, his relationships with contemporaries, and his influence on successors. Dalton the man emerges clearly, in an essay by Frank Greenaway, as a modest, rather retiring man, who never married, but who was an excellent teacher of young people, yet someone who suffered from the disadvantage of intellectual isolation. D. S. L. Cardwell in his introduction stresses the importance of Dalton's early interest in meteorology and in the physics of gases in conditioning his attitude to atomism, and accounts for his simple approach by his love of teaching, and his fondness for playing with models. Dr Cardwell follows this up by a discussion of Dalton's place in the development of a Manchester scientific community.

A. Rupert Hall's paper *Precursors of Dalton* is a clear statement of the novelty and usefulness of Dalton's atomism as compared with the ideas of Newton, Boyle and Descartes, while Henry Guerlais's contribution is a wide-ranging and scholarly assessment of the background to Dalton's theory. More specific aspects of Dalton's antecedents are given by Arnold Thackray in his discussion of the development of the Newtonian approach to quantified chemistry and by B. B. Kelham in his paper on late eighteenth-century atomic theories. Archie Clow considers the industrial background to Dalton, coming to the conclusion that the chemical industries operating in and around Manchester had no direct impact on Dalton. In his essay *Berzelius and the Development of the Atomic Theory*, C. A. Russell comments on the differences between Dalton and Berzelius in their concept of atoms and how they should be represented, but emphasises the role that Berzelius, as the leading chemist of his time, played in popularising the atomic approach, particularly through his adoption of alphabetical symbols for the elements, and his accurate determinations of atomic weights. E. L. Scott and William H. Brock both discuss Dalton's relationships with individual scientists—Mr Scott pointing out the importance to Dalton of the intellectual companionship of William Henry, and Dr Brock discussing Dalton's attitude to Prout's hypothesis.

A further group of papers is concerned with Dalton's other scientific achievements. Professor Manley assesses the importance of his work on meteorology, which was one of his early enthusiasms, pointing out that his research on the air-water vapour system was significantly new. Robert Fox traces the antecedents of Dalton's theory of heat, demonstrating how Dalton's mistaken views arose, while W. V. Farrar discusses Dalton's contribution to the development of structural chemistry, maintaining that, though his ideas in this field were naïve, his approach, with its emphasis on model studies, was the one which was to prove fruitful in the light of later theories of bonding.

A general survey of Dalton's influence on chemistry is contributed by Harold C. Urey, while more specialised papers by M. P. Crosland and two Russians, Yu. I. Solov'ev and L. P. Petrov, consider the impact of the atomic theory on French and Russian scientists.

The other essays are less easily classified: Mrs Farrar's survey of Dalton's scientific equipment effectively disposes of the myth that his apparatus was crude—it was well up to the standards of the time, and not cheap—he spent £200 at one time on the purchase of supplies. An interesting sidelight on the practice of Dalton's time is the use of interchangeable brass fittings in pneumatic apparatus—the fore-runners of the modern standard glass cones and sockets. W. D. Wright, in a fascinating paper, discusses Dalton's recognition of his own colour blindness in the light of modern theories of the mechanism of colour perception, while the late Sir Cyril Hinshelwood, in what is in many ways the most stimulating essay in the collection, points out the danger of 'spurious quantification'—of attempting to replace 'difficult qualitative judgements' by 'inadequate mechanical counterparts'. Sir Cyril, while recognising the value of the quantitative approach in deepening our understanding, is concerned with the existence of the qualitative experiences of our inner consciousness. This paper is essentially a plea for the recognition of the value of both qualitative and quantitative approaches, and of the danger of the undue neglect of either. It could be read with profit by both scientists and non-scientists.

Altogether this is a most interesting collection of papers, which in its diversity of approach and style is perhaps the epitome of modern British writing on the history of science.

University of Strathclyde John R. Hume

The Industrial Archaeology of Dartmoor, by Helen Harris, DAVID & CHARLES, Newton Abbot, 1968, pp 239, ill, maps and diagrams, 50s.

If the bleak uplands of Dartmoor have hitherto seemed to the un-initiated to be an unfruitful hunting ground for the industrial archaeo-logist, this impression will now be firmly dispelled by Mrs Harris's most readable and comprehensive work. The moorland itself and its immediate surroundings have seen the rise, and in most cases the fall, of industries whose range was surprisingly wide and whose scale was often considerable.

Metal mining led the way. In the twelfth century Dartmoor was Europe's largest source of tin, and it came to boast four stannary towns, although more recently, with the emphasis turning to copper and arsenic, the mines could not compete in importance with those of Cornwall and the Tamar Valley. Granite quarrying was widespread, and the china clay industry still flourishes. Peat working on a commercial scale was several times attempted, but always foundered through lack of transport facilities. The peripheral region had its quota of corn mills, wool mills dependent on the moorland sheep, and some paper and edge-tool mills. A solitary gunpowder factory adorned the centre of the moor. Of the many water leats, domestic and industrial, the 17-mile Plymouth leat of 1591 and others are remarkable for the skill of their early engineers. The turnpike road, and indeed the wheeled vehicle, came late to Dartmoor, and many of the ancient pack-horse tracks across the moor may still be traced. The rise of granite quarrying, china clay working and large-scale peat works resulted in a number of highly individual railways. Finally, Mrs Harris gives an admirable survey of a subject too often ignored by the industrial archaeologist: agriculture. Always an uphill pursuit on the moor, where even the most intrepid nineteenth-century improvers met their Waterloo, it has influenced the area's history as deeply as any other activity, and left remains which, if not as spectacular, are equally worthy of study.

Of the vanished monuments, we may particularly lament the 70-ft waterwheel at Taw River mine, and deplore the needless depredations of the military. But, though much has perished, much remains, and the moor is still adorned by such highlights as the blowing houses, the water leats, Sticklepath forge, and the egregious Haytor granite tramway. The surviving remains of each industry are enumerated, and their history, working and place in the economy concisely described. The text is complemented by an informative gazetteer of sites. A number of the maps, in spite of their generous scale, are less detailed than one would like. There are some good photographs, especially the nineteenth-century views of Poldice mine's wheel and stamps, and the aptly-named Gem mine nestling under Brunel's timber Walkham Viaduct.

No book of this sort can be exhaustive, for space demands some degree of selection. Two granite quarries do not find the mention which they perhaps deserve—Christow and Wilminstone, both large enough to have possessed locomotive-worked tramways. Mrs Harris refers to the Cann Wood railway, but neglects the canal that preceded it and the slate quarry it served. Nor does she discuss the railway (a branch of the Plymouth and Dartmoor, or a separate system?) from Swell Tor and Foggintor to the Tavistock–Princetown road. Turnpike roads, so essential in improving access to the moor, are dismissed in less than a page; and their milestones—and the ancient crosses at Sourton and Shaugh Prior, re-used as direction posts—are ignored. Then the word *trackway*, which generally appears in its normal meaning of foot-or horse-path, sometimes signifies, disconcertingly, a railway track. Finally, apart from a few parentheses in the text, there are no direct references to sources of information: nothing but a skimpy bibliography that surely lists only a tithe of the material used.

But these few shortcomings cannot detract from the value of the book as a whole. It is a worthy companion to Frank Booker's *Industrial Archaeology of the Tamar Valley*. The two areas adjoin; in both, mining was the principal industry; but in most else the contrast is great. Compare the highway of the Tamar and its tributary canals and railways with the lengthy, uncertain and tedious communications of the moor; the market gardens and horticulture of the valley with the painful agriculture of the uplands. In Dartmoor, man seems puny and nature omnipotent. The picture that Mrs Harris paints, through the medium of the surviving remains, is the very human one of man's struggle against the powers of nature, to tame them for his own profit and benefit. This is the very stuff of industrial archaeology.

University of Hull M. J. T. Lewis

Early Agricultural Machinery, by Michael Partridge, HUGH EVELYN, London, 1969, pp 30, ill, 16 pp colour plates, 63s.

This book, in common with most of Hugh Evelyn's publications, is of a commendably high standard in appearance, presentation and printing. It is intended to be a popular history of agricultural implements and machinery with most of its emphasis on British usage and practice. What a great pity then, that a book, which is obviously directed at a public which will be inevitably largely ignorant of farm implements, should contain so many errors of fact, so much loose interpretation and such poor technical descriptions. It is a necessity above all for such a work, however simple and superficial, to be accurate. This requirement is singularly lacking.

Mr Partridge, who, no doubt, wrote this book with the best of intentions, has a knowledge of farm machinery and especially tractors, which is revealed as one reads on, to be scanty in the extreme. He devotes, in the limited space available, an inordinate amount of attention to implements which were no more than examples of man's misguided ingenuity, for example, Mann's reaper, the Blackburn digger, the Marquis of Tweedale's ploughing engine, not to mention that supreme example of sheer idiocy in engineering, the Darby steam digger. All these (and there are others), were designs (if that is the right word) which were completely abortive, mere figments of disordered imaginations; they were born of nothing, they achieved nothing, and had no effect whatever on the mainstream of farm mechanisation. Surely machines of more historical significance could have been chosen with benefit to all concerned? It seems that Mr Partridge's undoubted talent as an illustrator (his colour prints are very attractive) has been allowed to take precedence over his judgment as a historian. His text, regrettably, shows little or no trace of originality and is, in the main, merely a rehash of the three modern authors listed in the bibliography, with the addition of inaccuracies which appear to be his own. For example, on p 13 he states in connection with Bell's reaper that 'no reaper was ever sent to America from Britain', whereas Fussell (one of Mr Partridge's authorities), quotes Slight, a contemporary writer, as stating categorically that four machines were exported to the USA as early as 1834.

To be fair, while on the subject of Bell, he does give the Reverend gentleman due credit. Bell was definitely the first with a practical reaper, for McCormick himself admitted that his own was not a good machine until after 1841. Mr Partridge is incorrect in stating that the Crosskill-Bell reaper had a side delivery added; this was a feature of the original. In fact, the Crosskill, which was a success in its day, was Bell's with an improved cutter bar. Until the advent of the self-raking principle the Crosskill-Bell was by far the most advanced design on the market. Another error in this same chapter occurs when the author states that when McCormick died in 1884 he had become a rich man 'since the family had developed the International Harvester Co'. This is a blatant mistake as IHC was only created in 1902 with the amalgamation of the McCormick interests with the Deering Harvester Co and three smaller manufacturers. A careful perusal reveals many more inaccuracies, but it is not until one reads Section 12 on tractors that the full extent is made apparent. The author has, unfortunately, accepted as his authority the Rev Philip Wright's book, *Old Farm Tractors*, and has made a paraphrased precis of its contents; Wright's book is perhaps the worst travesty of historical reporting it has ever been my misfortune to read. I will forbear to bore the reader of this review by undue recapitulation, but such arrant nonsense should not pass without some comment. To cite examples: the Ivel tractor had twin cylinders not twin engines; the idea of using tracked vehicles dates from Edgeworth's patent of 1775 not Cayley's of 1825; the Ideal tractor was only notable for its lack of success, very few being made, and the Austin Cultitractor was imported from the USA. The description of a motorplough as a 'Boon type plough' is novel but not of much value except to one with a wide knowledge of tractors. The Boon was, in fact, a little-known and late addition to the ranks of those hybrids known as motorploughs, all of which, fortunately, descended into oblivion with great celerity.

In conclusion, very nice presentation, excellent colour prints for which the author can claim much credit, but as a popular history of farm mechanisation, this book is of very little value.

Pocklington Charles L. Cawood

The Village of Ecclesfield, by David Hey, THE ADVERTISER PRESS LTD, Huddersfield, 1968, pp 133, ill, maps, 25s (2s post and packing if ordered directly).

For whom should the parish history be written? Some consideration is due to subscribers, representing the alert general interest, but time has shown how even this audience may change in its approach, just as the need for such grass-roots material has grown among social and economic historians. A balance between anecdote and rigour is sometimes hard to strike, and some writers in this field manage altogether to avoid such an antithesis. Mr Hey at least goes some way towards striking the mean, although some sections, notably those on poor relief and crime, show an over-popular approach.

Ecclesfield is now one of Sheffield's northern suburbs, hardly separated from the city's twentieth-century expansion. Mr Hey samples the development of the original distinct community from its agricultural beginnings through, in turn, its increasing specialisation in nail-making and, later, filemaking. By use of probate inventories, Hearth Tax returns and the 1851 census he illustrates social and economic patterns over four centuries, prevented to some degree by shortage of other material from providing the support these sources are apt to need. While accepting that such a book rarely pleases everyone, the industrial historian may well seek a fuller treatment of secondary metal manufacture. Indeed, agrarian historians have come increasingly to recognise the importance of part-time industrial earnings to small farmers of many periods, and, in turn, the social historian may wish to test how far such a reserve of industrial skills provides a basis for later developments.

A set of maps of varying quality comes loose with the book, and sixteen half-tone plates are bound between the main text and the appendixes, their captions being grouped, rather awkwardly, on the succeeding pages. As some of these plates appear more significant to the author than to this reviewer, perhaps some economy here might have afforded an improved treatment of the maps.

University of Sheffield D. W. Crossley

The Compleat Collier . . ., by 'J.C.', FRANK GRAHAM, 6 Queen's Terrace, Newcastle-upon-Tyne, 3rd edn 1968, pp 55, 6s. **Blundell's Collieries: Technical Developments 1776-1966,** by D. Anderson, HISTORIC SOCIETY OF LANCASHIRE & CHESHIRE, 1967, pp 66, ill.

Coal mining, as befits what was once a great national industry, has been well served by its historians and commentators. At no point is this more so than in technological development, where Galloway's *Annals of Coal Mining and the Coal Trade* is surely still one of the very best technical histories for any British industry. The two booklets reviewed here are both contributions to the history of mining thus conceived, though they differ widely in age and purpose.

The *Compleat Collier*, first published in 1708, is here reprinted between stiff paper covers as a facsimile reproduction of Richardson's edition of 1845. Along with the account of mining in Simpson's *Hydrostaticks* (1672) it is one of the earliest expository works on the 'whole Art of Sinking, Getting and Working Coal-Mines' that we have. It is based entirely on experience in the great northern coalfield of Tyne and Wear, but since this district was generally in the vanguard of technical development, it may be taken to represent the best mining practice of its day. 'J.C.' treats such subjects as drainage, winding and the sale of coal in the dialogue form so popular in treatises of the period. Though later books dealing with the northern coalfield are inevitably fuller, the *Compleat Collier* is of particular interest for its appearance before Newcomen's crude but mighty steam engine liberated colliery engineers from the worst uncertainties of drainage. Thus it looks at the technology of 'Nef's revolution' and has in fact been frequently drawn on by historians of early mining progress. Reprinted at this price it ought to be quite irresistible to all interested in the subject.

Mr Anderson, a modern mining engineer and surveyor, has for long been engaged on a history of the collieries of the Blundell family situated at and around Wigan. In a series of notable articles in the *Transactions of the Historic Society of Lancashire & Cheshire* he has placed us all in his debt by offering us a first-class social, economic and technical history of this important group of mines. The present pamphlet is in effect an offprint of the article dealing with the changing technology over almost the last two hundred years of mining. Aided by a judicious choice of (mainly) old photographs and some excellent diagrams and drawings, the author covers every aspect of mining development. Doubtless his description of the engines used for pumping, winding and haulage will be of the most interest to industrial archaeologists, who will cherish the photographs of early beam engines (though they are not the actual ones used by the Blundells). Coal mining has left its most obvious physical heritage in the shape of waste tips and the often mean rows of monotonous collier houses. But it was not without its own architectural dignity, as witness the fine headgear illustrated in plate 4 or the truly noble engine house at Pemberton Colliery (plate 8).

As collieries close, the familiar mining landmarks which those of us who grew up in coalfields regarded as immutable are being swept aside. Mr Anderson's booklet is an example of a concern for the past which is scholarly and meticulous in detail while also succeeding in recapturing the wider physical impact of coal mining on the environment.

University of Strathclyde Baron F. Duckham

Our Contributors

DR M. J. T. LEWIS is Staff Tutor in Industrial Archaeology, Department of Adult Education, University of Hull. Cambridge classicist. Books on temples in Roman Britain, on the Festiniog and Pentewan railways, and (soon to be published) on early wooden railways.

W. N. SLATCHER, a Cambridge graduate, did research in history of science at Manchester. Now Leverhulme Fellow in the History of Technology, Imperial College. Putting finishing touches to doctoral thesis on Aire & Calder Navigation.

DR P. N. JARVIS is Liverpool graduate. Interests include medieval castles and Cistercian industrialism. Part-time platelayer on Festiniog Railway. Does some extra-mural lecturing on Industrial Archaeology.

DR ARTHUR E. J. WENT has a doctorate in zoology. He is scientific adviser to the Fisheries Division, Department of Agriculture & Fisheries, Dublin, and an expert on the past and present of the Irish fishing industry.

P. T. L. REES graduated from University of Nottingham in 1968 after reading Classics with Archaeology as a subsidiary subject. Now studying for Certificate in Education and hopes to take up teaching post in the East Midlands.

MISS LARCH S. GARRAD, PhD, AMA, is Assistant Keeper at the Manx Museum. She takes an active part in organising the field work of the Field Section of the Isle of Man Natural History and Antiquarian Society. Together with four fellow members of the Society she is writing an 'Industrial Archaeology of the Isle of Man' for David & Charles.

Notes and News

Heritage at Work

We feature below the first of a series of occasional items on industrial sites where traditional crafts or modes of operation are still carried on as in the past. In this issue Mr K. Howarth, 25 Red Bank Road, Radcliffe, Lancs, writes about a remarkable survival in the Lake District. His fine illustrations show bobbin manufacture at Stott Park Mill, Finsthwaite.

Stott Park Bobbin Mill

About a mile north of Newby Bridge is Stott Park Bobbin Mill, one of the few traditional industries that Lakeland still possesses. The firm of E. & W. Coward dates back to 1875 when Mr William Coward, grandfather to the present Mr J. R. M. Coward (partner) came to Stott Park. The first building on the site could have been a cottage or farmhouse, as there is evidence that the buildings were used as a cornmill at some time. The oldest structure is built of typical Lakeland stone, local stone again being used when extensions were added in 1880. The earliest part is still represented, narrow windows of the 'domestic' type being of note.

Originally, the wood was handturned, the only power being a wide breast waterwheel at the back of the factory, but today only the race remains. The waterwheel was abandoned in 1880 when the new extensions were built, part of the reorganisation including the installation of a steam engine, which replaced the waterwheel.

Lengths of timber litter the forecourt of Stott Park Bobbin Mill, Finsthwaite

Interior of the mill, showing a maze of belts carrying power to the various machines

This steam engine worked until 1946, when an electric motor took over. Today the steam engine still remains in working order, at the back of the works. Built in 1880, at the time of the extension, it is a single-cylinder horizontal engine with injector, condenser and 7-ft flywheel. It was supplied by W. Bradley, Brighouse, Yorkshire. Steam was raised in a Cornish boiler which is still in use, supplying the necessary heat for drying timber laid on trays above the boiler, in a room known as the kiln. The tall brick chimney from the boiler is still intact at the rear of the works near the old mill race.

The production of bobbins from the raw wood, even though partially mechanised, still requires a great deal of traditional skill. Mr J. Ivison, partner in the firm, recalls how as a youngster he was paid 2¼d per twenty lengths for 'bleeding' (releasing the sap by removing several strips of bark) which stopped the wood from becoming rotten.

The main types of wood used at the mill are: silver birch (which is used as soon as possible); alder (which is suitable for some jobs; although poor, it is very light); and sycamore, which owing to its superior quality does not have to be bled. 'Bleeding' or 'chipping off' used to be carried on from Martinmas to Whit Sunday when it is said the sap ran naturally. Timber around sixteen years old is preferred by the workers at Stott Park.

Today only a handful of men are employed at Stott Park, although forty or fifty men have been employed there in the past. The timber is cut into short lengths and dried in the kiln, a hole is bored through the centre of each piece and finally the wood is turned. The workers, several feet deep in wood shavings, and unconscious of the web of belts and pulleys inches above their heads, work happily as is shown by Mr James Graham who has worked at Stott Park for forty-eight years. When the finished bobbins are dropped from the lathe they fall into a basket known locally as a 'swill'. The swill is made of plaited pieces of wood shaving and forms a firm, solid dish. The oldest machine on which turning is still done dates back to 1876, being built by W. A. Fell, Paisley & Bridge Iron Works, Windermere.

Although there is a great deal of fine dust in the air, surprisingly bobbin making is a healthy vocation. Today, there is little demand for the knee-deep accumulation of wood shavings in the works; occasionally local farmers use it but of course, in the days of the steam engine, wood shavings were an excellent fuel. Wood is supplied through timber merchants today and re-distributed in the form of bobbins all over the country from this little works, which can produce up to 300 gross of bobbins a week. The big advantage that a small firm like Stott Park has over its competitors is that it can undertake to do small orders, whereas the larger manufacturers find it uneconomical even though they may be using synthetic materials instead of wood.

Drilling wood ready for turning

The CBA and the National Organisation of Industrial Archaeology

Dr Angus Buchanan, Bath University of Technology, writes as follows:

At the Bath Conference on Industrial Archaeology in November 1968, grave concern was expressed about the lack of an adequate national organisation for pursuing the objectives of industrial archaeology. It accordingly appointed a steering committee with a mandate to discuss with the CBA and other interested bodies the possibility of strengthening the industrial archaeological functions of the CBA, or to consider the formation of an independent Council for British Industrial Archaeology, and to make a report of its deliberations. In the course of fulfilling the first part of this programme, the committee had a long consultation with representatives of the CBA, as a result of which it was felt that it would be useful to publish some factual information about the CBA in order to remove current misunderstandings about its role in industrial archaeology.

The Council for British Archaeology is a body which exists to represent the interests of archaeological societies in Britain. It was established in 1944 and in 1967 it had 338 organisations affiliated to it. Each constituent organisation is represented on the national council, which meets twice a year, and on its Regional Group. There are single regional groups covering Scotland and Wales and thirteen groups for England. Each of these groups is represented on the Executive Committee, which holds four or five meetings annually. The income of the council in 1967 was £15,448 12s 2d, of which £10,000 came from a government grant, £595 10s 0d from affiliated organisations, and over £4,500 was derived from CBA periodicals and publications. The council has a staff of five and an office at 8 St Andrew's Place, Regent's Park, London, NW1. Its periodicals include the *Calendar of Excavations*, issued monthly from March to September with a summary of the season's fieldwork published later in the year, an annual *Archaeological Bibliography for Great Britain and Ireland*, an *Annual Report*, half-yearly lists of *Current and Forthcoming Offprints*, and *British Archaeological Abstracts* (twice yearly). The council supports six period research committees and a scientific research committee. It makes annual grants for the publication of important archaeological papers and administers awards for training in field techniques and research on behalf of the Carnegie United Kingdom Trust and the Margary Research Fund.

The CBA has made a contribution to industrial archaeology in Britain too. A research committee in industrial archaeology was set up as early as 1959 and has recruited its membership ever since from amongst the people who are most actively engaged in the study of the subject. This committee meets twice a year and discusses a wide range of subjects, from urgent matters of preserving industrial monuments to less pressing issues such as the possible design of postage stamps commemorating important industrial structures. The membership now stands at forty-five, and from the outset the chairman of the committee has been Professor W. F. Grimes.

The development of industrial archaeological activity and the increasing urgency of measures to preserve industrial monuments led the research committee to appoint an advisory panel from amongst its number to recommend for preservation industrial monuments included in the National Survey or notified by affiliated societies or private individuals. The advisory panel is also making a systematic review of industrial monuments, county by county, giving assessments of the relative merits of monuments. The recommendations of the panel are confirmed by the research committee and are then passed to the appropriate Ministry or local planning authority. The panel at present consists of fourteen members under the chairmanship of Professor Grimes. It meets twice a year on the same day as the research committee, and during 1968 it made nine recommendations for scheduling and forty for listing industrial structures.

The National Survey of Industrial Monuments was set up in 1963 by the Ministry of Public Buildings & Works in conjunction with the CBA, which had been urging the need for such an investigation upon the Ministry. The Ministry appointed Mr Rex Wailes as consultant to carry out the survey. In 1966 the Ministry invited the CBA to take over the direction of the survey which would continue to be coordinated by Mr Wailes whose salary and expenses, together with the administrative costs and travelling expenses of the panel and research committee, would be met by a government grant of £2,000 for a period of three years. This arrangement has now been extended.

In addition to these functions, the CBA and its regional groups have promoted conferences and other activities to which industrial archaeologists have been attracted. The conference on *Problems of Urban Recording* in March 1968, for example, was supported by 125 people including many involved in the study of industrial archaeology. The council is now planning to hold a conference on *The Future of Industrial Archaeology* in London on Saturday, 11 October 1969. It is much to be hoped that industrial archaeologists will attend this conference in great numbers in view of the importance of its theme.

Committee for the Recording and Study of Historic Engineering Structures Before and During Demolition

Dr Stanley B. Hamilton of the Newcomen Society has asked us to print the following letter:

During the demolition of old structures to make way for new it must from time to time transpire that, for a brief period (sometimes of only a few days), some interesting detail is exposed or evidence comes to light as to how the old structure was put together. Too often, before anyone who would recognise the significance of the exposure knows of it, and however willing those in charge of the work might have been to co-operate, that opportunity has been lost forever. A committee of the Newcomen Society for the Study of the History of Engineering and Technology has accordingly been set up to consider how such loss of historical evidence can be prevented.

It should be made clear at the start that preservation is NOT the aim of the committee: nor is the assessment of architectural merit or social significance; other bodies attend to these worthy objects. In the first instance, and to limit the field to manageable size, the committee proposes to concentrate on:

(a) Structures erected before (say) 1870, of cast iron or wrought iron, alone or combined with masonry and timber.

(b) Early reinforced concrete before (say) 1914.

It is requested that engineers willing to help will:

(1) Make this fact known to the Hon Secretary of the Newcomen Society at the Science Museum, South Kensington, London, SW7.

(2) Give early warning of the threat of demolition to any structure with which they are concerned that, by age or association, is likely to be of interest.

(3) Let a member of the committee see drawings and documents that explain the construction.

(4) Allow access to the structure at an

appropriate stage of demolition.

(5) Permit photographs or sketches to be made.

(6) Allow old drawings no longer needed to be taken for filing in the Science Museum.

Research Inquiries

The Editors will be pleased to publish readers' research inquiries from time to time. We hope this will provide a useful means of co-ordination and interchange of ideas.

Stroudwater Navigation

M. A. Handford, Department of Economic & Social History, University of Bristol, 67 Woodland Road, Bristol 8, is engaged in a research project on the Stroudwater Navigation and would be grateful for any information or details of records. Readers who can help are asked to contact him direct.

Pre-Engineered Buildings

The Griswold, Eshleman Company, Public Relations Executives, 1 East Wacker Drive, Chicago, Illinois 60601, are anxious to obtain information relating to pre-engineered metal buildings. They are particularly interested in the origins of the 'standing' or 'welted seam' roof and thought that readers might be able to provide details of when these types of roofs were first used and when the 'standing seam method' evolved. They would also be grateful if readers could refer them to any other organisation or institution which might be able to help them.

Turnpike Roads

Norman Mutton, Wolverhampton College of Technology, St John's Square, Wolverhampton, is seeking help about a problem relating to turnpike roads. He is sure that other workers must have met, as he has in south Shropshire and north Worcestershire, references to posts or stones being set up by turnpike trusts to indicate the beginnings and endings of exceptionally steep hills, over which carriers were allowed to use an abnormal number of horses without penalty. The problem is simply one of identification. What did such posts or stones look like? Has anyone definite evidence that any existing stones were indeed set up for that purpose? Probably there was nothing like a standard design, yet they must have been readily recognisable wherever they occurred. Mr Mutton poses a related point of interest about operations on steep hills. Where were the horses kept? Was it in a nearby stable ready to assist heavy coaches or loads (for a fee), in a manner analogous to a railway banking engine? Or did each carrier take enough spare horses to cope with any incline he might meet on the journey? Mr Mutton would welcome any references or illustrations from readers on these interesting relics.

Classifying Industrial Monuments

Following the article entitled 'The Classification of Industrial Monuments' in Vol 6 No 1, Mr P. J. Riden, 18 Mill Lane, Wingerworth, Chesterfield, Derbyshire, has written to us as follows:

I was most interested to read the article on the classification of industrial sites as I have been interested in this problem for some time. Not only do we need some kind of standard classification like the one suggested, but also a new method of compiling an index of sites to supplement or modify the NRIM. The simplicity of the system and its basis on the SIC are two of its outstanding merits, but perhaps with more single-digit subdivision more precision could be obtained without loss of simplicity. The heading 701 might be subdivided as follows:

701.0 Railways in general
.1 Standard gauge

.2 Narrow gauge
.3 Broad gauge
.4 Underground railway
.5 Rack railway
.6 Cable railway
.7 Overhead railway
.8 Monorail
.9 Horsedrawn railway

As the question of motive power hardly arises in the case of *Communications* (either being explicit in the class number or so various as to be impossible to classify), the idea of combining class numbers could be used here in a slightly different way. Thus a tramroad at a colliery would be 101.1.701.9; railway staithes by a river navigation, 705.4.701.1; and a canal at a gunpowder mill, 273.0.750. Such figures would be no more complicated than OS grid references.

If the three- or four-digit system was adopted for the industry classification, the addition of two more numbers for the site would give each record card a unique reference. The first of these might consist of the two digits for the county (such as the NRIM already uses) followed by five for the site number within the county. Finally the eight-figure grid reference would complete the classification. The following is the reference of a hypothetical milestone near Chesterfield, Derbyshire: 705.1/12.00371/SK 341632. Such a method would give greater scope for expansion than the system used at present by NRIM. Cards could either be indexed by county or industry.

I outline below a further possible breakdown of sections within the *Communications* heading:

702.0 Roads in general
.1 Turnpike or post road
.2 Packhorse road
.3 Drove road
.4 Military road
703.0 Road transport in general
.1 Tramway
.2 Trolleybus
.3 Motorbus
.4 Other vehicular transport
704.0 Docks and harbours in general
.1 Dock
.2 Harbour
.3 Wharf
.4 Basin
705.0 Canals and inland navigation
.1 Narrow canal
.2 Broad canal
.3 Ship canal
.4 River navigation
.5 Navigable dyke or drain
706.0 Air transport in general

Tasker Collection

Tasker's Waterloo Ironworks near Andover was established in 1813. Over the past twenty years the firm has succeeded in retrieving from all over the country examples of bygone Tasker workmanship of every kind, showing the development of rural industry and technology since the early nineteenth century. It included the largest collection of steam traction engines, as well as threshing machines, horse gears and numerous varieties of ploughs and other agricultural machinery.

Change in ownership of the firm meant dispersal of the collection and an appeal was launched at the eleventh hour to save as much as possible. Hampshire County Council offered temporary storage space and land suitable for a permanent building at the site of their projected Museum of Hampshire Rural Life at Chilcomb House, near Winchester. The Appeal Fund was most successful and at the auction in February this year spent over £13,000 on eleven of the twenty-six traction engines and about two thirds of the 159 lots. One of the Appeal Fund's trustees, Mr Robin Butterell, said that many enthusiasts and United States buyers decided not to bid because of the intention to keep the collection together. (See David & Charles' book on the firm)

Museum of Telecommunications & Electronics

Mr W. Dudley White, a technical author of Crestland Wood, Alresford, Colchester, Essex, has written a monograph suggesting the need for a museum specialising in exhibits illustrating the development of telecommunications and electronic engineering, the early stages of which 'are now passing into history'. 'It is highly desirable', writes Mr White, 'that coming generations of engineers working in these branches of technology should be able to see examples of the methods used by their predecessors.'

In the past a good deal of obsolete plant was scrapped without regard to its value as an illustration of one stage in the development of a technique. But thanks to efforts of a number of industrial firms and a growing interest in industrial archaeology, some early equipment has been preserved, either in private and industrial collections or at the Science Museum in South Kensington.

The main aim would be to display, in as dynamic a form as the material merits, the key developments in radio, broadcasting and television, radar, data handling and transmission. The secondary aim would be to convey the meaning and purpose of electronics to the wider public.

Mr White suggests that Chelmsford had strong claims for the site of this proposed museum. The building in which Marconi carried out his work 1899–1912 still stands in Hall Street. In excellent preservation and virtually unaltered since that time, 'it would make a highly appropriate and useful part of the accommodation required'.

IA in a Primary School

Natural Science in Schools, Vol 6 No 2 (Summer 1968) contains a most interesting article by Oliver Aston of Harlescott Grange County Junior School, Shrewsbury, entitled 'Industrial Archaeology: Historical and Scientific Links at Primary Level'. Mr Aston wastes little time on the philosophy of the subject, and unlike many adults working in industrial archaeology, immediately equips his youthful workers with boots and maps. 'Discovery which begins and ends in books is, at the primary stage, of no great value', writes Mr Aston, 'and after the full exercise of their own resources, the children will turn to books and are helped to use them to complete what can be a very comprehensive survey.' Environmental studies have long held an important place in modern educational theory, but in practice are stultified by numerous difficulties both real and imaginary which the teacher has to face. Not so Mr Aston, for he backs up his opinions with case-studies of work undertaken by himself and his pupils and writes at length on the scope for future applications in the junior classroom. Clearly there

Hydraulic crane at Broad Street

Broad Street Goods Depot, prior to closure 1968

are more problems with younger children than with sixth-formers (especially if let loose on a derelict industrial site), but Mr Aston has done good service in alerting primary school teachers to the value of industrial archaeology as a teaching and learning medium.

Greater London

Mr Paul Carter has written telling us of latest developments in the capital. The outcome of the inaugural meeting of the Greater London IA Society was the election of a Steering Committee of eleven, who are to decide the exact aims and functions of the new society, draw up its constitution and report back to the general body of people interested. The main aims are to provide a really good communications system, writes Mr Carter, so that everybody knows of all the activities in the area. This will be partly achieved by a professional-type bulletin, to be published once a month if possible. There will be one or two one-day conferences on industrial archaeology in the area annually, plus a couple of full-day demonstrations on site of the various methods of recording. It is also contemplated to have a number of visits of various types to stimulate interest.

The society may undertake or assist in the production of a film on monuments in London and it has offered its help in the possible restoration of a beam engine house, containing four compound pumping engines (J. Watt & Son, 1864) at Crossness Sewage Treatment Works, being considered by the Greater London Council for preservation. The building not only contains its four engines, but also has some very fine cast-iron work, similar to that at the better-known Abbey Mills Pumping Station.

Mr Carter has sent some fine photographs of monuments surveyed by the Thames Basin Group over recent years and we reproduce three of them here. The Broad Street railway goods depot of the LNWR dates from 1868 and was closed recently. It has a number of interesting features, including a magnificent hydraulic crane. The shot of warehousemen at St Katherine Docks, Stepney (just before closure last October), shows the limited amount of space in a building dating from 1828. Here too the Thames Basin Group carried out a detailed photographic record, which has been deposited with the National Monuments Record and a full report is now being compiled.

Preserving Cornish Waterwheels

A. J. Stoyel, Hon Secretary of the newly formed Cornish Waterwheel Preservation Society writes:

Cornwall is in the process of losing the last of the waterwheels and associated machinery which have been a feature of the county for centuries. The Cornish Water-Wheel Preservation Society has been formed in order to save some of the best examples of these before the opportunity is lost for ever. It is hoped to start work on several projects in Cornwall, repairing and restoring some of this machinery to working condition, and the following illustrate the scope and urgency of the task.

In Trevaunance Coombe, St Agnes, on a site designated for a new car park, stands a small set of Cornish stamps. Such stamps were used in their hundreds to crush tin

Workmen in bonded warehouse (c 1828) at St Katherine Docks, closed in 1968

ore in Cornwall and the basic design has not changed for centuries. Of the handful which has survived, however, not one has any degree of security. The society intends to dismantle, remove, and re-erect this particular set on a suitable site, replacing whatever is necessary to enable it to work again.

The old tin yard at South Crofty Mine is to be demolished within the next few weeks and the society has received the generous offer of the old wooden dipper wheels, one of which is 12 ft in diameter. These used to lift the tin-bearing slurry to higher levels during the concentrating processes and they are now unique, although once common to all the old Cornish tin-streaming works. The society intends to take this chance of salvaging them.

On a remote site near Blisland stands the largest waterwheel on the mainland of England. This wheel, which is 50 ft in diameter, used to work iron flat-rods for a mile and a half to pump water from a china clay pit. Although it was not built in Cornwall, it is the last of the great waterwheels which were part and parcel of Cornish mining. Emergency repairs must be carried out in the next few months or this wheel will collapse.

The obvious bias towards the mining industry in these examples reflects the urgent need for preservation in this particular field but does not indicate a preoccupation with it. The dismantling, removal, and re-erection of one of the last examples of horse-driven gear in the county, from a farm near Altarnun, is another imminent project which demonstrates just how wide are the interests of the society.

Volunteer labour will be used wherever possible but the financial assistance which can be attracted will also be a crucial factor in determining how many of these previously-neglected relics of Cornwall's history can be saved. The annual subscription is 10s 6d, with a junior subscription of 5s 0d for full-time students aged 14 and over, and the society is confident that, given the support that its aims deserve, it will be able to preserve for the future some of the fine relics from Cornwall's past that are at present being neglected or broken up for scrap.

Cornwall County Museum Appeal

For 150 years the Royal Institution of Cornwall has sponsored, financed and administered the Cornwall County Museum in Truro and during the long period has acquired a reputation as one of the best regional museums. It has numerous important collections and has become the natural centre for students of every aspect of the county's history and archaeology. The museum is invariably busy with casual visitors, researchers and organised school parties and the premises are also used by numerous local societies.

In the early years of the nineteenth century, when the Institution was founded, the mine and the smelting house, the foundry and beam engine were the symbols of Cornwall: men like Davy, Trevithick and Gilbert represented the spirit of inquiry which underlay the industrial activity. Industrial history and archaeology are well represented, and indeed metals and mining are reflected in much of the museum. There is the famous ingot of tin which was dredged up from Falmouth Harbour, the Roman ingot from Carnanton and the medieval one from Fowey. There is a comprehensive and unrivalled collection of smelting-house marks and examples of miners' primitive tools. The Mineral Gallery houses a unique geological collection, containing numerous metal ores found in Cornwall.

The museum has now entered a new phase of development and an Appeal Fund has been launched to provide new facilities for storage, staff and public accommodation as well as complete redecoration of the building. The appeal was directed with success toward the Institution and county and over £14,000 has been raised. It is now being widened and all who are sympathetic to things Cornish are invited to contribute to the Appeal Fund target of £28,000. The Secretary of the Appeal Committee is H. L. Douch, County Museum & Art Gallery, Truro, Cornwall.

Southampton University IA Group

At a recent meeting of the Southampton University Industrial Archaeology Group, Mr Brears of the Hampshire County Museum Service spoke on the technique of the pottery industry in the immediate post-medieval period. While there are considerable remains of brick, tile and terracotta works in Hampshire, the production of good domestic pottery was somewhat restricted, but Mr Brears drew attention to three main areas. First, the extreme north-east of the county, second, an area straddling the Dorset border at Verwood in the west, and third, the Fareham district. With the increasing interest in the collection of pottery, including examples from the Victorian period, knowledge of Hampshire products may well increase and the work of other potteries and the sites of their kilns may come to light.

After Mr Brears's talk, the chairman of the group, Dr Edwin Course, drew attention to their exhibition on view throughout March in Winchester City Library. This was also displayed in other centres in and around Southampton. Fieldwork includes the listing of Hampshire windmills and watermills, preparatory to a gazetteer being compiled by one of the group, Mrs Monica Ellis of Colden Common. To date, significant remains of about 140 mills had been recorded. Work is also in progress on breweries and on the whiting industry. It is hoped that when the gazetteer of mills is ready for publication, the group will undertake a survey of roads, including milestones and tollhouses.

York

Mr Stanley Tyson, Westwood, 27 Carr Lane, Acomb, York, who recently contributed a note on the work of W. Thomlinson Walker, a York ironfounder, continues to produce some excellent short monographs on industrial archaeology in the area for the Department of Liberal & General Studies, York College of Further Education. His *Industrial Archaeology In and Around York* contains details of several hundred sites under the headings: brickyards; buildings; bridges and aqueducts; canals; hydraulic power; quarries; tunnels; water engineering; windmills; watermills; cast iron; and railways. Mr Tyson has also produced a two-page *Industrial Archaeology Perambulation Around York*, which is a circular tour of the industrial features of the city, easily undertaken on foot and which can be joined at any point along the route. It includes many nineteenth-century buildings normally overlooked by the visitor and even by the trained architect or industrial historian.

Steelmaking in Sheffield

The Steel Times Annual Review 1968 contains an article entitled *Early Steelmaking in the Sheffield Area* by K. C. Barraclough, joint Hon Secretary of the Sheffield Trades Historical Society, which outlines the development of the industry in the town and district since the late seventeenth century. The article provides interesting, detailed information on crucible steelmaking.

Salisbury & South Wiltshire

Bulletin No 11 of the Salisbury & South Wiltshire IA Society contains details of spring and summer programmes undertaken by members. Field survey work carried out by the society is very varied. A photographic survey of the mills of A. Laverton & Co, Westbury, was undertaken, prior to disposal and sale of premises. The company records are being deposited with the Wiltshire County Record Office. At Wilcot near Pewsey a forge operated by eighty-year-old Mr S. Williams was recorded and some interesting hand tools discovered. Arrangements are in hand for a research programme into the history of R. & J. Reeves Ltd, an agricultural engineering firm and ironfounders, established in 1808. Mr D. A. E. Cross, Hon Secretary of the society, is investigating mills in the county which produced hydro-electricity. The summer excursion concentrated on the Poole, Wareham and Isle of Purbeck districts, where a variety of features were visited.

Somerset Hemp-spinning Mill

Mr R. J. Shepherd, a director of David & Charles, has sent some notes and photographs of the plant of the small hemp-spinning mill known as Dowlish Ford, in the Somerset countryside near Ilminster, which he owned until twenty years ago. The machinery, dating from the last quarter of the nineteenth century, was torn out in a hurry in 1940 when the mill was requisitioned for war production, and only the photographs and Mr Shepherd's recollections remain.

The power-producing and transmitting plant is probably more interesting than the spinning machinery which differs little in principle, though much in detail, from its modern equivalent. The power source for the whole plant was a Hick Hargreaves

Mill pond and hempmill buildings at Dowlish Ford

Hemp preparing room

horizontal condensing engine of 200 ihp, turning over at 50 rpm and fed with steam from three Lancashire boilers at a pressure of 60 lb per sq in—a most soothing machine to watch. The flywheel was 6 ft in diameter, of cast iron. Its segmented rim carried teeth which geared into a much smaller pinion on the line shafting, which at that point had a speed of 200 rpm. The rim segments were detachable, to assist renewal. The whole assembly was finally tightened up with oak wedges. The engine was extremely reliable right up to the end, and though hardly economical in steam its maintenance costs were minimal. How a mere 200 hp drove all the heavy machines involved puzzled successive owners, but it did, even when most of them were working together; the indicator diagrams showed consistent power.

Power was transmitted to the machines (no electricity being available) throughout the rambling old buildings by shafting—there must have been 400 or 500 ft of it—carrying pulleys which drove through belts on to the individual machines. At one point the buildings turned through roughly a right angle, so that the shafting had to follow suit: for many years a set of five ropes ran over a grooved pulley on each shaft and passed round two grooved drums placed almost vertically on the corner between them (see the photographs). The ropes wore out quickly and the bearings of the drums could only be kept cool by the application of enormous quantities of oil, so the arrangement was replaced in the 1920s by bevel gears, which proved much less expensive. At another point where a right-angle drive was required, but where only a low power had to be transmitted, a pair of bevel gears with hornbeam teeth was used. These needed renewal in time, but on the whole were efficient.

Drying yarn in steam-heated room at Dowlish Ford

Fitting-shop and mechanics at work

Crank and part of flywheel of Hick Hargreaves engine at Dowlish Ford

North East

Mr D. Wilcock, Secretary of the Durham IA Group has sent us news of the activities undertaken by members recently. The winter programme was completed in May and consisted of lectures, films and visits on subjects such as coal mining, glass making and wagonways. Trips were made to a steam-powered pumping station, a coal-shipping harbour, a steel works and the Durham County Archives Office. The summer programme for 1969 included a group survey of wagonways, old colliery sites and industrial housing.

The Sunderland Group of the North East Industrial Archaeology Society has held several joint meetings with the Durham Group and has also pursued a very successful programme of its own. A Sunderland town survey is well underway and the local planning department has shown great interest in the work and is keen to have a copy of the final map and record.

Stourbridge Foundry

Norman Mutton of Wolverhampton College of Technology writes:

The Black Country is notably cavalier in its treatment of historical material. There is an urge to go forward with little regard for the past; not a bad thing in itself, this does make difficulties for those interested in industrial archaeology for it tends to the destruction of relics irrespective of their value or importance as historical documents.

One notable relic, of national and not merely of local importance in my view, is the Stourbridge Foundry with its unique wrought-iron and cast-iron roof truss system devised and developed by John U.

Rastrick (1780–1856). The foundry was designed and built by Rastrick in 1820–1. It was one of the first major projects of his association with the Stourbridge ironmaster, James Foster (1786–1853). Rastrick had become managing partner of the Stourbridge Ironworks of John Bradley & Co, of which Foster was part-owner and in complete charge, and Foster and Rastrick expected, and in fact realised, a vast expansion of their foundry business. For many years the Stourbridge Ironworks and Foundry remained Foster property, but the character of the firm and the work now carried on has, not unnaturally, changed over a century and a half and most of the old works is now destroyed.

The foundry however still survives, although altered. Some years ago it was taken over by a firm of ironfounders so that it has reverted to its original purpose. In 1968 the chimney stack, of considerable visual appeal, was demolished, and one or two of us expressed fears over other possible alterations, especially to the roof. It must be stressed that the present owners are anxious to maintain the character of the fabric so far as possible, and have in fact gone to some expense. Attempts to interest the planning authority, the Worcestershire County Council, in taking positive steps to schedule the building have not been successful. Like many other towns, Stourbridge is changing rapidly, and the area by the east end of the old ironworks complex is now having a ring road constructed by it. Other changes will surely follow and it would be pleasant to feel that there was no danger to the foundry, even if the ownership should change. I suggest that action by the County Council to schedule the building is the best way to ensure this.

A final point, and one very much to the credit of the County Council, is that it has just scheduled the Georgian gothic house, 7 Lower High Street, Stourbridge. This house, also threatened by the ring road development, was built for and occupied by Gabriel Bradley, the father of John Bradley who founded the firm owning the ironworks and foundry. Gabriel's widow lived there and when she remarried, her second husband, Henry Foster, and their children including James Foster, also lived there. It is a house of considerable architectural character (Professor Pevsner declares it the best in the whole town) but it also has these important industrial associations and its preservation should be a spur to preserve the Stourbridge Foundry.

Portsmouth Scrap Yard

Dr Ray Riley of Portsmouth College of Technology has been carrying out a survey of the Warblington Street premises of Thomas Barnes Ltd, a metal merchandising firm. The works comprise a scrap yard (still in operation) and a smithy which ceased work in 1966. The scrap yard contains a massive shearing and punching

Brick-built tyre oven at Portsmouth

machine, weighing 10 tons, by Scrivens & Co of Leeds, built 1870–90. Initially installed in Portsmouth Naval Dockyard, where it was used for shearing and punching rivet holes in ships' plates, it was moved to its present locale in 1934. It was probably originally steam-powered although it is now driven by an electric motor. The vertical motion for punching and cutting is achieved by cams placed on the ends of the main shaft and the two operations are carried out at different ends of the machine. Holes up to ½ in in diameter can be punched through ¼-in plates, while the 13-in shearing edges will cope with a similar thickness. Swing gantries can be employed to support sheets being punched or cut.

In the yard outside the smithy stands a brick-built tyre oven, thought to have been constructed c 1900 and used until 1956 to heat metal tyres fashioned in the smithy. The 3 ft 6 in radius tyre plate on which the hot tyres were fitted on to wooden wheels, and the metal trough from which water was taken to cool the tyres, are both *in situ*. The oven had two iron doors, since once the tyre was in position it had to be rotated to achieve an equal overall temperature. All that remained within the smithy were two furnaces, a swedge stand by Allday & Sons, London and some miscellaneous furnace equipment.

Economic History Society: IA

As usual the Economic History Society, as part of the proceedings of its annual conference (held at Durham University during the Easter vacation), arranged visits to places of interest to industrial archaeologists: the lead mines in Weardale and the remarkable staithes of the planned coal port of Seaham Harbour attracted a great number.

Scrivens' shearing and punching machine

Lock gates at Seaham Harbour with staithes in the background

Scottish Society

The Scottish Society for IA held its first annual business meeting on 8 March in the University of Strathclyde. Following the election of office-bearers two papers (illustrated by slides) were read on 'The Rise of the Scottish Cotton Industry' (by J. Butt) and on 'Ports & Harbours in Galloway' (by I. Donnachie). The society hopes to increase its efforts to co-ordinate work by individuals and local societies in Scotland and steps have been taken toward the establishment of a Scottish Archive of Industrial Monuments to be based on the Royal Commission on Ancient & Historic Monuments of Scotland in Edinburgh.

From the Newsletters

Manchester Region IA Society *Newsletter No 1* (Spring 1969) contains a useful check-list of CBA Report Cards received, classified under the headings of Power, Transport, Raw Materials, Manufacture and Industrial Housing. Dr R. Hills summarises the findings of a coal mine survey undertaken in the summer of 1968, which included the recording and photographing of winding engines at a number of collieries and the Bickershaw brickworks of the Midland Brick Co. A survey of central Manchester by the society is being actively encouraged by the City Planning Department. Bristol IA Society's *Bulletin Six* (April 1969) gives details of four projects being undertaken this summer: paper mills of the Bristol region; turnpike roads (completing the fieldwork begun in 1967); a systematic survey of the Kingswood area; and the lead industry of the Mendips, under the supervision of Dr Angus Buchanan. CBA Group 2 has produced *Industrial Archaeology in Wales Newsletter No 5* (1968–9) virtually a one-man effort by its editor Douglas B. Hague. It contains a useful bibliography of books on industrial archaeology in Wales as well as reports from local societies working in the field.

T. T. HAY

Watermills in Japan

JAPAN is a country of contrasts, none more striking than the technical achievements and outlook in twentieth-century industry, developed from European practice, compared with the long-established methods and attitudes introduced from the Chinese mainland since the fourth century. A particular example of this is the extensive use of water power, both in hydro-electric installations using turbo-alternators, and in farming communities where simple waterwheels are used for grinding and polishing rice. The reasons for these anomalies are largely historical in that Japan retained a feudal system with a policy of isolationism towards the outside world until the middle of the nineteenth century. When the feudal system collapsed the Japanese set out to achieve in a few decades what had taken centuries to develop in the western world.

According to the Nihou-shoki (*Ancient Chronicles of Japan*) the first watermill in the country was made by a priest from the Kingdom of Koma in Korea in 610. The Nihou-shoki also mentions that in 670 a watermill was constructed and used in the making of iron and this was apparently introduced from China. It seems that from about the seventh century watermills came into general use for grinding cereals, husking or polishing rice, one type even being built into a ship and used for polishing rice.

In Japan today mills are still working which have not changed in design or method of construction since they were first introduced into the country. There is no evidence that horizontal waterwheels were ever known in Japan. This could mean either that the Chinese developed the vertical wheel and gearing without the evolutionary stage of the horizontal wheel which occurred in Europe or that they had progressed well beyond the horizontal wheel before watermills reached Japan.

The primary need for watermills in the eastern world was to polish rice, the staple food in many areas. This consists of removing the husk and is analagous to our need to peel potatoes. A pounding rather than a grinding process is used, and the equipment (illustrated on p 369) is very similar to the ore stamps for the preparation of lead for smelting or drop hammers for forging, used in this country up to the nineteenth century. As the rice polishing equipment could be driven conveniently by a vertical waterwheel—and gearing was not essential—it is possible that the horizontal wheel was never needed and thus never invented.

Grinding was also required to make rice and maize flour for the preparation of cakes and noodles. For this gearing was required to transmit the rotation of the vertical waterwheel to the horizontal mill-stones. Having developed the vertical waterwheel for polishing rice, it was a comparatively simple step to adapt it for grinding (illustrated on p 370). In Europe, mills for grinding corn evolved from rotating hand querns, to Greek and Norse mills with horizontal wheels, to Roman mills with vertical wheels and gearing, and thence to the ultimate developments of the nineteenth-century watermills.

Even today all forms of mill can be found still in use. One hundred miles south of Tokyo, in the Izu peninsula, there are several working waterwheels, polishing and grinding rice, and one notable example driving a sawmill at Kawaino (illustrated on p 369). A very fine example of a mill with both polishing and grinding equipment stands by a farmhouse/restaurant at Hiekawa on the sky-line highway, a popular tourist area (illustrated on p 370). As an attractive commercial showpiece for visitors, this mill is likely to remain, but ideally it should be put in the hands of the Japanese equivalent of our Ministry of Works or National Trust to ensure its preservation.

Locally available timber—pine, cedar, oak and bamboo—is used in the construction of the buildings, waterwheels and equipment, nails and iron fittings being almost non-existent. Even so the waterwheels last for some fifteen years before they need rebuilding or renewal, and polishing and grinding equipment has given over a hundred years' service. The simple peg gearing and bearings of hard bamboo last surprisingly well; thus there has been no desperate need to seek better materials. The basic design of the grinding equipment is remarkably similar to illustrations which have survived of Roman mills; yet these eastern designs could be much earlier than that which the Romans evolved.

As in this country, the owners and operators of Japanese mills are very proud of their association with waterwheels and their family

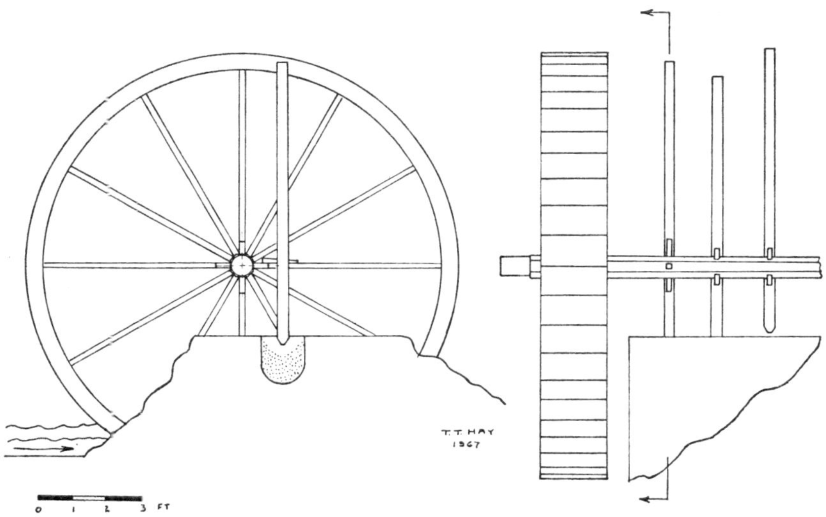

Rice polishing mill, Odawara, Japan

tradition of milling, and are pleased and flattered that others from the 'outside world' share their enthusiasm. However, as maintenance and repair costs of water courses, buildings and equipment increase, and quicker, more compact and efficient electric or engine-powered equipment becomes available, so Japanese watermills become uneconomic and are fast disappearing. For example a small electrically-driven rice polisher (illustrated on p 418) can handle in an hour what a water-driven mill takes twenty-four hours to polish.

The Engineering Department of the National Science Museum in Tokyo is anxious to preserve a typical example of a working watermill as a 'national cultural asset' and although it has a dismantled mill in store, as yet they have no site on which to re-erect it. The waterwheel is very much a part of the traditional Japanese landscape (see p 369) and appears in many wood-block prints. It is an ornamental feature, full size or in miniature, turning in many parks and gardens. However, from the archaeological point of view it is the mill and milling equipment which needs preservation as well as the waterwheel.

Since the middle of the last century Japan has established an industrial society equal to and beyond that of any developed country in the world. If the current motto of one Japanese electronics firm, 'Find out the best practice in the world and improve on it', had been applied centuries ago to the watermills which were adopted from China, it is interesting to speculate what the inventive Japanese mind and skilled craftsmanship might have produced.

Plates, see pp 369–70 *and also* Notes and News, p 418–19

ANGUS BUCHANAN

The Cumberland Basin, Bristol

THE Cumberland Basin (illustrated on p 371) was named after the Duke of Cumberland, the son of George III who was made a freeman of Bristol in 1803 and who became King of Hanover in 1837. The name was given to the entrance basin of the Floating Harbour, that important improvement in the port of Bristol which was officially completed on 1 May 1809. The Floating Harbour had been constructed by the Bristol Dock Co formed under the Bristol Dock Act of 1803, and it had taken exactly five years to complete. The engineer was William Jessop, a distinguished figure in the first great epoch of the civil engineering profession, who had many canal and dock works to his credit. The fact that his name is less familiar today than those of some of his contemporaries is probably due to his great natural modesty.[1] Jessop was responsible for the plan which was finally adopted, after a generation of argument, for the improvement of the port of Bristol. The object of this scheme was the conversion of the tidal courses of the Rivers Avon and Frome in the centre of the city into a wet dock at permanent high-water level, so that ships could remain afloat at all states of the tide. It was this feature which caused the improved port to become known as the 'Floating Harbour'.[2]

The Floating Harbour was provided with three entrances: Cumberland Basin, Bathurst Basin, and the Feeder Canal. The latter admitted barges and other river traffic from the Avon Navigation connecting with Bath and, eventually, the Kennet & Avon Canal. The Bathurst Basin gave access via the New Cut to the upper half of the harbour. Only the Cumberland Basin could deal with the largest vessels, and it was intended from the beginning to be the main entrance to the harbour. The basin was excavated from the clay of Rownham Meads in a southwards bend of the River Avon before it swept north-west

THE PORT OF BRISTOL:
Location of Cumberland Basin
Urban area, 1968
Scale
0
1
2
miles
N
Avonmouth Docks
Portishead Dock one mile
RIVER AVON
Pill
Filton
Sea Mills
B R I S T O L
RIVER FROME
Clifton
Gorge
Suspension Bridge
Floating Harbour
City Docks
Cumberland Basin
Area shown in figure two
New Cut
Bathurst Basin
Feeder Canal
Totterdown Lock (derelict)
Netham Dam
Crews Hole
Conham
BJHB 1968

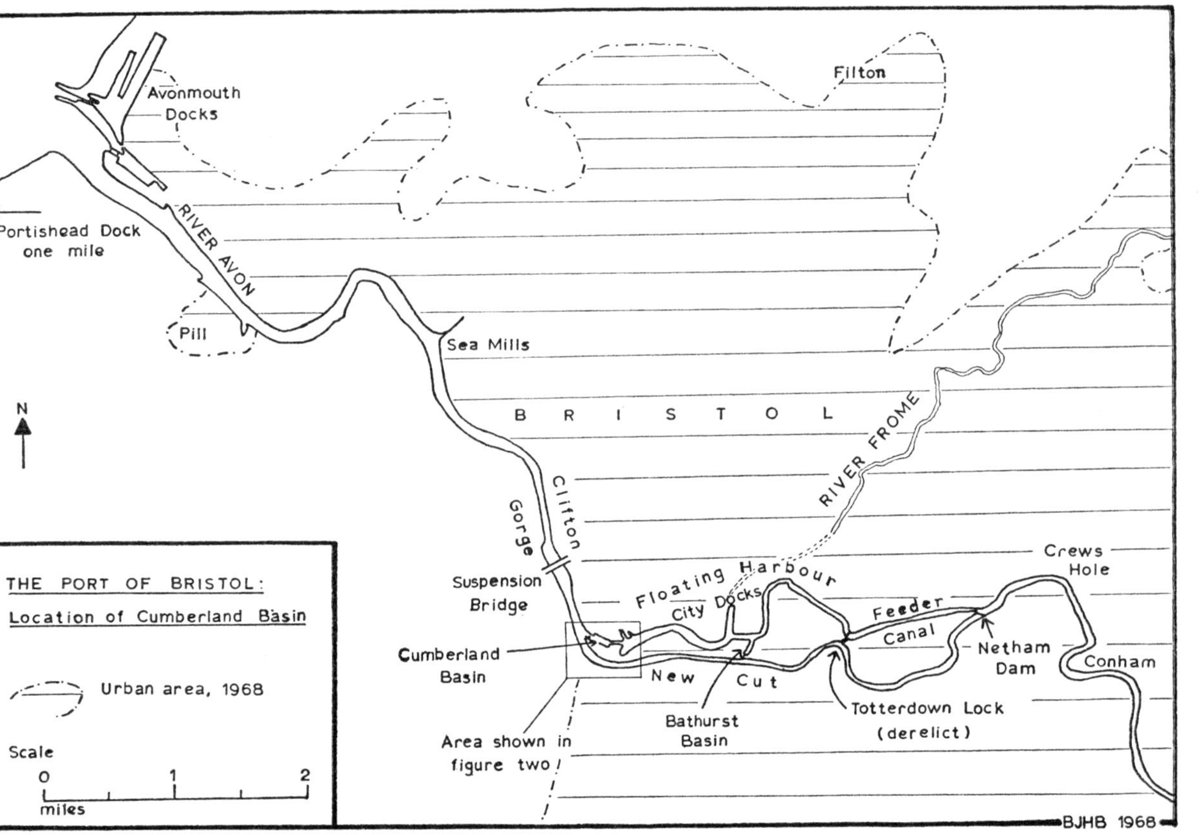

Fig 1

into the Clifton Gorge. Jessop had originally planned for it to cover an extent of 6 acres, but as an economy measure at a time when the costs of the whole enterprise were beginning to mount alarmingly over his estimates, the size was reduced by a third to 4 acres. He was also obliged by the instability of the sub-soil to line the whole of the basin with masonry, which he had not intended to do.[3]

Another modification in the design was a reduction in the number of locks. Although Jessop appears, from early drawings of his scheme, to have thought in terms of a single entrance lock at either end of the basin, the Act of 1803 specified four—two entrance locks from the river and two junction locks between the basin and the harbour and the Merchants' Dock respectively. In the course of construction, however, amending legislation allowed the junction with the Merchants' Dock to be omitted. The Merchants' Dock was an enclosed wet dock which had been constructed at Hotwells in 1765 but had never been popular with ships using the port because of its distance from the city centre. The other three locks were built as planned, the two entrance locks being almost at right-angles to the river with a narrow pier separating them. The northern entrance lock and the junction lock were 45 ft wide, while the southern entrance lock was only 33 ft wide. The only one of the three to survive in anything like its original shape is the now disused junction lock.

Many modifications have been made to the Cumberland Basin since it opened to shipping in 1809. The first major alteration came in 1844–8 when the southern entrance lock (illustrated on p 371) was reconstructed to designs prepared by I. K. Brunel. It was completely rebuilt to a width of 54 ft; most of the additional width was taken off the south side because of the narrowness of the central pier between the two entrance locks. The size of this pier limited any extension to the length of the new lock, but Brunel sought to increase its operating capacity by the arrangement of the gates. He designed novel single-leaf gates constructed in wrought-iron on the 'caisson' principle of containing air chambers which enabled the gates to become partially buoyant and thus more mobile. The gates hinged into large recesses on

THE CUMBERLAND BASIN, PORT OF BRISTOL
Line of old railway to Canons Marsh
RIVER
AVON
North Entrance Lock
Old North Entrance Lock
Grid Iron
CUMBERLAND BASIN
Old Hydraulic Power Station
Junction Lock
Merchants Dock
Hotwell Dock
Mardyke
FLOATING HARBOUR
Brunel's Lock
Rownham Ferry
Railway
B
A
Tobacco Warehouses
Old Junction Lock
Hydraulic Power Station
Underfall Yard
Underfall Dam and culverts
Ashton Swing Bridge
NEW CUT
N
Scale
0
1000
yards
(all roads omitted)
BJHB 1968

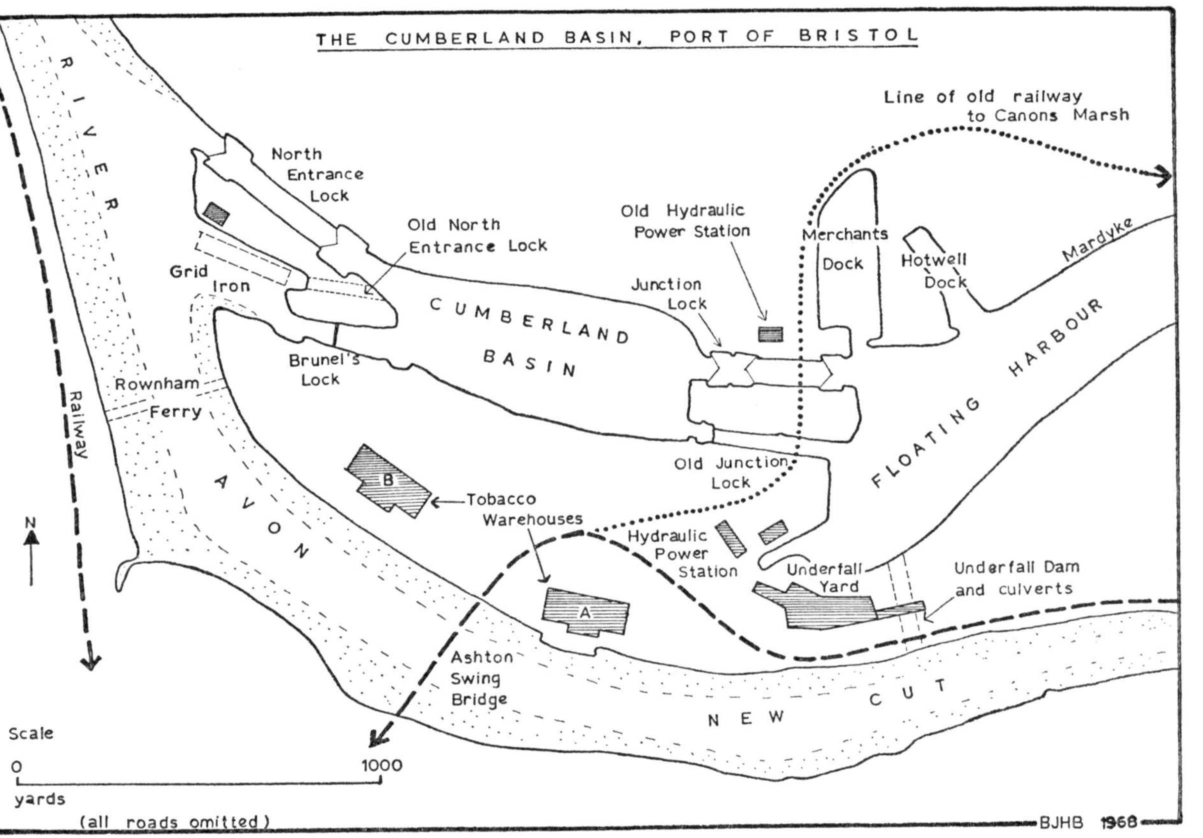

Fig 2

the southern side of the lock and were worked by chains running through channels in the masonry to manually-operated 'crabs'. The whole lock was strongly constructed and was designed with a semi-oval cross-section across the base. The masonry, gate recesses, and apertures for the winding chains, can still be clearly seen at low tide; so can the hinge which carried the outer gate. The gates themselves, however, have long-since disappeared as the lock has not been used for many decades and it is now permanently sealed by a concrete wall across the middle of the lock pit.

The new lock, which has always been known as 'Brunel's Lock', required a new swing bridge to span it, and Brunel provided this also. His design is interesting, both for its characteristic ingenuity and for the fact that it incorporates a feature which he later developed successfully on a large scale for his railway bridges at Chepstow and Saltash. This is the cylinder made up of plates of wrought-iron, two of which are used in the bridge which survives at the Cumberland Basin. There is, however, difficulty in identifying which bridge it is because there are two on the site, virtually the same in design and size. The engineer's reports in the 1870s show that Thomas Howard, when he was engineer to the Dock Committee, removed Brunel's bridge and put it over the newly enlarged northern entrance lock. He then found it necessary to put a new bridge over Brunel's Lock, and it seems likely that he went back to Brunel's drawings for his design. If this is a correct reconstruction of what occurred, the genuine Brunel swing bridge is that by the northern lock (rarely swung now), while the bridge over Brunel's Lock is a later imitation dating from c 1875.[4]

Another contribution of Brunel to the Cumberland Basin was the *BD6*, the scraper-drag-boat used from the 1840s to the 1960s for removing deposits of mud from the walls of the basin so that it could be raised by conventional dredging and scoured into the Avon through the culverts at the Underfall Yard. Brunel first recommended the use of such a boat in his report to the directors of the Dock Co in 1832, and he designed his first experimental scraper-boat soon afterwards. This was a complete success, and led to the construction of the *BD6* in 1843. The dismantled parts of this ingenious craft are now in Bristol City Museum, although the hull itself was beyond hope of repair after its long working life and had to be scrapped. A smaller replica of the *BD6* was at work until recently in Bridgwater Dock.

Great changes were made in the Cumberland Basin during the 1870s, when Thomas Howard rebuilt the northern entrance lock, cut a new junction lock, and installed hydraulic power to operate the gates, bridges, and other machinery. By altering the alignment of the new northern entrance lock Howard decreased the angle with the river, which had become a major operational hazard of the port. He also managed to increase the length of the lock from 200 ft to 350 ft and widened it from 45 ft to 62 ft. The new lock was opened in 1873.[5] The central pier between the two entrance locks was greatly enlarged as a result of this alteration, particularly when the redundant part of the old northern lock was filled in. The river-wards mouth of this old lock now provides one end for the 'grid-iron', the platform of timber beams (installed in 1884) on which minor repairs can be carried out on vessels at low water. Another by-product of Howard's new lock was the replacement of Rownham Ferry across the River Avon, the northern terminus of which was demolished by the work on the lock. A new position was found for the ferry just up-river from Brunel's Lock. It was made redundant by the Ashton Swing Bridge and has been disused for many years, but the roadway leading down to the ferry can still be seen on both banks of the river at low water.

At the eastern end of Cumberland Basin, Howard's new junction lock was constructed to the same dimensions as the new entrance lock, and on the site which had been intended for a lock but omitted from the original scheme in 1804–9. The completion of this in 1871 made the southern junction lock redundant, so that it was sealed at the end closest to the basin and used for mooring small craft. On the northern side of the new junction lock Howard built the engine-house for the steam plant to power the hydraulic equipment which he installed in the basin. These were still early days in the development of hydraulic power techniques, and the British specialists in this field, Sir William Armstrong's Co, were called in to provide it. Within ten years the equipment was proving inadequate for the rapid extension of the use to which it was put, and a new set of steam engines was installed in the red-brick engine-house in the Underfall Yard which still provides power for the remaining hydraulic machinery in the Floating Harbour. The Underfall Yard, where Jessop had dammed the original course of the Avon to the south-east of the Cumberland Basin, was developed from the 1840s onwards as the centre for the workshops and maintenance yard for the port, and it still performs these functions for the City Docks.[6] Meanwhile, the first hydraulic engine-house was taken out of commission, but the pennant sandstone building still stands, its Italianate accumulator tower giving it a curiously ecclesiastical appearance.

Another series of modifications was made at the Cumberland Basin as a result of the completion of the Ashton Swing Bridge in 1906. This bridge carried a road and a railway on two separate decks across the River Avon, and the railway was then carried over the two junction locks and on via Mardyke to the goods yard and warehouses at Canon's Marsh. Two small swing bridges were provided over the locks, but as these were removed in 1967 following the closure of the Canon's Marsh extension, they have passed beyond the province of industrial archaeology. The railway across the lower deck of Ashton Swing Bridge is still open for traffic with the wharves on the southern side of the Floating Harbour, but the top deck has been dismantled and the bridge has not been swung for many years.

A more recent and visually more dominant change came in 1965 with the completion of the new Cumberland Basin road scheme, carrying a dual-carriageway road over the River Avon and the entrance to the Floating Harbour, with multiple intersections. The pier of the Plimsoll Bridge, as the swinging section of the fly-over has been named, has been built on the central reservation between the northern entrance lock and Brunel's Lock. The whole complex of new roads has interfered remarkably little with the Cumberland Basin, and the fly-over provides incidentally some vantage points from which the various features of the basin can be conveniently viewed.

When the basin was excavated in Rownham Meads there were no buildings in the fields, but many followed the completion of the work, and the water was soon ringed with a variety of buildings. Some of these were official premises of the Dock Co and of the Dock Committee which succeeded it, like the dockmaster's house on the southern side of Brunel's Lock which was demolished to allow the construction of the fly-over. The dockmaster now has an office on the central reservation. Other buildings were warehouses or the work of speculative builders, and as the various modifications were made, these were bought and demolished. Thanks partly to the new roadworks, the basin is now almost entirely free of adjacent buildings, although three large tobacco bonded warehouses loom starkly on its southern approaches. These were built between 1905 and 1919, and despite their brick exteriors, they are early examples of British steel frame and reinforced concrete construction.

The Cumberland Basin still operates as it has done for 160 years, locking vessels through the entrance lock between half-tides, and passing them on through the junction lock into the Floating Harbour. The task is performed much more efficiently and rapidly now than it was when Jessop completed the basin. Yet the volume of traffic is dwindling, as vessels are increasingly tempted to use the newer dock facilities at Avonmouth rather than tackle the tortuous 8-mile journey up to the City Docks. It seems likely that long before the end of this century the whole of the Floating Harbour will have become obsolete, so that the city of Bristol will find itself with a large-scale industrial monument in its centre. It is to be hoped that when this time comes the city will consider sympathetically the preservation of the harbour as an amenity, and that the Cumberland Basin in particular, with all its engineering and commercial associations, will receive the careful treatment it deserves as the embodiment of a distinguished part of the local industrial heritage.

References

1 L. T. C. Rolt, *Great Engineers* (1962), ch 3, gives a valuable biographical sketch of William Jessop.

2 R. A. Buchanan & Neil Cossons, *Industrial Archaeology of the Bristol Region*, Newton Abbot (1969), ch 2, 'The Changing Port', give a general account of the Floating Harbour. For a more detailed treatment of the historical aspects see R. A. Buchanan, 'The Construction of the Bristol Floating Harbour' in a forthcoming issue of the *Transactions of the Bristol & Gloucestershire Archaeological Society*.

3 Jessop explained his problems at the Cumberland Basin to a Committee of the House of Commons on 25 April 1807; the abstract of this account and the subsequent cross-examination is in Bristol City Archives, 11168(15).

4 This reconstruction is based on references to the bridge in the *Engineers' Reports* preserved in the archives of the Port of Bristol Authority. I am deeply grateful to the officers of the PBA for allowing me free access to these valuable archives.

5 W. G. Neale, *At the Port of Bristol*, Bristol (1968), vol 1, 26, gives a useful tabular summary of the size of successive locks, although his figure of 35 ft for the width of the original southern entrance lock is an estimate based on Ashmead's Map of Bristol (p 4) whereas the Act of 1803 specified 33 ft.

6 F. D. C. Jeffery, 'Summary of a Survey of the Workshops and Machinery at the Port of Bristol Underfall Yard, Bristol', *BIAS Journal*, no 1, Bristol (1968), gives a detailed review of this fascinating collection of machines.

Plates, see p 371

HARRY W. HODGSON

Packhorse Roads in Todmorden

TODMORDEN, a small town on the borders of Lancashire and Yorkshire, was at one time a market town concerned with wool and other agricultural products, though the soil was poor and shallow and not conducive to crop rotation. The wool was spun and woven in farmhouses, and the pieces taken by packhorse to neighbouring towns such as Halifax and Rochdale or even farther afield to Manchester. As a 'gap' town over the Pennines, Todmorden was the gathering place of several important packhorse roads running between Lancashire and Yorkshire, and it is these roads which are the subject of our survey.

Over a period of several years the writer has walked the moors surrounding the town and has been impressed by the way the old roads have been preserved and their extent. He saw many miles of roads in their original condition just as they were when they were used by the trains of packhorses. They are all on the uplands, not in the valleys, mostly between 500 and 1,000 ft OD. Unlike most of the other packhorse tracks in the country, they have not been incorporated in the modern road systems but were left untouched when new roads were constructed in the Calder Valley in the early nineteenth century.

Previous to this date, the valleys were swamps and subject to frequent flooding; even today flooding in the Calder Valley is a major problem and extensive remedial work is being carried on by the River Board to minimise the effects of flood water. Because of the swamps and frequent floods, the packhorse roads avoided the valleys and only came down to the river level in order to cross the valley. The result was that the new roads had little or no effect on the old packhorse roads, and there they remain gradually becoming overgrown or becoming natural water courses, except on the hillsides.

The writer felt that these roads should be recorded, as far as was possible, and photographed before they disappeared entirely, and the need for this was seen during the time of the survey (1966–7), as one packhorse road was overlaid with tar macadam in order to give easier access to a hill farm.

These roads were, of course, designed and made by the local men using the local gritstone found in abundance on the hills and admirably suited to road making. The stones vary in size but are mainly between 18 in and 2 ft across in the form of a truncated triangle, being placed head to toe along the road. The stones are from 6 to 9 in deep, though the builders would not hesitate to place a stone on the road which was thicker than this if it should be suitable otherwise.

A walk along these tracks fills one with admiration for the skill of the builders and almost awe at the sheer physical effort which went into the building of the tracks in the remoter parts of the borough. The usual method of construction was to have these larger stones along the centre of the track and a pathway about 1 ft wide on each side where this was deemed necessary, though where the track was over firm soil the secondary track was not constructed. In one or two instances the track was much wider than this and capable of taking a wheeled vehicle, notably near the towns.

Space will not allow for more than a brief description of one or two of the more typical roads in the area and of some of the more interesting buildings still to be seen along them.

The tracks are lined with dozens of old farmhouses, many of them dating from the seventeenth century and some even earlier, and a number of them in their prime, centres of industry and considerable settlements so vividly described by Daniel Defoe in his accounts of his journey through these parts. We visited some houses which at one time were surrounded by cottages and housed over a hundred inhabitants.

The Reddishore Scout Road is one of the important links between Yorkshire and Lancashire and appears on Sheet 244 NE ref 19/9495. We begin the inspection of the road at the Todmorden boundary where the track travels roughly NNW for about 1½ miles and is clearly marked all the way. For the most part the road is typically packhorse (illustrated on p 372) as described earlier, though at one point the natural rock has been levelled and used in preference to a formally constructed track.

At a point about three-quarters of a mile from the boundary several roads join and the junction is marked by an interesting guide post. The post (illustrated on p 372), made from local gritstone, is some 2½ ft out of the ground, 9 in thick, and marked by incised letters which give the distances from Todmorden, Rochdale, Burnley and Halifax, all of them less than those on modern maps. If we compare the distances on other guide posts (there are two on the next road we propose to describe), we see why they are called 'guide posts' rather than 'mile posts', since although the distance between the post under discussion and the next one is over 2 miles, the numbers marked on the stones differ by only 1 mile. The posts are very old but in excellent state of preservation as may be seen from the illustration.

At this point we have the choice between dropping down the rather steep hillside to Bottomley or following the track along the top of the hill to Strines Gate End, Walsden. The latter, though interesting, has not as much to offer as the other, which is now overgrown and the stone track itself can only be seen in patches. From the modern Class A road between Todmorden and Rochdale, the road is known as 'Bottomley Road' as it leads to the village of that name. At one time this village was of considerable importance, but it is now rather shabby, though it possesses some good examples of seventeenth-century houses. The road itself is one of the best preserved packhorse roads in the borough and is of the wider type which would take a wheeled vehicle.

After Bottomley the track is lost in the fields, though it may be found on the map marked as a footpath. It appears again at North Hollingworth Farm and from there to Hey Head Road it is clearly traced as a single-stone track, well made and crossing the various streams by means of culverts. One of these streams is used to drive a waterwheel, a fast turbine, for Birks Mills in Walsden.

Saltersrake Gate is so named because it was the route by which salt was taken from Cheshire into Yorkshire. There is a similar track to the south west of the borough known as 'The Limers' Gate' along which lime was taken from the Craven area into Lancashire. This track is now completely overgrown and very little of the stonework can be seen. Saltersrake Gate on the other hand can be traced along its entire length from North Hollingworth Farm to Hey Head Road. There are no buildings along the road as it runs through moorland, but at Shurcrack (229 SE 56/23), where the road passes between two walls, there is a guide post, similar to that on the Reddishore Scout Road, slightly slimmer in section and a shade taller out of the ground, with distances to Halifax, 'Roachdale' [sic], and Todmorden marked on it. From this point the road passes to Hey Head Road and is lost until it reappears in the village of Lumbutts (illustrated on p 372).

The villages of Lumbutts and Mankinholes are of great interest to the antiquarian, being at one time thriving centres of industry. (Mankinholes was known as a wool town and early mentioned in the Wakefield Court records.) There are a number of well-built and well-maintained seventeenth-century houses in the villages and several stretches of packhorse tracks.

One thing which has puzzled the writer is the presence of a third guide post, this time giving the distance to Halifax and Heptonstall. It is roughly the same as the other two, perhaps not as well finished, with the letters more crudely cut, but it is none the less a genuine guide post. The strange thing is that there is no mention of the post on any map that the writer has been able to consult, not even on the large-scale (25-in) map of the village and he feels that there should be some indication that the post is there, even if it does not serve any useful purpose. The other two posts are useless so far as giving accurate information, though they are of undoubted antiquarian importance.

Apart from the tracks in the villages, there is a good packhorse bridge in the centre of Lumbutts, and in Mankinholes there is one of the finest water troughs that the writer has ever seen. It is over 20 ft long and can accommodate a dozen horses or cattle at once. It would be the last point at which a string of packhorses could be watered before going over the long road to Cragg Vale or on to the London

Road. This last is still so marked on Ordnance maps and runs along the valley past the Stoodley Pike monument, though the stone track has now almost completely disappeared.

From Mankinholes there is a packhorse track going over the moors to Cragg Vale and thence to Sowerby and Halifax. For the most part this track (illustrated on p 372) is in an excellent state of preservation and a perfect example of the way the old tracks were constructed. At the top of the hill is a large stone post, some 8 ft out of the ground, which acted as a guide for travellers. It is known locally as the 'Long Stoup' (or Stoop), and is a landmark for miles around. Just beyond it are several smaller posts which act as guides for the track during snowy weather. We say 'act' in the present tense as they are still of use to the walker in winter.

Withins New Road, an old road which runs from Hey Head Road to the top of the moor, is worth mentioning, although it is not a packhorse road, nor is it a public road at all. It was constructed at the behest and at the expense of the Fielden family (the same family as John Fielden, the 'Ten Hours Act' man) during the cotton famine of the 1860s. There was little or no work for the cotton operatives at this time and rather than distribute charity, the Fielden family created work by constructing this road. It is some 2½ miles long, well made at the time, now rapidly deteriorating through neglect (it serves no useful purpose), but it acts as a reminder of this famous local family and their attitude to their workers.

There are many more miles of track which can be traced, some with the stones still exposed and usable, others overgrown or incorporated in the modern roads. One such is the ancient 'Long Causeway', a road which in its day was one of the most used and important of all the roads between Yorkshire and Lancashire. It ran from Pontefract to Clitheroe and thence to Lancaster and was the route by which the de Laceys governed their extensive territories. In later times it was used to carry goods between the counties.

Only in occasional spots do we see any of the original track, simply because it was so well used. Modern roads have followed the old track for the most part, but we can still see short stretches of the packhorse road where a detour has been made to avoid a steep hill. One such stretch can be seen at the border between Lancashire and Yorkshire at Stiperden (229 NW 16/28). Here the modern road follows the datum line in a wide sweep while the old road dips down to Stiperden House and up to the site of Stiperden Cross. Parts of Stiperden House are of great antiquity. The writer was shown round the ground floor by a previous occupant who pointed out the lintel of the 'new' part, dated 1643! This house must have been a regular calling place for travellers on the Long Causeway.

In conclusion and as an example of some of the many interesting items of antiquarian interest along these old roads, Mount Cross should be mentioned. There are several crosses along these roads, some marked by a site only, others as simple upright stones and others, by far the minority, as cruciform. Examples of the simple upright pillars can be seen at Cross Stone, and alongside the Burnley/Halifax Road at Mereclough, known as 'Maiden's Cross', and a spurious cruciform cross at Cross Farm, Mankinholes.

A genuine cruciform cross in an excellent state of preservation can be seen at Shore above Todmorden (229 NW 92/27). This cross is some 8 ft out of the ground, shaped along its entire length as if to fit in a socket, though set directly into the ground and topped by a circular head shaped into a Greek-style cross. The whole is of a single piece of stone and in spite of acts of vandalism in its long history, it is still upright, standing where it must have stood for hundreds of years. Opinions differ as to its exact age. It bears all the marks of Saxon or Celtic origin, though it may be a medieval copy. It is certainly pre-reformation, as Todmorden was well to the fore in adopting the reformed worship, and it is most unlikely that such a cross would be constructed after the mid-sixteenth century.

Map Reference

All the roads mentioned in this survey will be found on the six-inch Ordnance Survey map, Nos 229 and 244 (1950 edition).

Plates, see p 372

B. P. LENMAN AND E. E. GAULDIE

Pitfour Brickworks, Glencarse, Perth

THE broken brick piers of the original Tay Bridge, which fell in December 1879, still show above water, but while the disaster of the bridge's collapse has attracted the attention of historians it has only recently been discovered that the bricks used in its construction have their own story.

On the estate of Pitfour, in the parish of St Madocs, on the flat clay lands of the Carse of Gowrie in the 1830s, Sir John Stewart Richardson of Pitfour, like other improving landlords of the Carse, had recognised the impossibility of increasing farm yields without efficient drainage of the heavy soil and some reclamation of the River Tay's encroachment. Finding traditional methods of drainage, chiefly by the construction of ditches lined with twigs, inadequate, and the cost of transporting drainage tiles, which had come into use in other parts of Scotland only within the last three years, prohibitive, he proceeded from 1837–8 to make tiles from the clay of his own land. He erected drying and moulding sheds, kilns, and a horse-driven clay mill, and by April 1840 he was advertising the tiles for sale.[1] From the start Sir John had hoped to manufacture for sale as well as for his own use and, despite a prejudice in some circles against tile drainage in clay land,[2] demand for Pitfour's products increased more rapidly than had been expected. Bricks and tiles which, in 1839, had been advertised at a price per 100, by the opening of the 1840 season, were being priced per 1,000. The 1839 advertisement explained that a second of the Marquis of Tweeddale's patent machines, driven by steam, and a new steam engine, as well as additional buildings for drying and burning, had been installed.

That it had been difficult to maintain supplies to meet consumer demand can be deduced from the words 'it is hoped that those persons requiring tiles and bricks may now have a regular supply'[3] which

② Tay Rail Bridge
③ Tay Road Bridge
④ Forth Rail Bridge
⑤ Forth Road Bridge
Built-up Area
Railway
NORTH
River Tay
River Earn
ARBROATH
CARNOUSTIE
DUNDEE
BROUGHTY FERRY
TAYPORT
NEWPORT
WORMIT
Errol
PERTH
Glencarse
Cottown
FIRTH OF TAY
NORTH SEA
ST ANDREWS
CUPAR
LOCH LEVEN
ALLOA
STIRLING
KIRKCALDY
DUNFERMLINE
FIRTH OF FORTH
FALKIRK
QUEENSFERRY
Leith
EDINBURGH
Bruce Lenman 1968

Fig I

appeared in the advertisement. Mechanisation came slowly to brick and tile manufactures. The most common machine around 1840 was the pug-mill, a barrel-shaped container in which clay was churned by blades on a turning wheel. This process of churning the clay probably accounts for the existence of a freestone mill-wheel of 6-ft diameter, and 9 in thick, with a square hole in its centre and slots in its rim that may have held iron blades, which remains on the site today close to the engine shed. It probably dates from a late stage in the site's history, but something like it must have been in use from the start.

Bricks with a substantial frog or hollow face on them were not made successfully by machine until after 1850, but efficient tile-making machines were being developed from the 1840s. Richardson's enterprise owed much of its success to the fact that, in supplying his own need for materials for agricultural improvement, he was supplying the needs of landlords and farmers over an area which included all Angus and Perthshire, in the whole of which there was no other brickfield. Carse tenant farmers up to this period had for the most part not attempted the drainage of their land, neither stone nor timber being cheaply available to them. The usefulness of Sir John's project was recognised by the agriculturalists of the Carse of Gowrie, Stormont and Strathearn, 300 of whom attended and subscribed to a public dinner in his honour 'from a sense of the obligation under which they lie to him for his attention to their commercial interests'.[4]

Sir John's own commercial interests extended beyond agriculture to the patronage of bleaching and printing works near Perth. He was a partner of the bleaching company at Ruthvenfield until 1830 and proprietor, with Robert Smythe of Methven, of the bleachfield at Huntingtower, which was let after forty years' operation by the firm of Richardson & Co to Wm Turnbull & Son.[5] While other textile industries of Perth shrank in importance throughout the nineteenth century, affected by the collapse of the West of Scotland cotton trade, the bleachfields, serving a much larger area of linen and cotton manufacturers, survived and flourished. As the coarse linen and jute trade of Dundee increased its production rapidly, the resultant growth in population brought about a sharp demand for housing which strained supplies of traditional building materials to the point where, from about 1865, the use of brick instead of stone was considered. Although the typical Dundee tenement, like the typical Dundee warehouse and mill, continued to be stone-built, brick was increasingly used for interior load-bearing walls; and, after the introduction of a public water supply in 1875, the necessity for bringing sanitation to existing buildings caused the widespread addition of inelegant brick WC towers to the backs of stone-built tenements.

Sir John had, from the first, made some bricks at his tilefield, witness his early advertisements in the *Dundee Courier*,[6] probably most of them for agricultural use. But the period of industrial expansion in the neighbouring town, preceded by railway development in the Carse[7] and the consequent demand for brick for station houses and signal boxes,[8] created a market which caused the original emphasis of the firm to change from tile to brick production.

Labour for the brickfield seems to have been found from Sir John's own tenants within the parish, where the only employment other than agricultural labouring was some hand-loom weaving carried out during the winter months for Dundee linen manufacturers who supplied yarn and paid for webs on collection. Power-loom weaving was introduced into Dundee in the 1830s and grew rapidly from 1850. Although it did not completely exclude hand-loom weaving until the first world war, it steadily reduced the possibility of making a living by its practice. Sir John's tenants, then, missing the income from weaving to which they were accustomed, provided for him a labour force for the brick-field without any need for him to build bothies or industrial cottages on the site. Those cottages now to be seen near the site are clearly of the pre-industrial period.

It was customary for a brick-works owner to employ as *moulder* the head of a household, who could undertake in his turn to supply a woman to assist him as 'walk-flatter', with a number of children to carry bricks and push wheelbarrows.[9] Brick- and tile-making was a seasonal industry, closing down of necessity when frost and rain would have spoiled the bricks, and opening again each spring. It was not as conveniently adapted to the intervals of farm work as hand-loom weaving, an indoor winter occupation, but it allowed for some flexibility in the working year and made a convenient addition to the income of a cottar family. The amount of the wage earned depended entirely on the rate at which a family was able to work, because the moulder was paid by output. Evidence given to the commissioners appointed to enquire into working conditions in brickfields seemed to show that children were overworked by their fathers in a way that few employers would have demanded.[10]

The first mill to regulate the hours of females and young persons employed in brickfields was introduced in 1867. It can hardly have been coincidence that it was in this year that Sir John Richardson chose to consider the lease of his land to a coal, lime and brick company in Dundee. The population of St Madoes, like all the villages in the Carse, had declined throughout the nineteenth century. If the use of children were forbidden there was no additional source of adult male labour to draw upon. This made one of two courses necessary. Other labour must be attracted from elsewhere by the building of housing and the payment of wages competitive with those paid in Dundee where the demand for labour was still high; or modernisation and mechanisation of processes must be introduced so that the labour force could be reduced. Both of these courses proved unattractive to Sir John, now a man of seventy, because of the heavy outlay they would involve. He was unlikely to see a return for such expenditure during his own lifetime.

From the end of the American Civil War Dundee's need for closer contact with world markets had aroused discussion of the possibility of bridging the River Tay. Capture of the contract for the supply of ten million bricks for the erection of the proposed new bridge encouraged Robert Small & Co of Yeaman Shore to take the lease of Pitfour brickworks.

The lease between Sir John Richardson and Small is described as a Clay Lease. Under it Small took a 21-year lease on the clay deposits on 16½ acres of land at Pitfour. His administrative headquarters and coal and lime yard remained at Yeaman Shore in Dundee. By 1867 this site was cut off from the Tay owing to land reclamation in connection with the railway from Dundee to Perth. Before the railway embankment was built Yeaman Shore had been a favourite spot for dumping building stone for Dundee from quarries farther up the river Tay, like Kingoodie near Invergowrie. Sandstone blocks were dumped in the shallows at high tide and recovered as needed at low tide. At first, Robert Small seems to have discounted the idea of using the river to transport raw materials or brick. His lease envisaged the construction of a tramway or light railway from the Dundee & Perth Railway station at Glencarse, due north of the brickfield, to a new complex of kilns and other buildings to be erected by Small.

The lease specified that agricultural land was to be re-soiled once the clay had been stripped off it. Brick spoil not used to build the track of the tramway was to be spread on the land before the soil was replaced. Small had the right to use existing roads subject to repairing any damage owing to the extra traffic he placed on them, and to preserving existing access to the fields. He was to pay 5d to the landlord for every cubic yard of clay extracted, as well as £20 per annum for the land for his tramway with its sidings and junctions, and £5 per annum per imperial acre for land covered by buildings or being dug for clay. Small had the right to use existing gravel or open a new gravel pit to build the tramway embankments,[11] and in 1868 he also leased from Sir John, for £35 per annum, a small freestone quarry at Cottown, a farm just north of the brickfield.[12] By 1870 Small had accepted an offer from Sir John of a lease of the house and garden of Upper Mains of Pitfour to run for the same period as the lease of the brickfield. The house became the residence of the partner in Robert Small & Co who was responsible for managing the brickfield.[13]

Further development on the site saw the extension of the tramway to the bank of the Tay. This southern extension was designed for shipping out finished bricks by barge. A lease of 1871 between the company and Sir John provided for the construction of a southern extension to the tramway along the line of an existing strip of woodland. The lease laid down that when the tramway emerged on to the reclaimed land between the wood and the river it was to be elevated on an embankment as high as the existing river embankment. It was to cross the landward ditch north of the reclaimed land on a brick arch. There was even a clause in the agreement envisaging the construction of a second watertight embankment parallel to the new railway embankment, such that the river embankment could be removed between the ends of the two new embankments to form a small tidal harbour. This was never done. The pier envisaged in the lease as the first stage of development seems also to have been the last.[14]

In 1871 a Dundee newspaper described the already substantial development on the site. The paper ascribed the idea to Robert Small himself, who had recently died. The actual plans were drawn up by Mr John Dick, described as the managing partner of the firm, after a tour of all the principal British brickworks. It was constructed according to principles patented by the Germans Hoffman and Licht. F. Hoffman had in 1858 patented the first continuous circular kiln which had a series of openings permitting the fire to be moved from one to another. Without the fuel economy effected by this design a site like Pitfour, whose nearest source of coal was in the mining areas of South Fife, would scarcely have been a practical proposition. As it was, all fuel had to come in by rail.

The kiln was in the form of an arched passage like a railway tunnel divided into sixteen chambers, each capable of taking several thousand bricks. They were so arranged that air entering the kiln passed through the chambers of bricks already burned, absorbing their surplus heat and reaching the chambers which were in course of burning at a high temperature. From there the air circulated to chambers where newly-made or green bricks were stacked, making them completely dry and hard before the fires were applied to them. Finally it was expelled, along with the furnace smoke, from the chimney placed in the centre of the kiln. By means of a system of dampers air could be diverted to any part of the kiln. The top of the kiln was a common earth floor from which the furnaces were fuelled. Coal was thrown in handfuls down 350 tubes set into the earthen floor and leading to the kiln. The coal was turned to gas before it reached the bottom of the tube.

When the newspaper article was written there was still only one brick-making machine at work on the site. This was itself fairly progressive. As late as the 1870s brick-making in the south of England was still often almost entirely a hand industry,[15] despite the fact that brick-making machines, which cut ten bricks at a time from a length of clay, on the model of a sausage machine, were being introduced into Britain from mid-century.[16] The bricks manufactured at Pitfour do not in fact seem to have been wire-cut. They bear all the marks of having been stamped out by a mechanical press.

According to the newspaper another brick-making machine was to be installed shortly, as well as machines for making pipes, tiles and other products. What was called 'a sort of revolving carriage' was being built to convey newly-made bricks from the brick machine to the first floor of the building in which it was housed, adjacent to the kiln. There the bricks were stacked to dry after being removed from this early type of conveyor belt by men and boys. The dry bricks were then taken to the kiln by wheelbarrow, but there were plans for using a mechanical hoist on this job. A powerful horizontal steam engine drove all the machinery in the brickfield, as well as hauling up the waggons from the clay pit.

Robert Small & Co had rights to beds of clay 15–17 ft deep over 20 acres of land. Part of the licence for the Hoffman and Licht patent gave Robert Small & Co exclusive rights to it in an area stretching from Montrose to a considerable distance beyond Perth. In other words the company was secured against rivals in a large part of eastern Scotland, including urban centres like Montrose, Brechin, Arbroath, Forfar, Kirriemuir, Blairgowrie and Perth. In 1871 the Pitfour site was hard at work on the order for the Tay Rail Bridge brickwork. In full working order the site could produce several thousand bricks daily.[17]

The whole brickfield was under the control of John Dick, its designer, who lived nearby at Upper Mains of Pitfour. With Robert

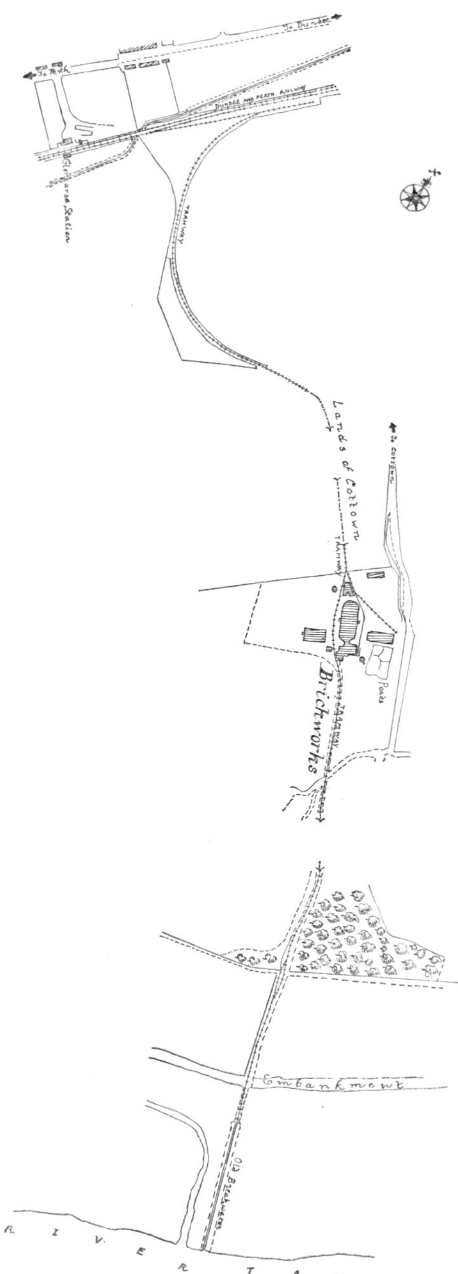

Blackadder, a Dundee architect, and Frank Collier, a nephew of the late Robert Small, Dick was one of the three partners in the firm after the death of its founder.[18] Obviously a great brickfield like this, with long earthworks attached to it, created problems for neighbouring farmers. At the southern end of the tramway the new embankment interfered with drainage on the fields comparatively recently recovered from the river. As early as 1871 Robert Small & Co had to agree to construct a new drain and outlet through the river embankment under the supervision of a Perth engineer.[19] More problems arose when in 1879 the company wished to strip clay from the farm of Dumgreen. This was a new area for them, situated to the south east of the kiln, and it involved a new branch line on the tramway. The clay lease required them to raise the existing road alongside Dumgreen Farm above the new tramway on a stout brick bridge at least 12 ft wide with parapets. The bridge, erected on brick spoil, stands there to this day, leading to a mink farm situated just south of the old brickfield.[20]

Fig 2 Plan of Pitfour Brickworks, 1888 (total length of site c 3,000 yd)

By 1888 Frank Collier had become sole partner in Robert Small & Co, and a lease between him and Sir James Richardson of Pitfour, heir of Sir John, gives some idea of the state of the brickfield and the problems it created around that time. The lease confirmed Collier's rights on the tramway, buildings and kiln and clay excavations. It shows that he had ceased to use the south tramway, apparently relying exclusively on the north tramway and the Caledonian Railway at Glencarse. Sir James Richardson was to have the use of the south tramway for moving manure, subject to undertaking upkeep of the track, until Collier chose to resume use of it. Collier's decision may have been connected with his own increasing involvement with the Caledonian Railway. In 1889 construction of the new Caledonian station in Dundee—the West Station—was begun. Its design and construction was handled not from Glasgow, but from the District Office in Perth by the District Engineer, Thomas Barr, and his assistant E. C. Moon.[21] The contract for the brickwork went to that good client of the Caledonian Railway, Frank Collier. Since the demolition of the West Station in 1966 most of the bricks have been used to build up approach roads to the roundabout where some of the traffic crossing the new Tay Road Bridge enters central Dundee.

The firm's relationship with Sir James seemed healthy enough in 1888. The only complaint the latter expressed in the new lease was the way employees of the brickfield poached his estate. He tried to deal with this by requiring the company to forbid its employees to keep dogs and by asking Collier to sack any employee guilty of poaching.[22] Records survive of payments from the company to the laird of Pitfour from 1868 to 1890, and it is clear from them that the brickfield, once it was in full operation by 1871, yielded an income of £200–£400 a year to the laird, who made occasional use of its facilities and whose farmlands were systematically re-soiled as they were stripped of clay.[23]

Robert Small & Co were well placed to sell bricks in both Perth and Dundee. Their lease of 1888 suggests that they were manufacturing coke and cement as well as bricks, tiles and other pottery products. Frank Collier did not prove a successful entrepreneur in the long run.

In 1895 he retired from the company, which split into the Dundee Coal & Building Supply Co, now Taylor Brothers, and the Pitfour Brick & Tile Co Ltd. The latter continued to operate. In 1912 it had orders outstanding for 300,000 bricks to Messrs Milligan of Kilmarnock, when the land on which the brickfield stood was acquired by a business rival, Alexander Bell Scott Fraser, brick and tile manufacturer of Inchcoonans near Errol. After buying the land from Sir Edward Austin Stewart Richardson of Pitfour, he served notice in September 1912 on the Pitfour Brick Co which, after a legal delaying action, agreed to remove the plant, steam engine, drying floors, pipes and machinery and vacate the site, as it was obliged to under the lease of 1888.[24]

Fraser of Inchcoonans insisted that the buildings be left, but he never seems to have operated the site as a brickfield. Tenement building in Dundee virtually came to a standstill by 1900. This was part of a general crisis in the provision of working-class housing, which had ceased to be a profitable field for private enterprise in the early twentieth century. The market for bricks was shrinking. Fraser concentrated on his Inchcoonans brick and tile works. He tried to sell land at Glencarse to the Caledonian Railway in 1914. This land had been the part of the tramway adjacent to Glencarse station. The Caledonian Railway refused to buy but disputed Fraser's boundary claims.[25] There were other financial complications, more annoying than significant, such as the assessments levied by Pitfour Water Committee. As late as 1920 Fraser was paying these with reluctance, protesting that as he did not use the water he should not be charged for it.[26]

Curiously enough, when state subsidies for council housing led to the early building of a brick housing scheme at Logie in Dundee in 1919, there was no move to reopen Pitfour. There was a desperate shortage of building materials in Britain at the time. One Dundee councillor alleged that 6 stone quarries within 5 miles of Dundee and 75 per cent of the many brickfields within 20 miles of Dundee were closed. He appealed to the government to give a capital grant to assist the opening of some of these.[27] This was not done. Much of the state subsidy vanished into increased costs for building materials. Bricks remained scarce in the Dundee region. Shortly after building Logie, Dundee Corporation built the Taybank Scheme of avowedly more expensive stone because brick was less obtainable. London bricks were actually used on some early Dundee Council housing schemes.[28]

An expert had advised Fraser in 1914 that it was not worth reopening Pitfour.[29] This remained true throughout the inter-war period, despite the high price of building materials at various stages. This was partly due to the considerable capital investment required to reopen a site like Pitfour, and partly because of certain drawbacks in the brick it produced. As compared with fire-clay bricks it was expensive and unsuitable for rough-casting or harling as it is called in Scotland. There was a glaze on the face of Pitfour brick. Frost was able to get in behind it and kick off the face and the harling.

In the immediate post-war period there were suggestions in Labour circles in Dundee that the brickfield be reopened to provide work for the unemployed and bricks for council houses.[30] These suggestions came to nothing. By 1926 the site was being leased by the trustees of the now deceased Fraser as a poultry run and grazing ground for stock.[31] By 1933 Messrs Alexander Fraser, Brick & Tile Manufacturers, Inchcoonans Brick & Tile Works, Errol, sold the Pitfour site with the significant proviso that it never again be used for a brick or tile works. The wheel had come full circle since the expansive days of the 1870s.[32]

Much of the site remains. Fraser of Inchcoonans took up the rails of the tramway just before the first world war, but the track of the light railway can clearly be traced from what was a siding at Glencarse station, along a sizeable embankment in a field, to the Pitfour Errol Road. South of this road the tramway bed is clear and marked by small stone posts with grooves cut in their tops. These stones may be the remains of a signalling system. Where the tramway enters the brickfield proper a complex of remains can be distinguished. At the eastern corner of the site is an overgrown, circular kiln made of stock bricks of various makes, none of them from Pitfour. Almost certainly this is a fragment of the earliest kiln erected by Sir John Richardson. Due south of this kiln are two ponds which are probably the flooded remains of very early clay excavation on the site, for they were there when Robert Small & Co were operating the brickfield. Indeed, brick pillars remain in the lower pond where they must have carried the rails of a tramway over the water to a nearby field being stripped of clay at a later stage in the site's history. After crossing the pond the rails went under an existing road through a small brick bridge into a field where the clay lay. Much the most striking remains are those of the great Hoffman Licht kiln, for all that its earth roof has sharply accelerated the process of colonisation of the ruins by scrub woodland. All that is left of the engine shed is a brick wall. Beside it sits the great millstone. Southwards the track of the tramway dips through a series of cuttings until it emerges on a brick-ballasted embankment which crosses the reclaimed land on the bank of the River Tay until it meets the old river embankment. Coastal accretion in the shape of mud consolidated by rushes marks the site of the old jetty. Over this once daring development in the building supply industry of Tayside broods an atmosphere of decay and desolation.

References

1 *Dundee Advertiser*, 14 April 1840.
2 Vide J. Duncan, *Remarks on Land Drainage*, Edinburgh (1849).
3 *Dundee Courier*, 30 July 1839.
4 *New Statistical Account of Scotland*, x, 626.
5 *NSA*, x. 1034 Bricks from Pitfour were also supplied to the bleachfield at Pitcairn.
6 *Dundee Courier*, 30 July 1839.
7 The Dundee & Perth Railway was opened in May 1847.
8 Station buildings themselves were usually of stone with the notable exception of Dundee West Station, built of Pitfour brick.
9 G. P. Bevan, *Manufacturing Industries of Britain*: Ceramics, 203
10 E. R. Pyke, *Human Documents of the Industrial Revolution*, 156–65
11 Clay Lease dated 8–9 December 1868.
12 Quarry Lease dated 8–9 December 1868.
13 Richardson to Small, 30 August 1870, and Small to Richardson, 3 September 1870.
14 Minute of Agreement dated 22 May 1871.
15 Vide G. P. Bevan, *The Industrial Classes and Industrial Statistics* (1876), 155–67.

16 T. K. Derry and T. I. Williams, *A Short History of Technology*, Oxford (1960), 590.
17 *Dundee Advertiser*, 3 August 1871.
18 Vide address given in lease dated February 1873.
19 Agreement of 25–6 August, and W. Paterson's report, 22 May 1873.
20 Minutes of Agreement, 25–6 June 1879.
21 For this information we are indebted to Mr David Walker, DA, FSA (Scot).
22 Talk between Sir James Richardson and Robert Small & Co, 20–2 June 1888.
23 Robert Small & Co in Account with Sir John S. Richardson, 1868–90.
24 Minute of Agreement between A. B. S. Fraser and the Pitfour Brick & Tile Co Ltd, 13 June 1913.
25 Correspondence etc, re Pitfour Railway.
26 Ibid.
27 *Dundee Advertiser*, 15 December 1920.
28 Ibid, 7 January 1921.
29 Fraser to Messrs Wilson Carnegie & Co, 7 January 1914.
30 Information supplied by Mr J. Malcolm, Dundee.
31 Minute of Lease dated 15, 18, 20 and 22 January 1926.
32 Missive of Sale, 1933.

MARINETTE BRUWIER, ANNE MEURANT AND CHRISTIANE PIÉRARD

Le Grand-Hornu

THIS *article originally appeared in* Industrie, *the monthly journal of the Federation of Belgian Industries, as part of the issue for January 1968. We are grateful to Kenneth Hudson who not only sought permission from the Federation so that we could reprint it but also provided us with this translation.*

The Industrial Revolution and Coal-mining in the Borinage

In the first chapter of his masterly essay, *The Economic History of World Population*, Carlo M. Cipolla writes that 'a new kind of history' began with the Industrial Revolution of the eighteenth century, 'dramatically and completely different from anything that went before; deep chasms were created in the continuity of the historical process'. The transformation of society was certainly of this order of importance. The spread of modern technology destroyed the old world and gradually and painfully a new breed of man has begun to emerge.

The beginnings of the Industrial Revolution in England have received careful attention from scholars for many years now. In France and Germany research has produced some interesting published work, but it has come only comparatively recently and is far from abundant. In Belgium a number of studies are in progress, but serious work has so far been confined to a few parts of the field. It is already clear, however, that in Belgium the roots of modern industry go deeper than in other Continental countries. In particular, advanced coal-mining techniques were in use in the Borinage as early as the eighteenth century.

In England, as elsewhere, the mechanisation of the textile industry had great problems to overcome, but the first steam engines, the so-called fire engines, were accepted much more rapidly. This type of engine was most frequently used for pumping. The original version was produced by Thomas Savery in 1698, but it was its successor, developed by Newcomen in 1705 or 1706, which was of practical value. Newcomen engines are known to have been working in Germany and Hungary in 1722, and there was one at Tilleur, in the Liège coalfield, in 1720. Five years later, Gédéon Desandrouin set up the first Newcomen engine in Hainault, at Lodelinsart. This was the famous Fayat engine. Nevertheless, this new technique was very slow to establish itself around Liège and Charleroi. Even in 1812 the first area had only ten steam engines and the second twelve. On the other hand, although the first modern pumping engine in the Borinage began working only during the period 1734–40, there were thirty-nine between 1740 and 1790, with twenty in operation at the time of the French Revolution. Their reputation was so considerable that the Boussu engine was used to illustrate the entry 'machine à feu' in the *Encyclopédie* of Diderot and Alembert, and mining engineers from the Borinage visited the coalfields of Charleroi and the north of France as consultants.

Why was progress in the Borinage so much more rapid than elsewhere? It seems probable that gravity-drainage of the pits was more difficult to achieve here, on account of the stratification and of the level nature of the ground. Deeper coal seams may also have been worked in the Borinage, where mining had been in progress for centuries, with Louis XIV's inspector, Bernier, emphasising the importance of the industry in this locality. Coal production was certainly rising fast during the second half of the eighteenth century and, according to the first statistics to be prepared by the post-revolutionary French government, it was three times higher in the Borinage than around Charleroi.

In 1810, coal production in the Jemappes *département* represented 30 per cent of the French total. Traditionally, coal from the Borinage was exported to France through La Haine and then, as early as 1750, by the road leading to Paris by way of Valenciennes. There was certainly competition from the rich mines around Anzin, but imports of English coal, cut off from their French markets at the time of the

Revolution, amounted in 1830 to no more than 10 per cent of the 510,749,637 kg imported from Belgium, three-quarters of it from the Borinage. Borinage coal was also exported to Flanders. To make this possible, and more particularly in order to by-pass the French customs in Condé, a road was built from Saint-Ghislain to Barry, at which point it rejoined the road from Tournai to Ath. This is an indication of the importance of the coal trade and of the all-important role which coal from the Borinage played in the industrial expansion of Flanders, of the port of Antwerp and of the north of France, where several different types of steam engine had a steadily increasing appetite for fuel.

Insufficient emphasis has been placed on the part played by the Borinage in the first phase of the Industrial Revolution, not only in Belgium, but in France as well. The size of its coal trade provided at least a partial explanation of why the Borinage engaged hardly at all in any other kind of economic activity. In particular, it failed to develop metal industries. There was, moreover, a close link between the coal trade and the production of coal. From the eighteenth century onwards a number of merchants had put capital into the modernisation of the pits, especially into the installation of steam engines. One curious fact is worth noting in this connection. De Gorge-Legrand appeared in Hornu for the first time, in the Revolutionary Year X, as a merchant dealing in coal.

Le Grand-Hornu and Henri De Gorge-Legrand

Hornu was a very old *seigneurie* belonging to the abbey of Saint-Ghislain. It had coal mines as early as the thirteenth century. A very large number of pits, certainly not deep, are mentioned from this time onward. In 1747 a concession to mine coal was given by the abbey to a merchant from Mons, Pierre-Toussaint Durieu. It involved the whole of the western part of the village. Another contract, drawn up in 1778 on behalf of Charles Godonnesche and several partners, concerned the eastern part. It marks the real beginning of the exploitation of Grand-Hornu, which covered 963 hectares and in 1810 had one steam engine (for pumping), horse-driven winding gear and 230 employees. At that time there were two other mines at Hornu. At one, Le Champret, the concession was let to a man called Gendebien, the father of the well-known revolutionary of 1830; the other was run by the wealthy Mons merchant, Hardempont.

After the coal mines at Wasmes and Warguigmes had obtained, in 1769, a road which gave them a direct link with the roads from Valenciennes and Barry to Tournai, Hornu, situated only a few kilometres from La Haine and from the Mons Canal, at Condé, was exceptionally well placed at the centre of a communications network. Bavay could be easily reached through Wasmes and Warguigmes.

Yet, despite these advantages, the business controlled by Godonnesche was in a far from prosperous condition. In 1800 we find him complaining bitterly about the greed of the merchants, and in 1810 his widow sold le Grand-Hornu to one of them, Henri De Gorge-Legrand. He was 36 and in 1800, when he married Eugénie Legrand at Lille, he held the somewhat vague, and hardly brilliant, position of *garde magasin des chauffages*, a supervisor of fuel stocks. His family came from the old French province of Hainaut and does not seem to have been particularly well-off or distinguished. The Legrands on the other hand were important wholesale merchants. They provided their daughter with a dowry of 20,000 *livres*, a larger sum than De Gorge was able to show for himself. His own belongings amounted to 13,833 *livres* in money, goods and securities, together with two small pieces of land.

De Gorge-Legrand had no success with the sinking of two new pits. Like Godonnesche he was concentrating too much on the northern part of the area. However, with the help of the master-miner, Saussez, and a group of experienced workmen, he persevered, and a third and fourth pit further to the south struck very rich seams. This was the success he had been waiting for. Between 1815 and 1830 ten more pits were opened and the production at le Grand-Hornu rose from 16,000 tons in 1808 to 100,000 tons in 1829. When De Gorge died in 1832, his property was valued at 1,200,000 francs for the mining installations, 646,000 fr for the concession, and 445,000 fr for credits with merchants, totalling more than three-quarters of the whole assets of the community. Bearing in mind that the 305 *bonniers*[1] of woodland at Colfontaine, reckoned to yield 628,570 fr a year, were also linked to De Gorge-Legrand's industrial enterprises, as a source of timber and fuel, we can see that it was industrial property which formed the core of his fortune. It included no more than 80,000 fr in paper funds, in the form of state loans.

It would be useful to be able to compare De Gorge-Legrand with his peers. Nicolas Warocqué, who made a fortune from his coal interests at Mariemont, estimated in 1838 that he was worth 4 million francs, excluding real estate. We have, as yet, no similar information about d'Hardempont or Legrand-Gossart or the Colenbuens, whose mining activities, formerly part of the Produits de Jamappes, were believed in 1830 to be worth 2 million francs at least.

An Industrial Empire

Henri De Gorge-Legrand did not owe his reputation solely to his wealth. The *Revue Encyclopédique*, published in Paris, devoted an article to him while he was still alive, and in 1830 there were reports of visits by French engineers who were interested in the techniques he had been using. In his *Dictionnaire géographique de la Province de Hainaut*, Philippe Vandermaelen is never tired of mentioning the work of De Gorge-Legrand. He was made a member of the Senate in 1831 and he would certainly have added to his achievements if he had not died in the cholera epidemic of 1832, when he was 58.

He had no children, and his widow, Eugénie Legrand, took over the running of the business for a while, before leaving it to her nephews. The Legrand and Rainbeaux families formed a private company which remained in existence until 1951, when coal mining in the area came to an end. They continued the work which had been begun by the founder of the enterprise, building houses for the workers and modernising the installations. The statue which they erected in 1855 to the memory of Henri De Gorge is a splendid symbol of the exceptional stature of the man.

What impressed his contemporaries and causes us to marvel even today was, on the one hand, the creation of an integrated industrial empire, and, on the other, the planning and building of a *cité ouvrière*, a town for his workpeople, with amenities which were remarkable for the time.

We know very little about the chronology of all this. By 1820, at the latest, De Gorge had added a machine-building workshop to his coal-mining enterprise, to be followed later by a foundry. In the workshop there was a steam engine which drove five lathes and a number of other machines, and in the foundry there was a mobile crane which had six men to look after it. The most up-to-date techniques were used, but the most important aspect of De Gorge's pioneering was his attempt to integrate the different parts of the business. His workshops made equipment for his mines, but they also carried out work for the outside market. They manufactured steam engines of all kinds and even locomotives. It would be interesting to study the beginnings of the rope-works set up just outside Le Grand-Hornu by the Englishman, James Hall Greeve. Was it Henri De Gorge who persuaded Greeve to come? We might add that in 1829–30 De Gorge installed a horse-drawn railway, the first of its kind in Belgium, to link his pits to the Mons Canal, at Condé.

The task of the houses in the *Cité* was to provide the business with a supply of strong arms. In order to attract workers by means of 'previously unheard-of comfort', as De Gorge wrote in 1829, 425 houses were built, providing living accommodation for 2,500 people, 'of whom 500 came from France, attracted by the bonuses which were offered to them'.

'Everything has been admirably arranged, both for walking and for relaxation,' wrote Vandermaelen. The steam pumping engine made it possible to circulate hot, tepid and cold water. There was a bathing establishment and a dance-hall, and, as a philanthropist who was convinced of the value of popular education, De Gorge insisted on having schools for his workers' children and listed the newspapers and periodicals which could be found in the community centre. In the eyes of men of good will at the beginning of the nineteenth century, enlightened paternalism was destined to solve the formidable social problems of the age.

It is certain that, compared with many other working-class houses built at this time, those at le Grand-Hornu had many progressive features. But, as time went on, they lost their modern flavour. In the investigation which Seebohm Rowntree made in Belgium during 1907–9 the houses built by De Gorge were placed only in the second category. By then larger houses, with better living conditions, had been designed elsewhere for people of a comparable social level. There were also taverns to be found in De Gorge's town and it would be interesting to establish the relationship between the gin business operated by Pierre Descotte, who collected the coal-tax at Pâturages, and the mining concern at le Grand-Hornu.

From the 1920s onward, as a result of the law making education compulsory, young men left the mines in the Borinage. *Corons et colonies*—workers' barracks or colonial settlements—was the local phrase for the communities set up by De Gorge. Must all these monuments of mining history disappear because they preserve awkward evidence of difficult and humbling days in the industrial past?

The Industrial Revolution was a significant stage in human development. It resulted in rapid and impressive progress, it subjected whole nations to great and unforeseen stresses. If we keep at least some of its more important survivals, we are far better placed to study technological change, to understand the conditions under which people lived and to make a contribution, similar to that which is already evident in other countries, to the development of a modern humanism, which can do much to increase our understanding of the processes of civilisation.

The Workshops at Le Grand-Hornu

Commissioned by De Gorge, the architect Renard designed a group of buildings of exceptional architectural quality, including an assembly shop, foundries, stores and an administration block. Although these buildings were in use for more than a century, few alterations were made to them and their present delapidated condition is due entirely to neglect during the past twelve years. They are a quite remarkable survival from the early days of the Industrial Revolution.

The buildings used for constructing the machinery needed in the mines surround an elliptical courtyard, which is about 100 metres from the pithead. Its longer axis runs north–south. It is beautifully proportioned, 140 m × 80 m, and the workshops and offices are placed around its perimeter. The main entrance is on the southern side. The ends of the ellipse consist of a continuous arcade, perfectly regular and with no upper storey. The arcade is roofed with slates and the shelter produced in this way was used for storing iron, oil and patterns and for garaging the fire engine. The buildings were along the longer sides; on the west, the assembly shop, now in ruins, and on the east the offices. These higher blocks harmonise successfully with the rest. The offices are lit by sixteen tall windows, arranged on both sides of a carriage entrance, which has a gable above it and suggests a private house rather than an office building. The basement, one should note, is skilfully planned to provide large, light rooms.

The workshop began operations in February 1831. It manufactured steam engines, as well as a wide range of mining machinery. This building, which is now only a shell, is 70 m long and 28 m wide. It is constructed, like the whole complex, of bricks rendered with a yellowish stucco. The quoins are made to resemble stone. The first of the seven bays facing on to the courtyard housed the steam engine which provided power for the factory. A tall square chimney rises from it. The remaining six bays lit the workshop itself.

Between the bays there are eight columns of blue stone, with Tuscan capitals. Tradition has it that they came from the Abbey of Saint-Ghislain, which originally owned the land below which the coal was mined. Inside the buildings, brick pillars form the other side of the arcades. The vaulted roof, formerly supported by the columns and pillars, has collapsed. The system of vaulting used to roof the workshop at le Grand-Hornu had two advantages. It was in perfect harmony with the pillars and it allowed the greatest possible height to be achieved with this particular material.

Seen from the courtyard, the grouping is impressive but, despite its size, the excellent proportions and the skilful distribution of the various masses prevent it from being overwhelming. The colour of the stucco intensifies the unity of the composition, by making use of the play of light and by emphasising certain architectural features.

In the centre of the courtyard is the cast-iron statue of De Gorge, erected by his successors in 1855. Some parts of it have disappeared. In a manuscript note on le Grand-Hornu, compiled in 1888, Louis Lepreux says that representations of a miner's lamp and tools, and of machine-gears, were placed at De Gorge's feet. The base of the statue is in Soignies stone, and carries the dedication. The statue is much damaged, but it preserves its noble appearance.

The 'Backyard'

The southern entrance to the courtyard forms a quadrilateral—which Lepreux calls 'the backyard'—joined on to the ellipse. It contains the former stables and stores. The façade, which is in a very plain neo-classical style, opens directly on to one of the streets of the town. On both sides of a wide porch with three arcades there is a low building, with semi-circular bays, which functioned as a store. The angles are emphasised by two small structures, higher than the rest, and surmounted by dove-cotes. The store rooms at the entrance are particularly interesting. The ground floor and the first floor are divided up by small cast-iron columns, supporting a vaulted tiled ceiling carried on narrow iron beams. These areas were in use until 1957 and were preserved in their original condition. In this courtyard one can see a weighing-machine and a cart, both abandoned and derelict.

When looking at this group of buildings one is reminded very strongly of the monumental project which Ledoux undertook at Salines de Chaux and which was partially completed between 1775 and 1779. His intention was to group his pavilions around a circular courtyard, but only half the scheme was completed. The rows of pavilions were separated from one another by paths radiating from the centre of the courtyard. They were designed to provide housing for the workers and to accommodate certain of the operations of the works. In the centre of the courtyard stood the director's house, demolished in 1918. This was flanked by long workshops, with a décor that depicted aspects of the salt industry. The architect's attempt to give prestige and grandeur to a functional building at once recalls le Grand-Hornu. Ledoux had an industrial town in mind but his attitude to the work was Utopian. His aim was to give each dwelling a different form, corresponding to the occupation of the person who lived in it. Similarly, each public building was to reflect its function in its appearance. This whimsical ambition, coupled with lack of funds, caused the completion of the building to be deferred for ever.

The Town[2] *of Le Grand-Hornu*

Planned industrial towns are rare before 1850. The first examples were the result of the private initiative of industrialists and philanthropists who were anxious to remedy the deplorable conditions under which industrial workers were forced to live. It was only much later that state subsidies became available, either by granting of loans to local bodies or by constructing cheap housing directly. We will confine ourselves here to giving examples of what was being done by contemporaries of De Gorge.

In France the glassworks at Baccarat had gone to a great deal of trouble, as early as 1750, to build good houses for its workers. A hundred years later this company was providing rent-free accommodation to 224 workpeople. Many industrialists at that time were interested in following the example of Mulhouse and of le Grand-Hornu, if one is to believe a letter addressed to De Gorge in 1831 by a Frenchman who appeared anxious to do something similar on the outskirts of Paris.

In 1835, André Koechlin had built thirty-six houses, each with a garden, at Dornach, near Mulhouse, for people employed in his factory. The project was reasonably successful, but it was only after 1853 that it became really important. By 1862, the *cité* of Mulhouse, designed by the architect Müller, contained 560 houses, along avenues 11 m wide, with pavements and trees on each side. Mulhouse had a great influence in France during the last third of the nineteenth century.

We are not aware of anything on this scale in Great Britain during the same period. The research being carried out by industrial archaeologists, more extensively in Britain than elsewhere, may help us to fill this gap in our knowledge. Societies established to finance the construction of cheap housing came into existence fairly rapidly in England, but it was philanthropists and commercial undertakings, not industrialists, who brought them into being.

In Belgium one should mention the work done by Liévin Bauwens, the pioneer of the cotton industry in Ghent. In 1802 he set up a second factory on the premises of the Premonstratensian Abbey at Tronchiènnes, near Ghent, and at the same time began building houses for his workers. At Verviers, Simonis and Biolley, the textile manufacturers embarked on a housing programme in 1808, but did not carry it any further before 1833. Le Grand-Hornu, which had more than 400 houses by that date, was consequently well in the lead. Between 1830 and 1850 a number of other firms built subsidised housing for their workers, but without giving it the design or importance of a town.

The plan of the town of le Grand-Hornu, like that of the factory, was the work of the well-known architect, Bruno Renard. It covers the site of the mine and forms an approximate rectangle, 500 m × 400 m. The streets are wide, nearly 12 m, dead straight and paved. The width increases as one approaches a cross-roads. Green open spaces formed part of the plan, the chief of which was the main square, Place Verte. Originally it contained a bandstand where the town band gave concerts twice a week during the summer months. Some distance away there was a second square, facing De Gorge's own residence.

Construction of the houses began in 1819. Evidence for this is to be found in the leases preserved among the Grand-Hornu papers in the State Archives at Mons. By 1825, 175 houses were inhabited. On 1 September 1832, 395 houses were let and 27 under construction, with plans for the work to continue further.

The houses, all built to nearly the same design, were planned to accommodate a family in reasonable comfort. Each is on two floors and has a cellar. The average floor area is 55 sq m and the height 9·5 m. There are six rooms, three downstairs and three on the upper floor. A garden of between one and two *ares* goes with each house, and contains a coal house, where the family kept the waste coal which was supplied cheaply by the company. An oven and a well were provided for every ten houses.

The houses were constructed of brick, rendered, like the workshops and offices, with a yellow stucco. The door-steps, the air-vents and the string-course running below the upper storey are in dressed stone, or in some imitation of it, since stone was an expensive material. The lintels of the doors and windows are of oak, painted to look like stone. An estimate for the work shows that the floors of the houses built in 1867 rest on a framework of ten laminated iron girders, whilst the earlier houses had to content themselves with fir.

The doors and windows are occasionally round-headed and have fairly wide jambs. Some of the windows still keep their original simply-made wooden shutters, and there are two or three examples of old doors, with the upper and lower halves opening independently. Some of the doors have considerably projecting cornices above them.

The most commonly found type of house, and the smallest, has only one door and one window on the ground floor, with two windows upstairs. The larger houses have two windows downstairs and sometimes three.

A Complete, Self-contained Town

The houses were not for sale, but were rented by the week. They were inhabited by families of between six and ten people and often by a lodger as well. The parents and the older children worked in the mine or the workshops, and the company had the right to possession of the house if an employee was dismissed. The correspondence of De Gorge contains interesting information about this.

This may have given the company some protection against strikes and it may have discouraged political activity among employees, but, on the other hand, it brought not inconsiderable advantages to the workmen and their families. According to Lepreux, a butcher's shop, a bakery and a general store sold 'better quality goods at lower prices'. Was this a benevolent application of the truck system, which produced such opposition elsewhere? Washrooms and baths were provided, with hot water laid on. Houses were made available to nuns, so that they could run a school for girls, and similar facilities existed for the boys. The town possessed meeting rooms, a free library, a band and a fire brigade. Medical care, wine and meat for people who were ill was partially financed by the company, and a hospital, staffed by nuns belonging to the order of St Vincent, was established in 1858. A cemetery was laid out in 1853.

Although it was a little distance away from the town centre, De Gorge's house formed part of the total composition. It was substantial and ornamented with pillars. After his death his heirs rapidly abandoned it to the manager of the company and built a much larger house, dignified by the name of *château*, in a park, or more accurately, a large garden, behind the office block. One should also add that the family vault was constructed within the precincts of the town.

This complete, self-contained town has not entirely disappeared with the passing of the coal industry. The tenants have bought their houses and still live in them, after making certain modifications which, from the aesthetic point of view, have not always been entirely fortunate. In the early nineteenth century the businessman who was responsible for building a factory, a railway station or a museum demanded a building with style to it, rather than something merely functional. Conventions began to form: churches were Gothic, private houses took on the noble appearance of the Italian Renaissance. This conscious imitation of ancient taste did nothing to solve the problems presented by the new industries. It misunderstood or underestimated the potentialities of contemporary materials.

Bruno Renard (1781–1861) had already made a name for himself when De Gorge commissioned him to work at le Grand-Hornu. He had recently returned from Paris, where he had studied under the famous masters of the Empire style, Percièr and Fontaine. The façade which he designed for the Piat-Lefèvre carpet factory at Tournai, divided up by Ionic columns and statues and surmounted by a pediment, suggested a large public building rather than an industrial establishment. But, for le Grand-Hornu, Renard was prepared to simplify his cherished principles. If his town with the modest houses produced its effect by nothing more than the perfect alignment of its buildings and by its sheer mathematical distinction, the works itself owes its grandeur to the elliptical plan, more majestic than functional, to its splendid proportions and to the restrained character of its component parts.

It was to an academic language, given new life at le Grand-Hornu as a result of being made flexible and free from dogmas, that the new industrial age turned in order to proclaim its power. Communication at this time belonged entirely to the architect, not to the engineer. Industry had not yet discovered a style for itself.

The history of technology is still in its infancy. It is certain, nevertheless, that an architectural creation such as le Grand-Hornu will find a significant place in any future assessment of nineteenth-century achievement. Its interest is as much for the economic and social historian as for someone whose main concern is with architecture or technology. One very rarely comes across a nineteenth-century industrial complex as complete as le Grand-Hornu which has survived without thorough-going renovation.

A study in depth of this remarkable example of architecture and town planning might well be the first important piece of research within the field of industrial archaeology to be carried out in Belgium. Our country has so far all too little to show in this direction, at a time when in England the Council for British Archaeology has sponsored several projects to record, protect and preserve early industrial monuments.

Notes

1 A *bonnier* or *bonier* was a land measurement formerly used in Belgium and the North of France. It was a somewhat vague measure equivalent, according to the locality, to between 64 and 148 *ares*, 1 *are* being 100 square metres.

2 'Town' is only an approximate translation of the French *cité*, for which no exact English rendering exists. *Cité*, in this context, implies a planned, compact grouping of buildings, a piece of controlled urbanism.

Bibliographical notes

The Industrial Revolution, as it affected the Borinage, is dealt with by Marinette Bruwier in a contribution to *La Révolution Industrielle en Belgique*, which is shortly to appear, under the editorship of Professor Pierre Lebrun, of Namur.

Among general works on the coal-mining industry, one should mention particularly the monograph by G. Decamps, *Mémoire historique sur l'origine et le développement de l'industrie houillère dans le Bassin du Couchants de Mons*; R. Darquenne's book, *Histoire économique du département de Jemappes* (Mons, 1962–4), and Vanden Eynde's study of the Warocqué family, published in *Musée de Mariemont, Exposition Raoul Warocqué* (Mariemont, 1967).

The records from Le Grand-Hornu are preserved in the State Archives at Mons and have been indexed by Professor H. Watelet, now of the University of Ottawa. The results of his work in this field are to be found in *Inventaire des archives des sociétaires et de la societé civile des Usines et mines de houille du Grand-Hornu* (Brussels, 1964). Professor Watelet has been preparing a doctoral thesis on coal mining and in 1963 he read a paper on Henri de Gorge at a symposium on the coal industry which was held at the University of Lille. This paper was published in 1967. Research in the archives of Le Grand-Hornu and in other material at the State Archives at Mons, and in the documents of the Administration des Mines in the National Archives, has made it possible to present a much fuller assessment of Henri de Gorge.

A note on the *cité*, written by a teacher, Louis Lepreux, in 1888 is valuable. It is No 548 in the Le Grand-Hornu papers. It has to be supplemented by other important manuscript material, such as the weekly lists of leases, which exist from 1825 onwards, and by other unpublished documents which are to be found among the accounts and letter-files. Other works to be consulted are on workers' housing: A. Raffalovich, *Le logement de l'ouvrier et du pauvre: Etats-Unis, Grand-Bretagne, France, Allemagne, Belgique* (Paris, 1887); on the salt mines at Chaux: M. Raval, *Nicolas Ledoux, architecte du Roi* (Paris, 1945), and on Bruno Renard: A. G. B. Schayes, *Histoire de l'architecture en Belgique*, vol 2 (Brussels, no date).

Hainaut-Tourisme, no 7 (July 1963), contained an article on Le Grand-Hornu by Christiane Piérard.

Plate, see p 373

Sawmill, Kawaino, Japan (1967) with 18 ft diameter breast-shot waterwheel

Rice polishing mill, Odowara, Japan. The octagonal shaft is gear-driven from an undershot waterwheel 13 ft in diameter by 2 ft wide. The stamps are 4 in square and 10 ft long; the rice containers are 16 in in diameter and 18 in deep

See 'Watermills in Japan', pp 321–4

Watermill at Hiekawa, Japan, has overshot wheel 14 ft in diameter by 1 ft wide

Rice grinding machinery, Hiekawa. The stones are 20 in in diameter and the main drive gear wheel 30 in in diameter with 26 teeth 2½ in long by 1½ in wide

See 'Watermills in Japan', pp 321–4

Brunel's Lock at low tide. One of the two caisson gates closed against the sill in the masonry, and was swung open into the recess on the left

View over Cumberland Basin looking up towards the Floating Harbour. The old junction lock is on the right and its 1871 replacement on the left, with the original hydraulic engine house on the side

See 'The Cumberland Basin, Bristol', pp 325–33

Road to Long Stoup looking towards Lumbutts Village with Todmorden in the background

Reappearance of the old road at Lumbutts Village near to a guide post which is omitted from the Ordnance maps

Reddishore Scout Road, typical stretch of packhorse road. Note the chisel marks on the stone nearest the camera, perhaps the last piece of repair work done to the road

Guide Post on Reddishore Scout Road. The girl is 5 ft tall, which helps to give some idea of the size of the stone. Made from local gritstone, the distances are deeply cut. Age doubtful but certainly an old post

See 'Packhorse Roads in Todmorden', pp 334–9

General view of Le Grand-Hornu from the air. This shows the position of the workshops, with the small yard on the left and most of the 425 houses which De Gorge-Legrand built for his workers between 1819 and 1832. (Copyright: Charles Léva. This aerial photographer is authorised by the Ministry of National Defence)

See 'Le Grand-Hornu', pp 354–68

Stacksteads station. Lancashire & Yorkshire wooden style. Notice the island platform, all wood construction, and size of the awning. The subway entrance is on the right

Summerseat station. East Lancashire style. Notice the round topped windows, the open-air waiting area now fronted by a wood and glass panel, the worked corner stones, the plinth stone, and the low platform

See 'Aids to Recording (5): The East Lancashire Railway—The Bury to Bacup Section', pp 377–87

An East Lothian corn drier: hopper and iron levers in the loft (*top*); *the furnace* (*bottom left*) *and the drying bin and hopper beneath* (*bottom right*)

See 'An Early Corn Drier at Whittingehame Mains, East Lothian', pp 388–91

Section of curb used to support dry brick wall of pit shaft

Sough (probably eighteenth-century) revealed during opencast working at Newman Spinney, Derbyshire, in 1965. It is c 180 ft from the surface. Note the wooden prop (right of centre) supporting the roof

See 'Bell-Pits and Soughs: Some East Midlands Examples', pp 392–7

P. T. L. REES

Aids to Recording (5)

The East Lancashire Railway—II: The Bury to Bacup Section †

THE SECTION of line from Clifton Junction to Bacup via Bury was begun as the Manchester, Bury & Rossendale Railway, and was incorporated in 1844. The scheme proposed a junction with the Bolton line at Clifton to give access to Manchester, although at that time Rawtenstall was the most northerly point considered. Mills supplied most of the traffic for which cheap quick transport to Manchester was of the utmost importance. The engineer appointed was Mr C. E. Cawley; Mr Smithells, the secretary, became the manager of the Lancashire & Yorkshire Railway after 1859. However, local interests were expanding and even before the line was opened the name had been changed to the East Lancashire Railway, and extensions via Stubbins were being made to Accrington and hence to Colne and Preston. Indeed, when the line opened in September 1846, the ELR had direct access to Liverpool. In the valley itself the line was first extended to Newchurch in February 1848, and then to Bacup in November 1852. Seven years later the L & YR took over the line and worked it as a separate unit until 1923. There is little surprising in an analysis of the gradient; the line rises gently to a summit at Bacup. This station was in fact the highest on the L & YR system, 801 ft above sea level.

---

† *The first part of this article by Paul Rees appeared in IA vol* 6 *no* 3, *which also gives his bibliography.*

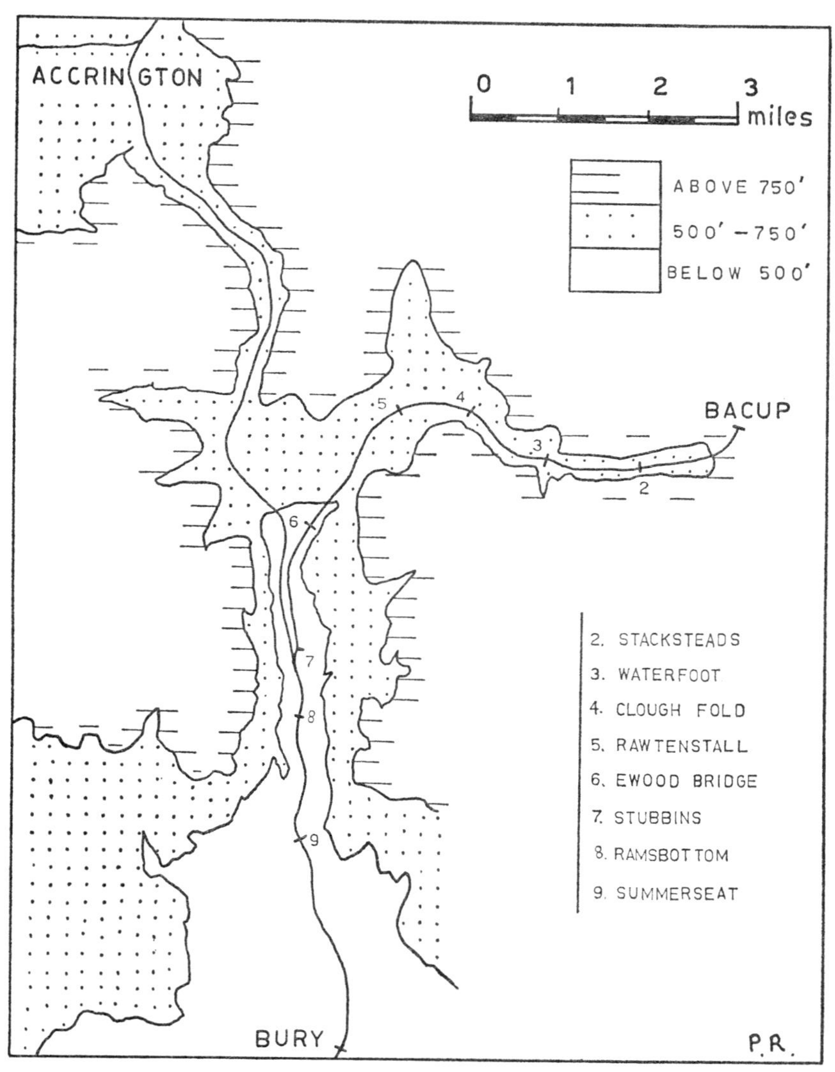

Fig 1 Relief map of the East Lancashire Railway: Bacup to Bury section

Station Types

1 *East Lancashire*

The basic type has already been discussed. The most notable characteristics are the open-air waiting area, the semi-circular arched windows and doorways, the plinth-stone and the worked corner stones. The exterior joists, especially noted on the goods sheds, are common and may well have supported weather boarding as at Clough Fold.

2 *Lancashire & Yorkshire*

Style 1 is basically a copy of the ELR style, usually early in date, probably not later than 1860.

Style 2 is typical of the whole L & YR region. Small stones or brick construction, many irregular and pokey offices, frosted glass in square plain windows, excessive ornate ironwork, and many blank walls. Wood is common, some stations being built completely of this material. Covered platform awnings exhibit a peculiar toothed effect. This style dates, as will be shown, to the last decade of the nineteenth century, and stations along the line where this style is exhibited seem to form part of a refurbishing plan designed for the whole line. The giant goods shed at Waterfoot dates to this era.

Present State of the Line

The Bacup to Rawtenstall section is closed and all services now terminate at Rawtenstall. From here to Bury a shuttle service gives connection to the electric service to Manchester via Radcliffe. Conductor guards are employed; the stations are unoccupied and their condition is deteriorating rapidly. Moves are afoot to replace the old structures by bus stop shelters. The Clifton to Bury section is closed.

Bacup (see Fig 2)

Of the early ELR phase only a long blank wall remains, pierced by

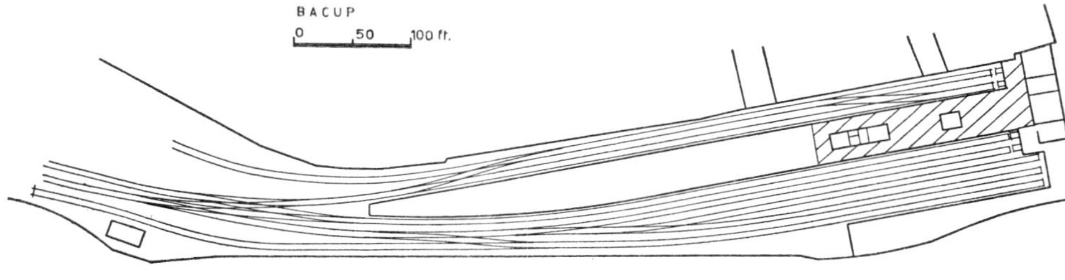

Fig 2

two arch-topped doors which lead into Manor Street and Spring Street. The original entrance seems to have been at the side; the L & YR rebuilding has positioned it at the end of the platform. The old low station platform can be seen as unfinished courses in this wall, running for some 50 yd in length.

An article in the *Rossendale Free Press*, 11 October 1902, comments on the first railway station at Bacup: 'the waiting rooms were cold ramshackle affairs made out of two dwelling houses which stood there when the line was opened. The platform was long and narrow, with one side on which to get in and out of the trains.' The account continues with a complaint about the lowness of the platforms both at Bacup and other stations on the line. They were not of course raised until the L & YR refurbished the line in the 1890s. This rebuilding is in the typical L & YR style: the offices and entrance hall are of the local stone, well dressed; the platform structures and all-over roof are of glass and wood. The entrance itself can only be described as pokey and inconvenient.

After this rebuilding there were no significant additions or alterations: the station is as it was left in the prosperous years of the 1890s. The goods shed has been recently demolished, and the yard is overgrown and unused. The track has been lifted. Certain small buildings on the periphery still stand; of these one at least may be of ELR date.

Stacksteads (see Fig 3)

The six-inch maps of 1844 and 1851 show Stacksteads station as a structure on the up side at the site of the present signal box. No trace of it remains; presumably it was one of Mr Perring's third-class halts. There was a complaint about the lowness of its platforms in the early years; this is recorded in the *Rossendale Free Press*, 11 November 1902.

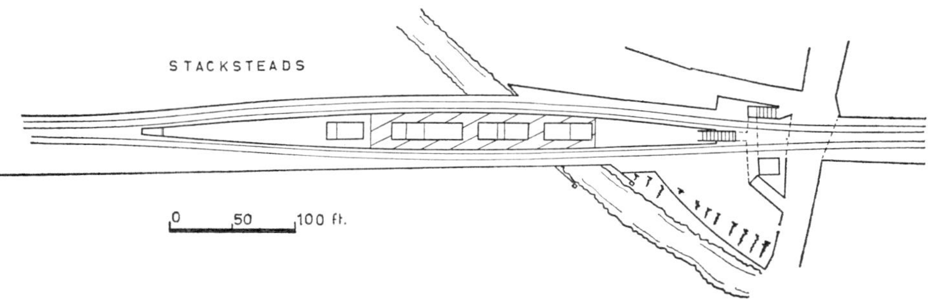

Fig 3

The one period structure now standing (illustrated on p 374) is of L & YR style 2. The platform is a single full-height island supporting the wooden station buildings. The plans of the station, prepared about 1932, show two blocks of buildings, but of these only the eastern is now standing. The only stone structure was the urinals, next to which there was a curious building, the purpose of which is not yet understood. It is a hut with three sides open for the upper half of their full height, and filled in by railings. The floor of the structure is at rail level, ie cut down into the platform and access to this is down stone steps. Gas lamps are of a standard L & YR pattern: a subway under the level crossing also gives access to the station. The signal box is of contemporary date to the station—that is the 1890s.

Waterfoot

No trace of the ELR can be found here, although the six-inch maps of 1844 and 1851 indicate a station structure on the site. Indeed a goods shed and yard are also indicated of which nothing remains. This was presumably demolished when the present structure was built, and the new goods yard opened at Newchurch one mile or so to the west. The size and style of this yard and its associated warehouse suggest a date in the prosperous years at the end of the last century.

The present station is of L & YR style 2 design, small stones, and brick being used in the make-up. The line runs parallel to the main road at this point, about 20 ft above it. Consequently the station is built on two levels, the lower giving access to the village through an opening that is all too easily mistaken for a shop door. At the lower level the booking and parcels offices open on to an entrance hall which leads directly to the staircase up to the platforms. At this level are the offices and rooms, built unusually on the down side, presumably because of the awkward layout of the site. Dating must surely be to the last decade of the last century.

Clough Fold

Neither the maps of 1844 and 1851 nor the timetable for 1849 indicate a station at Clough Fold. Yet in the ELR style there remains what was probably the stationmaster's house, set back from the station across the Irwell. It exhibits the usual features of the ELR, and introduces a style of weather boarding otherwise unknown. The style of this and the general condition of the house (it is unoccupied) suggest that it is original. This weather boarding may well have fitted on to the 'outside joists' feature noted elsewhere. We must presume a date shortly after 1851.

The present station buildings are of the L & YR style 2, built completely of wood, standing on the centre of the full-height island platform. At some time the western block was taken down exactly as at Stacksteads. Goods accommodation here was quite extensive until it was transferred to Waterfoot. The nearby gasworks seem to have been built in conjunction with the railway; no division can be found between its land and that of the railway company. The date for these is c 1890, as elsewhere.

Rawtenstall

The down-side buildings are quickly dealt with. They consist of two periods of L & YR wooden buildings, the earlier partly contained by the later. The earlier has parallels at Summerseat, and seems to date from c 1890. Phase two with its ironwork typifies the later style and dates to the extensions made later during that decade. The up-side buildings are of earlier date and origin. The ELR style extends through the whole structure, which consists of three parts. The stationmaster's house and the original station buildings stand to the south of a L & YR addition which now constitutes the booking hall.

The 1844 and 1851 maps indicate both of these structures, so they can be certainly assigned to Mr Perring. The filling in between them and the booking hall are in L & YR style I and should date to some time between 1860 and 1880.

Goods facilities were available from the opening of the line in the large yard and goods shed adjacent to the station. The shed was considerably extended by the L & YR probably during the 1890s.

Ewood Bridge and Edenfield

The station at Ewood Bridge falls into none of the usual types. The entrance is from the road, which crosses the lines by a bridge at the south end of the platforms. The platforms are of full height, and the structure of the buildings seems to be built on this so that the date must be after the 1890s. In support of this late date can be cited Harrison and Sale, who state that 'a flight of steps descend to the station' and not that it was unique in being built on two levels. Presumably in its early years the station was no more than a 'third-class halt' built all of wood.

The windows are square, the stonework massive and well worked. The style if anything could be a copy of the L & YR wooden style in stone, even providing accommodation for the stationmaster in the station buildings. The only parallel for this is at Summerseat where the accommodation so provided was an extension of the original structure. Here the same squat square style is again in evidence.

The goods facilities are of late L & YR wood design; the shed is now used as storage accommodation for a local firm. On the up-side platform the only structure is a modern bus-stop-type shelter.

Stubbins

The style of this station is pure ELR, with the exception of the raised platforms, placed north of the old low platforms, which constitute a ramp to the new ones. The open-air waiting area is not in evidence here; perhaps the exposed position of the buildings necessitated the inclusion of a real waiting room in the design. This, the porters' room and the booking office are all at platform level. Beneath them, opening on to the road, which crosses at right angles to the track under its embankment, is the stationmaster's accommodation. Square windows here, in an otherwise pure ELR design, show that Mr Perring was not averse to their use, and this fact might have some bearing on the date of the structure at Ewood Bridge. The awning has been removed, but its point of attachment has left traces. There are no structures on the up side; and there may well have been none owing to the narrowness of the platform, required by the junction with the Accrington branch. The covered subway is at the far end of the platform. Thus passengers for down trains have to walk the length of both platforms in getting from the station buildings to their trains.

Ramsbottom (see Fig 4)

All styles of building are represented here at what was, apart from the termini stations, the most important station on the line because of its position as changing station for the Accrington and Bacup branches.

The down-side structures are L & YR style 2 in design, showing all its features. The booking hall is large and cavernous with a skylight above, and the blank wall which supports the awning runs for a considerable length down the platform, showing that passengers were once

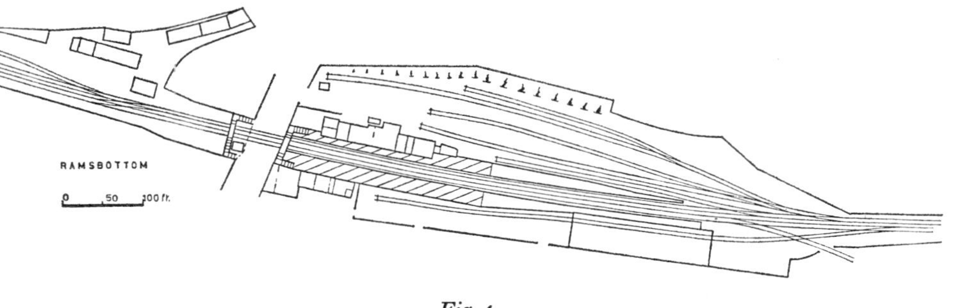

Fig 4

numerous. Indeed, there was in use here until 1966 a L & YR destination finger indicator for all down trains.

On the up side there are the original buildings. These were the stationmaster's house and the booking offices. The separate nature of these buildings was destroyed by the construction of more offices between them as at Rawtenstall some time between 1860 and 1880. Finally in the 1890s a third phase brought the L & YR style 2 across the platform, in the form of further offices with a wooden frontage.

The goods shed is of ELR origin, and was demolished in December 1968. The extensive network of sidings north of the station laid out in the period of prosperity at the end of the last century was being removed at the same time.

Summerseat (see Fig 5)

The down-side structures consist of a L & YR wooden shed and awning of the same pattern as Rawtenstall phase one, that is, built soon after the platforms were raised in 1890. The iron footbridge also dates to this era.

The up-side buildings (illustrated on p 374) stand on the original low-height platforms and the difference between the two heights is easily visible. The structure is pure ELR in style apart from an extension made to the living accommodation at the back in the 1890s. It conforms well to Mr Perring's general plan, although the open-air waiting area was filled in by the L & YR to give more comfort to the waiting passenger. All in all this is the best example of the ELR style to be found anywhere; the windows are arched, the corner stones worked, and the awnings an integral part of the roof design. The whole design is far more pleasing than the L & YR styles typified by Ramsbottom.

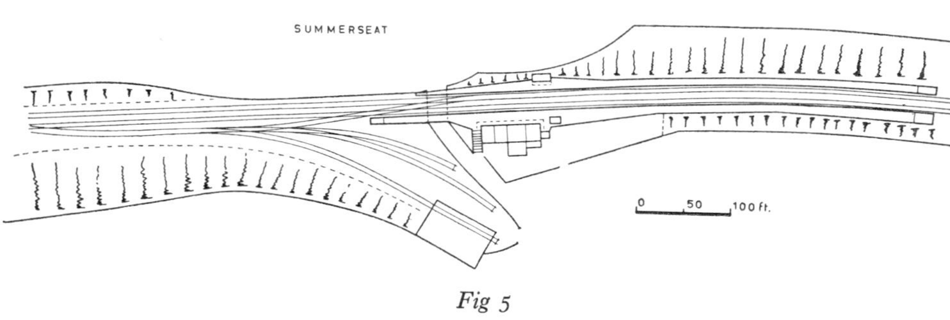

Fig 5

That the structure actually dates to the opening of the line is in doubt. Harrison and Sale, in their *Guide* of 1848, refer to Summerseat as a roadside halt and state that such halts were built only of wood, or wood and brick. Conjectural dating must be the 1860s, when traffic from the village had proved itself worthy of permanent accommodation.

Bury (Bolton Street)

Bury station was once the headquarters of the ELR. It now boasts three through platform faces and a double bay for Manchester-bound traffic.

The original ELR buildings still stand practically unaltered, used as offices for BR staff. The platforms are of course higher than when the buildings were erected, and an L & YR awning has been added. Apart from this and the rearrangement of the offices and entrances, the structure is as it was in 1848. The island platform, from which all services now operate, is similar to those found at Stacksteads and Clough Fold: for this a date of c 1890 seems reasonable. A rebuilding was effected in the 1950s, removing the entrance to a new building on the Bolton Road itself. In this the ELR crest, taken from the old entrance hall, is displayed.

I have given here an account only of the stations of the branch, in order to make something comprehensible from the masses of material available. Conclusions that can be drawn are not unexpected. After a slow start the ELR built itself a fine headquarters and a series of tasteful stations. The L & YR take-over came in a period of increasing trade. Further building was put in hand. By the end of the century a complete refurbishing of the whole line was required to cope with the increasing trade. The opening of the Bacup to Rochdale and the Bury to Holcolme Brook branches in the 1880s, together with the increasing services to Manchester, must have been of great benefit.

Until the era of nationalisation the line held its own, especially in the field of goods transport. Since then the advent of an efficient road system has caused this to dwindle to next to nothing. Diesel trains never captured the dying passenger traffic. The decision to close the upper section of the branch was neither unexpected nor really troublesome. The only worry is for the archaeologist, who must continually fear the demolition of his evidence.

Note

The station plans have been redrawn from the LMS rating plans c 1930. In conjunction with the plates, they illustrate the three basic styles of construction found on the ELR. In all the plans, the up-line, ie to Bury and Manchester, is at the bottom.

Plates, see p 374

A. FENTON

An Early Corn Drier at Whittingehame Mains, East Lothian

THE ESTATE of the Earl of Balfour in East Lothian can claim two Scottish firsts: the introduction of the combine harvester to Scotland, and the setting up of the first corn drier.

The combine harvester was made by the firm of Clayton & Shuttleworth Ltd and was bought from them by Lord Balfour in 1932. It was in regular use at the farm of Whittingehame Mains till about ten years ago, and its present coat of camouflage paint bears witness to wartime service. According to the book of working instructions, this is an E5 model, dated 12.5.1932. In use it was towed by a tractor, and the machinery driven by its own engine. The farm-grieve at Whittingehame Mains enjoyed working it and said it was like steering a ship through the cornfields. It is now in the care of the National Museum of Antiquities of Scotland.

As a necessary concomitant to the combine harvester, Lord Balfour installed a corn drier. The first one he put in was at the farm of Cairndinnis, on the west side of Traprain Law. It was transferred a year or two later to Whittingehame Mains where it remained in use until 1966, and is now being replaced by the new owner of the farm, Mr T. H. Hepburn-Wright. The following details were gleaned in the course of a visit in January 1967.

Heat was provided by a brick-built coke-burning furnace (illustrated on p 375), about 4 ft high × 3½ ft wide. This was surrounded by a metal cover that led the heat from the furnace into the drum of a fan, c 4 ft in diameter by 1 ft 6 in wide, with a belt drive attached to a dynamo (see Figs 1 & 2). The fan has a plate reading 'The Cyclone Fan, Matthews and Yates Ltd, Cyclone Works, Swinton, Manchester' with specifications as follows: Size No 15, Type No Heavy 6, Fan No

10117, Date 1926. If this date applies to the whole drier as well as the fan it would appear that its installation at Cairndinnis has antedated the arrival of the combine harvester by six years, perhaps in anticipation of this event.

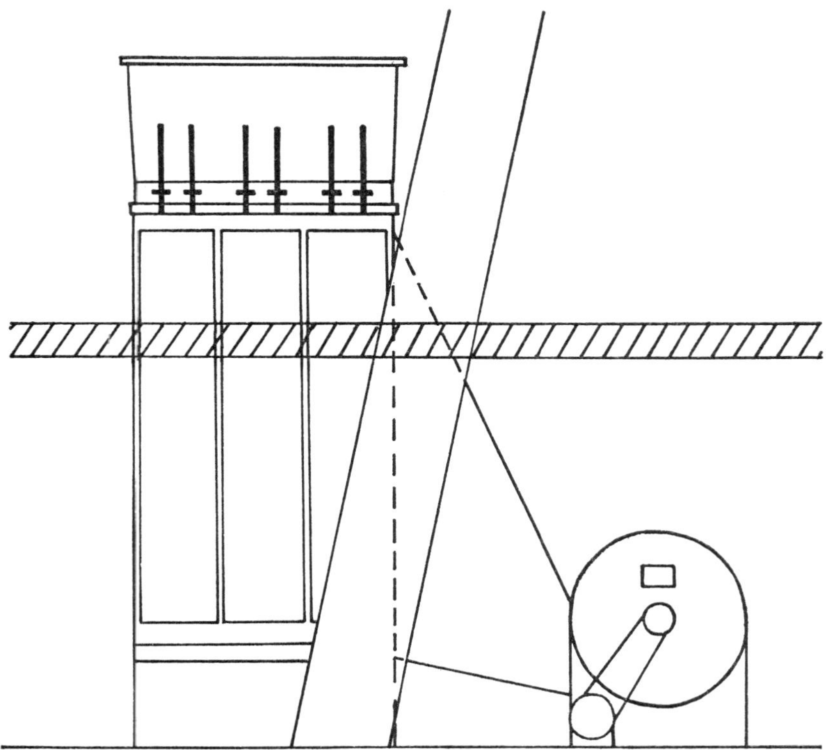

Fig 1 The Whittingehame Mains corn drier, showing (right to left) *the fan and dynamo, the metal vent, the drying bin, and the hopper with iron levers above. There is a grain elevator in front*

The fan blew air into the corn-drying bin through a metal vent, 2 ft deep where it joined the fan, and splaying out to 10 ft deep where it joined the bin. Transverse metal plates inside the vent helped to direct the flow. The drying bin (illustrated on p 375) is 10 ft deep × 6 ft long × 4 ft 10 in wide, with a hopper above and another below. The topmost hopper, in the loft (illustrated on p 375), received the grain for drying from an auger or a travelling belt, depending on whether it came straight from the sacks or from the reserve storage hoppers. To let the grain through, iron levers controlled openings in the base of the hopper, and one section could be opened by a wooden lever from the barn below. The grain did not fill the whole bin but was contained between two parallel walls of perforated metal sheets at each side, in a layer about 7 in thick. The corn was retained in these walls by two wooden flaps at the bottom, each of which could be opened by turning an iron lever. When the bin was full the upper hopper was closed and not opened again till the dried corn had been let out into the hopper

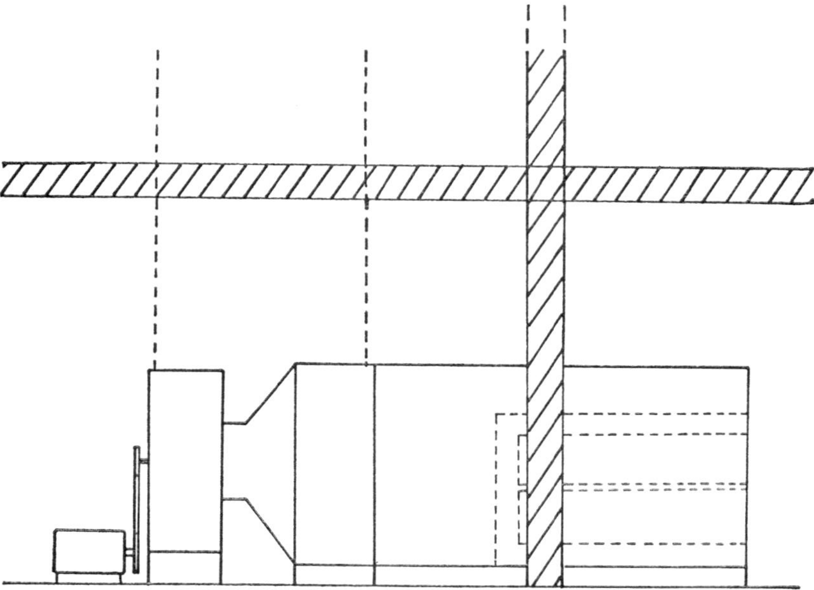

Fig 2 The Whittingehame Mains corn drier, showing (right to left) *the furnace, fan, and dynamo with belt drive. End view*

lying under the bin and below the level of the barn floor. An elevator belt with buckets took the dried grain back up to the loft for further treatment.

The drier was kept fully occupied during the harvest season, sometimes by night as well as by day if the quantities of grain built up too much. It was capable of reducing the moisture content from about 20 per cent to 16 per cent in half an hour, at a temperature of c 180 degrees. The hot air was cut off by a plate at the end of the drying period, and cold air put through for about ten minutes. It dried 200 acres of grain from the farm itself in 1966, and also part of the crops of neighbouring farmers.

Plates, see p 375

A. R. GRIFFIN

Bell-Pits and Soughs: Some East Midlands Examples

FOR THE industrial archaeologist, coal mining is normally an unrewarding study. Once a mine is closed, its shafts are covered or filled in, and usually its surface plant and buildings are removed. Occasionally an engine house might be left standing (sometimes converted to another use). For example, an old winding engine house on Birchwood Lane, Somercotes, was converted into a cottage which is still occupied. At least one early nineteenth-century headstocks still stands at South Normanton on the Nottinghamshire–Derbyshire border. In fact, both headstocks and winding engine house still stand at the old Winterbank Colliery which closed in 1889, but usually all that is left of an old pit is a mound of debris and a filled-in shaft. The underground arrangements are lost to sight; although in at least two cases they can be traced on the surface. The first of these was the subject of an article in *Colliery Engineering* in 1955.[1] Aerial photography revealed a series of bell-pits in a field at Wollaton, Nottinghamshire. In the second case, shallow pillar and stall workings have left their mark on the surface pattern of a field at Coleorton, Leicestershire.

However, from time to time, underground workings are revealed during opencast coal operations but because of the speed at which the work is done, they quickly disappear. Fig 1 shows a group of bell-pits in the Tupton (or Low Main) Seam at Heage, near Denby, Derbyshire. In the bell-pit method of working coal, a shaft was sunk down to the coal seam and the coal was then extracted from around the base of the shaft until the sides were in danger of giving way. Seen in section, such a pit is bell-shaped, hence the name. When the sides showed signs of giving way, the pit was abandoned and another sunk nearby, the debris from one being used to fill the next. During opencast operations, the soil is removed from the seam, and the bell-pits can then be seen because the debris with which they are filled is lighter in colour than the coal seam.

At Denby the pattern is confused because interspersed among the old (possibly sixteenth-century or earlier) coal bell-pits which are usually between 12 and 20 ft in diameter, there are also some shafts sunk chiefly for iron ore at a much later date (late eighteenth or early nineteenth century) which are considerably smaller.

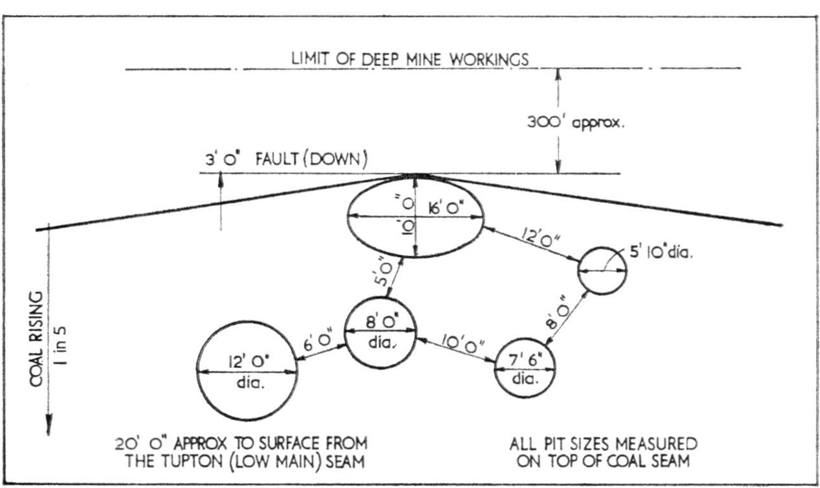

Fig 1 Group of bell-pits at Salterwood opencast site, Heage, near Denby

The largest bell-pit at Salterwood was oval in shape (see Fig 1), measuring 16 ft × 10 ft at the top of the seam and 19 ft × 12 ft at the base. The shaft was approximately 20 ft deep. Oval shafts are rarely found, most bell-pits being circular. On some sites, indeed, they are absolutely regular circles, although there is no apparent reason for this.

As it became necessary to sink deeper, bell-pit working became intolerably wasteful of labour. At the next stage of development headings were driven out into the seam. Such workings exist in the Silkstone Seam at Denby (about 145 ft below the Tupton) which are probably mid-eighteenth century since the rate of extraction was very low—only about 25 per cent. The headings, about 3 ft wide, were separated by pillars about 9 ft wide. At a later stage of development, 50 per cent extraction was common. Later still, when the headings (or stalls) had reached the boundary set by difficulties of ventilation, it was sometimes the practice to work back to the pit bottom extracting the pillars. This was called working in the 'broken' (as distinct from working in the 'whole'). There are possible indications of this practice on the site at Denby, too, probably dating from the late eighteenth century, although these may be early long-wall workings.

On another site at Newman Spinney, near Barlborough, where opencast production took place in 1965–6, approximately 90 per cent of the area of coal in the Clowne Seam had been virtually fully extracted, with irregularly-shaped pillar and stall workings on the remainder of the site running up to the outcrop. It seems likely that the whole area was worked by pillar and stall, and that the pillars were then extracted except where the workings were so shallow that this would have been dangerous. The seven small licensed mines currently working in North Derbyshire all employ the pillar and stall system. In one or two cases the pillars are later extracted, but only where there is plenty of cover. In the case of the old Newman Spinney workings, the maximum depth was approximately 180 ft from the surface and they had to be drained, as at Denby.

Keeping the workings reasonably dry was the main problem facing the early mining engineer. Before the invention of the steam-driven pump the principal method of drainage was to drive water levels (usually called adits, or, in the Midlands, soughs) below the level at which the coal was to be worked. In the bell-pit era, a ditch was sometimes dug through the field and the pits were then sunk along the line of the ditch. Similarly, on an opencast site near Alfreton a 12-in square wooden drain, presumably sunk from the surface, has been found. With deeper workings, the water level had to be driven underground and where the sough was long, shafts needed to be sunk at intervals for ventilation purposes. As early as 1552, the Willoughbys of Wollaton drove a sough over a mile in length;[2] whilst another one, driven in stages between 1703 and 1774 by Sir John Molyneux and others to drain workings on the Derbyshire–Nottinghamshire border between Westhouses and Teversal, attained a length of approximately 5 miles.[3]

The plate on p 376 shows the sough at Newman Spinney, which marks the lowest point of the old workings. All the coal worked lay between the sough and the line of the outcrop of the Clowne Seam which was approximately 300 yd to the west of the sough. As will be seen from this illustration, the sough was supported by a single row of wooden props and, considering how little support was given to the roof, it has stood very well. Later soughs were usually supported with props and bars, although some—especially nineteenth-century ones—were lined with bricks.

During excavation of the Silkstone Seam at the Salterwood opencast site (near Denby), a section of a wooden curb (or crib) was found recently (see plate on p 376). Curbs were used during sinking operations to support the timber laggings lining the shaft. The section found at Denby is not a sinking curb, however, because it bears impressions of bricks. It is clearly a section of a bricking curb, which was a support fitted in any shaft with a permanent brick lining. The shaft for which the curb was made was most probably 8 ft in diameter, which may be deduced from the drawing (Fig 2), and is quite likely to have been unmortared.[4]

When the Children's Employment Sub-Commissioner visited the Derbyshire–Nottinghamshire coalfield in 1841 he noted that many shafts were lined with unmortared bricks. One reason for using dry bricks was to facilitate their recovery and re-use when the pit was exhausted. Coal was wound out in hazel baskets (or corves) hooked on to a hempen rope which swung freely, and when men rode the shaft, the corves were removed and short chains were attached to the hooks, forming a series of loops through which they passed their legs. The loaded corves sometimes struck the side of the shaft and dislodged

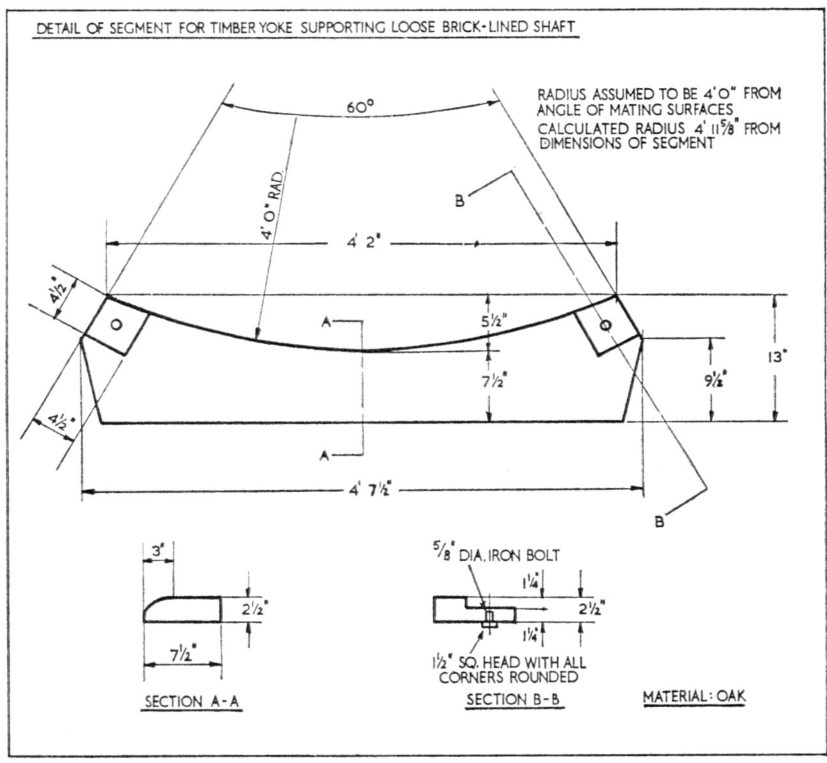

Fig 2 A wood segment found on Salterwood site, near Denby

bricks, which made it dangerous. For example, John Fisher was riding the shaft at Newthorpe Common, Nottinghamshire, when the dry brick wall gave way, throwing him out of the chain. He fell 35 yd to the pit bottom and was severely injured.[5]

It is unfortunate that, because opencast coal production is carried on at speed using heavy equipment, much evidence is lost. Where artefacts are found, for example, it is usually impossible to say where they came from—and sometimes their use can only be guessed. Another difficulty is that most old workings are 'backfilled', either deliberately or by the natural process of subsidence, and this obscures, where it does not obliterate, the old workings. The bell-pit discussed earlier was cleaned out by hand specially for the purpose of this paper.

Acknowledgments

I wish to acknowledge the co-operation of my colleagues Mr G. Jago and Mr W. Hyder of the NCB Opencast Executive, Mr I. Scattergood of the NCB North Derbyshire Area, Mr R. Storer and Mr G. Batey of the NCB, North Nottinghamshire Area.

Notes

1 F. A. Henson and R. S. Smith, 'Detecting Early Coal Workings from the Air', *Colliery Engineering* (June 1955), 256.
2 R. S. Smith, 'Huntingdon Beaumont: Adventure in Coalmines', *Renaissance and Modern Studies*, vol I (1957), 119.
3 *Chatsworth Estates Plans*, EM 378,381 (added) and 1052.
4 For shaft curbs see H. W. Hughes, *A Textbook of Coalmining* (1904), 113, 125, 135
5 *Children's Employment Commission (Mines)* (1842), First Report, App Pt II, 304–5.

Plates, see p 376

Book Reviews

View North: A Long Look at Northern England, by Frederick Alderson, DAVID & CHARLES, Newton Abbot, 1968, 283 pp, ill, 50s.

The writer begins by telling of the folly of a student friend who, when together they walked the length of Hadrian's wall, attempted to convince Northumbrians and Cumbrians that he was one of them by way of a cloth cap, strong plug tobacco and affected speech. Such tactics are of course not unknown and more recently Lord Hailsham, prior to the publication of *The North East* (HMSO, 1963), enraged, annoyed or amused northerners when on a visit to the region he arrived cap in hand. Was this therefore yet another work that would do much for the cloth cap image of the north and about which many are extremely sensitive?

Regionalism tends to be one of the more abstract branches of geography but it was clearly ignored when the southern boundary to *View North* was drawn. For to include references to Derbyshire and north Staffordshire and to rely heavily on Arnold Bennett, especially in earlier chapters, is stretching bounds rather more than most schoolboys would. Many schoolboys would however still agree with the reasons given for the location of the south and central Lancashire cotton industry. But can the establishment of a major industry be explained in such terms as the existence locally of cheap coal, a damp climate and Liverpool? Might not schoolboys also add that 'Lancashire "faces" the USA'?

The promise, in the preface, of a patchwork survey that will aid the study of industrial archaeology calls for a close examination of the quality of both 'patchwork' and 'survey'. Unfortunately the design is such that some readers will be in danger of losing their way in the rapid jumps from one district to another or from topic to topic. This could result from too much having been attempted in too short a work.

One can anticipate northerners being embarrassed by the patronising terms that appear in the earlier pages and by the north–south comparisons that are drawn. The lowest note that is struck is when Worcester, a type Midland city, is dismissed in the space of a few lines as having little character, an uncertain future and 'barely distinguishable from so many further south'. Might there not be many from the more 'positive' nineteenth-century back-to-backs who find the 'blossomy country' attractive and who can find as much delight in a skyline of the Malverns as in that of the Cheviots or any other northern range.

Chapters devoted to *Home* and *Work* indicate the author's interest in Lancashire and Yorkshire and in spinning and weaving. But what were the work conditions of the coal miners of Northumberland, Durham, Cumberland, Yorkshire or Lancashire? Or of the haematite miners of West Cumberland and North Lancashire or those who won ironstone in Cleveland? One might have reasonably expected these and other industries to have been dealt with in some detail.

Trade and strikes are acceptable surveys and the snippets from the past plus brief references from present-day reports, guides and Acts that are scattered throughout the author's text produce a greater degree of unification than what precedes it. *Play* and *Chapel* are more superficial and the writer's objectivity, especially towards Methodism, must be questioned frequently. *School* is another more competent study though factory schools might have been treated more fully.

Shop will be the most rewarding chapter in the book for many readers, especially the vivid description of a CWS grocery branch of the 1930s. We must hope that Frank Atkinson may eventually find space for such a 'store', and particularly the counter, in the Industrial Archaeological Outdoor Museum at Beamish.

The final chapter, *Figures*, is used to good effect to offer much that one expected to find in earlier chapters. Sixty-four pages of photographs also improve the work but only as much as prints do when presented in four self-contained blocks. The text makes no reference to the photographs. The index when tested was found to be 'thin' and references that are labelled as no more than 'HMSO, 1966' are irritating.

The book will act as an introductory background volume for those who have yet to discover the industrial north of England. For those interested in industrial archaeology it may point to fruitful lines to pursue or to references that might open up new fields.

University of Newcastle-upon-Tyne J. W. Bainbridge

New Inventions. A Comprehensive Survey of Scientific and Technical Progress in the Arts, Science and Manufactures as published during the Reign of Her Majesty, edited by Maurice Richards, HUGH EVELYN LTD, 1969, pp 72, ill, 18s.

That this little book hardly makes serious claim to live up to its grandiloquent title is at once apparent from a comparison of its length with the extent of the subject with which it purports to deal. The publishers in fact do not make plain the purpose its modern compiler had in mind or what were the sources from which the various descriptions of inventions were taken.

If not a serious survey of nineteenth-century technology it can be regarded as a charming collection of Victoriana; some characteristics of the age were perhaps better displayed in its actual and attempted mechanical innovations than in anything else. Its keenness to improve the minor conveniences of life, to preserve privacy, to avoid fire and seasickness contrast with the daring of the early aeronauts, the jingoism with which terrifying devices of war were dreamed up by military amateurs of every nation. We laugh at Popoff's circular warships only to shudder with the horror of hindsight at Maxim's new gun; amused at new devices for trying to reduce the discomforts of railway travel by the most improbable means, we are brought up against inventions as influential for the future as Eastman's lightweight (5 lb) camera or Bell's telephone.

To some extent this reads as a technological fun-book having some emphasis on the water closet and such interesting ideas as that for the collection of horse manure by drivers while a vehicle remained in motion and the ground unsullied—a scheme which would 'in no way inconvenience the horse'. Yet some more interesting reflections arise; the extent to which the amateur, non-scientific inventor still found an outlet for his talents, the immense solemnity with which the trivial or the humorous subject for invention was treated, the gullibility of a public which had become almost drunk on the wine of continuous innovation. All these remind us of aspects of the period for which more serious works on technological innovation have little space. The illustrations are delightfully and often amusingly redolent of the period.

University of Liverpool J. R. Harris

Robert Owen and the Owenites in Britain and America. The Quest for the New Moral World, by J. F. C. Harrison, ROUTLEDGE & KEGAN PAUL, London, 1969, pp x + 392, ill, 70s.

We are used to finding in Professor Harrison's work a great deal of erudition coupled with exceptional lucidity of thought and clarity of language, and once again we are not disappointed. This volume on the thought and the practical activities of Owen and the Owenites represents indeed a monument to the author's learning: a great mass of recent literature, together with some unpublished material, has been brought together between the covers of this book and the bibliography, running to some 107 pages, is the best so far in a field which seems to have attracted more than the usual quota of competent compilers. And as the author lets his mind play on one facet of Owenism after another, the reader is content to follow him in his concise summaries and his balanced judgments.

Yet Professor Harrison is less at ease with his theme than with any of the earlier ones he has tackled. Perhaps this owes something to the shape of the book itself. After a brief chronological introduction, it is not strictly historical, but is organised according to different aspects of the Owenite teaching, each chapter containing both a discussion of the theory and a description of the practice, if any. The main divisions are those dealing with philanthropy and poor relief, socialism, Millenialism, education, community building and the wider social movements. Such an arrangement cannot avoid certain obvious dangers. The story jumps backwards and forwards in time in a confusing manner; there is much overlap and repetition; and while some sections, like those on education or community building, allow the author to take an Olympian view by drawing upon a huge store of material already available, in others he had to do the tedious groundwork himself. These latter include the social origins of the communitarians, the finances and profitability of New Lanark, and the early influences on Owen's own thought, which the author traces to the Scottish Enlightenment—an emphasis which may not command wide assent but which this reviewer, for one, would wholeheartedly support.

The main problem, however, lies in the subject itself and is merely focused by the method of presentation: in spite of the author's intention to make this an integrating study, integrating theory and practice, the United Kingdom and the USA, there seems to be no obviously necessary link between the different aspects of Owenism itself. It is possible to agree with Owen's view of education without necessarily concurring with his economics; one could assent to his views on religion without necessarily supporting communal settlements; and one could accept his millennial view of the future without necessarily accepting his stand on the Factory Acts or on the management of cotton mills. In this, Owenism is diametrically opposed to the closely interlocking thought systems of other contemporary Socialists, from St Simon to Marx and even to Lassalle. Indeed, Owenism has transferred the eclecticism normally associated with the Conservative stance, which does not have to be logically consistent if it merely defends the *status quo*, to the camp of the critics, where it is bound to lead a much more precarious existence.

The last two sentences of the book are in the form of a statement, but they really pose a question, not consciously answered by the author: why did Owenism become a relic, rather than a legacy after the death of Robert Owen? Or in the light of the above, one could put the question differently: how did Owenism manage to unite so much support for so disjointed a programme for so long? The answer is in part that its support did, in fact, fluctuate widely, according to which phase was foremost, and that many people passed through its ranks quickly or accepted only one or other facet of the master's teaching. But it is also true that its widespread and sustained appeal arose from the fact, shown up convincingly by the author, that far from being eccentric, Owenism fitted surprisingly well into the framework of its age.

Its literature, for example, whether of the self-help and improving, or the sectarian variety, was part of a large and successful literature of the same type. The factory village settlement in Britain, and the communitarian settlements in the USA, formed successful models for Owen's ideal communities. Owen was not the only factory master to seek to supplement the poor law by philanthropy, nor even the only one to support community settlements. The critics of the classical political economy at the time, taking a line very similar to Owen's, greatly exceeded in number those who were prepared to accept its narrow premises or its dismal conclusions. The Halls of Science had obvious contemporary parallels—and so on.

The social experience, as Professor Harrison rightly emphasises, had changed so fundamentally in the years 1800–40 that no one could take the new capitalism to be quite as firmly established as it has become since, and questioning criticism was found in many different quarters. In this context, many of Owen's ideas seemed much more reasonable than they appeared in retrospect to Marx or to the marginalists. Who can fail to see the parallels, at a similar economic stage, of the Chinese communes and the Owenist settlements? Again, with certain of our inbred prejudices removed in the approved Owenite manner, are not Owen's views on education, on religion or on the position of women, commonplaces among that modern liberal opinion which draws its inspiration, as did Owen, from the eighteenth-century Enlightenment?

Above all, Owenism as a socio-economic programme, offended no one. It implied a voluntary withdrawal, rather than an imposed change, on society; it put moral conversion first, and social revolution after, always an attractive proposition to the Establishment in times of uncertainty.

There was therefore something in Owenism to satisfy those who looked for an intellectual criticism of society, something to attract the philanthropist, much to attract the main victims of industrialisation, the working population, and something even for those who needed a millennial solution for their despair. Each of these traits has survived separately, in different forms. But as a composite movement, it might have been adequate for the bad years before 1850; it could not survive thereafter.

University of Sheffield Sidney Pollard

The Industries of Scotland, Their Rise, Progress and Present Condition, by David Bremner, DAVID & CHARLES, Newton Abbot, reprinted 1969, pp 535, 84s.

So many reprints have been published in recent years that an addition to the number is bound to be regarded suspiciously by reviewer and reader alike. Both will ask if the work is worth reprinting. David Bremner's *The Industries of Scotland* might seem unlikely to pass the test. About the author, a journalist, virtually nothing is now known. He published a series of articles in *The Scotsman* in 1868. In the following year they were revised and published in one volume, now reprinted. The perceptive reader might expect the worst from these origins: 530 pages on Scottish industry by a mid-Victorian journalist is not of the most obvious value to readers of a century later.

Such an impression would be wrong, for, though the book has been virtually unobtainable for many years, it has been persistently used by modern historians. There are good reasons for this continual usefulness. The work is comprehensive. With the one notable exception of the chemical industry, most branches of the complex Scottish industrial structure of those days are covered. More important, the documentation is good. Bremner is not content to speculate on an industry's origins, nor is he the admiring traveller so typical of a generation earlier. He culls information from a variety of sources. Few are unusual (the Statistical Accounts loom large); nor are they necessarily those which modern historians would use; and at times quotations are unnecessarily long-winded. But its documentation distinguishes the book from much contemporary writing and is probably the reason why the detectable errors in Bremner are not numerous. But Bremner's greatest achievement is in his use of case studies of particular firms. Most of his essays follow a similar pattern. They begin with a description of the industry and move to an investigation of firms. Of course, even this approach has defects. The emphasis is overwhelmingly technical. It describes conditions of production, but is weak on commercial problems and on distribution; sometimes the discussion of firms can lapse into a mere catalogue, of the numbers they employ or of when the works were built. In short, Bremner is always about to tread the primrose path to sterile particularism. To his credit he proceeds much less far in that direction than many of his contemporaries.

Many can use this book with profit. For those engaged in local studies, among them industrial archaeologists, Bremner, especially in his case studies, provides information not readily available except by delving into frequently inaccessible local records. Similarly helped will be those who have interests in any aspect of Scotland's industrial history in the nineteenth century. Regrettably, that history is still unwritten. For years Bremner has been a leading guide to the important period around 1870, when the Scottish economy was at the peak of many international achievements. Now more will be able to follow Bremner in his conducted tour around the industries and firms which lay behind these achievements. For making the guide freely available once again, the publishers and Dr Butt and Mr Donnachie, who provide a brief but useful introduction, are to be thanked.

University of East Anglia R. H. Campbell

Struktura: en bok om strukturförändringarna inom Värmlands industrie förr och nu, Rolf Adamson and others, VÄRMLANDS MUSEUM, 1968, pp 182, no price.

For more than 300 years, the south-western province of Värmland has been of great importance in the development of Sweden's iron and steel industry, and from the nineteenth century onwards, its engineering, timber and wood pulp industries have also made substantial contributions to the national prosperity, with the textile, glass, tobacco and food-processing industries also expanding and profitable.

To commemorate the fiftieth anniversary of the founding of the Värmland Engineers' Association, the Värmlands Museum decided to sponsor and publish a symposium describing the economic changes which have taken place in the province since the sixteenth century. The resulting book, issued as a major supplement to the museum's normal Yearbook, is the work of nine specialists and gives an excellent picture of the way in which the area has continuously adapted itself to technological progress and innovation and to new demands in the world market.

Struktura is an authoritative work, clearly and concisely written, well documented and attractively illustrated. The last two contributions are of particular interest to the industrial archaeologist. Torsten Althin, the former director of the Technical Museum in Stockholm, provides a valuable commentary, which he calls 'Three Generations', on the outstanding ironmasters and engineers who were active in Värmland from the middle of the nineteenth century until the middle of the twentieth, men like Gustav de Laval, Carl Johan Nilson and Albert Bergström. Marie Nisser and Gunnar Sillen are responsible for the final section, a photographic panorama of the industrial environment, which shows both the small-scale installations of the eighteenth century and the massive enterprises of the twentieth. Värmland is rich in industrial monuments and the generous selection offered here has been sensitively photographed and well annotated.

There is a great deal to be said for a book of this kind, in which the whole time-span of a region's industry is described between the same covers, in such a way that a reader or a visitor can get his bearings easily and make sense of what he finds and sees. Similar volumes for other parts of Europe would be most welcome.

Bath University of Technology Kenneth Hudson

The Engineering Industry of the North of Ireland, by W. E. Coe, DAVID & CHARLES, Newton Abbot, for the Institute of Irish Studies, 1969, pp 224, ill, maps and diagrams, 50s.

When the new economic history of Ireland is eventually written, historians will have to explain how it was possible for the Belfast region to develop into a thriving industrial area while the rest of the country was stagnating. A useful beginning has been made with Dr Coe's study of the Belfast engineering industry. (The title is a shade misleading.)

The rapidly growing cotton industry of the late eighteenth and early nineteenth centuries and, later, linen manufacturing and ship building gave the necessary impetus to the industry. But firms faced stiff British competition. Those with enterprise survived by diversifying and selling in the expanding export market. By the end of the century Belfast manufacturers were providing a huge variety of products—spinning machines, tea dryers, tobacco presses, stable fittings and heating and ventilating plants amongst them.

In an all too brief section (pp 129–36) Dr Coe discusses the decline of industries in the rest of the country, and points to the explanation, the smallness of the home market. Belfast's success was undoubtedly due to its entrepreneurs having so energetically sought outlets for their products in the British and world markets.

If there are faults in this book they are to be laid at the door of the publisher. To do justice to the subject the writer should have been given a great deal more space, and it is irritating to have to search for the footnotes at the back of the book. Those readers seriously interested in engineering in Northern Ireland would be well advised to turn to Dr Coe's original PhD thesis for fuller documentation.

Queen's University, Belfast J. M. Goldstrom

Our Contributors

THOMAS T. HAY is a mechanical engineer employed by the Heavy Organic Chemicals Division of Imperial Chemical Industries Ltd at Wilton, North Yorkshire, responsible for maintenance and commissioning of petro-chemical plants.

ANGUS BUCHANAN is Director of the Centre for the Study of the History of Technology at Bath University of Technology, and co-author (with Neil Cossons) of *Industrial Archaeology of the Bristol Region.*

HARRY W. HODGSON was born in Selby, Yorks, educated Pontefract Kings School, Durham University and Lincoln Theological College, and worked for some time as a mining engineer and surveyor in Yorkshire where his interest in transport and engineering began. He worked as a parish priest in the Halifax district from 1934 and is at present Vicar of Todmorden and Rural Dean of the Calder Valley where the packhorse roads are situated.

BRUCE LENMAN is a graduate of Aberdeen and Cambridge universities, and lectures and directs Local Research Programme in Department of History, University of Dundee; secretary of Abertay Historical Society and its IA section; currently engaged in SSRC-sponsored project on sources of capital for industrial development in east-central Scotland.

MRS ENID E. GAULDIE is a graduate of St Andrews University where she wrote a thesis on Scottish bleachfields; has been employed in the Local Research Programme of the Department of History of the University of Dundee for a couple of years working on aspects of the history of the jute and linen industry, and is currently working on an SSRC project.

KENNETH HUDSON, Senior Lecturer at the University of Bath, is the author of many books and articles on local history and industrial archaeology and was editor of this journal till 1 January this year.

P. T. L. REES graduated from University of Nottingham in 1968 after reading Classics with Archaeology as a subsidiary subject.

ALEXANDER FENTON is Assistant Keeper, National Museum of Antiquities of Scotland, Edinburgh, Secretary of Society for Folk Life Studies, and co-editor of *Tools and Tillage* (a journal published in Copenhagen).

A. R. GRIFFIN works for the National Coal Board as Area Industrial Relations Officer, North Notts Area; also holds an appointment as the Special Lecturer in Industrial History and Industrial Relations in the University of Nottingham, and is author of several works on the history of mining, at present working on *An Industrial Archaeology of Coalmining.*

Notes and News

Editorial

In reviewing the first year of our editorship it is only right and proper that we should thank our subscribers for their support and our contributors who have provided us with a welcome flow of articles and notes. Would-be contributors are requested to write for our conventions, which give useful hints on the way that we would like the material prepared for us. Would all local societies and IA sections' secretaries also contact us if they wish to be included in the list of local societies which is published annually, and if they could send us copies of their publications we would be glad to bring them to the notice of a wider public. For the guidance of those proposing to write, the following are the copy dates for *Notes and News*:

Not later than 1 October for the February issue.

Not later than 1 January for the May issue.

Not later than 1 April for the August issue.

Not later than 1 July for the November issue.

Subscribers may also like to know that there has been, during this last year, a fruitful liaison with *Transport History* and this is particularly useful as the number of books for review and notice increases. We have tried as far as possible to extend the coverage of books reviewed and publications noticed. In the next volume we propose to start an annual bibliography of books and articles likely to interest our readers.

The future of industrial archaeology and its relevance in local and regional studies is increasingly being debated. We would like the journal to continue to provide a forum for information and opinions and we hope that it can be a medium of co-ordination for everyone interested, no matter how superficially, in the history of industry and technology. The greatest amount of speculation has naturally been about the creation of a national society and the form it should take. Perhaps, without prejudging the outcome of these discussions too much, we should state our support for a national society which makes membership open to individuals as well as corporate bodies such as existing societies. A completely federal society with membership only open to societies has been widely canvassed. This would certainly have the advantage of being representative but its weaknesses are fundamental. It would be difficult for it to channel the enthusiasm of individuals and small groups, and the problem of how it was to be financed would not be readily solved.

It is certainly clear that the creation of a national society would involve further rationalisation. For instance, it might be reasonable for the Bath Conference to be formally regarded as the annual meeting of such a society. Informally, it is already so regarded. Naturally, the future of this journal also enters the issue. Without wishing to pre-empt the place of any national society's journal, it seems to us that it would be unnecessary duplication to bring into existence another publication unless its readership, policy and coverage were radically different from our own. Many of our readers may not know that the journal has been regarded as a clearing-house for general enquiries of the kind that ought to be dealt with by the executive and secretary of a national society; few of these ever get into print; inevitably, and no doubt our opinion would be confirmed by our predecessors, much of our time has to be spent on what are strictly non-editorial duties.

JB
ID

Preservation Corner

We continue our series of preservation features with details of an exciting new project for an open-air industrial museum being formed around the relics at Ironbridge Gorge. Within the boundaries of Telford New Town designated in 1968, the Ironbridge Gorge Museum Trust hopes to preserve for ever the unique industrial monuments of Coalbrookdale and neighbourhood as part of the national heritage. May we again remind our readers that we will welcome contributions and illustrations of local preservation projects.

Ironbridge Gorge: A Living Museum

Much of Coalbrookdale and the Ironbridge Gorge in the Severn Valley survives from the eighteenth century. No early industrial area in the world can compare in importance with this part of Shropshire: modern iron smelting, metal railways, canal inclined planes, Coalport china—all had their origins here and all have left remains as monuments to the pioneers of the Industrial Revolution. Here Abraham Darby I was the first to smelt iron with coke, probably the most important breakthrough in the early phases of the Industrial Revolution. The old furnace he used dates back to 1638 and survives as it was enlarged by his grandson to cast the members of the first iron bridge.

John Wilkinson, the great ironmaster, Thomas Telford, the father of civil engineering, Richard Trevithick, the pioneer

Focal point of the Ironbridge Gorge Museum: the first iron bridge with its 100-ft span dates from 1779

The old furnace at Coalbrookdale built in 1638 where, in 1709, Abraham Darby first smelted iron with coke

locomotive designer and many others came to work at Coalbrookdale, as the only place in existence where there was the technical knowledge and skill to make their theoretical ideas into practical inventions. Both furnace and bridge form part of the projected museum complex, and both can be seen in their original setting. In fact much of the entire area preserves features as they were in the eighteenth century. There are period Georgian dwellings, workers' cottages, churches and inns strung along the Dale and essentially the industrial community remains vigorous and thriving without spoiling the rural quality of its setting. It is the Museum Trust's intention to preserve the entire area in its living state.

The nucleus of this unique museum already exists. It occupies 300 acres close to the famous Iron Bridge and work has started on the restoration of industrial and domestic buildings of the period lying within it. In 1959, the Coalbrookdale Co itself established a works museum which now houses a most interesting collection of material associated with the development of the company over a period of 250 years. It also has an open-air section which includes a dam, an eighteenth-century warehouse surmounted by a cast-iron cupola with a clock, Darby's original furnace and another early furnace. Railway exhibits include early rails and trucks and a nineteenth-century locomotive.

The Coal Brook, from which the Dale and surrounding area takes its name, runs through the site which the Museum Trust plans to expand so that it serves as a focus for the area to be conserved. The Trust has already accepted responsibility for whole sections of the area where industrial monuments are in most danger. The museum will ultimately illustrate the multifarious industrial achievements of the area—the Iron Bridge itself, a canal incline, ceramic works including brick and tile production, the Coalport china kilns and a clay pipe works, early tramroads and railways, housing, shops and public houses—a three-dimensional display on a scale never before attempted in Britain.

A Coalbrookdale token coin, value one halfpenny. Industrialists found it necessary to circulate their own coins because of the shortage of small change in the late eighteenth century

The museum area is to be sub-divided into three main complexes—Coalbrookdale, Ironbridge and Blists Hill. The latter affords an opportunity for the development of perhaps the most ambitious open-air industrial museum in the world. The Blists Hill site occupies some 100 acres and contains the famous Coalport incline, the remains of iron, clay and tile works, as well as numerous other mining and geological features. On this site it is proposed to establish many of the industrial relics at present in isolated situations and which, by virtue of their location, would be destined for destruction. The industries will be roughly grouped under the headings of transport, coal, clay and iron.

Clearly this project will involve considerable expenditure both now and in the future. A great deal of material has been collected and much voluntary effort expended on the project. But in order to obtain the services of a professional curator and other staff necessary to a project of such size and significance, funds are urgently needed. An estimated £1 million will be needed to restore or reconstruct the relics within the museum area. An appeal has been launched for this vital project.

Details of the project can be obtained from The Secretary, Ironbridge Gorge Museum Trust Ltd, Priorslee Hall, Oakengates, Shropshire. Readers may be interested to know that an association, known as the Friends of the Ironbridge Gorge Museum, has been formed and membership is open to any interested individual, family or society. The Secretary of the Trust will be pleased to forward information on request.

The recently excavated top transfer section of the Coalport Inclined Plane, showing the boiler house stack in the background

Beam engine built in 1851 which is to be brought from the Lilleshall works nearby for erection in the Museum area. This interesting engine is featured in Notes and News, *February 1970 issue.* (*Photos courtesy Ironbridge Gorge Museum Trust Ltd*)

Seal of the Ironbridge Gorge Museum Trust, based on the design of the token

Lea Valley Conference

Mr P. J. Huggins has sent us a report of activities at a conference on the archaeology of the Lea Valley held at Capel House, Waltham Cross, on 15 March 1969. The scene was set by Denis Barker and John Carr who traced the influences of geology and geography on the land-use pattern and transport links, including navigable waterways. Denis Smith described the area of his Lower Lea Valley Industrial Monument Survey, which stretches from the Thames to Waltham Abbey. He showed examples of the fine buildings and machinery still extant in the valley.

Barry Sheldon and Roland Adamson explained the proposals of the Lea Valley Regional Park Authority, which include the establishment of a Museum of Industrial Archaeology based on the Abbey Mills sewage pumping station at West Ham. W. Branch Johnson, who was responsible for the survey of industrial monuments in Hertfordshire, stressed the need for close co-operation with managers of local firms and for 'swotting up' of information before visiting plant. The meeting concluded with a forum.

A handbook which includes a full report of lectures and additional papers on the Lea Valley area is being reprinted and can be obtained from P. J. Huggins, Enfield College of Technology, Queensway, Enfield, Middlesex, at a cost of 10s, cheques to be made payable to the London Borough of Enfield.

Bristol School Projects

H. M. Stedman, Head of the History Department, Hartcliffe School, Bristol, has written telling us of industrial archaeology fieldwork undertaken by groups of fifth-year pupils in and around the city. One of their first major projects was a preliminary survey of the 'Great Western' Cotton Mill at Barton Hill built beside the Feeder Canal in 1837, which has since been demolished.

This was followed by a variety of field surveys, including toll-houses and a local brewery. 'When we worked in Bedminster in the summer of 1966', writes Mr Stedman in the school newspaper, 'we knew the Mill Lane area was soon to be redeveloped. This threatened the circular urinal that was cast in Glasgow and erected in the 1890s. The view from inside the dome was a most striking example of cast-iron work.' Thanks to the work of Hartcliffe School's IA workers, however, Bristol Museum has since decided to preserve it.

Conference on Victorian Studies

A conference on Victorian Studies arranged by the Departments of English Studies and Economic History was held at the University of Strathclyde, Glasgow, 19–21 March. A wide range of lectures on Victorian society and technology was delivered, including 'Technology and Utopia' by I. F. Clarke (Strathclyde), 'Science and the Industrial Revolution' by Professor Peter Mathias (Oxford), 'The Evolution of the Early Victorian Factory' by David Walker (Dundee) and 'Victorian Sanitary Engineering' by J. R. Hume.

James Reid: Millwright

We were sorry to hear of the death in April, at the age of 81, of Mr James Reid of Alness, Easter Ross, who was well known as a millwright and agricultural engineer throughout the northern Highlands, as well as in the North East.

A native of Foveran, Aberdeenshire, James Reid was born near a meal mill and from his boyhood was passionately interested in mills, waterwheels, steam engines and all the paraphernalia of the millwright's art. After leaving school in Dyce he worked on a farm, but soon afterwards apprenticed himself to a local millwright. Mills and milling became not only his life's work but his hobby as well.

As a young journeyman he went to Edin-

The late Mr James Reid, millwright, beside a traction engine at a Highland Show

burgh with a firm of milling engineers, for whom he installed large plants, waterwheels and turbines throughout southern Scotland and Ireland. In 1912 he went to Ross-shire and started his own business in Invergordon. A few years later he moved his business to Bridgend in Dingwall, where he took over a disused watermill as his headquarters. It was not long before the threshing and meal mills he built at Bridgend gained a reputation for efficiency and durability among farmers all over the North.

James Reid knew mills and millwrights far and near and nothing delighted him more than to tell in his homely Buchan dialect of mills long derelict and millers long passed away. He frequently contributed articles on mills and mill engineering to agricultural journals and newspapers. Even in his eightieth year he had the energy to pay a summer visit to the Orkneys to look at old mills and waterwheels. Some of the fine models of mills and farm machinery which he so skilfully made as a hobby are now in the Scottish Country Life section of the National Museum of Antiquities of Scotland in Edinburgh, and well worth seeing.

The Engineer in Society

The above is the title of a paper and discussion in the *Proceedings of the Institution of Mechanical Engineers* (Vol 183, 1968–9) which is of great interest not only to those in the profession but others concerned with the teaching of the history of engineering and technology. The author, Anthony Vickers, maintains that although technological potential is developing more rapidly than ever before, the social and economic implications remain too often unrecognised. The paper, which is endorsed by authorities in a wide range of activities at home and overseas, analyses the impact of different sources of energy for electric power generation, of containerisation in transportation and of developments in the iron and steel industry.

Economist's View

The Economist ran a feature in its 24 May issue entitled 'Industrial Britain's Great Remains' describing the rise and progress of industrial archaeology and the development of museums of technology in Britain. 'Industrial archaeology', it wrote, 'is just ceasing to be regarded as a hobby for harmless lunatics: the Treasury has been contributing all of an annual £2,000 for a survey of industrial monuments which can then, if they are worth it, come under official protection provided always that the survey manages to find and list them before the demolishers do.' The article continued: 'There is continual gnawing worry that outstanding industrial monuments and machinery are being destroyed without record because their importance is not appreciated by their owners or by demolishers and redevelopers. Ignorance is the chief enemy; since the monuments are in declining and forgotten industries, the natural process of replacement and modernisation inevitably take their toll. So do natural decay and vandalism, especially in out of the way sites and on canals. In city centres, urban redevelopers wreak havoc; sometimes it is very difficult to find new uses for a bulky 19th century warehouse.'

Much of the work of the CBA and the MPB & W, together with the NRIM, university departments, local societies and individuals is frustrated by lack of central organisation and this is perhaps the point most stressed by *The Economist*: 'If industrial archaeology is worth serious study, should we not be doing something less haphazard about it?'

Kirkcaldy Factory Chimneys

Mr Walter Stephen writes:

The year 1828 saw the first steam engine made in Kirkcaldy, a 6-hp machine used to drive lathes and other machines in a foundry. This was still in use in 1872. Engineering, ship building, iron founding and steel forging establishments were set up, mainly in the period 1850–70, each being equipped with at least one steam engine and chimney stack. Today no steam engines are in use in Kirkcaldy, although a few factories still use coal-fired steam-raising plant. Many of the buildings are still in existence but are often much altered from their original appearance and function.

Three principal types of chimney can be discerned. In plan these are square, octagonal and circular. Square chimneys are unquestionably the oldest. An examination of the OS 25-inch map (1855) shows that all but 2 of the 24 factory chimneys mapped were square, and the position of the 2 circular chimneys on the outskirts of the town indicates their recent construction. The 1894 map, at a scale of 1:500, shows 35 square, 3 octagonal and 26 circular chimneys. Remaining today are 14 square, 2 octagonal and 17 round chimneys.

The square chimneys are modest in scale and plain in appearance. Typical dimensions are an outside measurement of 6 ft at the base and a height of 30 ft, with almost vertical sides. The chimney at the Invertiel works of the Forth & Clyde Roperie Co Ltd was probably the oldest chimney in the area until blown down in the gale of 14 January 1968. The largest chimney of this type, and one of the latest, is the one at the same company's Hendry's Mill, where a new 200-hp engine was installed in 1856, with a suitable chimney. This one is on a much larger scale, being 170 ft high with a pronounced taper. At the base, the outside measurement is 12 ft.

Octagonal chimneys represent a transition from the square to the circular type. These were never common, only 3 being shown on the 1894 OS 1:500 map. There are 2 survivals, both erected in 1866; the one at the Bennochy works of N. & N. Lockhart is 120 ft high with a decorated top. At nearby Kinghorn, another octagonal chimney with a plain top was built in 1858. This measures 9 ft 4 in in diameter at the base, tapering to 4 ft 6 in, and 135 ft high.

The first circular chimney was erected at the Whitebank Foundry in 1851; the new developments of later decades almost without exception incorporated chimneys of this type. Some had ornate tops but most, like the example at the Abden works of Robert Stocks & Co Ltd, were plain. This example, built in August 1866, is 155 ft in height, with a diameter of 12 ft at the base, tapering upwards.

All the surviving factory chimneys in the area are built of brick, although some of the earliest were of stone and a few of the square type are of stone for the first 20 ft above ground level. The local tradition is of building with freestone and whinstone and it seems likely that the progression from square, through octagonal, to circular chimneys was a development in the handling of an unfamiliar building material which held out the possibility of greater flexibility and taller structures than the massive masonry of tradition could tolerate.

The typology of factory chimneys in the Kirkcaldy area appears to be well established. Superficial observation leads one to think that a similar typology may exist in the west of Scotland and in the West Riding of Yorkshire. Detailed local studies might show whether this is the case and whether the dates agree with those observed in Kirkcaldy.

Large square chimney at the Invertiel works of the Forth & Clyde Roperie Co Ltd

Round chimney stack of the Abden works of Robert Stocks & Co Ltd, built 1866

Another Welsh Beam Engine

Following the note in vol 6 no 2 about the Cornish beam engine at the Dorothea slate quarries near Caernarvon, Mr D. E. Bick, 13 Rotunda Terrace, Cheltenham, has written to us as follows:

I was pleased to see that the Dorothea engine is being preserved, but it is not, in fact, the only remaining example in Wales. There is another at the Old Glyn pit near Pontypool. It is a rotary engine and stands well back from the shaft. The pumps were operated by bell cranks and flat rods. The engine house, dated 1845, built of local stone, is roofless and all of the machinery is exposed to the elements. Close by is a complete vertical winding engine with the drum high up above the cylinder. These engines provide a fine and probably unique example of nineteenth-century colliery pumping and winding equipment.

Mr Bick's photograph of the Old Glyn engine shows that it too is a worthy candidate for preservation, either in situ or in a museum.

Beam engine and engine house, Old Glyn Pit

The Gas Industry

A. J. Spackman, Lecturer in Fuel Technology, Enfield College of Technology, Queensway, Enfield, has prepared a memorandum on the history of technology of the gas industry. The present rate of change in this industry, he writes, is so rapid that the need to preserve records and suitable items of plant machinery is being lost sight of in the rush for the incinerator and demolition contractor. There is an urgent need to begin a central reference collection relating to the gas industry and for the establishment of a national centre co-ordinating all aspects of study of the history of this industry. A number of colleges, universities, professional engineers and individuals are interested in this aspect of the gas industry, and people within the industry itself are anxious to help, providing it does not hinder the urgent need to re-equip much of the country's industry. Readers interested in the archaeology of the gas industry, including private manufacture in country houses and factories, are asked to contact Mr Spackman for further details of activities and surveys.

More Pictorial Sources

Kenneth Lindley, 6 Woodthorpe Lane, Sandal, Wakefield, writes:

I was interested to read the item in the May issue following up my article on wood engravings as sources of information. The remarks about cataloguing are particularly important, as they indicate some considerable weakness in our approach to the whole concept of art galleries.

Regarding sources of information, old postcards are of considerable interest. It has often seemed to me strange that the earliest postcards often portray industrial scenes rather than the obviously 'picturesque' subjects to which we have now become accustomed. I have a number of these in my own collection, including some rare stereo 'pairs' bought in a second-hand shop.

On the same theme, Dr D. Chapman of the School of Business Studies, University of Liverpool, says that 'because of the death of a generation of photographers using large format cameras, quantities of lantern slides are finding their way into junk shops'. Many of these have historic value and Dr Chapman has collected some 400 in the field of Liverpool and Merseyside shipping in the last two years.

Japanese Molinology

Mr Thomas Hay, author of the finely illustrated article in this issue on Japanese watermills, has written telling us of his visits to Japan and how he was able to gather the material for his survey. An engineer with ICI, Mr Hay in 1966–7 was engaged in the design of a petro-chemical plant. This design was licensed by the Japanese fibres firm, Teijin Ltd, for the production of Para-xylene, a raw material for the synthetic fibre Terylene.

Mr Hay worked on the design in this country and afterwards went to Tokyo for four months in 1967, where he spent most of the time in the design offices of Teijin Ltd, advising and assisting with the detailed mechanical design and equipment specifications for the construction of the plant in Japan. Towards the end of 1967 he returned to Japan and spent one month at Tokuyama in the south west of the country, where the plant was built.

At weekends and during his travels Mr Hay (with his Japanese colleagues) visited any watermills that could be found, taking photographs and talking about mills and milling with the local farmers and anyone who could give information. Mr Hay also visited the National Science Museum in Tokyo and talked about mills with Mr Aoki, Head of the Mechanical Engineering Department.

Mr Hay has also recently visited Canada, where he had an opportunity to carry out some 'mill-hunting'. We look forward to another article on his Canadian findings.

An electric-powered rice polisher, Oniyanagi near Odawara, Japan

Rice polishing mill, Sakashita, Japan, photographed in 1967. The undershot waterwheel is 5 ft in diameter by 1 ft wide

Museum of Applied Arts & Sciences, Sydney

J. L. Willis, Director of the above museum, has written telling us of the role industrial archaeology will play in the future in Australia. He writes:

Although the Museum of Applied Arts & Sciences was established in 1880 (as the Sydney Technological Museum) it did not occupy its present building and site until 1893. However, since its establishment it has been collecting items of transport, industrial machinery and other objects associated with industry. Unfortunately, like most museums today, limited finance, staff and space dictate a policy of preservation which restricts the selection of objects only to those that are of highest historical and technological importance. Similarly the recording of information is generally restricted to these major objects and the part they played in the development of the country. The more detailed history and recording in this field is carried out by the numerous historical societies in each state of Australia.

During the past ten years many specialised museums have been formed in New South Wales in such fields as tramways, railways, motor cars, aircraft—as well as a Horse Era Museum. The establishment and growth of these museums will ensure that the historical and technological developments in these fields will be recorded and preserved for future generations to study.

The involvement of the National Trust of Australia in the field of industrial archaeology is fully supported by the museum and will complement the work it has successfully performed over the past eighty-nine years.

IA Film Group

An IA Group of the British Industrial & Scientific Film Association was formed in May. Its purpose is to examine existing film material and to encourage further films to be made in order to keep a record of important items of historic industrial technology before they are destroyed. The formation meeting on 22 May at the Shell International Centre saw a selection of interesting and valuable films sponsored by Shell, the NCB, Messrs Peek, Frean & Co, and Courtaulds Ltd. These included: *The Wheelwright* (demonstrating the traditional method of making a cart-wheel); *The Tidemiller* (a working tidemill); and *Winding at Old Mills* (a record by the NCB of a steam winding engine at Old Mills Colliery, Somerset).

Bradford

Bradford Technical College is forming an IA group under the direction of George Ingle and Derek Pickles. Much of old Bradford is being destroyed and little is known generally about the early industrial history of the area. The group hopes to contribute towards the permanent recording of buildings and machinery and provide a means of co-ordination for those interested in the industrial archaeology of the region.

Ice Houses

Mr E. P. Griffith of Hexham has written telling us of his interest in ice houses in Northumberland, where he has been carrying out a survey. Ice houses were used by larger country houses for preserving foodstuff and fish before the days of refrigerators and were often remarkably efficient.

Just north of Hexham are three mansions which still have good examples—Beaufront Castle, Sandhoe Hall, and Stagshaw Close House. Beaufront is the most interesting as it is in original condition. Here an outer door leads to a vaulted passage 15 ft long which ends in a drop to the 10 ft square floor of the 'house'. Stone-cut channels in the floor provide for 'run-off'. The interior is of well-finished stone and the vaulted ceiling is 15 ft above floor level. Sandhoe is similar, though modern alterations have been made to put the ice house to some other use. Stagshaw has an unusual anteroom instead of the traditional passage and has been insulated with earth as well as stone.

Ice was usually obtained from natural or artificial ponds, the latter being created by damming a convenient stream. The dam and remains of the sluice for the Sandhoe ice house can still be seen, while Beaufront was supplied from a natural pond nearby. Ice was lifted from the pond and carted off to the ice house, where it was covered with straw before meat and dairy produce could be stored. An ice house at Nunwick Hall was in use until 1910 and was often effective in the month of July.

(Similar ice houses can be found in most parts of the countryside adjoining mansions. The doocot or dovecote was another —somewhat less scientific—means of preserving food throughout the winter and can often be seen near the ice house. Editors)

Beaufront Castle ice house: the entrance

Tinplate Making

In *Iron & Steel* (April 1969) is an illustrated article by Norman Mutton on the operation of a tinworks at Hampton Loade in Shropshire 1822–6—the only one known in that county. The experiment in tinplate making was the work of James Foster, the Stourbridge ironmaster, but after only four years it was abandoned and the site became a charcoal ironworks.

The Kidwelly tinplate works in Carmarthenshire is the subject of a short paper in the *Carmarthen Antiquary* (vol V, 1964–9) by W. H. Morris. This works was erected by Charles Gwynn in 1737 at Bank Broadford in the valley of the Gwendraeth Fach. There was abundant water for cleaning and power and the coastal location facilitated the import of Cornish ore.

Teach-In

St Katherine Docks, now owned by the GLC and currently the subject of a re-development competition, was the venue for a practical session undertaken by members of the Greater London Industrial Archaeology Society on 13 July. After a tour of this most interesting dock system the party split up into smaller groups to discuss and apply techniques including photography, recording, surveying and what to look for in both buildings and equipment.

The Mineral Water Industry

Patrick Matthews, a pupil at Downside School near Bath, and an enthusiastic member of the Archaeological Society, has written to us about a local mineral water manufacturer. Like similar plant elsewhere, the former works are virtually unrecognisable 'and all that remains today would suggest a perfectly ordinary farm'. Behind the house, about a mile north of Stratton-on-the-Fosse, is a large building which was the actual mineral water works of Thomas Hignell & Co. Hignell came to the district from Bristol and established the firm c 1886, which eventually did a wide trade throughout the surrounding towns and countryside. It supplied most of the public houses in the area, as well as the local shops. About 1900 the firm had a staff of six, besides two horses and two wagons. Mr Matthews possesses one of the only two known surviving bottles from this firm.

On the same topic Harold Gregory of Buckley, Flintshire, who originally raised the discussion about the 'pop industry', has sent some photographs of early 'pop' bottles, including the Codd patent glass marble-stoppered bottle (the invention of Hiram Codd c 1870) with wooden opener. This was used by the local firm, Gregorys of Buckley, described in the *Notes and News* section (pp 195–6) of the May issue of *Industrial Archaeology*.

The Trident

F. D. C. Jeffery of 5 Salisbury Road, Redland, Bristol, writes:

On page 202 of vol 6 no 2 there is an interesting comment by Mr G. D. Peach about a trident, with accompanying photograph.

In the early 1900s (c 1909–12) I used to see this type of implement used in the water meadows and ditches of the village of Hoo which formed a part of the Stoke Saltings. This is in Kent on the north shore of the Long Reach of the River Medway.

The implement was called an 'eel spear' and was used by plunging the trident part deep into the wet, almost liquid, mud with a slight twisting motion. When withdrawn there was almost always an eel wrapped around its prongs; it was quickly unwrapped and put into a pail or basket.

I found it intriguing to watch this form of fishing. No doubt some expertise was

Codd's patent 'pop' bottles in 5 oz and 10 oz sizes

necessary in the way it was done apart from deftness in using the spear but to a young boy the sureness of the catch was next to miraculous.

I cannot remember whether the particular eel spears which I saw used were in fact plated in any way as there was a lot of mud on them; but I can imagine their owners would take good care of them, and brass was a common form of protection for both iron and steel. Certainly the shape was exactly that shown in your illustration.

Short Reviews

The National Trust has recently produced an attractive booklet entitled *Conway Suspension Bridge* by Douglas B. Hague, which commemorates the opening in 1826 of Thomas Telford's most successful 'Gothic' bridge. Although dwarfed by the Menai Bridge (begun in 1819), Conway followed it closely in detail, having a span of 327 ft. In 1958 a new bridge was opened and only through the action of the National Trust was Conway saved.

Wiltshire Industrial Archaeology (One/1969) is the first issue of the transactions of the Salisbury & South Wilts IA Society. Besides recording the actual research of members, ranging over unusual milestones, little-known railway projects, hydro-electricity, and cast-iron gravestones, it contains a thought-provoking feature on future trends in industrial archaeology by Kenneth Hudson, society president. Copies (price 6s) are available from the Editor, Berry Cottage, Bradley Lane, Holt, Trowbridge, Wilts.

The Transactions of the Teeside IA Group entitled *End of an Era* (vol 1 no 1) is naturally concerned with local industry and its three main articles deal with various aspects of the iron trade in the area. Two features deal with the Cleveland iron industry and the third provides a case study of the Ayresome Ironworks of Gjers, Mills & Co Ltd, founded in 1869.

List of Industrial Monuments in the care of Local Trusts, Societies, or Groups

The CBA is compiling a list of industrial monuments in the care of local trusts and other specially constituted bodies. If readers know of any examples which are accessible to the public would they please communicate with the Secretary, Miss B. de Cardi, CBA, 8 St Andrew's Place, Regent's Park, London NW1, giving the following particulars:

name of the monument;
its approximate date;
its location, parish and county;
its nature and special interest;
its accessibility to the public;
the name and address of its owner, trust or society.

Transport History

The contents in the November issue of *Transport History* (vol 2 no 3) are as follows: 'Southampton and the Railway Mania, 1844–7' by D. J. Rowe; 'The Development of Cross-Channel Trade at Weymouth, 1794–1914: Geographical and Operational Factors' by P. J. Perry; 'Railway Electrification on Tyneside, 1902–67' by K. Hoole; 'The Aviemore Line: Railway Politics in the Highlands, 1882–98' by Neil T. Sinclair, and 'The Shropshire Omnibus Association: A Note on a Producers' Co-operative' by John Hibbs. There are also extensive sections of book reviews and *Notes and News*. The editor is Baron F. Duckham of the Department of Economic History, Strathclyde University, and the journal is obtainable from David & Charles at an annual subscription of 42s (for three issues) or 15s per copy. A free supplement in the form of a facsimile reproduction of the *Bibliography and Priced Catalogue of Early Railway Books* compiled by S. Cotterell in 1893 was sent out with the July issue to all those who had subscribed to vols 1 *and* 2 of *Transport History*. New subscribers can back-date their subscriptions.

LOCAL SOCIETIES ACTIVE WITHIN THE FIELD OF INDUSTRIAL ARCHAEOLOGY

ABERTAY HISTORICAL SOCIETY: INDUSTRIAL ARCHAEOLOGY SECTION
Secretary: B. P. Lenman, 21 Strawberry Bank, Dundee.

BATH & CAMERTON ARCHAEOLOGICAL SOCIETY
Secretary: Peter J. Greening, 61 Pulteney Street, Bath.

BATH UNIVERSITY OF TECHNOLOGY: CENTRE FOR THE STUDY OF THE HISTORY OF TECHNOLOGY
Director: Dr R. A. Buchanan, Northgate House, Bath.

BATLEY MUSEUM SOCIETY: INDUSTRIAL ARCHAEOLOGY GROUP
Secretary: Mrs. Joyce M. Ashworth, Richmond House, Town Street, Birkenshaw, Bradford.

BERKSHIRE ARCHAEOLOGICAL SOCIETY: INDUSTRIAL ARCHAEOLOGY GROUP
Secretary: J. Kenneth Major, 2 Eldon Road, Reading.

BLETCHLEY ARCHAEOLOGICAL & HISTORICAL SOCIETY
Secretary: Mrs S. S. Jarvis, 1 Wordsworth Drive, Bletchley, Buckinghamshire.

BRISTOL INDUSTRIAL ARCHAEOLOGICAL SOCIETY (BIAS)
Secretary: Neil Cossons, City Museum, Queens Road, Bristol 8.

BRUNEL SOCIETY
Secretary: S. A. Urry, Brunel University, Kingston Lane, Uxbridge.

CORNISH WATER-WHEEL PRESERVATION SOCIETY
Honorary Secretary: A. J. Stoyel, 3 Aneray Road, Camborne, Cornwall.

COUNCIL FOR BRITISH ARCHAEOLOGY, GROUP 2: INDUSTRIAL ARCHAEOLOGY SECTION
Secretary: Douglas B. Hague, Edleston House, Queen's Road, Aberystwyth.

COUNCIL FOR BRITISH ARCHAEOLOGY, GROUP 9: INDUSTRIAL ARCHAEOLOGY SUB-COMMITTEE
Secretary: J. Kenneth Major, 2 Eldon Road, Reading.

CUMBERLAND & WESTMORLAND ANTIQUARIAN & ARCHAEOLOGICAL SOCIETY: INDUSTRIAL ARCHAEOLOGY COMMITTEE
Joint Secretaries: M. Davies-Shiel, Lilac Villa, Lake Road, Bowness-on-Windermere. Dr J. D. Marshall, Department of History, University of Lancaster.

DERBY GROUP FOR INDUSTRIAL ARCHAEOLOGY
Secretary: R. Moore, 661 Osmaston Road, Derby.

DEVON INDUSTRIAL ARCHAEOLOGY SURVEY
Secretary: Michael Dower, Dartington Amenity Research Trust, Central Office, Skinner's Bridge, Dartington, Totnes.

DOWNSIDE ARCHAEOLOGICAL SOCIETY
Secretary: Dom Philip Jebb, Downside School, Stratton-on-the-Fosse, near Bath.

DURHAM INDUSTRIAL ARCHAEOLOGY GROUP
Secretary: D. Wilcock, 26 Bede Terrace, Bowburn, Durham.

EAST LOTHIAN ANTIQUARIAN & FIELD NATURALISTS' SOCIETY
Secretary: George Murray, 10 New Winton, Tranent.

EAST RIDING AGRICULTURAL MACHINERY PRESERVATION SOCIETY
Secretary: H. E. Kirk, Louvain, Rowley Road, Little Weighton, Hull.

EDINBURGH: OLD EDINBURGH CLUB
Secretary: Miss Catherine H. Cruft, 6 Bruntsfield Crescent, Edinburgh 10.

FORFAR & DISTRICT HISTORICAL SOCIETY
Secretary: G. C. F. Laird, 7 Wyllie Street, Forfar.

GLASGOW SPELAEOLOGICAL SOCIETY
Secretary: S. F. Thomson, 120 Lochlea Road, Glasgow, S 3.

GLOUCESTERSHIRE SOCIETY FOR INDUSTRIAL ARCHAEOLOGY
Secretary: Dr T. E. Edwards, ICI Fibres Limited, Gloucester.

GREATER LONDON INDUSTRIAL ARCHAEOLOGY SOCIETY
Secretary: Paul Carter, 20 Chestnut Grove, Sudbury, Wembley, Middlesex.

HAMPSHIRE FIELD CLUB AND ARCHAEOLOGICAL SOCIETY
Assistant Secretary: Mrs S. M. Course, Department of Archaeology, University of Southampton, Southampton S09 5NH.

HISTORICAL MODEL RAILWAY SOCIETY
Secretary: J. N. Slinn, 5 Cloister Mews, Theale, Reading.

HUDDERSFIELD INDUSTRIAL ARCHAEOLOGY SOCIETY
Honorary Secretary: Robert Whitehead, 119 Coniston Avenue, Dalton, Huddersfield.

INDUSTRIAL STEAM PRESERVATION GROUP
Chairman: C. D. Topp, Gurney House, Leazes Terrace, Newcastle-upon-Tyne, 1.

IRISH SOCIETY FOR INDUSTRIAL ARCHAEOLOGY
Secretary: K. A. Mawhinney, 34 Lakelands Close, Blackrock, Co Dublin.

IRONBRIDGE GORGE MUSEUM TRUST LIMITED
Honorary Secretary: E. Thomas, Priorslee Hall, Oakengates, Salop.

ISLE OF MAN NATURAL HISTORY & ANTIQUARIAN SOCIETY: FIELD SECTION INDUSTRIAL ARCHAEOLOGY GROUP
Secretary: Dr Larch S. Garrad, Manx Museum, Douglas.

LEICESTERSHIRE INDUSTRIAL HISTORY SOCIETY
Secretary: D. L. Alderton, 18 Toller Road, Quorn, Loughborough.

LINCOLNSHIRE LOCAL HISTORY SOCIETY: INDUSTRIAL ARCHAEOLOGY GROUP
Secretary: N. C. Birch, Stanede, Thorpe Lane, South Hykeham, Lincoln.

MANCHESTER REGION INDUSTRIAL ARCHAEOLOGY SOCIETY
Secretary: R. L. Hills, Department of History of Science & Technology, Institute of Science & Technology, Manchester 1.

NORTHAMPTONSHIRE INDUSTRIAL ARCHAEOLOGY GROUP
Secretary: Geoffrey H. Starmer, 17 Mayfield Road, Northampton.

NORTHERN CAVERN & MINE RESEARCH SOCIETY
Secretary: K. Walls, 33 Gledhow Avenue, Roundhay, Leeds 8.

NORTH-EAST INDUSTRIAL ARCHAEOLOGY GROUP
Secretary: Michael Wheeler, Bowes Museum, Barnard Castle, Co Durham.

NORTH-WESTERN SOCIETY FOR INDUSTRIAL ARCHAEOLOGY & HISTORY
Secretary: Mrs P. Paget-Tomlinson, City of Liverpool Museum, William Brown Street, Liverpool 3.

PEAK DISTRICT MINES HISTORICAL SOCIETY
Secretary: Mrs P. E. Lunn, 28 Kembourne Road, Sheffield, S7.

PETERBOROUGH INDUSTRIAL ARCHAEOLOGY GROUP
Secretary: John David, Peterborough Technical College, Park Crescent, Peterborough.

POOLE (WEA) INDUSTRIAL ARCHAEOLOGY GROUP
Secretary: A. J. A. Cooksey, 18 Parkstone Avenue, Parkstone, Poole.

PORTSMOUTH COLLEGE OF TECHNOLOGY INDUSTRIAL ARCHAEOLOGY SOCIETY
Secretary: Dr R. C. Riley, Department of Economics and Business Studies, Portsmouth College of Technology.

RAILWAY & CANAL HISTORICAL SOCIETY
Secretary: J. R. Harding, 38 Station Road, Wylde Green, Sutton Coldfield.

ROCHDALE INDUSTRIAL ARCHAEOLOGY GROUP
Secretary: D. Ternent, 149 Ashfield Road, Rochdale.

SALISBURY & SOUTH WILTSHIRE INDUSTRIAL ARCHAEOLOGY GROUP
Secretary: Donald A. E. Cross, College of Further Education, Salisbury.

SCOTTISH SOCIETY FOR INDUSTRIAL ARCHAEOLOGY
Secretary: Dr John Butt, University of Strathclyde, Department of Economic History, McCance Building, Richmond Street, Glasgow C 1.

SOUTHAMPTON INDUSTRIAL ARCHAEOLOGY GROUP
Secretary: Robert Lawrence, c/o Henderson Bearings Limited, Savoy House, Junction Road, Totton, Southampton.

SOUTHAMPTON UNIVERSITY INDUSTRIAL ARCHAEOLOGY GROUP
Secretary: Dr E. Course, Extra-Mural Department.

SOUTH-EAST WALES INDUSTRIAL ARCHAEOLOGY SOCIETY
Secretary: W. G. Hughes, 96 Wenallt Road, Rhiwbina, Cardiff.

STAFFORD INDUSTRIAL ARCHAEOLOGY SOCIETY
Secretary: F. Brook, Staffordshire College of Technology, Beaconside, Stafford.

SUNDERLAND INDUSTRIAL ARCHAEOLOGY GROUP
Honorary Secretary: Stuart B. Smith, Sunderland Museum, Borough Road, Sunderland.

SUSSEX INDUSTRIAL ARCHAEOLOGY STUDY GROUP
Secretary: K. C. Leslie, Little Broadmark, Sea Lane, Rustington.

SWANSEA INDUSTRIAL ARCHAEOLOGY SOCIETY
Secretary: T. M. Lloyd, Department of Economic History, University College, Singleton Park, Swansea.

TEESSIDE INDUSTRIAL ARCHAEOLOGY GROUP
Secretary: Roger L. Pickles, 15 Cromwell Terrace, Thornaby, Stockton, Teesside.

THAMES BASIN ARCHAEOLOGY GROUP
Secretary: Miss Betty Powell, 73a Southwark Bridge Road, London SE1.

WEST LOTHIAN COUNTY HISTORY SOCIETY
Secretary: B. C. Skinner, 10 Randolph Cliff, Edinburgh 3.

WIND & WATERMILL SECTION OF THE SOCIETY FOR THE PROTECTION OF ANCIENT BUILDINGS
Secretary: Mrs M. Dance, 55 Great Ormond Street, London WC1.

WOLVERHAMPTON COLLEGE OF TECHNOLOGY: IDUSTRIAL ARCHAEOLOGY GROUP
Secretary: Norman Mutton, Department of Management & Business Studies, St John's Square, Wolverhampton.

WOLVERTON & DISTRICT ARCHAEOLOGICAL SOCIETY
Secretary: R. J. Ayers, 13 Vicarage Walk, Stony Stratford, Wolverton.

Index: Volume 6 of Industrial Archaeology